Southeast Asian
Specialties

Southeast Asian Specialties

A Culinary Journey

Rosalind Mowe (Editor)
Günter Beer (Photographer)
Peter Feierabend (Art Director and Design)
Martina Schlagenhaufer (Desk Editor)
Michael Ditter (Project Co-ordinator)

Culinaria

KÖNEMANN

Abbreviations and quantities*

1 g	= 1 gram
1 oz	= 1ounce = about 25 g
1 lb	= 1 pound (16 ounces)
1 cup	= 8 fl oz (250 ml) liquid measure
	= 8 oz (250 g) heavier foods such as granulated sugar and rice
	4 oz of light foods such as flour and powdered sugar
1 pint	= 2 cups or 16 fl oz
1 quart	= 2 pints
1 jigger	= 1 fl oz (3 tablespoons)
1 Tbs	= 1 level tablespoon
	= ½ oz (15–20 g) dry ingredients
	½ fl oz (15 ml) liquids
1 Tsp	= 1 level teaspoon
	= 3–5 g dry ingredients
	= 5 ml liquid measure

Non-metric measurements are American, not imperial. Do not combine American and metric quantities in the same recipe.

Recipe quantities

If no other indication is given, each recipe serves four (except for drinks when the quantities are for one). The portions are rather small because they are intended to be served as several small dishes, not one large entrée, and all are eaten with rice.

Instructions for use

Coconut milk

This is the liquid extracted from freshly grated coconut. The grated coconut is squeezed for the first pressing without additional water or with only a small quantity. The result should be a thick milk. The same coconut is mixed with more water and squeezed again to produce a thin milk. Both thick and thin milks are used in cooking; thin milk is always added first and the thick milk is only at the end of the cooking process. One coconut with the brown husk that adheres to the white meat will produce about 2 cups (500 g) grated coconut. Without the husk, there will be about 2 oz (50 g) less.

Tamarind juice

Tamarind pod pulp is pressed into blocks and sold in oriental food stores. The quantity required is softened in hot water and the liquid obtained is used as a sour flavoring.

© 1998 Könemann Verlagsgesellschaft mbH
   Bonner Strasse 126 · D–50968 Cologne

Photography Assistant:	Markus Bassler, Barcelona
Studio Photography:	Arena Studios Pte. Ltd., Singapore
	Klaus Arras Fotodesign, Cologne
Food stylist:	Fanny Seah, Singapore
Maps on p. 11–12:	Astrid Fischer-Leitl, Munich
Translation of headings into Chinese:	Dr. Boesken & Partner, Ostasien Service, Hamburg
Production Manager:	Detlev Schaper, Cologne
Reproduction:	CLG Fotolito, San Martino Buon Albergo

© 1999 for the English Edition:
Translation from the German: Josephine Bacon, Monica Bloxam, Clare Charters, Simon Dalgleish, Paul Fletcher, Pierre Gottfried Imhof, Debra Nicol, Christine Shuttleworth, Dafydd Rees Roberts
Production of the English Edition: Chanterelle Translations, London
Project Coordinator: Bettina Kaufmann
Assistant: Kristin Zeier
Printing and binding: Neue Stalling, Oldenburg

Printed in Germany
ISBN 3-89508-909-5

10 9 8 7 6 5 4 3 2 1

Contents

Lain padang lain
belalang,
lain lubuk lain
ikannya.

Other fields, other
insects; other seas,
other fish.

Indonesian proverb

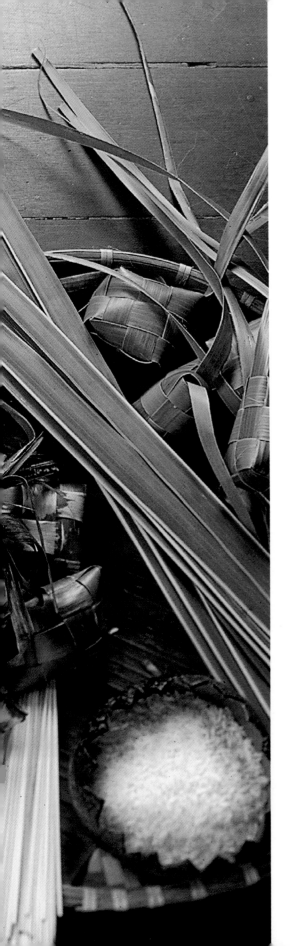

The simple truth of the common expression, "Other countries, other customs," in its Indonesian version or in any other, was demonstrated to us at the latest when we arrived at a village of the Orang Asli, the indigenous Malayan forest-dwellers. We were welcomed with genuine friendliness and freshly brewed tea — served in rather dubious-looking tin cans whose patina made it clear that they were a well-used and much loved teaset! Now we knew why Father Anthony, to whom we owed our introduction, had begged us, not long before, to accept whatever was offered to us so as not to hurt our hosts' feelings.

It wasn't the first time on our travels from Singapore through Sumatra, Java, Bali, and Eastern and Western Malaysia that the photographer, his assistant, and myself had experienced the selfless hospitality of local people, offered as soon as the reason for our visit became known. The strong impression this made on us helped us get over the difficulties with which we had to cope — whether it was the hordes of insects, the antediluvian sanitary arrangements, or the obstinate and uncomprehending guides who were so reluctant to leave the well-trodden tourist routes.

Our journey through Singapore, Malaysia, and Indonesia wasn't simply a culinary exploration of a tropical paradise. It also represented an opportunity to explore the delicate equilibrium of a more-or-less voluntary, centuries-old co-existence of different cultures in one of its everyday aspects — through cookery. (How unstable this equilibrium might be was made clear by the disturbances in Java in the spring of 1998.) This was a most appropriate starting point, given that for the West it was the precious spices of the region which had aroused their covetous interest and had subjected the inhabitants of these islands to the oppressive attentions of the rival colonial powers. The imperial masters brought with them the colonists, traders, and foreign workers of various nationalities, which is why today there is hardly any other part of the world which has such an important, profound, and complex relationship to the art of cookery.

Rosalind Mowe

Singapore

新
加
坡

食不厭精，膾不厭細。
食饐而餲魚餒而肉敗，不食。
色惡不食，臭惡不食。
失飪不食，不時不食。
割不正不食，不得其醬不食。

Eat healthy food, prepared with care.
Avoid spoiled items and improperly treated ingredients.
Never eat between meals, make sure the food is properly shared out, and that the sauces are in harmony.

Confucius

The downtown area on the Singapore River is always busy, even at night.

Preceding pages: a cook at the Raffles Hotel with his Peking Duck.

"Ni chi bao le ma?" The question "Have you eaten yet?" is a customary greeting when people meet, and in Singapore they don't so much talk about the weather as about food. With such a great variety available all day and nearly all night, eating is almost considered a kind of national pastime—unofficially of course.

This devotion to food may be a relic from the days of the early immigrants, when life was hard and no one could be sure where their next meal was coming from. Settlers from China, India, Indonesia, and Arabia, who usually came to Singapore for economic reasons, brought with them their own cultures and hence their own recipes, though they also proved quite willing to look further afield than the rim of their own plates. So the cooking of the largest ethnic groups, the Chinese, the Malays, and the Indians, developed a very individual, Singaporean character. The Europeans—mainly British, Portuguese, and Dutch—also left their mark on these cuisines which have also had some effect on the foods of the mother-country. The best-known examples of this phenomenon are ketchup and rijstafel, but there are many more.

At first there were hardly any restaurants in this British trading post, established on the sea route to the Spice Islands by Sir Stamford Raffles in 1819. People ate at home, although they availed themselves of the services of the many pedlars who brought cooked food to the door, on pushcarts or in baskets hung from the ends of bamboo poles carried on their shoulders. In addition to food, these street vendors carried miniature kitchens with them, and many even had little wooden stools on which to seat those customers who wished to enjoy their noodles on the spot. They would cry out their wares, or their assistants would precede them, announcing the noodle-seller's arrival by striking two sticks of bamboo together. There were also stalls at which you could eat in the open air, and coffee houses that were kept comfortably cool with aid of fans.

Today, officially certified food-sellers ply their trade in so-called "*hawker centers.*" There are also countless eateries and food stalls which offer a great diversity of dishes to suit any pocket.

新加坡的中餐 Chinese cuisine in Singapore

A Chinese meal is usually a communal affair. Whether people eat out or at home, the food is always shared between the diners and any guests. Depending on the number of people, there will be three or more dishes to accompany the bowl of rice, which will consist of meat or poultry, fish, vegetables, and soup. Everyone helps themselves and composes their own meal. It would completely go against Chinese custom to select and to eat a whole dish for oneself.

Chicken, duck and pork, and all kinds of stewed and braised meats are extremely popular in Chinese cooking. The Chinese also love seafood, and they are particularly fond of soup. Rice, however, is the principal staple, while noodles in every shape and form, cooked in every possible way, provide quick snacks between meals, as do the ever-present steamed buns and ravioli-like pockets called dumplings, which are stuffed with a variety of fillings. Health-conscious Chinese are always anxious to preserve or re-establish the harmony of forces (Yin and Yang) within the body, and they take this into account when choosing what they eat. Steaming, stir-frying, braising, deep-frying, grilling, and broiling are among the preferred methods of cooking. Various sauces, soybean pastes, and oils provide stimulation to the tastebuds. China tea is considered to be the most suitable beverage to accompany this kind of food.

Nowadays, many Singaporean Chinese families use a plate, fork, and spoon, rather than eating from a bowl with chopsticks. Knives are never used, and in any case, they are unnecessary. Meat and fish is usually served in bite-sized pieces, but if necessary, it can be cut up with spoon and fork, and the spoon is used for the rice. Little dishes of chili sauce and chili peppers sliced into thin rings are available for anyone who finds the food too bland, as the tastes of Chinese have not been unaffected by the availability of spicy Malay and Indian foods.

Right: freshly steamed *shao mai* — a type of open-topped dumpling, filled with ground pork, shrimp, and mushroom, and garnished with crab roe

To gladden the heart
Dim sum

One of the stories told about the origins of *dim sum* retraces them back to the moods of the Dowager Empress Tzu Hsi (who died in 1908), the fifth concubine of Emperor Hsien Feng and mother of his only son. Bored with her food, she ordered her servants to prepare something special, and they invented these *dim sum* in order to "gladden her heart."

Dim sum are served for breakfast or lunch. The dough pockets may be steamed in bamboo baskets, fried in a wok, or baked. They may be savory or sweet, and are served with quantities of tea. The atmosphere in a *dim sum* establishment is relaxed and informal. Special serving carts, containing a selection of these delicacies, are pushed through the restaurant and people simply stop the waiter when they spot something they would like to try. A diner can eat as many dishes as he or she likes, and the waiter notes everything down on the bill, which is left on the table. Unfortunately, more and more restaurants have abolished these serving carts and have replaced them with set menus.

The buns and dumplings are prepared using different kinds of wrappers, such as:
- a *wonton* skin made of wheat flour, egg, and water
- a spring roll pancake made of flour, water, and salt
- a dough of wheat flour and cold or boiling water
- a bread dough for the buns, made of flour, yeast, water, and sugar
- a translucent "cellophane wrapper" made of flour, pork fat, cornstarch, and boiling water

The filling may consist of any of the following ingredients, alone or in combination: broiled or barbecued pork, ground pork, shrimp, veal, bamboo shoots, peas, chives, green onions (scallions), mushrooms, and ginger root.

The Empress must have certainly have been kept amused by these exquisite culinary morsels. For thirty-nine years she was the real ruler of China—her own son died without an heir, and her adopted nephew, whom she then made emperor, was only a few years old when he acceded to the throne. Tzu Hsi was always praised for her drive and initiative, her beauty, her charm, and the elegance of her manners.

Above: The stacks of bamboo steaming-baskets are in use around the clock, and their constantly changing contents will always find a taker. The large steamer contains freshly made *cha shao bao* , steamed buns filled with ground barbecued pork seasoned with oyster sauce and soy sauce.

點
心

Shao mai: steamed open dumplings with pork, shrimp, and mushrooms, garnished with crab roe.

Zha nai huang bao: deep-fried dumplings filled with lotus paste, on a garnish of omelet and cucumber.

Cha shao bao: ground barbecued pork, seasoned with oyster sauce and soy sauce, wrapped in dough and steamed.

Chun juan: small spring rolls with a vegetarian filling of grated carrot, white turnip, and mushroom.

Xiao long bao: steamed dumplings, Szechuan-style, filled with pork and garnished with a pea.

Cha shao su: ground barbecued pork in a pie-crust, glazed with honey and baked in the oven.

Xia jiao: steamed rice-flour dumplings with a filling of fresh shrimp and minced bamboo shoots.

Jiu huang zhu juan: fried dumplings with a filling of shrimp and chives, served on a banana leaf.

Pi dan zhou: rice gruel, oysters and ground pork, with thousand-year-old egg, green onions, and rice or shrimp crackers

Guo tie: deep-fried steamed dumplings, filled with ground pork, Chinese (Napa) cabbage, green onions, and ginger.

Ma Ti Tiao: deep-fried pastries with a vegetarian filling of water chestnuts.

Zha yun tun: finely chopped pork with shrimp, wrapped in a wonton skin, and fried.

Jin xu qu yu dai: dried scallops cut into very fine strips and fried

Xiao mang xia tong: small fried rolls filled with a mango and shrimp purée and sprinkled with sesame seeds

Zha sheng hao: fried oysters, served simply but effectively in their own shell

Luo bo gao: fried slices of a sweet dessert made with grated white turnip.

Ming xia jiao: steamed and deep-fried "ravioli", filled with fresh vegetables and chopped water-chestnuts.

Zhu rou su: baked pastries, filled with ground pork, shrimp, winter mushrooms, and chives.

Jiu cai jiao: steamed rice-flour pastries, filled with ground pork, shrimp, water-chestnuts, and chives.

Dai zhi shao mai: steamed rice-flour dumplings, with a shrimp filling, garnished with scallops, and crab roe.

Suan tian xia: deep-fried balls made with cornstarch, ground pork, and shrimp, in a sweet-and-sour sauce.

Fen Chang: steamed rice-flour dumplings, filled with broiled pork and shrimp or mussels.

Zhi bao ji: chicken breast, marinated in a mixture of oyster sauce and soy sauce, and fried in packages.

Niang dou fou: tofu coated with a paste of pork, shrimp, fish, and mushrooms, and fried

Lian hong bao: steamed buns with a filling of lotus paste, garnished with yolk of salted egg.

Nuo mi ji: glutinous rice with chicken, sausage links, and winter mushrooms, wrapped in a lotus leaf and steamed.

Feng zhua: marinated chicken feet braised in oyster sauce, sprinkled with sesame seeds.

Niang la jiao: quartered bell peppers and halved chili peppers, filled with a fish stuffing and braised.

Nuo mi ci: balls of glutinous rice, filled with a paste of peanuts, sesame, sugar, and butter, and rolled in grated coconut.

Dan ta: little puff pastry tartlets with a golden-yellow filling of sweetened egg custard.

Mang guo bu ding: chilled mango cream gelatin dessert (made of puréed and diced mango) in a mango syrup.

Longyan dou fu: chilled almond milk gelatin dessert garnished with a longan poached in syrup.

咖啡店的早點 Breakfast in the coffee-shop

Only a few of the old-time coffee-shops of the 1930s, 1940s, and 1950s have survived to the present day. Once they were an integral part of the cityscape, and were to be found on almost every street corner. The location was chosen to ensure the better circulation of air. The clientele consisted mainly of men who left China without their families. They would congregate at the coffee-shop to eat breakfast still wearing their pajamas. A boy would take the order, which he would repeat in a loud voice so that the kitchen staff could hear it too. The menu was simple, and consisted of:

• toast with margarine, sprinkled with raw palm sugar (jaggery).
• a slice of bread covered in egg jam, a custard made of egg, sugar, and coconut milk

When breakfast is prepared for a customer it is not unusual for the owner or a member of his family to lend a hand.

The kitchen almost always opens onto the seating area, so you can watch the preparation of the breakfast you have ordered.

• soft-boiled or hard-boiled eggs

The coffee was very strong and drunk with sugar and condensed milk. The shops also served tea and malted beverages diluted with water or milk. All the drinks were served in thick china cups. It was a common sight to see a customer drink his coffee from the saucer into which he had poured it to cool it down. Underneath every table was the obligatory spittoon.

Over the years, spaces in the coffee shops, were rented to food stall-holders who cooked and served such items as noodles, fish, and pork or chicken gruel, on the premises to supplement the choice of food on offer for breakfast.

These days many people breakfast in the food halls near the markets. These are particularly handy for housewives, who take out a cooked breakfast back to their apartments after shopping in the street markets for the family groceries.

Egg jam

This has little to do with the fruit purée usually known as jam. It is more like a kind of custard, made with eggs, sugar, and the milk of a large grated coconut, in which 10 eggs are used to one pound of white sugar. This is then flavored with pandanus leaf (or perhaps a vanilla bean.) The mixture is stirred vigorously over hot water for 20–25 minutes, which dissolves the sugar and ensures the ingredients are well amalgamated. This custard is then strained through a sieve into a bowl or pan, which is covered and left to stand for four hours in a water-bath. Egg jam will keep for several days in the refrigerator

A slice of toast with egg jam is still standard breakfast fare in the coffee shops

There are no pop-up toasters or espresso coffee machines here, but they do just fine without them.

Nowadays, the breakfast menu is more varied, but still bears little resemblance to the kind of foods which people in the West associate with breakfast, with the exception of milky coffee. Cereals, bacon and eggs, and hash browns have not yet invaded.

Top: In the coffee-shop, coffee and water are usually poured into a cup that already contains milk and sugar.
Left: the custard is only left untended for the picture, because egg jam is stirred constantly while cooking.

Here are a few of the most popular breakfast items eaten by the Singapore Chinese:
- *Yu tiao* — long strips of dough, twisted and deep-fried.
- *Chye tau kwei* — "fried carrot cake", which isn't really carrot cake at all but is made with daikon radish and rice flour. It is first steamed, then sliced, and the slices are fried until crisp with minced garlic and beaten egg. It is served topped with a sweet sauce. There are several variations on "fried carrot cake."

- *Chu cheong fern* — steamed rice-flour pancakes, rolled and cut into strips, seasoned with soy sauce, chili sauce, and sesame oil, and garnished with finely chopped green onions (scallions) and toasted sesame seeds.
- *Chi kwei* — steamed rice-cakes sprinkled with spicy ground pork and pickled vegetables, one of the few meat dishes served at breakfast.

China Tea

Wherever you go among the tradition-conscious Chinese, at business establishments and in domestic households, hot tea is always available. It is kept warm in padded woven baskets, and a visitor is more likely to be offered hot tea than a cold drink. A predominantly male clientele meets in tea-clubs and tea-houses to discuss or to read about politics and the topics of the day while leisurely sipping at their tea. Small snacks are served with the tea, which is always drunk without cream or sugar.

For the Chinese, tea-drinking can be a real social event. Tea-tastings are held in much the same way as wine-tastings are held in the Wes. The tea is sipped thoughtfully and judged not only on taste but also on color and aroma. Top-quality teas are served in a "smelling cup.". The tea is then poured into a new cup and the aroma inhaled from the empty cup.

At a Chinese wedding, the tea ceremony is of great importance, because before the bride can be admitted into the groom's family she first has to wait upon her father-in-law and mother-in-law, and then on the groom's older siblings and relations, offering a cup of tea to each in turn. In exchange, each of them gives her a *hong bao*, a small red package containing money. The groom then performs the same ceremony with the bride's in-laws, in her parents' home. The ceremony is repeated on birthdays and at the New Year. All this goes to show what a central role tea plays in Chinese culture.

In the trade, tea is stored in canisters, although very precious, aged teas are kept in earthenware jars. At home, the best way to preserve a good tea is to put it into a resealable plastic bag and store it in the vegetable compartment of the refrigerator.

Tea and the seasons

Spring: The tea is now rich and full.
Summer: This tea is less highly esteemed, as a higher proportion of tannin in the leaves makes it bitter. Several cups of it are good for whetting the appetite.
Fall: This tea has a more marked scent and a long-lasting flavor, but it is more bitter than the spring or winter tea.
Winter: This tea is harder to find, as the harvest is limited. In many tea plantations, no crop is harvested in winter, as it can reduce the spring harvest. The plants are in a growth phase, and the tea is finer in aroma.

The traditional tea-set includes a bowl to receive the hot water from rinsing the teapot.

The pot is warmed with hot water (which at the same time enables fermented tea to be rinsed.)

The required quantity of tea leaves is put into the pot and hot water added.

The pot is passed several times over all the bowls so that each receives exactly the same strength of tea.

In a specialist store, tea is measured out and packed according to customers' requirements

Utensils for the preparation of tea

Teapots should be of either china or earthenware. The Chinese city of Yixing is very famous for its handmade earthenware teapots. The region's sandy clay, used for making the Yixing teapots, turns green or reddish-brown when fired. Flowery, aromatic teas are best brewed in china teapots. Earthenware teapots tend to hold the aroma, which might spoil the aroma of subsequent teas brewed in the pot.

Large teacups have saucers and lids, and are used both for brewing the tea and for drinking it. The lid is lifted just a fraction at one side of the cup, which helps stop the tea leaves getting into the drinker's mouth. These cups have a handle. Small delicate bowls of china or earthenware are ideal for tea-drinking. The people of Chaozhou, for instance, brew tea in small earthenware teapots and drink it from thimble-sized cups of the same material. These diminutive tea-sets are known as "Kung Fu" tea since the art of preparing tea in this way takes time and a great deal of skill, almost as much as the martial art of the same name.

A pot or bowl for the rinsing water is always at the ready.

Another pot is needed as a slop-bowl for the tea remaining when the cups have been filled. Tea is not usually left to steep in the pot.

Bamboo utensils are used to eliminate possible impurities from the tea-leaves. Hard stems and old leaves make the tea bitter.

The traditional way of preparing tea

- Boil freshly drawn water.
- Place the tea leaves in the pot, half-fill the pot with boiling water, then pour it away. This process also rinses of the tea-leaves, although it is only necessary for fermented teas.
- Refill the pot with boiling water, cover it with the lid, and pour hot water over the outside of the unglazed earthenware pot. When the water on the outside has dried off, the tea is ready. (If the pot is not made of unglazed earthenware, you can let it stand for 3 minutes by the clock)
- Pour hot water over the cups as well.
- Place the cups close together, in a row or circle, and pour the tea while constantly moving the pot from one cup to the next, so that the tea in each cup has the same strength.
- Pour more hot water into the pot, without adding tea leaves. This can be done no more than twice, depending on the type of tea. While doing so, any remaining tea must be poured from the tea-pot into the slop bowl before the water for the next brew is added

Tea and used tea leaves are sometimes left standing in earthenware pots, in order to improve the patina.

Special teas

祁門茶

Keemun (qihong): the champagne among black teas, low in tannin and delicate and mild in flavor. This tea goes very well with sweet and spicy desserts.

龍井茶

Lung ching (longjing): (Dragon Well tea) A green tea which is pleasantly cooling in warm weather. A choice tea with an unmistakable aftertaste.

鐵觀音茶

Ti kwan yin (tie guanyin): This is the most famous of the Oolong teas. As a semi-fermented tea, it has the body of a black tea and the taste of a green tea

鍾山小珠茶

Zhengshan xiaozhong (lapsang souchong): A black tea which is smoked, pan-roasted, rolled, fermented, roasted, and rolled again.

寶珠茶

Baozhong (pouchong): a lightly fermented tea, sometimes used as a basis for jasmine tea. It comes in rag-paper packages.

壽梅茶

Sau mei: this green tea is popular with the Cantonese, who serve it with *dim sum.* (The name means "eyebrows" a reference to the shape of the long leaves.)

白毛珠茶

Bai mo dan: The leaf-buds are rubbed, giving the surface a fibrous and downy appearance, and they are then tied together in bundles. A very light green tea.

龍珠茶

Loong chu: This mild green tea is produced in a similar way to *bai mo dan.* One ball is enough for four cups. The temperature of the water should be 176°F (80°C).

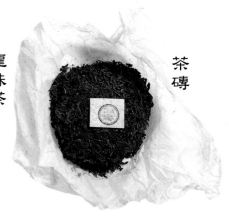

茶磚

Brick tea: This tea is popular with Chinese nomads because of its transportability. Broken-quality leaves of various teas are pressed into different shapes.

Hei zao (Mandarin): black dates are sedative and strengthen the blood (Cantonese: *hak choe*).

Hong zao (Mandarin): red dates are also good for the blood and are said to be muscle relaxants (Cantonese: *hung choe*).

Naturally healthy
Healing herbs

草藥

The Chinese have a long tradition of natural healing. There are records of diagnostic methods and herbal prescriptions dating back to 500 BC. The word "herbal" is, however, misleading, as bark, roots, seeds, leaves, and fungi are also used. If health is nothing but the perfect harmony of Yin and Yang, disease requires the re-establishment of the lost equilibrium. In this, nutrition and medication are closely linked. Both food and medicine can be categorized as "warming," "cooling,", and "neutral." Should the balance of Yin and Yang be disturbed, the healer will determine the cause by observing the patient. The color of the complexion, the iris of the eyes, and the tongue are checked, as are breathing and pulse. He will establish the diagnosis, prescribe the remedy, and send the patient to the herbalist who will dispense the medicine. The ingredients not only have to be accurately weighed, but the mixture has to be steeped in exactly the right amount of hot water, must stand for a precise amount of time, and the tea must be drunk at the right time of day. The herbs can be infused like a tea, or they may be boiled in soup (decoction), or taken in the form of pills made from the pulverized ingredients.

Yuan rou (Mandarin): dried longan have a relaxing, soporific effect and are good for the blood (Cantonese: *longan yok*).

Mi zao (Mandarin.): honey dates have a beneficial effect on the lungs (Cantonese: *mut choe*).

Gao li shen (Mandarin):Korean ginseng promotes vitality and the immune system; it can be prescribed pure or mixed into food (Cantonese: *ko lai sum*).

Pao shen (Mandarin): ingested with other herbs once a week in chicken or pork soup, American ginseng has a tonic effect (Cantonese: *pao sum*).

Ju zi (Mandarin): the fruit of the box-thorn (*Lycium barbarum*) lowers blood pressure and cholesterol levels, is good for liver and kidneys, and improves the sight (Cantonese: *kei chee*).

Ci shi (Mandarin): seeds of the Indian waterlily (*Euryale ferox*), which open up into a flower shape during cooking, are diuretic and good for the spleen (Cantonese: *see sut*).

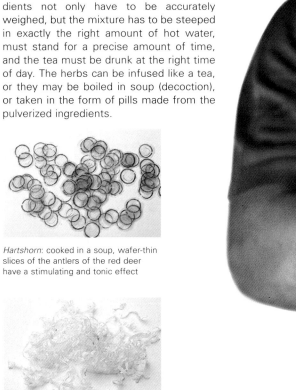

Hartshorn: cooked in a soup, wafer-thin slices of the antlers of the red deer have a stimulating and tonic effect

Bai her (Mandarin): the dried leaf-buds of a species of lily (*Lilium brownii*) strengthen the lungs and ease coughs (Cantonese: *bak hup*).

Lian zi (Mandarin): the seeds of the Indian lotus flower (*Nelumbo nucifera*) prevent diarrhea and insomnia (Cantonese: *lin chee*).

Lin yeung (Mandarin): antelope horn reduces fever; children can be given 2 grams boiled with sugar.

Dang shen (Mandarin): the roots of the Chilean bellflower *(Codonopsis pilosula)* have a tonic effect, particularly on women (Cantonese: *dong sum*).

Peiqi (Mandarin): the astragal root *(Astragalus membranaceus)* is an ingredient in many prescriptions as it provides vital energy *(Chi)*. (Cantonese: *puk*

Dang gui (Mandarin): angelica root *(Angelica sinensis)* is useful in menstrual disorders, after childbirth and during menopause (Cantonese: *dong kwai)*.

Yu zhu (Mandarin): the rhizomes of Solomon's seal *(Polygonatum officinale)* help ease coughs and dry throat (Cantonese: *yok chok*).

Fu shen (Mandarin): *Wolfiporia cocos,* a fungus which grows on the roots of conifers and deciduous trees, is a sedative and diuretic (Cantonese: *fook sun*).

Huai shan (Mandarin): the tuber of this yam *(Dioscorea opposita)* is prescribed for lack of appetite, diarrhea, coughing, and asthma (Cantonese: *wai san*).

Dong chong sia cao (Mandarin):the fungus *Cordyceps sinensis* strengthens the kidneys and lungs, and cures night sweats (Cantonese: *dong chong chou*).

"Dust pearls" are ground into powder, mixed with water, and drunk in order to improve the complexion. They are also used as an expectorant.

Exotic remedies

Sea-horses
Dried sea-horses *(hai ma)* come from the Chinese provinces of Canton (Guandong) and Fujian, as well as from Indonesia. A broth made from whole sea-horses simmered with with one or two other remedies cools and detoxifies the body. People who suffer from rashes or who want to get rid of acne can drink this and do their kidneys good at the same time.

海馬

蝎子

Scorpions
These special scorpions *(xie zi)* are bred in the province of Shandong and exported all over the Chinese diaspora. They are said to cure nervous twitches, muscular cramps, and boils.

壁虎

猴頭蘑

Geckos
(Bi hu), these are sold in pairs of male and female. The reptiles are dried, and skewered so that the body remains flat. The head is removed before they go into a chicken soup cooked in a steamer. As long as the gecko retains its tail, men will not refuse a bowl of this soup. Women have no fear the loss of the tail, and they take the soup to give their skin tone a boost. Ground into powder, the geckos become a medicine which can be given to children who suffer from asthma. Geckos can also be steeped in wine for a certain amount of time, and the resulting potion consumed.

Monkey head
Monkey head *(Hou tou mo)* — these fungi grow in pairs in the Szechuan mountains. As they are very nutritious they are prepared as vegetables, and not only satisfy hunger but at the same time stimulate the circulation of the blood and prevent cancer, particularly cancer of the stomach.

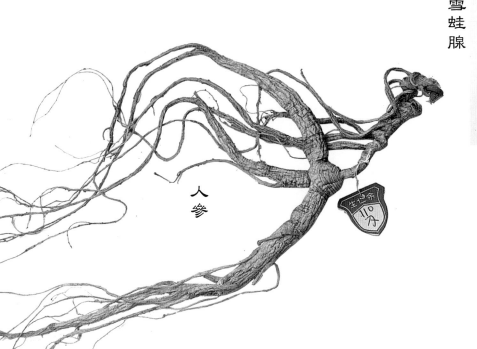

雪蛙腺

Hasma
Dried snow-frog glands *(xue wa xian)* are imported from northeast China. Cooked in a sweet soup, they are supposed to strengthen the lungs. Winters are very severe in the snow-frog's habitat, and last for months. In order to survive, the male frogs have to hibernate together with the females. During this time their mouths stick together and the female provides the male with a glandular secretion without which he would freeze to death.

人參

羚羊角

Antelope horn
Unlike the antlers of the red deer, antelope horn *(ling yang jiao)* is said to be cooling, and it is therefore used to reduce fever. Two grams of finely-shaved antelope horn boiled with a little sugar in a double saucepan can even be given to small children. To produce the wafer-thin white shavings the dark, uneven, outer layer of the horn is first rubbed down and then smoothed with a stone, before paper-thin layers are sliced off with a stainless-steel blade.

Ginseng
Ginseng *(ren sen)*, which grows in China, America, Canada, and Korea, is a costly universal panacea. Wild ginseng is very expensive, but even cultivated ginseng costs a great deal, because it takes five or six years to reach maturity. Scientists in Singapore have, however, succeeded in reducing the ripening period of ginseng root to four weeks. Before taking ginseng the body should be put into a neutral state, by drinking barley water, for example. For ginseng to have its full effect it is advisable not to drink any tea for three days before and after taking it, nor should one eat amaranth, fish, beans, or radish (daikon). The effects of ginseng last for 24 hours. Earthenware pots and dishes and porcelain spoons must always be used, never metal utensils. Wild Chinese ginseng (which is also cultivated now) has to be prescribed by a physician. It is said to stabilize the blood circulation and to act as a sedative on the mind and the senses.
American ginseng can be found in the temperate zones of the United States and Canada. It has cooling properties. The best variety comes from the forests of Vermont and of New York State. Korean ginseng is particularly beneficial for the old and frail. It regulates the fluids and temperature control mechanism of the body, strengthens the heart, and stimulates the mind
The Chinese name for gingseng means "human-shaped root" and some of these roots bear an uncanny resemblance to a tiny human being.

虎骨膏

Tiger Balm
(Hu gu gao) This ointment was invented by the brothers Aw Boon Haw and Aw Boon Par, the sons of a Chinese herb-seller, and it first conquered the Singapore market in 1926. Despite its name, the manufacture of the balm represents no threat to the endangered tiger, for it contains only menthol, camphor, cloves, peppermint, and cajeput oil. It is said to be effective against a whole series of ailments, among them headaches, rheumatism, lumbago, insect bites, and muscular pains. It is available in two strengths, the greater being red in color and the lesser, white. The Chinese word for "tiger" is *haw*, and this is probably the reason for the name. This misunderstanding has nonetheless added something of a mysterious aura to the product, which together with its old-fashioned packaging and a highly effective marketing campaign has made Tiger Balm famous throughout the world.

The most popular herbal soups

Six-herb soup
Pork or chicken is cooked in a double-boiler with:

- *Yu zhu* (rhizome of Solomon's seal (*Polygonatum officinale*)
- *Huai shan* (yam tuber (*Dioscorea opposita*))
- *Dang shen* (bellflower root (*Codonopsis pilosula*))
- *Lian zi* (seeds of the Indian lotus flower (*Nelumbo nucifera*))
- *Ci shi* (seeds of the Indian waterlily (*Euryale ferox*))
- *Yuan rou* (dried longan, a fruit similar to the lychee nut).

Four-herb soup
Pork or chicken is cooked in a double-boiler with:
- *Huai shan* (yam tuber (*Dioscorea opposita*))
- *Fu shen* (*Wolfiporia cocos* fungus)
- *Ci shi* (Seeds of the Indian waterlily (*Euryale ferox*))
- *Lian zi* (seeds of the Indian lotus

補
湯

Pleasant and useful

Soup as medicine

A person is ill if the harmony of Yin and Yang within the body is disturbed, and health will return as soon as this harmony is restored. To achieve this, whatever is in excess must be reduced and whatever is insufficient must be increased, or neutralized by matching one factor with its opposite. As elementary as this sounds, it is a science in itself, because it means that every medicine and every type of food has particular characteristics which need to be known. Meat, sea-food, vegetables, and herbs, everything is either "warming," "cooling," or "neutral.". Chicken, mutton, and beef, for example, are warming meats, and if the body's system is already in a balanced state, this effect must be neutralized by cooking these meats with cooling herbs or vegetables. Duck, frog, and rabbit, on the other hand,

are said to be cooling meats, while pork is neutral. When meats are cooked with cabbage or cauliflower (cooling), garlic and ginger (warming), the desired neutralizing effect will be produced.

A further factor in the classification of food and natural remedies is "humidity." It is unhealthy to accumulate too much humidity in the body. That is why oysters, shrimp, corn, mangoes, and coconut, which produce "humidity," must be neutralized with potatoes, carrots, apples, milk, or honey.

This type of elaborate preparation, in which traditional remedies are cooked together with meats, seafoods, dried or fresh fruits, and vegetables to produce a thick soup or clear broth, has many applications. It can revitalize, rejuvenate, strengthen the body's organs and support their function, improving blood circulation, regulating the amount of heat and humidity in the body, act as a sedative and improve the complexion. Most medicinal soup recipes result in a clear broth from which the few herbs are removed before it is drunk. The meat which has given its flavor to the liquid is served separately with soy sauce. The Chinese believe that eating an animal organ

strengthens the corresponding part in the human body, and they therefore eat every part of the animal, including the internal organs (variety meats) and feet.

As with herbal teas, these "herb soups" are only effective if they are consumed on a regular basis, and this is another reason why they are a constant feature of festive meals consisting of several courses. A few of these soups are taken just before going to bed, when the body is in a relaxed state and is better able to absorb and make use of nutrition.

The medicinal soups are either prepared in a clay pot, in which the ingredients simmer gently for three to four hours, or in a double-boiler, which consist of a lower pot filled with water and a close-fitting upper part which holds the soup. In the double-boiler the soup simmers very gently. This enables the Chinese person eating the finished soup to feel that he or she has benefited from the essence of the ingredients. Chinese herbal medicine is now practiced in many western countries, and many western physicians believe in its beneficial effects.

The medicinal ingredients for black chicken soup (in Chinese herb stores you are given the exact amount for one chicken):
1 *Yuan rou* (dried longan)
2 *Yi mi* (pearl barley)
3 *Huang jing* (monk's pepper root)
4 *Ju zi* (boxthorn fruit))
5 *He shou wu* (buckwheat rhizome)
6 *Dang shen* (Chilean bellflower root)
7 *Lian zi* (seeds of the Indian lotus flower)

烏
雞
湯

Hai ji tang, black chicken soup, does indeed call for a black hen or rooster, which is supposed to have a particularly warming and strengthening effect. The meat is simmered in water for two hours in a double-boiler, together with all the other ingredients (see left). The broth is drunk and the chicken meat served separately with a light soy sauce.

湯 **Winter melon and other**
Soups

In restaurants Winter melon soup is served in scooped-out melons lavishly decorated with Chinese numbers or Chinese characters. The expense, one could even say, the extravagance of this exercise, is so great that the soup has to be ordered in advance. You can, of course, make Winter melon soup at home, although you may have to make do without the artistic decoration. You should select a winter melon (winter gourd) at least 12 in (30 cm) in diameter, to hold all of the ingredients. As the amount of soup depends on the size of the melon, the quantities given in the recipe opposite are only approximations. For the same reason, the volumes have been given in cups, the basis of which is a standard American cup measure of 8 fl oz (250 ml).

It is not advisable to make this soup in an ordinary saucepan, as the extended cooking time (five hours!) is not without its effects on the finished soup, though this affects not so much the taste as its medicinal value. Properly prepared, the soup is believed to have a detoxifying and purifying effect on the body.

The wintermelon is a large, pale green muskmelon which can be found in Chinese markets. The skin is a wonderful pearly green color when fresh.

Dong gua tang
Winter melon soup

1 winter melon, about 12 in (30 cm) long
chicken broth (enough to cover the ingredients to be cooked in the melon shell)
1/4 cup cubed chicken breast
1/4 cup shiitake
1/4 cup bamboo shoots, thinly sliced
1/4 cup diced, mild smoked bacon
1/4 cup cubed abalone
1 sliced fresh root ginger
2–3 green onions (scallions), sliced in rings
1 Tbs Chinese rice wine
1/4 cup lotus seeds, soaked, bitter green center discarded
salt

Rub off any wax coating on the melon. Slice off the upper quarter of the melon and set aside to be used as a lid later on. Scoop out the seeds and flesh with a spoon. The seeds will not be used, but some of the flesh is cut into cubes and used as an ingredient in the soup. Pre-cook the scooped-out melon for 15 minutes in the prepared chicken broth.

Soak the shiitake mushrooms in water for 30 minutes, squeeze them dry, and mince them. Put the mushrooms, bamboo shoots, diced chicken fillets, and ham into the melon, together with the flesh of the melon, ginger, green onions, wine, and lotus seeds. Pour over sufficient broth to cover the ingredients. The melon should not be filled to the brim. Cover the melon with its own lid and steam for about five hours, or until the melon is cooked and translucent. Add the abalone and the salt ten minutes before the end of cooking. If you can get them, small melons in which the soup can be served in individual portions are ideal for parties.

Cai tang
Clear vegetable soup

4 cups (1 l) chicken broth
5 1/4 oz (150 g) Chinese (Napa) cabbage, each leaf sliced into 1 in (3 cm) pieces
or
7 oz (200 g) Chinese leaf vegetables (such as bok choy or pak choy) sliced or torn into 1 1/2–2-in (4–5 cm) pieces
1 medium carrot, peeled, and sliced into 1 in (2 cm) thick slices
3 green onions (scallions), sliced into 1 1/2 in (3 cm) lengths
1 Tbs soy sauce
salt to taste
pepper

Bring the chicken broth to the boil, add the vegetables and green onions; return briefly to the boil. Season with soy sauce, salt and pepper, stir, and serve piping hot.

As a variation, add 8 medium shrimp when the vegetables are half-cooked, or fish steaks marinated in soy sauce and Chinese rice wine (or sherry), 15 minutes before serving. Do not let the fish overcook.

西
洋
菜
豬
骨
湯

Xi yang cai zhu gu tang – Pork rib soup with watercress

菜
湯

Cai tang – Clear Vegetable Soup

Ji shang tang
Chicken soup

1 large boiling fowl
or 4 lb 8 oz (2 kg) chicken carcass, neck and wings
12 cups (3 l) water
2 pieces peeled ginger root, cut into
1/2 in (1 cm) thick slices
1 green onion (scallion), sliced into 1 in (2 cm) pieces

Put the chicken or carcass into a large saucepan, together with ginger and green onion, cover with water, and bring to the boil. Skim off the scum, reduce the heat, and allow the broth to simmer for 2 hours. Strain through a sieve, then pour back into the pot and reheat before serving.

Xi yang cai zhu gu tang
Pork rib soup with watercress

1 lb 5 oz (600 g) pork spareribs cut into
1 1/2-2 in (4–5 cm) pieces, trimmed of fat
5 cups (1 1/4 l) water
14 oz (400 g) watercress
2 Tbs light Soy sauce
1 Tsp salt (or to taste)
pepper
4 tsp (20 g) boxthorn fruits (optional)

Trim the roots and stalks of the watercress, wash and drain it.
Put the spareribs in a saucepan with the water and bring to the boil. Reduce the heat and simmer gently for 30 minutes. When the ribs are almost done, add the watercress, soy sauce, salt, pepper, and boxthorn fruits if using.
Simmer for a further 10 minutes and serve hot.

Huang gua tang
Yellow cucumber soup

1 medium-sized yellow cucumber,
peeled and diced
1 lb 2 oz (500 g) ham hocks, trimmed of fat
3 Chinese honey dates
6 cups (1 1/2 l) water

Bring all the ingredients to the boil in a large saucepan, reduce the heat, and simmer for 2 hours. Remove the bones. Salt the soup and serve hot.

Shu mi tang
Corn soup

2 large fresh corn cobs or
1 can baby sweetcorn (1 1/4 cups) (255 g)
2 egg whites
5 Tsp milk
3 cups (750 ml) chicken broth
1 Tsp salt
2 1/2 Tsp cornstarch mixed with 5 Tsp cold water
or chicken broth

Garnish
2 Tbs fried onion rings or
2 Tbs finely chopped lean fried bacon

Strip the corn from the cob or drain the tinned corn. Beat egg-whites until stiff, add the milk, and beat it in. Bring the chicken broth to the boil, add the corn, and salt.
Bring the soup back to the boil, stirring constantly, and thicken with the cornstarch mixture. Remove the pan from the heat and fold the beaten egg whites into the soup. Stir again and serve hot, garnished with fried onion rings or chopped fried bacon.

玉
米
湯

Shu mi tang — Corn Soup

33

麵條 Noodles

Noodles are eaten at any time of day, and feature in both simple and very lavish meals. Noodles may be made of wheat or rice flour and can be bought fresh or dried in various shapes and sizes. Wheat noodles can be made with or without eggs. The famous cellophane noodles are made from mung beans. In Chinese cooking, handmade noodles are only served at very important festive meals, as machine-produced noodles are of perfectly satisfactory quality. Noodles can be used in many ways. They can be stir-fried, served in soups, or with rich meat sauces, but also simply dressed with a light soy sauce or sesame oil. Chicken, roast duck or pork, fish, shrimp, vegetables, beansprouts, and various kinds of mushrooms are popular accompaniments to a dish of noodles, all served in a spicy sauce.

Cutting, coiling, and deep-frying

To make a noodle dough, you will need all-purpose flour, water, potassium carbonate (potash), salt, and eggs. Depending on the use for which the dough is intended, varying proportions of these ingredients are kneaded into a firm but elastic dough. This is rolled out evenly, cut into flat strips of varying width, and steamed. If the noodles are to be dried, they have to have their moisture content removed in a low oven.
For wrappers, the dough is first cut into wide strips, and then into squares for wonton or circles for dumplings.

To make *yee fu* noodles, fresh noodles are cooked, carefully drained, and then fried. For this, 1 lb 6 oz (600 g) of noodles are put into each perforated metal cylinder, which is then plunged for one minute into very hot oil (383°F (195°C)). This cooks the noodles in round "nests" which are used for the preparation of *sub gum mee*. Sprinkle the "noodle nest" with a little water and fry, stirring to separate the individual strands. In the meantime, cook vegetables, meat, or seafood in a sauce thickened with cornstarch. Pour the sauce over the noodles and serve.

Fujian mian: fresh, yellow egg noodles made with wheat flour, for soups and for frying

Sheng mian: fresh, thin egg wheat flour noodles for soups, or served with soy sauce or sesame oil

Yi mian: dried thin egg noodles made with wheat flour (used in the same way as *sheng mian*)

Kuo mian: fresh egg-noodle strips made with wheat flour, for soups or for dipping in sauces

Dong fen: cellophane noodles made of mung bean flour. They become transparent when cooked.

Mi fen: dried rice vermicelli for soups, for frying, or for serving with rich sauces

Gan mian: dried thin wheat flour and egg noodles, for soups and for stir-frying

Yun tun pi: for wonton fried or cooked in broth, the noodle dough is cut into squares.

Yun tun pi: wrappers for steamed dumplings like *shao mai* are cut out into circles.

蝦仁麵

雞蛋 Eggs

In Chinese cuisine, eggs are not just an important ingredient in cooking and baking but are a subject in themselves. The eggs of hens, ducks, geese, and quail are all eaten, and with eggs, as with so many things in the larder and cellar, the harder it is to get hold of them the better they seem to taste. For the Chinese one of the main attractions of this symbol of luck and fertility is its smooth, rounded shape, devoid of corners or edges, a shape which they see in some way as the expression of well-being itself. In their efforts to make the very most of the qualities of the egg in cuisine, and to ex press this symbolic meaning, the Chinese have made many discoveries, and these have also been adopted in Singapore. Hen's eggs, for example, are marbled, smoked, or dyed red. A steamed egg sauce prepared with ginger juice and rock candy is eaten to soothe and strengthen the lungs.

Cha ye dan: For marbled eggs the shells of hard-boiled eggs are tapped so that a network of cracks appears in them. Water, soy sauce, black tea leaves, and star anise are boiled up together, and the eggs are simmered for some time in this liquid, to allow the color and aroma to penetrate the cracks. When the shells are peeled, the eggs have a marbled appearance. Such an egg can be eaten as a snack, as a starter, or as part of a cold platter.

Lu dan: Smoked eggs are not actually smoked but owe their color and flavor to a marinade of soy sauce, sesame oil, sugar, and salt. They are simmered in the shell for some time on a low heat without any fat. The eggs are left for several hours in this marinade after cooking. Hen's eggs used for *lu dan* are only cooked for as long as it takes to hard-boil the whites while leaving the yolks a little soft in the center. They are served the same way as marbled eggs.

Hong ji dan: Red is the color of joy, which is why red-colored, hard-boiled hen's eggs are given to friends and family when their new baby is one month old. Red eggs are also used as offerings when asking the gods for a favor, and women who go to the temple with a red egg usually hope for a son. Superstitious parents do not give their children red eggs when they are taking examinations as a red circle signifies zero (the lowest grade.)

Xian dan: Salt eggs. A duck's egg cannot be kept as long as a hen's egg, but because the shell is tougher it can be subjected to complex preserving processes. One of these requires the raw eggs to be laid down in salt and covered with a layer of fine black, burnt earth. This earth is removed before boiling and the egg is thoroughly washed. The boiled egg is served with rice or rice gruel. The egg white is quite salty, but it isn't eaten alone but rather used as a condiment. The egg yolks are used in moon cakes. Raw salt eggs can be beaten, mixed with ground pork, and steamed.

Pi dan: These are the famous so-called ":Thousand - year-old" eggs. They are duck eggs which have been preserved in a mixture of chalk, ash, salt, and rice husks for 2-4 months. At the end of this period, the egg-white has turned to a translucent black and has the consistency of a thick jelly, and the yolk has taken on a gray-green color. When the egg is "ripe", the ash coating is removed, and it is washed, peeled, then cut in half and served with pickled ginger, as an appetizer or as part of a cold platter. Rice-gruel can be served with it. In a famous Cantonese "three-egg" recipe, a thousand-year old egg is steamed together with beaten hen's eggs and salted duck eggs.

An chun: The delicate, little quail's eggs in their pretty speckled shells are hard-boiled, peeled, and served as an accompaniment to hot-and-sour soups. Because of their size, they are also a popular garnish on cold platters, for which they are preferred to boiled hen's eggs due to their decorative effect. Quails' eggs preserved in the same manner as thousand-year-old eggs are a special delicacy.

Tea eggs cooking in a mixture of water, soy sauce, and black tea.

Choosing hen's eggs

When buying eggs, quality inspection starts with the shell. The important thing is not the color but that the egg should be intact, and — you may find this surprising — clean. While we in the West may think of bits of straw and other impurities as the signs of really happy free-range hen (which may well inspire an enterprising chicken-farmer to apply a little "make-up" to his eggs!), in Singapore people consider clean eggs to be a sign of careful management. Unfortunately, the freshness of an egg is something that can only be tested at home when it is broken. Fresh eggs have a well-rounded yolk in a viscous, clear egg-white which is not watery and runny.

Storing hen's eggs

Fresh eggs which are refrigerated immediately in their original packaging will keep for 4 to 5 weeks, as long constant changes of temperature are avoided, as these may affect the consistency of the egg white. Egg whites will keep for up to four days in the refrigerator, in an air-tight container, but egg yolks are best stored in water in an air-tight container, and will keep no longer than 1–2 days.

The Spring Roll

春卷 Poh piah

In the West, there is no other dish that is as symbolic of Chinese cooking as the spring roll. Nowadays, it has become standard fare in every supermarket freezer. But it has traveled a very long way to get this far. The spring roll probably originates from the Chinese province of Fujian, on the coast of southeast China, opposite Taiwan. Emigrants who passed through Taiwan before spreading through the whole of Southeast Asia took the spring roll along in their baggage, so to speak. The spring roll was traditionally eaten at a time when there was a surplus of fresh vegetables in the markets. The name "Spring Roll" indicates the importance of the new season, after the winter, with its reduced choice and reliance on preserved varieties, is finally over. On its way to the West, the spring roll not only changed its appearance but also its content, and ingredients for the filling have been adapted to regional conditions and preferences. What remains is the mainly vegetarian character of the filling, in which meat is not the essential ingredient.

So much for the "spring" part of the name. The "roll" is a wafer-thin pancake made with a dough of wheat flour, water, and a little salt, which can be made with or without eggs, as preferred. The ingredients are mixed together and kneaded to obtain a soft, smooth dough, which should not be too soft but should form a firm yet elastic ball. This ball of dough is then rolled onto a hot skillet and quickly lifted off again, so that a thin layer of dough sticks to the bottom. Three pans are used, and the first pancake will be ready when the third hits the pan — as long as the chef has sufficient dexterity, speed, and practice. If you do not feel up to the high art of making spring-roll wrappers, you can make thin egg pancakes from a dough made from 6 medium eggs, 2 cups (250g) all-purpose flour, about 1⅓ cups (325 ml) of water, and a pinch of salt. This batter should be liquid enough to be of pouring consistency, as it must be poured into the pan.

The filling consists of three elements — a basic vegetable-and-meat mixture, the seasonings, and a garnish, which is served separately. For the basic mixture, grated bamboo shoots and jicama are cooked together with shrimp, ground pork, garlic, and fermented soybeans in a shrimp-and-pork broth. The sweet sauce, chili paste and garlic paste must be spread over the pancake very thinly, and it is then sprinkled with fried shallots and garlic. A green salad leaf or thin piece of dough is then arranged on the pancake as a base for the filling, and to give the roll more body. For the garnish, there is a choice between blanched beansprouts, grated cucumber, finely-shredded omelet, crabmeat, cooked shrimp, sliced wind-dried Chinese sausage, little pieces of sole, and coriander (cilantro) leaves. The meat can also be omitted altogether.

Pie tee

To make these crunchy fried shells or nests, prepare a thin batter from ground rice, tapioca flour, eggs, and water. Leave it to rest for at least 20 minutes as you would any pancake. The special long-handled metal shell-mold which is used to shape the shells must be left in hot oil for a minute or so to heat it up.

To make the shell, dip the shell-mold into the batter and then immediately plung it into the hot oil. As soon as the shell is cooked and lightly browned, it will loosen itself from the mold. Lift the shell out of the oil and carefully place it on kitchen paper to drain. When all the shells made in this way have cooled, they can be stored in an airtight container. This means that the crunchy shells can easily be prepared in advance.

The filling is the same as for spring rolls. The shells are garnished with shrimp, finely-shredded omelet, and coriander (cilantro) leaves and stems, and served with a chili and garlic sauce.

Plenty of practice is needed in order to get the dough into the hot pan fast enough, and for the rhythm to be established.

Wafer-thin commercially manufactured spring-roll wrappers are sold by weight.

Start the spring roll with a piece of thin dough for reinforcement

Now for the spicing: chili and garlic paste and sweet sauce

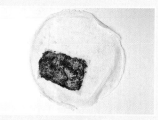

Only now are the seasonings mixed together.

Next the vegetable and meat mixture is arranged neatly on the wrapper.

For the garnish there is a choice. These are blanched beansprouts, …

…followed by finely shredded omelet strips, …

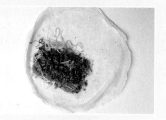

…and then fried or dry-fried, minced shallots and garlic, …

…topped with fresh coriander leaves.

Now the lower edge is folded tightly over the filling…

…and first the left and then the right side folded toward the center…

…to obtain a neat rectangle

Now the whole wrapper is rolled up and turned seam side downward, to make a neat package.

Slice the roll, using a sharp knife.

黃豆 Soybean

Today the products of this versatile bean can be found everywhere, and it appears not only in the familiar form of sprouts, soy sauce, beancurd, or tempeh, but also in disguise, as "vegetable protein," "emulsifier," "lecithin," or "vegetable oil," playing its part in spreads, dairy products, canned fish, candies, desserts, and much more beside. Soybean has a venerable history and has no need of anonymity. Soybeans have been known for almost 5,000 years in China, and they quickly spread throughout the whole of the Asia, as they make an important nutritional contribution where meat and milk products are scarce. It was only, however, toward the end of the 19th century that this valuable protein arrived in Europe and America. This bushy annual, which grows to a height of about 32 inches (80 cm), requires more or less the same climate and soil conditions as corn and grapevines — high temperatures and moderate rain in summer and fall, and light, neutral soil. Most of the world production of soybeans is grown between the 25th and the 45th parallels, at altitudes of around 4000 ft (1000 m) above sea level. The USA, Canada, and Brazil have now overtaken China in Soybean production, which in the West is fully mechanized. Soybeans are often grown as monocultures, with all the disadvantages that this entails, such as the use of chemical fertilizers and pesticides. The recent development of genetically-engineered varieties of soybean is another consequence of this state of affairs.

Despite their great nutritional value, fully-grown soybeans are rarely used as a vegetable because they require long soaking and a cooking time of up to 24 hours! That is why the fresh sprouts are preferred. Most of the harvest is processed into beancurd and tempeh, using agents such as molds and bacteria to break down the beans into these foods which are among the staples of Southeast Asia and are now gaining more and more recognition in the West. Soy milk, made from soaked, cooked beans, resembles cow's milk, and from a nutritional point of view is an ideal milk substitute, for those allergic to cow's milk. It is also drunk in its own right, hot or cold, with or without sugar. The beans can also be ground into flour and pressed to obtain oil. And where would the cuisine of the orient and Southeast Asia be without its famous soy sauce?

Soybean sprouts

Black soybeans are imported from Thailand and Myanmar (Burma).

The beans are washed and spread out in deep baskets with slatted bottoms, and covered with plastic sheeting. They are sprayed with cold water every four hours, and by the second day they have already begun to sprout. During their growth, the sprouts remain covered, to protect them from sunlight and air, as they would otherwise become green and spindly. They grow in days, so the use of growth-promoting chemicals is unnecessary. By the fourth day, the sprouts are 90 percent grown, and on the sixth day they have reached the required size. Before the baskets of sprouts can be sold, the top layer of green leaves is trimmed off. These are used as feed for chickens and ducks. One basket yields about 154 lb (70 kg) of sprouts, and the output of a medium-sized business is 60 baskets a day. The best soybean sprouts are short, clean, crisp, and white, without any green leaves. Sprouts should never be eaten raw, nor should they be cooked for too long. Stir-fried soybean sprouts with green onions (scallions) and ginger are a popular vegetable dish. They are also often added to soups.

Soybean sprouts should not be confused with the better-known mung beansprouts, which are used in spring rolls or combined with noodles. Both types of sprouts can be kept for a few days in the vegetable compartment of the refrigerator, in a closed container to which a little water has been added, or one which is lined with damp terrycloth. Both types may be bought fresh, though mung beans sprouts are easier to find.

Dou ban jiang

Salted soybeans are a popular condiment throughout the region. They are used crushed, either on their own or mixed with crushed chili peppers and garlic. They are made from cooked soybeans which have been placed in large jars and heavily salted. Wheat flour and a fungus starter are added, then the mixture is left to ferment for 45 days. The fungus starter, a mold, reacts on the top layer, which turns black. When this layer is removed the light brown beans underneath can be decanted and pasteurized.

Dou chi

A similar process is used to turn black soybeans into a very strongly flavored condiment. Dried black beans are cooked and spread out for four days, then mixed with wheat flour, salt, and a mold starter. Any mold clinging to the surface is washed off with water, then the beans are drained, and stored in jars for 45 days. When they are fully fermented they have a powerful aroma and must be washed before use. They are used sparingly to enhance the flavors of fish and beef. The flavor is said to be an acquired taste.

The soybean is in the process of turning into beancurd (from top left to bottom right): fresh soybeans, soaked soybeans, ground soybeans, soy milk, and mashed curds before pressing.

Meat from the fields

Tofu

Tofu (beancurd) can be made with various kinds of soybeans, the important factor here being a particularly high protein content and the qualities which give the finished product an appetizing look and pleasant aroma. Soybean oil and animal feed are made from different varieties of Soybean. In Singapore, tofu is generally made with beans imported from Canada.

The manufacturing process starts with the washing of the raw soybeans, which are then soaked in warm water at about 90°F (32°C) for three to four hours. The soaking period must not be too long, as the beans would otherwise start to ferment. The soaking process facilitates the subsequent stages, particularly the extraction of milk. More water is added to the soaked beans

before they are ground to a pulp in a stone mill, with the addition of oil. Stone-grinding creates less heat, and this is an important factor as heat impairs the quality of the finished product. Furthermore, this type of milling increases the homogeneity of the finished beancurd. The oil is added to stop the formation of foam during the production of the pulp.

The pulp is then cooked for 30 minutes at a temperature of 219°F (104°C). The milk (80%) is separated from the solids (20%), which can then be used as animal feed or as meat extenders for the food industry (in hamburger, for instance).

A skin forms on the hot milk, which is then removed and dried by being draped in folds over a pole. It is eventually sold as dried beancurd sticks (*fu chok.*)

If the soy milk is further processed while it is still hot, the end-product is a firm beancurd, while if the milk is allowed to cool down the beancurd will be soft. For the next stage a coagulant, calcium chloride or

calcium sulfate, is added to the milk, and acts in the same way as rennet does on cows' milk, curdling the soy milk. The curds are then broken up as in cheese-making and poured into smaller molds lined with cheesecloth. The soy curd is pressed into the mold to remove excess moisture and to obtain the required thickness. After pressing for 25 minutes the beancurd is unmolded and allowed to dry off for a further five to ten minutes.

Tofu gonn, which is very dry and flat, is cut up into rectangular blocks and stored in a cool place

A second, thicker, moister quality of beancurd is cut into blocks 3 in (7.5 cm) wide, which are briefly rinsed in water to cool them and rid them of surplus coagulant, and then packed.

1 The prepared soybeans on their way to the stone-grinder. They must not soak for too long, otherwise they will begin to ferment.
2 The bean pulp is transferred automatically by conveyor belt to stainless steel vats, where it is heated to 220°F (104°C).
3 When a coagulant is added to the hot soy milk it curdles.

4 The curdled soy milk is broken up and put into molds lined with cheesecloth.
5 The cheesecloth is carefully folded over the curd and the mass pressed down until it takes on the required consistency.
6 After about 25 minutes, the curd has lost enough liquid and a worker cuts the pressed beancurd into rectangular blocks.

On the hot Soybean milk a skin is formed, which will be processed into *fu pei* and *fu chok*

Soy milk products

Fu pei — dried tofu skin
The skin formed when soy milk is gently heated in a wide, shallow pan is removed and arranged on a draining board to dry and solidify. The process is repeated until no more skin is formed. Meat and fish balls are wrapped in beancurd skin for frying.

Fu chok — dried tofu sticks
For this, the skin is not laid out flat but only drained and then draped in folds over a pole to dry out completely. This makes it so brittle that it has to be soaked before further processing. Small pieces of *fu chok* are a prized addition to boiled or braised dishes.

Tim chok — sweet tofu pieces
The very thick layer of curd left over after making *fu pei* or *fu chok* is dried, cut up, packaged and sold in rectangular 4 x 2 in (10 x 5 cm) blocks. It is slightly sweet, and is never eaten alone, but is cooked and added to other ingredients, particularly vegetables. It can also be frozen, or used as a garnish for dry-fried rice noodles. It must be soaked before use.

Tofu fa — soft tofu as a dessert
This is made of well-diluted Soybean milk with the addition of a little tapioca flour and coagulant, which gives it its soft consistency. This beancurd is served warm or cold, with a syrup flavored with almond extract.

Marinated tofu
These are small cubes of pressed beancurd steeped in spiced wine. *Nan ru* (red marinated tofu) can be used as a condiment, but also as an appetizer in the form of an accompaniment to rice or rice-gruel. *Fu ru* (white marinated beancurd) is an accompaniment whose taste can be enhanced with a few drops of sesame oil.

The slabs of beancurd are removed from the molds and dried for a few minutes, until they reach the consistency required by the end-user.

Tofu recipes for every taste

豆腐的各種烹調法

Tofu on its own is rather bland in taste, but this is precisely its strength, since when it is combined with different ingredients and condiments it tastes new and different every time.

Soft beancurd is an interesting addition to soups, and it can be steamed or even fried so that it is crisp on the outside and soft and melting on the inside. A very simple and extremely nutritious meal can be made by scoring the surface of a piece of tofu several times, sprinkling it with a little soy sauce and a few drops of sesame oil, then sprinkling very finely chopped green onions (scallions) on top and letting these ingredients soak in for a little while before steaming the beancurd and garnishing it with fried onion rings before serving.

Firm tofu is ideal for stir-frying and deep-frying and can even be stuffed, if it is cut in such a way as to make a pocket. It is solid enough to hold a filling of ground meat or fish. These stuffed pockets are used in soup, or fried for snacks. Another way of making such beancurd pockets is to fry the beancurd whole, then to halve it diagonally and cut pockets into each half, which are then filled with grated raw or blanched vegetables such as beansprouts, cucumber, salad, or carrots, and served with a mild or hot chili sauce.

Niang dou fu
Filled beancurd pockets

4 pieces firm white tofu
Cornstarch for dusting

Filling
8 oz (250 g) lean ground pork
12–16 bay shrimp, peeled and chopped
1 egg, beaten
4 Tsp light soy sauce
2 Tsp sugar
2 Tsp sesame oil
4 Tsp cornstarch
pepper
oil for frying

Combine all the ingredients for the filling and divide into 16 equal portions.
Quarter the four beancurd pieces. Make pockets by cutting deeply into one of the cut sides. Dust the pocket with cornstarch and carefully place the filling inside.
Heat the oil and fry 4 filled beancurd pockets at a time. Drain and serve with chili sauce.

Xia ren dou fu
Stir-fried beancurd with jumbo shrimp

2 blocks firm tofu, sliced into 16 pieces
5$\frac{1}{4}$–7 oz (150–200 g) jumbo shrimp, peeled and sprinkled with salt and pepper
1 garlic clove , peeled and chopped
1$\frac{1}{2}$ Tbs light soy sauce
1 red chili pepper, sliced into rings (or to taste)
salt to taste
pepper
2 Tbs oil

Heat 1 tablespoon of oil and fry half the garlic in it. When it is golden, add the shrimp and fry until pink. Remove from pan and set aside.
Heat the remaining oil and fry the remaining garlic. When golden, add the beancurd and lightly brown this as well. Return the shrimp to the pan and season with soy sauce, pepper, and salt. Stir, add the sliced chili peppers, and serve.

Hong shao dou fu
Braised beancurd

1 lb (450 g) soft tofu, cut into 1$\frac{1}{4}$ in (3 cm) cubes
1 green onion (scallion), sliced into 1$\frac{1}{4}$ in (3 cm) pieces
3 Tsp minced garlic
2 Tsp minced ginger root
4–4$\frac{1}{2}$ oz (120–150 g) button mushrooms
2 Tsp oyster sauce
1 Tbs dark soy sauce
1 Tbs rice wine
3 Tbs water or chicken broth
salt to taste
pepper
sesame oil
oil for frying

Heat the oil in a deep skillet and fry the beancurd cubes until they are crisp on the outside and tender inside. Drain and set aside.
Add more to the pan and sauté the garlic, ginger, and green onions . Add the mushrooms, stir briefly, and season with oyster sauce, soy sauce, wine, chicken broth, salt, and pepper.
Reduce the heat and add the fried beancurd cubes. Cover, and leave to simmer for about 10 minutes. Sprinkle with a few drops of sesame oil and serve.

Xia ren dou fu – stir-fried beancurd with jumbo shrimp

蝦仁豆腐

Sui rou zheng dou fu
Steamed soft beancurd with ground pork

2 blocks (1 lb 5 oz (600 g)) soft tofu
2 garlic cloves , peeled and chopped
2 Tsp fermented soybean paste (optional)
7 oz (200 g) ground pork
2 eggs, lightly beaten
salt
pepper
1 Tbs chopped green onions (scallions)
1 Tbs chopped coriander (cilantro) leaves
2 Tbs oil

Break up the soft beancurd into several pieces and drain it in a sieve.
Bring the water in the steamer to the boil. Heat the oil in a pan and fry the chopped garlic in it. When lightly browned, add the soybean paste and cook briefly. Stir in the ground meat and salt. As soon as the ground meat has colored, add the beancurd and mix well with the other ingredients. At first add only half the beaten eggs, mix well, then add more until the other ingredients are sufficiently well bound.
Season with salt and pepper. Place the mixture in a bowl about 2–2½ in (5-6 cm) deep and sprinkle with the chopped green onions and coriander leaves. Place the bowl in the steamer and steam for approximately 8 –10 minutes, or until mixture becomes firm.
If you are using soybean paste, reduce the quantity of salt as the paste is very salty.

Dou hua
Sweet beancurd dessert

10½ oz (300 g) soybeans
12 cups (3 l) water
1 Tsp powdered calcium sulfate, sifted
3 Tbs (45 g) cornstarch
½ cup (125 ml) hot water

Syrup
1¾ cups (420 g) sugar
1 cup (250 ml) water
almond extract (optional)

Wash the soybeans and soak for half a day or overnight. Drain.
Grind half the soybeans in a blender together with 1¾ cups (375 ml) water and squeeze the mixture in cheesecloth until the pulp is dry. Put the pulp back into the blender with a little water, process, and squeeze out again. Repeat this with the remaining beans.
Pour the soy milk obtained in this way into a deep pan, add the remaining water, and bring to the boil over medium heat while stirring constantly. Regularly skim the foam that appears on the surface.
Mix calcium sulfate (gypsum powder) and cornstarch in hot water until dissolved then pour into large heat-proof casserole or pan.
When the soy milk boils pour immediately over the cornstarch mix. Quickly remove all bubbles from the surface, cover the dish with a cloth, put a lid on top and let the soy milk thicken for 40 - 50 minutes. The result is a milky jelly.
For the syrup, bring water and sugar to the boil and stir until the sugar has dissolved. If the syrup becomes too thick it may be thinned again with almond flavoring.
Put a little of the beancurd into individual dishes, garnished with 2 tbs of syrup (or to taste). This sweet can be served hot or cold, and is as popular as a dessert as it is as a snack.

Zha fu pi juan
Fried beancurd skin roll

1 tofu skin (available from oriental food stores)
5–6 shiitake
5¼ oz (150 g) lean pork
5¼ oz (150 g) shrimps, peeled and sliced into three
4½ oz (120 g) carrots, scraped and blanched
1 shallot, peeled and sliced into rings
3 Tbs water
1 Tsp wine
1 Tsp light soy sauce
1 Tsp sugar
salt to taste
2 Tsp sesame oil
pepper
1 Tsp cornstarch, mixed with 2–3 Tbs water
2 Tbs oil

Soak the mushrooms in hot water for an hour, drain them, remove the tough stems, and cut the caps into thin strips.
Cut the pork into thin strips. Marinate for 20 minutes in a little light soy sauce, sesame oil, and pepper.
Stir-fry the shrimp in a little oil until pink. Drain and set aside.
Stir-fry the marinated pork strips in a little oil until done. Set aside.
Reheat the pan once more, add 1 Tbs oil, and as soon as it is hot, fry the shallot rings in it until they start to give off an aroma. Stir in all the cooked ingredients as well as the carrots and mushrooms.
Cook for one minute, add water and condiments, and mix well. Bind with the dissolved cornstarch while stirring constantly. Arrange the ingredients on a serv-ing platter and allow to cool. The filling should be only slightly moist.
Dab the beancurd skin with a damp cloth until it becomes smooth and can be spread out flat and cut into 6 - 8 triangles.
Divide the cooled filling into 6 – 8 portions.
Place one portion on the edge of a triangle. Wrap the corners over the filling and cover, fold in both sides to the center, and finish wrapping the roll.
Heat 1 tbs oil in a pan and fry the rolls in it, adding more oil if needed. These rolls can also be deep-fried.
Serve with plum sauce or chili sauce.

Zha fu pi juan – Fried beancurd skin roll.

炸腐皮卷

It always starts the same way: before the beans are soaked they are washed.

醬油 Soy sauce

Some of the proprietary seasonings used in Western Europe are made from raw materials which are clearly acceptable from the health point of view, as they are covered by government regulations, but which one would nonetheless not want to look at too closely. No one wants to think that what they are putting into their soup might be made from the residues of meat and fish processing, dried blood, and bonemeal extracts. This lovely mixture may have been boiled with hydrochloric acid, which then has to be neutralized with caustic soda or sodium carbonate, which produces salt. Unlike this chemical process, the manufacture of soy sauce uses mold cultures (Aspergillus soyae or Aspergillus oryzae). This method is time-consuming, however, and so as with naturally fermented soy sauce, there are also more quickly manufactured varieties available, made with the help of hydrochloric acid (by hydrolysis.)

For traditional enzymatic fermentation the soybeans are washed, soaked, and cooked under pressure in steel vats for 45 minutes. Lightly ground wheat and the required mold starter are then mixed in with the cooked beans. This mixture is put into culture-beds where it rests in an environment with controlled temperature and humidity. After 24 hours the beans are turned. After four days, as the mold grows, the beans take on a greenish color. They are then transferred into fiberglass tanks, covered in brine, and left to ferment for three months. At the end of this period, the first extraction of crude soy sauce takes place. More brine is added, and there is a second extraction, one month later, a process which is repeated for the third extraction.

At this point, the paths of the different soy sauces diverge. The saltier, light soy sauce is mixed with a preserving agent, pasteurized and stored in tanks for seven days to clarify before bottling. After extraction the dark sauce is not only mixed with a preservative but also with caramel, and then has to mature for a further month, before it too can be pasteurized and bottled.

The beans are cooked in two-ton pressure cookers for no more than 45 minutes.

The beans travel down a chute into the mixer, where the ground wheat and mold cultures are added.

The beans rest for four days while the mold cultures do their work. The beans are fermented in brine and what doesn't turn to sauce is sold in the market as "salted beans."

Jiang you ji
Chicken in soy sauce

1 oven-ready chicken 4 lb 8 oz (2 kg)
2 Tbs oil
2 slices root ginger, about (5 mm) thick
1 green onion (scallion), sliced into 3 pieces
1 Tbs wine rice
1/2 cup (125 ml) light Soy sauce
4 Tbs dark soy sauce
1/4 Tsp five-spice powder
1/2 cup (125 ml) water
1 Tsp sugar

Marinade
1 Tbs rice wine
1 Tsp finely chopped ginger root
2 Tsp light soy sauce
pepper

Wash the chicken thoroughly and dry well. Combine the ingredients for the marinade, rub them into the chicken, and allow to stand for 30 minutes. Heat the oil in a casserole and fry the ginger and green onion in it until the ginger is light-brown. Add the remaining ingredients and bring to the boil. Put in the chicken, bring the liquid back to the boil, then turn the chicken several times, basting each time with the hot liquid. Finally, braise the chicken in the covered casserole for 10 minutes on each side. Remove the chicken from the pan, allow to cool, and cut into serving portions. Pour sauce over the portions and serve.

Hong shao niu nan
Braised shoulder of beef
for 4 - 6 people

2 lb 3 oz (1 kg) shoulder of beef
3 Tbs oil
1 slice root ginger 3/4 in (2 cm) thick, grated
1 garlic clove , peeled and chopped
1 green onion (scallion), sliced into three pieces
2 Tsp sugar
2 segments star anise
1/2 Tsp Szechuan pepper
salt to taste
pepper
5 Tbs dark soy sauce
3 Tbs Chinese rice wine
11/2 Tbs mild vinegar
2 Tsp sesame oil

Heat the oil in a pan, and brown the root ginger, garlic, and green onions, then remove from the oil. Sear the joint on all sides to seal, then add the remaining dry ingredients to the pan and roast for a few minutes before adding the liquid.
Now transfer the meat and all the other ingredients into a casserole and fill up with water so the meat is just covered. Bring to the boil and skim the scum from the surface. Lower the heat and let the meat cook for three hours. As soon as it is tender and the liquid has boiled off, take it out, cut it into thin slices. Serve these on a platter, covered with the sauce.

While mostly mechanized, the business cannot entirely do without human labor.

After a further four weeks' rest, the dark soy sauce is also bottled.

蠔 Oyster sauce
油

Soy sauce has a competitor in oyster sauce, which is used with vegetables, meats, noodles, and mushrooms. It is often an ingredient in braised dishes, where its special aroma has an opportunity to develop. The extract obtained by boiling down oysters is imported from China or Japan and whisked for 20 minutes with sugar, salt, wheat flour, cornstarch, caramel, and water, which has to be filtered to ensure the quality of the finished product. This mixture is then cooked for an hour or so in a steamer. The cooked sauce is a rich, dark brown in color and has a creamy consistency. It is then filtered, and in order to minimize bacterial contamination, it is bottled while still hot, in sterilized glass bottles which are sealed in a vacuum in order to avoid the slightest risk.

Cornstarch, sugar, salt, wheat flour, oyster extract, and caramel (from left to right, top to bottom) are combined with water.

A bucket of caramel is added. The mixture is stirred and cooked for another hour, by which time the sauce will have reached the desired consistency.

Bottling takes place in a fully automated plant, and to the sound of tinkling glass thousands of bottles pass beneath the oyster sauce faucets every day.

芝麻 Sesame

Sesame is grown in China, India, Myanmar (Burma), Thailand, Vietnam, and Sri Lanka, as well as in South America and Africa. Even if it is only in fairy tales that pronouncing the words "open sesame" brings great riches, the value of these tiny (1/32 in (2 mm)) black or white seeds can be scientifically proven. They contain up to 60 percent oil and up to 30 percent protein. White sesame seeds improve sweet and savory dishes, while the black ones are used exclusively in candies, cakes, and desserts.

Both black and white sesame seeds are ideal for producing oil. A light oil is pressed from the raw seeds, while roasted sesame gives a dark oil. The light oil is neutral in flavor, and is of importance in margarine manufacture, but the dark oil has a nice, nutty aroma and is at home wherever Asian food is cooked.

Oil is pressed from whole or crushed sesame seeds, after it has been cleansed of all impurities, washed, and dried.

Sesame oil is as versatile as olive oil. It is ideal for cooking, and for marinades and dressings. A few drops are added to soups, noodles, meat, or fish.

Sesame oil is rich in vitamin E and polyunsaturated fats, and this aromatic oil is used for cooking, in marinades and as a condiment for soups, noodles, meat, or fish. A few drops are sufficient to impart its unmistakable taste to food. Sesame oil can be bought on its own or it can be blended with other oils. It is a good substitute for olive oil in dressings, particularly when the salad contains oriental vegetables. Used with a little soy sauce, and mixed with the juices of ginger and lime, it produces a spicy, aromatic dressing. Sprinkle toasted sesame seeds over the salad to make it even more special.

But sesame oil has other hidden talents. For some time after giving birth, Chinese mothers are given food fried in sesame oil as it is believed that the oil warms the womb, speeds healing, and prevents constipation. In India the oil made from pressing the unroasted seeds is used as a pomade, to keep the hair healthy, black and shiny.

1 Before the seeds are roasted, a machine removes foreign bodies and impurities. The half-hour long roasting time has to be carefully monitored.
2 The sesame seeds are transferred to big troughs to cool where they are turned several times so that the heat can escape more easily.
3 A check is again made as to whether the seeds have been over-roasted, as this would spoil the quality of the finished oil.

4 If the checks are satisfactory the roasted seeds go to the mill. The oil that pours out of the seeds is not yet free of residues.
5 The filtered oil is bottled. One ton of seeds produces about 22 gallons (300 liters) of oil. The residue is not wasted, as it provides an animal feed with a high protein content.
6 Nowadays, "open sesame" is no magic spell, but when roasted and pressed the seeds produce a wonderfully rich oil.

Condiments

Soy sauce and oyster sauce may be indispensable in Chinese cookery because together with the fish sauces they replace salt and are rich in protein and other nutrients, but they are not by far the only way of producing "tasty" food.

When people are used to food which is cooked rapidly and when meals consist of a variety of dishes all served together, they expect a variety of very different flavors, rather an amalgamation of tastes produced by long, slow cooking. Thus everything is welcome which can bring new, surprising accents to the food. This is why there is such a wide variety of sauces, pastes, pickles, and vinegars.

Hoisin sauce is thick, dark, and sweet, made from salted soybean paste with sugar, vinegar, and spices. It is used for dipping, but also as an ingredient in a marinade for grilled or broiled pork.

Dou chi: fermentation gives salted dried black beans so strong a flavor that they must be rinsed in water before use. They are cooked with fish or meat to enhance their flavor.

Dou ban jiang: the combination of salted soybeans and dates brings sweet and savory together. This is an ideal flavoring for bland foods.

Yu lu: fish sauce is made from anchovies or other small fish. It is very salty and can be used as a dip to which finely chopped chili peppers are added, or used to season food.

Jiang qing: light soy sauce is extracted from dried soybeans fermented with mold cultures, wheat flour, and brine. It is used as a dip and as a condiment instead of salt.

Hei jiang you: dark soy sauce is based on the same ingredients as light soy sauce, but is finished with caramel and matured for four more weeks. It is milder, and is also used to darken sauces.

Hao you: oyster sauce is made from cooked oysters, sugar, salt, wheat flour, cornstarch, yeast extract, caramel, and water. It is a harmonious addition to numerous sauces and dishes.

Jiang suan la jiao jiang: chili sauce with garlic and ginger is prepared from red chili peppers, garlic, and ginger, mixed with vinegar, salt, and spices. It is mainly used as a dip for seafood, but is also served with Hainanese Chicken Rice.

Mei zi jiang: Plum paste is made from plums, rice vinegar, sugar, and spices. It is served with roasted and fried dishes, cold dishes and grilled meats. It gives a special character to sweet and sour sauces and salad dressings.

Suan mei: Salted plums are pickled in a mixture of vinegar, salt, and spices. In judicious quantities, they are a worthwhile addition to steamed or braised dishes, particularly fish.

Fu ru: Small cubes of beancurd, pickled in wine, salt, and spices are a good accompaniment to steamed rice or rice gruel, which can be spiced up by the addition of a few drops of sesame oil.

La jiao jiang: chili sauce, here an extra-hot variety, is a thick preparation made from fresh red chili peppers, vinegar, salt, and sugar. It is used as a condiment and served on its own as a dip

Tian jiang: a thick, sweet sauce made from soybeans, sugar, wheat flour, and water. It is used as a dip for roasted meats, mixed with fried rice noodles and used as a condiment in spring rolls.

Bai cu: White vinegar is made from rice and is used in pickling, preserving, and cooking. It is stronger and more acidic than Western vinegars.

Hai cu: Black vinegar is made from glutinous rice and is milder than white vinegar. It is used as a dip or a condiment for braised dishes, which are traditionally served to women after childbirth.

蔬菜 Vegetables

The Chinese prefer their vegetables crisp and full of flavor rather than boiled in water until soft and mushy. All these finely chopped vegetables need is a quick stir-fry over high heat, with a touch of crushed garlic or ginger added. When leaf vegetables are cooked in water they are not boiled but merely wilted in hot water with a little oil added. This preserves the green color of the vegetable, which is then drained and seasoned with oyster sauce. Leaf vegetables used in soups are also pre-cooked in this way. The vegetables in herb soups are an exception, as they are simmered for a long time in the soup until they have imparted their healing properties to the liquid.

On the right: red and green chili peppers are thoroughly inspected before purchase.

Cucumbers, eggplant, loofahs, and okra make a nice dish of vegetables.

Here the green of bitter gourd and okra contrasts not only with the purple eggplant but also the white of the daikon radish and the red of the tomatoes.

菠菜

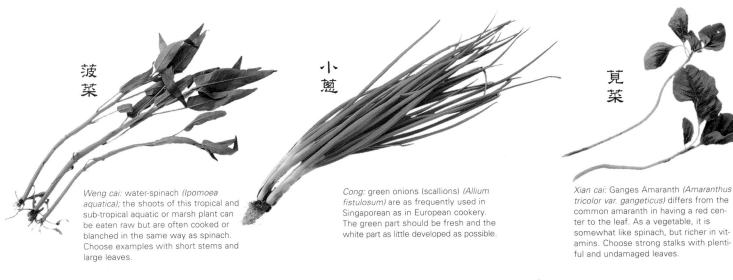

Weng cai: water-spinach *(Ipomoea aquatica);* the shoots of this tropical and sub-tropical aquatic or marsh plant can be eaten raw but are often cooked or blanched in the same way as spinach. Choose examples with short stems and large leaves.

小葱

Cong: green onions (scallions) *(Allium fistulosum)* are as frequently used in Singaporean as in European cookery. The green part should be fresh and the white part as little developed as possible.

莧菜

Xian cai: Ganges Amaranth *(Amaranthus tricolor var. gangeticus)* differs from the common amaranth in having a red center to the leaf. As a vegetable, it is somewhat like spinach, but richer in vitamins. Choose strong stalks with plentiful and undamaged leaves.

Jiw cai: Chinese mustard cabbage *(Brassica juncea)* can be found in many different varieties. Its strong taste can stand up to stir-frying or braising in a sauce with crabmeat. The Chinese also like it pickled in sour milk. Choose firm heads with immaculate stalks.

Vegetables are bought fresh every day. Here one can choose between garlic chives (front), snake-hair cucumbers (back left) and chili peppers (back).

Bai cai: Chinese white cabbage *(Brassica rapa var. chinensis)* comes in two varieties. It is popular for its strong stalks and is braised with other vegetables, mushrooms, and beancurd, when not stir-fried or used in a soup. Smaller plants are milder and more delicate.

大白菜

白菜

Da bai cai: Chinese (Napa) cabbage *(Brassica pekinensis)* is a leafy light green vegetable with white stems. It is stir-fried with garlic, or added to a clear soup. Chose firm, heavy heads without any brown discoloration.

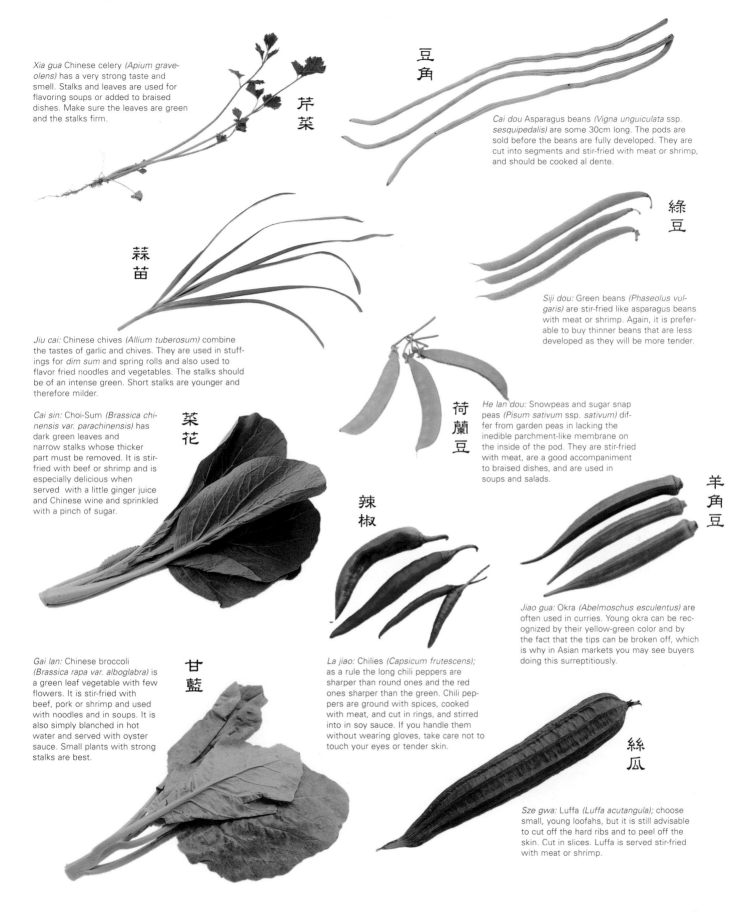

Xia gua Chinese celery *(Apium graveolens)* has a very strong taste and smell. Stalks and leaves are used for flavoring soups or added to braised dishes. Make sure the leaves are green and the stalks firm.

芹菜

豆角

Cai dou Asparagus beans *(Vigna unguiculata ssp. sesquipedalis)* are some 30cm long. The pods are sold before the beans are fully developed. They are cut into segments and stir-fried with meat or shrimp, and should be cooked al dente.

蒜苗

綠豆

Jiu cai: Chinese chives *(Allium tuberosum)* combine the tastes of garlic and chives. They are used in stuffings for *dim sum* and spring rolls and also used to flavor fried noodles and vegetables. The stalks should be of an intense green. Short stalks are younger and therefore milder.

Siji dou: Green beans *(Phaseolus vulgaris)* are stir-fried like asparagus beans with meat or shrimp. Again, it is preferable to buy thinner beans that are less developed as they will be more tender.

菜花

Cai sin: Choi-Sum *(Brassica chinensis var. parachinensis)* has dark green leaves and narrow stalks whose thicker part must be removed. It is stir-fried with beef or shrimp and is especially delicious when served with a little ginger juice and Chinese wine and sprinkled with a pinch of sugar.

荷蘭豆

He lan dou: Snowpeas and sugar snap peas *(Pisum sativum ssp. sativum)* differ from garden peas in lacking the inedible parchment-like membrane on the inside of the pod. They are stir-fried with meat, are a good accompaniment to braised dishes, and are used in soups and salads.

辣椒

羊角豆

Jiao gua: Okra *(Abelmoschus esculentus)* are often used in curries. Young okra can be recognized by their yellow-green color and by the fact that the tips can be broken off, which is why in Asian markets you may see buyers doing this surreptitiously.

甘藍

Gai lan: Chinese broccoli *(Brassica rapa var. alboglabra)* is a green leaf vegetable with few flowers. It is stir-fried with beef, pork or shrimp and used with noodles and in soups. It is also simply blanched in hot water and served with oyster sauce. Small plants with strong stalks are best.

La jiao: Chilies *(Capsicum frutescens)*; as a rule the long chili peppers are sharper than round ones and the red ones sharper than the green. Chili peppers are ground with spices, cooked with meat, and cut in rings, and stirred into soy sauce. If you handle them without wearing gloves, take care not to touch your eyes or tender skin.

絲瓜

Sze gwa: Luffa *(Luffa acutangula)*; choose small, young loofahs, but it is still advisable to cut off the hard ribs and to peel off the skin. Cut in slices. Luffa is served stir-fried with meat or shrimp.

細
瓜

Sair gwa: [Snake-hair cucumber] *(Trichosanthes cucumerina);* this thin-skinned cucumber is peeled, cut into slices and stir-fried with meat or shrimp. It has little nutritional value. Chose straight cucumbers if possible.

葫
蘆
瓜

Hu lu gua: (Lagenaria siceraria); the bottle gourd. The young immature gourds are succulent, the older ones too dry for use in cooking. The gourd is cooked like zucchini, and eaten in soup or pan-fried and served with pork or shrimp.

黃
瓜

Ging gua: Cucumber *(Cucumis sativus);* the Singaporean variety of cucumber is shorter and rounder than the short cucumber widely available in the West and develops larger seeds which have to be scraped out before eating. It is mostly eaten raw in salads.

苦
瓜

Ku gua: Bitter melon or bitter gourd *(Momordica charantia)* is recognizable by its rough and wrinkly skin. The bitter substances which give it its name are more pronounced in greener than in yellow-green specimens. To get rid of the bitterness the skin is peeled off, the seeds and inner membrane removed and the firm flesh cut into pieces, which are sprinkled with salt and allowed to stand for about 20 minutes before the salt is washed off and the flesh squeezed dry. Used boiled, fried, braised, or stuffed with a fish paste and then fried.

馬
蹄

Mati under their brown, flaky shell water chestnuts *(Eleocharis dulcis)* have a crispy, white, slightly sweet-tasting flesh, which can be used raw in salads, or in fillings, minced with ground pork and shrimp. The chestnut flour is used for binding. Make sure they are not bruised.

嫩
瓜

Miao gua: The young wax gourd *(Benincasa hispida),* shown here in an elongated, oval variety, is covered with a peach-fuzz and therefore has to be peeled before eating. The flesh is cut into pieces, which are then cooked in soups or braised with other vegetables. Larger cylindrical pieces are cored, filled with a stuffing of ground meat, and steamed or braised.

蓮
藕

Lian ou: Lotus root *(Nelumbo nucifera);* has to be thoroughly washed and the mud has to be brushed off before it is cut through at the narrow points. It is then peeled and cut into pieces or into slices which reveal a fascinating pattern. Braise with beef or cook together with pork ribs in a soup. Candied lotus root slices are one of the specialities offered during the Chinese New Year celebrations. Buy only whole roots without any holes.

冬
瓜

Dong gua: The winter melon, also called wax gourd *(Benincasa hispida),* can be found in the markets in both long and rounded forms. When used as a vegetable, it is peeled, the seeds and membrane removed, and it is cut up into pieces. Hollowed out and in one piece, it provides an ideal cooking pot for its own soup. In restaurants images of dragons or other significant symbols are carved into it. It should sound solid and not hollow when rapped with the knuckles.

南
瓜

Nan gua: The Japanese squash *(Cucurbita moschata)* is a tropical squash which comes in many different shapes, sizes, and colors. Unlike the summer squashes, it is harvested only when completely ripe, but still does not develop a hard inedible shell. The Japanese squash is nonetheless peeled and the seeds and inner membrane removed (the seeds are edible when dried and roasted). The flesh is cubed and stir-fried, or boiled in water and puréed. Check for rot at the base of the stalk.

Water-spinach cannot be too fresh when it gets to market

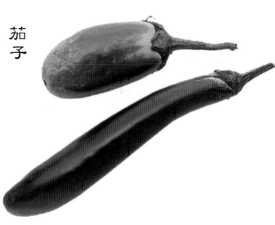

Qie zi: the eggplant *(Solanum melongena)* was already well established in Chinese stir-fry cooking long before it was known in the West. What many Westerners are unaware of is that eggplant is not necessarily purple, but also comes in light green, yellow, or purest white shades.

茄子

蘿蔔

Luo bo: Daikon radish *(Raphanus sativus)* is used in many ways in Chinese cookery. It can be cooked, stir-fried, braised, pickled, grated, steamed in a rice-flour dumpling and even carved. Choose heavy, undamaged specimens.

甘薯

Gan shu: Sweet potatoes *(Ipomoea batatas)* are not related to potatoes but to water-spinach. They can be cooked, steamed, mashed, and prepared like baked potatoes. The young sprouts and leaves are also used as vegetables.

黃瓜

Lao huang gua: Yellow cucumber *(Cucumis sativus)* resembles the green cucumber but is significantly larger and heavier. It is cooked unpeeled and the seeds do not have to be removed. In China you can buy sweet pickled yellow cucumbers. When buying yellow cucumbers, make sure they are heavy enough for their size and that they are firm all over.

芋頭

山藥豆

Sha ge: Jicama or yam bean *(Pachyrhizus erosus)* got its English name because the underground tuber, high in water content, resembles the yam, but the young shoots above ground can be eaten like beans (the ripened pods and seeds are supposed to be poisonous). Jicama is one of the the ingredients used for filling spring rolls, but it can also be eaten raw in salads. Smaller, younger tubers are usually less fibrous. Check carefully for signs of worm damage.

Yu tou: Yam (yuca) *(Dioscorea alata)* are harvested when the stems above ground have died down. They are cooked like potatoes but are particularly appreciated in sweet dishes. Their high starch content makes them a valuable food.

平菇

Shiitake, cloud-ears, and other
Cultivated mushrooms

The *Lentinus edodes* mushroom, called *dong gu* or *xian gu* in Chinese, is known as *shiitake* in Japan, and it is under this name that it has become known in English-speaking countries. It grows in forests, on the trunks of oak, pine, or beech, but it has been cultivated in China for over 2000 years, if traditional wisdom is to be believed. Until a few years ago, the method of cultivation remained almost unchanged. Freshly cut branches were bored and inoculated with the mycelium, which took six to twenty months to produce fruiting bodies. A new process has now been developed (see insert). Shiitake mushrooms are meaty, strong in flavor, nutritious, and rich in protein, vitamins, and minerals. They are said to possess aphrodisiac properties and to contain substances which regulate blood pressure and cholesterol levels. More recent studies on related fungi have even revealed tumor-inhibiting properties. However, at least 7 oz (200 g) of mushrooms a week would have to be consumed in order to derive any benefit. *Shiitake* taste best when fried, but they can also be braised; when boiled, they lose much of their intense flavor. When bought dried, they must be soaked before use. If they are cooked in a strong sauce they absorb all of its flavors. Other cultivated mushrooms are *mu er* (wood-ear mushroom) and *yun er* (cloud-ear mushroom) which owe their place in cookery less to their flavor than to their crunchy consistency. Paddi-straw mushrooms *(Volvariella volvacea)* are grown on rice husks or cotton waste.

Shiitake with garlic and green onion, braised in a brown sauce

Chao san gu
Mixed mushrooms

2 tbsp (30 g) dried shiitake, rinsed and soaked (soaking water retained)
1 Tbs oil
3 garlic cloves, thinly sliced
1 can (about 8 oz (230 g) paddi-straw mushrooms, rinsed and drained
1/3 cup (80 g) button mushrooms, washed, trimmed and sliced
2 Tbs wine rice
1 Tbs light soy sauce
3 Tbs oyster sauce
2 Tsp sugar
4 Tbs mushroom soaking water
sesame oil

Garnish
2 Tbs minced green onions (scallions)
a few sprigs coriander (cilantro) leaves

Trim the stalks from the soaked shiitake, leaving small mushrooms whole and cutting the larger ones in half. Heat the oil and fry the garlic till golden-brown. Add the *shiitake*, stir–fry for one minute, then add the paddi-straw and button mushrooms, and continue to stir-fry. Add the rice wine, soy sauce, and oyster sauce, sugar, and the soaking water. Reduce the heat and cook for about 8 minutes, stirring constantly, until the mushrooms are cooked and the most of the liquid has evaporated. Sprinkle with a sesame oil and garnish with chopped green onions and coriander leaves.

Dried *shiitake*

The cultivation of shiitake

Plastic bags filled with a mixture of sterilized sawdust and organic nutrients are cooled and then inoculated with mycelium in a special sterile filter chamber. The bags are closed, though not sealed, and left in an incubation chamber for eight weeks, at a temperature of 68 – 77°F (20 – 25°C). or until the first mushroom caps appear in the sawdust. The cover is then removed and the plastic bags pulled down so as not to impede the growth process. The temperature is now reduced to 59 – 64.5°F (15 – 18°C). The mushrooms are not watered during the growth phase, but are given water in the rest phase, which occurs for one minute four times a day. There are five crops a month from each bag of sawdust. The best yield is from the middle crop. After the fifth crop, when the sawdust in the bags has been blackened by oxidation, it is sold off as compost.

Niang bei gu
Stuffed mushrooms

3 1/2 oz (100 g) dried shiitake, washed and drained (soaking water reserved)
1 cup (250 ml) chicken or vegetable broth
1/2 Tsp cornstarch, mixed with 1 Tbs water

Filling
3 1/2 oz (100 g) ground pork
1 3/4 oz (50 g) chopped shrimp
2 Tbs grated carrots
or 2 water-chestnuts, peeled and finely sliced
1 Tsp sugar
2 Tsp light soy sauce
1/2 Tsp sesame oil
salt to taste
pepper
2 Tsp cornstarch

Garnish
2 Tbs minced green onions (scallions)

Cut the stalks from the soaked mushrooms. Combine all the ingredients for the filling, and divide into as many portions as there are mushrooms. Dry the mushrooms with a cloth and dust the insides of the caps with cornstarch. Put a portion of filling in every cap and steam for 5 - 8 minutes until the meat is cooked. In the meantime, bring the broth to the boil, thicken with the cornstarch, and pour the cooked mushrooms over them as a sauce. Garnish with chopped green onions.

Xiang gu li zi men ji
Chicken casserole with mushrooms and chestnuts

7 oz (200 g) chestnuts
1 oven-ready chicken 3 lb (1¼ kg)
6 dried shiitake, washed and drained (soaking water reserved)
1 Tbs sesame oil
4 slices fresh ginger, about 1⁄16 in (3 mm) thick
2 Tbs light soy sauce
1 Tbs dark soy sauce
1 Tbs oyster sauce
2 cups (500 ml) water (including mushroom soaking water)
2 Tsp sugar
¼ Tsp salt (or to taste)
1 Tbs cornstarch, mixed with 4 Tbs water
pepper

Peel the chestnuts. Bring the water to the boil in a saucepan and cook the peeled chestnuts for 5 minutes. Drain and remove the skins while still hot. Strip the chicken meat from the carcass and cut into bite-sized pieces. Trim the hard stalks of the mushrooms and cut the larger mushrooms in two. Heat the sesame oil and fry the ginger in it. Add the chicken pieces and the mushrooms and brown for 2 minutes. Add the chestnuts, pour on all the sauces and the water, then stir in the sugar and salt. Bring to the boil, lower the heat and simmer for about 20 minutes. Thicken with the cornstarch and season with pepper.

1 Button mushrooms
2 Oyster mushrooms
3 Abalone mushroom (*Pleurotus cystidiosus*)
4 Shiitake (*Shiitake*)
5 Nameko (*Pholiota nameko*)
6 Enoki (*Flammulina velutipes* – Velvet shank)
7 Paddi-straw mushroom (*Volvariella volvacea*)
8 Honshimeji (*Hypsizigus tessalatus*)

Honshimeji
(*Hypsizigus tessalatus*)

Nameko (*Pholiota nameko*)

From Chaozhou

China is a very large and varied country, and independent regional cuisines have developed in the various provinces, influenced by differing geographical and climatic conditions. These are reflected in the Chinese cookery of Singapore.

Chaozhou is a coastal region in the east of Guangdong province, where it borders the province of Fujian. The cooking of its inhabitants is influenced by the sea and also by Cantonese and Fujian cuisines. The most famous of their recipes is a braised goose which is cut into thin slices and served with a dip of chili, garlic, and vinegar. Goose liver and coagulated goose blood can be served as a side-dish. Other specialities are braised shark's fin and a mild, watery rice gruel, which was originally served with very simple accompaniments which have since become more and more refined: there are black olives, sweet and sour pickles, steamed peanuts, omelet with pickled spring turnips, steamed tofu, preserved vegetables, salted eggs, braised pork knuckle, little meatballs or liver dumplings, salted fish, fried anchovies, or squid.

Zhu gan rou wan
Pork and liver meatballs with rice gruel

3¹/₂–5¹/₂ oz (100–150 g) pork caul (order it from the butcher)
7 oz (200 g) pig's liver or chicken livers
10¹/₂ oz (300 g) ground lean pork
2 Tsp oil
3 oz (80 g) shallots, minced
1 small garlic clove, crushed
1¹/₂ Tsp dark soy sauce
1 Tsp sugar
¹/₂ Tsp salt (or to taste)
¹/₄ Tsp pepper

Wash the pig's caul carefully (it may be slightly damaged) drain and dry thoroughly. Fry the pork or poultry liver and then chop very finely.
Heat the oil and lightly brown the garlic and shallots, mix in the soy sauce, sugar, salt, and pepper. Remove from the heat and mix in liver and ground pork. When cool, form into walnut-sized balls. Cut the pig's caul into pieces 4 in (10 cm) square and wrap the balls in this with the edges well overlapped. Fry in a little fat over medium heat until brown. Serve with soy sauce or chili sauce.

Cai pu dan
Omelet with pickled baby turnips
to accompany rice gruel

4 Tbs chopped pickled baby turnips
1 garlic clove, crushed
3 eggs
oil for frying

Put a tablespoon of oil in a pan, fry the garlic and the baby turnips until the aroma develops. Remove from the pan and set aside. Beat the eggs, season with pepper, and mix with the fried turnips. Heat the oil in an omelet pan and make one large or two small omelets. Serve as a side-dish.

Hong shao e rou
Braised goose
for 6 persons

1 oven-ready goose (about 5 lb 8 oz (2.5 kg))
2 Tbs dark soy sauce
1 Tsp five-spice powder
10–12 garlic cloves, unpeeled
2 pieces star anise
2 cinnamon sticks
2 cups (500 ml) water
1 cup (250 ml) dark soy sauce
1 Tsp sugar
2 blocks firm tofu, sliced into 8 pieces

For the chili , garlic, and vinegar dip

2 garlic cloves , chopped
2 fresh red chili peppers, chopped
3 Tbs white vinegar
¹/₄ Tsp sugar

Rub the outside of the goose with the dark soy sauce and five-spice powder and leave to marinate for 20 minutes. In a wok or large pan, lightly brown the garlic cloves, star anise, and cinnamon in a little oil. Add water, dark soy sauce and sugar, mix together and place inside the goose. Cover the wok or pan and let the goose braise on a medium heat for one hour to 90 minutes. After 30 minutes, add the tofu pieces and baste the goose generously with the sauce. To make the dip, mix all the ingredients together.
When the goose is done, remove it from the pot and allowed to cool a little. Remove the meat from the bones and cut into thin slivers. Arrange the tofu pieces around the goose and pour the sauce over. Serve with the dip.

Zhu gan rou wan
Pork and liver meatballs

From Fujian

The southern Chinese province of Fujian is home to many ethnic minorities and its traditions and customs offer a colorful variety. Among the favorite dishes of the Fujian Chinese are Bak Kut The, a pork rib soup with spices, herbs, and garlic, braised belly of pork, oyster omelets, and noodles cooked with bacon and shrimp broth and garnished with squid, jumbo shrimp, and beansprouts.

Rou gu cha
Pork rib soup *(Bak kut teh)*

1 lb 5 oz (600 g) meaty pork ribs sliced into 3¹/₂ in (7 cm) pieces
5 cups (1¹/₄ l) water
1¹/₂ Tbs light soy sauce
1¹/₂ Tbs dark soy sauce
2 garlic cloves, unpeeled
salt to taste

Herb Mixture

10 white peppercorns
10 black peppercorns
1 piece star anise
5 whole cloves
3 cinnamon sticks
5 pieces *dang gui* (angelica root)
5 pieces *yu zhu* (Solomon's seal rhizome)
6 *ju zi* (buckthorn fruit)
¹/₂ Tbs fennel seeds

In Singapore, the herbs can be bought ready mixed in herb stores or supermarkets. If they are not available ready mixed, buy the ingredients from an oriental food store.
Pour the water into a large pan, add the light and dark soy sauces, garlic, salt, and the herb mixture, and bring to the boil. Add the ribs, bring back to the boil, reduce the heat, and simmer until the meat is done.
Serve with a bowl of light soy sauce mixed with freshly sliced red chili peppers. China tea (preferably Oolong, which comes from Fujian) is served as an accompaniment to aid digestion.

豬肝肉丸

Lu zhu rou
Pork belly
with steamed dumplings

1 lb 2 oz (500 g) pork belly in one piece
1 Tbs oil
2 garlic cloves , unpeeled
1½ Tbs thick dark soy sauce
3 cups (750 ml) warm water
1 Tsp sugar
salt to taste
1 bunch coriander (cilantro) (to taste)
fresh red chili peppers, sliced into rings (to taste)
mantou (steamed Chinese dumplings, available from Chinese supermarkets)

Marinade

1½ Tbs thick dark soy sauce
½ Tsp five-spice powder
pepper

Mix one and a half tablespoons of the dark soy sauce, five spice powder and pepper. Rub this into the pork belly and leave to marinate for 30 - 45 minutes.
Heat the oil in a Dutch oven or deep pot and lightly brown the unpeeled garlic cloves. Add the pork belly and brown for 5 minutes. Add the warm water, the remaining soy sauce, the marinade, and sugar. Cover and bring to the boil, then lower the heat and simmer until the pork belly is done. Salt to taste.
Steam the buns to warm them up. Halve the buns, in the middle put a slice of pork with a chili ring and a few coriander leaves, and eat like a sandwich.
If no Chinese steamed buns are available the pork can also be eaten between slices of bread.

Wu xian fen (five-spice powder) is a common mixture of cloves, cinnamon, star anise, fennel, and Szechuan pepper. Mixed with salt that has been heated a little in a dry pan, it can be used as a seasoning for roast chicken.

From Szechuan

Szechuan in southwest China is surrounded by mountain ranges. They provide a warm and humid climate in which fruit and vegetables thrive. As cattle are not used as beasts of burden the regional cuisine contains many recipes for beef. The climate, although ideal for agriculture, causes problems in keeping food fresh, which is why various methods of preservation such as drying, smoking, salting, and pickling have been developed. This could be one of the reasons why Szechuan cookery is so heavily spiced.

Gan bian si ji dou
Fried asparagus bean with ground pork

10½ oz (300 g) asparagus bean, sliced into 3 in (8 cm) pieces
oil for frying
3 Tbs oil
2 garlic cloves, peeled and minced
2 slices ginger root, chopped
½ Tbs minced mustard greens
½ Tsp dried shrimp, rinsed and chopped
4 Tbs cooked ground pork (or ground beef)
1 cup (250 ml) water
1 Tbs minced green onions (scallions)

Sauce

1½ Tsp sugar
1 Tsp dark vinegar
1 Tsp light soy sauce
½ Tsp dark soy sauce
a few drops of sesame oil

Fry the asparagus beans in a wok until they are slightly browned. Remove and reserve. Fry the garlic and ginger. Add the beans, mustard greens, shrimp, and ground pork, and stir. Add the water and simmer until the liquid has almost totally evaporated. Meanwhile, combine the sauce ingredients. Increase the heat, add the sauce, and cook until the aroma develops. Serve with green onions .

Gong bao ji ding
Roast chicken with dried chilies
for 6 people

4 chicken breast fillets, in ½ in (1 cm) diced
10 dried chili peppers (large, smooth ones , not crinkly)
1 cup + 2 Tsp (260 ml) oil

Marinade

1 egg
1 Tbs light soy sauce
1½ Tsp cornstarch
1 Tbs oil

Sauce

1 Tsp Chinese rice wine
1 Tsp vinegar
1 Tsp black vinegar
1½ Tsp sugar
½ Tsp dark soy sauce
½ Tsp light soy sauce
a few drops in sesame oil
1½ Tsp cornstarch, mixed from 2 Tsp water
4 slices ginger root
4–5 green onions (scallions), sliced into 2 in (5 cm) lengths

Marinate the diced chicken breast fillets for 20–30 minutes.
Cut the dried chili peppers into strips 1 in (2.5 cm) long and discard the seeds.
Heat the wok, add two teaspoons of oil, and quickly fry the chili peppers on a high heat, taking care not to let them get too dark, or they will develop a bitter taste. Remove and set aside.
Heat 1 cup (250 ml) of oil in a wok and fry the marinated chicken in it. When this is almost done, add first the sauce ingredients and then the cornstarch mixture, and heat until sauce thickens. Add ginger, green onions, and fried chili peppers, stir together and serve immediately.
The chili peppers are used to spice the dish but are not usually eaten.

来自四川

Rou gu cha (bak kut teh)
Pork rib soup

Gong bao ji ding
Roast chicken with dried chili peppers

排骨湯

宮爆雞丁

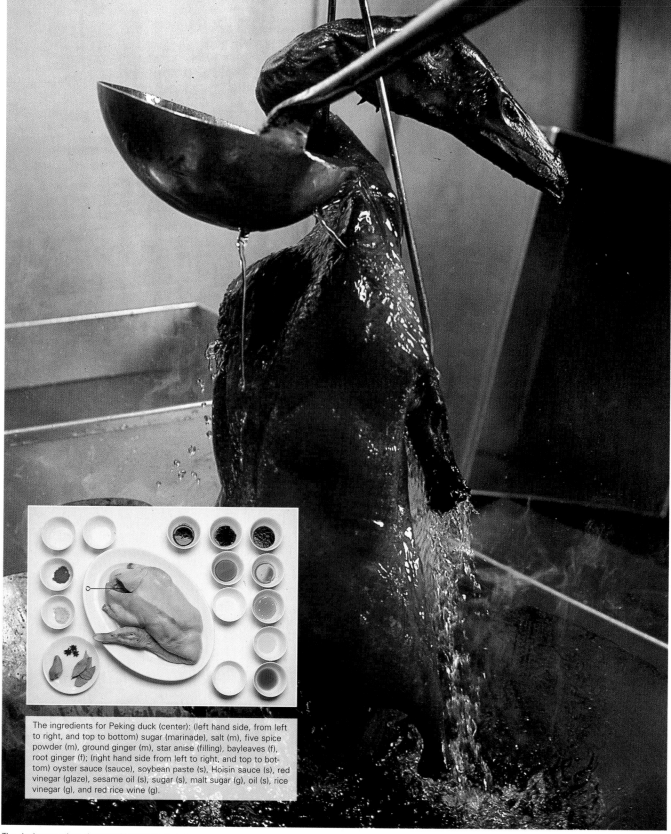

The ingredients for Peking duck (center): (left hand side, from left to right, and top to bottom) sugar (marinade), salt (m), five spice powder (m), ground ginger (m), star anise (filling), bayleaves (f), root ginger (f); (right hand side from left to right, and top to bottom) oyster sauce (sauce), soybean paste (s), Hoisin sauce (s), red vinegar (glaze), sesame oil (s), sugar (s), malt sugar (g), oil (s), rice vinegar (g), and red rice wine (g).

The duck gets a last shower of hot fat to give it a sheen, and the long and meticulous preparation is finally completed.

來自北京

Peking Duck

From Beijing

Beijing has been the capital of China almost without interruption since 1421, and has adopted the best from the cuisines of all the regions and developed this into its own style. The imperial cuisine of the Qing dynasty (1644 – 1911) produced a great many creative ideas which were then adopted by public eating-houses. Peking duck is the most famous local dish, but crispy-spiced chicken and mutton casserole are also specialities of the region. Peking duck is not a modern dish, it dates back to the Ming dynasty (1368 - 1644). The oldest restaurant to serve this tasty dish opened in Beijing 400 years ago! The ducks are specially raised for this purpose and have distinctive qualities. They are bred on farms in the vicinity of Beijing, where the water is good and the ponds are thick with plants. The duck is ready for slaughter at 65 days old,

Peking Duck and the Weather

Insiders know that Peking duck should only be eaten if the weather has been consistently fine for at least 12 hours before the meal. It takes a long time for the duck to acquire its appetizingly glistening sheen. The duck is first filled with air then brushed with a special glaze. As a result, it needs to be left to dry out in a well-aired place for several hours. That is why you see rows of ducks hanging up to dry at the best Chinese restaurants. However, if the atmosphere is very humid due to a prolonged spell of rain, the duck will not have completely dried out within the required time. This means that the skin will not be properly crisp and the whole effect of this delicacy will have been spoiled.

when it weighs at least 4½ lb (2 kg). For the last three weeks of its life it is force-fed on a rich mixture of different kinds of millet, mung beans, and wheat chaff. This period, so important for its life after death, must be spent sitting, which makes for thin skin and tender meat.

There are minor variations in the preparation of the Peking duck. Each famous restaurant swears by its own recipe, but the basic treatment, which involves scalding

the duck, glazing the skin, and hanging it up to dry before cooking, is always the same. In Beijing, air is pumped under the duck's skin before it is scalded in boiling water. It is then painted with a special glaze to produce the crunchy, deep red skin at a later stage. The duck is then hung in a cool, airy place to dry. When it is time to cook the duck, a measured amount of boiling water is poured inside it and the opening sealed before the duck is placed in the oven, where the water turns to steam and cooks the duck from the inside. In the meantime, the skin takes on a deep red color. The finished duck has tender meat and a crunchy, crispy skin. It is roasted for 40 minutes, during which time it must be turned several times, or preferably turned constantly on a spit.

Five minutes after the duck has been removed from the oven, the cook cuts it up into 120 pieces in such a way as to leave some skin on each piece. For a banquet, the remaining parts of the duck, such as the wings, tongue, feet, heart, and liver are used in various hot and cold dishes served as an appetizer. The Chinese love variety meats and believe that there is no part of the animal that is not fit to eat. Variety meats are often served in *dim sum*.

1 The duck is seasoned inside with sugar, salt, five-spice powder, and ground ginger.
2 Star anise, root ginger, and bayleaves are added, and the opening sealed with a small skewer.
3 Boiling water is poured over the duck for 5 seconds.

4 A wire loop around the head and wings of the duck facilitates handling and keeps it upright during roasting.
5 The glaze, made of malt sugar and different types of vinegar, will give the duck its characteristic color.
6 Having spent several hours drying off, and 40 minutes roasting in the oven, the Peking duck is almost ready.

With a broad sharp knife, separate the skin from the duck.

To remove the skin from the legs, they are first separated from the carcass.

The skin is cut into rectangles about 1½ in x 2½ in (4cm x 6cm).

The fat under the skin is removed, making the duck meat more digestible.

To serve, arrange a piece of crackling on a pancake...

...add a little bunch of green onions...

... spread with some of the prepared sauce...

...then fold the empty half of the pancake over the filling.

Beijing ya
Peking duck
Suitable for a banquet for 10 persons

1 duck (5 lb 8 oz (2.5 kg))

Marinade
2 Tsp sugar
1 Tsp salt
½ Tsp five-spice powder
½ Tsp ground ginger

Seasoning
2 tbsp (30 g) ginger root, peeled
3 star anise seeds
1 bayleaf

Glaze
1 tbsp (10 g) malt sugar
1 Tsp Chinese red vinegar
2 Tbs rice vinegar
2 Tsp Chinese red rice wine

Sauce
2 tbsp (30 g) sugar
1 Tsp oyster sauce
2 Tbs soybean paste
3 Tbs Hoisin sauce
2 Tbs sesame oil
1 Tbs oil

Pancake
22 Mandarin pancakes (see recipe opposite)

Garnish
22 pieces of green onion (scallion), about 2 in (5 cm) long (white parts only)
2 fresh red chili peppers, sliced into ⅛ in (3 mm) rings, seeds discarded (optional)

To prepare the duck, remove the giblets, clean the inside and the outside of the bird thoroughly, allow to drain, and pat dry thoroughly.

Mix the ingredients for the marinade carefully and cover the duck with it from the inside, making sure that none of it touches the skin. Leave for about 20 minutes.

Put the spices inside the duck and close it with a small skewer. Plunge the duck into fiercely boiling water for 5 seconds, remove, and immediately plunge into iced water for 5 seconds to stop the cooking. Remove the duck and dry it. Mix the ingredients for the glaze and paint the skin of the duck with it. This will give the finished duck its succulent, dark red sheen.

The duck is now hung up to dry in a cool place for 6 hours or so.

Mix all the ingredients for the sauce (with the exception of 1 tablespoon of the oil). Heat the oil in a pan, pour in the mixture, and bring to the boil, stirring constantly. Remove from the heat and allow to cool.

Heat the oven to 300°F (150°C). Roast the duck for 20 minutes, breast side upward on a rack over a roasting pan, then turn and roast for another 15–20 minutes. Remove the duck from the oven, heat a little oil, and pour over the duck.

Using a very sharp knife, carefully remove the skin from the breast, sides and back. Cut the skin into pieces approximately 1½–2 in (4 cm x 6 cm), carefully removing the fat with the knife.

To make the green onion bunches, cut the white parts of the onions into 2 in (5 cm) lengths and slice through four times at each end. Put the green onions into iced water and keep in the refrigerator until the ends curl. Drain well before use. Slip a ring of chili pepper over each end.

Mandarin pancakes
To make about 22 pancakes

2 cups (250 g) all-purpose flour
about ½ cup (125 ml) boiling water
1½ Tbs sesame oil

Sift the flour into a bowl, make a well in the center, and add the boiling water. Work the flour and water into a smooth dough and roll out on a lightly floured work surface to a thickness of ¼ in (5 mm). Use a round cookie cutter, about 3 in (7 cm) in diameter, to cut out as many circles as possible. Knead the dough scraps, roll them out, and repeat the process.

Brush half the dough circles with a little sesame oil and place the unoiled ones on top. With a rolling pin, roll out each pair into a circle 4½ in (12 cm) in diameter. Turn once while rolling out. Cover the pancakes with a damp kitchen towel to prevent them drying.. Heat a heavy skillet over a high heat for about 30 seconds. Reduce the heat to medium, and cook the pancakes without oil, one at a time. Cook about 1 minute on each side, flipping the pancake over as soon as bubbles form on the surface.

When all the pancakes are done, the two layers of each can be carefully separated, the pancakes piled on a platter, and served immediately.

Mandarin pancakes can also be frozen. To reheat, just steam them for 10 minutes from frozen or reheat for 3 minutes in the microwave oven.

Right: The classic way to serve Peking duck is in a wrapper of wafer-thin pancake, in which the crispy skin is combined with fresh green onions (scallions), a pinch of fresh red chili pepper, and the aromatic sauce.

How to serve Peking duck

In restaurants, Peking duck is usually served at the table by a waiter or waitress, but it is much more fun to do it yourself.

Place a pancake on your plate, dip the bunch of green onions (scallions) into the sauce, and brush the pancake with it. Then place a piece of duck skin on the pancake together with the green onion, fold the other half of the pancake over, and roll the whole thing up. Like this it's easy to eat by hand. If you only eat the skin, what happens to the meat? There should be no problem in using roast duck meat. It can be cooked with noodles, sir-fried with vegetables, or served as an appetizer with vegetables.

This way of serving Peking duck comes from a famous Beijing restaurant, the Quan Ju De. At one of its competitors, the Yi Fang, the duck is roasted a little longer at a lower temperature and the skin is served together with the meat. A lot of skill is required to cut the duck into 120 bite-size pieces all of which have some skin attached.

烙
餅

Cantonese roast duck and barbecued pork are beautifully displayed to tempt hungry customers.

來自廣東

Two versions of Cantonese duck

From Canton

As with the recipe for Peking duck, this Cantonese dish requires the duck to be plunged first into hot water, then into cold, and then patted dry. Use a pastry brush to coat the skin with dark soy sauce, then hang the duck up to dry for about two hours in a cool, well-ventilated place. The duck is now ready for roasting. The special touch is provided by the sauce of honey, vinegar, and a little cornstarch which is poured over the duck after it has been roasting for one hour. The duck is then returned to the oven for a further 10 minutes, turned, then left for another ten minutes, by which time it will have become a beautiful, dark mahogany color. The addition of a little red food coloring to the sauce further enhances the glaze by providing it with a russet hue.

Smoked duck

First marinate a dressed and drawn duck in a mixture of rice wine, salt, and pepper. Then hang it to dry in a cool, well ventilated space. For the next step, place the duck on a high rack set over a wok, having first piled loose tea leaves, dried boiled rice, and a sprinkling of brown sugar underneath the rack. None of these ingredients must be allowed to come into contact with the duck. Place a tight-fitting lid on the wok and increase the heat. As soon as steam starts to appear, turn off the heat, but leave the duck in the wok for a further five minutes. The duck is then steamed for an hour and finally deep-fried until the skin is crisp.

Above: Duck braised in dark soy sauce, water, five-spice powder, and sugar is boned and cut into bite-sized pieces before serving.

Left: A display of breathtaking skill when a chef carves a boned duck at breakneck speed, occasionally even whilst looking the other way!

來自海南 Hainanese Food

Many Singapore Chinese who originate from the island of Hainan on the southern coast of China entered the restaurant trade. Back in the days of colonial rule, many were employed as cooks in British households where they learned about western, and especially British, cuisine. Thus, oxtail and European-style chicken soups, as well as chicken and pork cutlets, have found their way into Hainanese cuisine. From their homeland, the Hainanese brought with them a recipe for chicken which, although still available in food centers, is now also served in top class restaurants. When you order for the first time, remember that western palates may have to become accustomed to the Chinese preference of serving chicken just a little bit pink.

Pork Cutlet Colonial Style

4 lean pork cutlets, about ½ in (1 cm) thick
2 onions, peeled and sliced into rings
3½ oz (100 g) cooked green peas
4 Tbsp all-purpose flour, seasoned with salt and pepper
1 egg, lightly beaten
Fresh white breadcrumbs from 5–6 slices bread

Sauce
1 Tbsp light soy sauce
1 Tbsp Worcestershire sauce
1 Tbsp HP sauce
1 Tbsp tomato ketchup
½ cup (125 ml) water
1 Tsp cornstarch, mixed with a little water

Lay cutlets flat and slice horizontally without cutting all the way through. Then fold open the cutlets to make "butterflies" and beat with a steak hammer. Roll the cutlets in seasoned flour, coat in the beaten egg, sprinkle with breadcrumbs, and press down .
Fry the cutlets on both sides until golden brown and set aside in a warm oven.
Combine the sauce ingredients in a pan, bring to the boil, and bind with the cornstarch mixture.
Garnish the cutlets with onion rings and peas and pour sauce over the top.

Hai nan ji fan – Hainan chicken and rice

Hai nan ji fan
Hainanese chicken and rice
(illustration on left)

1 x 3 lb 5 oz (1.5 kg) oven-ready chicken
2 green onions (scallions)
2 slices ginger root, about ½ in(1 cm) thick), crushed
sesame oil for sprinkling
2 Tbs (30 g) chicken fat or 3 Tbsp oil
1 slice ginger root (½ in (1 cm) thick), chopped
1 garlic cloves, peeled and chopped
12½ oz (360 g) rice, rinsed and drained
Salt

Chili sauce
4 fresh red chili peppers, chopped
3 garlic cloves, peeled and chopped
Juice of 4 limes
salt
pepper
1Tbsp grated ginger root (to taste)

Garnish
a few Chinese cabbage leaves
1 pickle, halved and sliced
green onions (scallions), white parts only, chopped
tomato slices
red chili peppers
fresh coriander (cilantro) leaves

Rinse the chicken inside and out and pat dry. Lay one slice of ginger in the chicken's cavity, and place the other in a large saucepan of water. Bring to the boil and place the chicken in the saucepan, ensuring that it is completely immersed. Do not cover saucepan. Bring the water back to the boil, reduce heat, and simmer for approximately 20 minutes. The meat should be a delicate pink and still moist.

As soon as the chicken is cooked, lift it out of the broth and rub it with sesame oil. When the chicken has cooled, loosen the meat from the bones and cut into bite-sized pieces. Pour the broth through a fine sieve and set aside.

To cook the rice, use the chicken fat to fry the chopped ginger and garlic. Remove ginger and garlic as soon as the fat has absorbed their flavors, and then fry the washed and drained rice until it becomes translucent. Then add one and a half times as much cooking liquid (chicken broth) as there is rice, add salt, and simmer gently until all the liquid has been absorbed.

To make the chili sauce, thoroughly combine all the ingredients. This sauce can be prepared in advance and kept in the fridge in a screwtop jar, such as a Mason jar, for several days.

Reheat the chicken soup before serving, add salt to taste as well as Chinese cabbage leaves and garnish with chopped spring onions.

To serve, arrange the chicken meat on a large platter over a bed of sliced cucumber, drizzle with sesame oil, and garnish with fresh vegetables and coriander leaves.

Serve with rice and chicken soup. The soup is often drunk throughout the meal.

Left: In the past, Hainanese dishes were only available in food centers, but they are now often served in restaurants.

来自湖南 Hunanese food

The central Chinese province of Hunan shares its southern border with the province of Guangdong, and is contained on three sides by high mountain ranges. The Hunanese are reputedly very hearty eaters and it is said that their rice bowls are larger, and their chopsticks longer than anywhere else in China. Like the Szechwanese, the Hunanese like their food spicy and are generous in their use of red chili peppers. Poultry is eaten frequently and in large amounts; the same goes for pork. Among the specialities of Hunanese cuisine are honey glazed ham (which is also exported), an unusual hot and spicy soup, and a beautifully presented soup with tender, finely chopped pigeon meat, traditionally steamed in bamboo bowls. These bowls are either made in Hunan itself or — a more recent development — imported from Taiwan.

Zhu teng tang
Pigeon soup steamed in bamboo bowls

1³/₄ oz (50 g) pigeon meat, chopped
3¹/₂ oz (100 g) lean pork, chopped
3 water-chestnuts, finely chopped
1 dried scallop, drained and finely chopped
1 Tbsp rice wine
1 Tbsp soy sauce
salt to taste
pepper
water
4 bamboo bowls

Combine all the ingredients except the water. Half-fill the bamboo bowls with the mixture and top up with water. Place the bowls in a steamer and steam for 45-60 minutes.

Xiang su ya
Crispy duck
Serves 4-6

1 oven-ready duck, about 1.8 kg (4 lb)
1 Tbsp rice wine
1 slice root ginger, 2 in (5 mm) thick, finely chopped
1 green onion (scallion), finely chopped
2 Tsp coarsely ground Szechuan pepper
1 segment star anise, seeds crushed
4 cups (1 l) oil
cornstarch
sesame oil
plum sauce

Rub the skin of the duck with rice wine, ginger, and green onions (scallions), and leave to marinate for 30 minutes. Then season with coarsely ground Szechwan pepper and star aniseed, and steam for approximately one hour, or until the duck is just done. Rinse off the seasoning, drain, and leave the duck to dry for 15 minutes.
Heat the oil in the wok. Sprinkle cornstarch over the duck, place it in the hot oil and reduce the heat.
When the duck is golden-brown all over, remove it from the oil and leave to cool a little. Carve the meat off the carcass and cut into bite-sized pieces. Arrange on a platter and drizzle with a small amount of sesame oil. If you like really hot food, sprinkle some more ground Szechwan pepper over the duck. Serve with a plum sauce dip.
Alternatively, roast the duck in an oven for 50 minutes. However, the result may be less crispy.
When the Chinese eat a whole duck or chicken, they first cut the bird into bite-sized portions which are then reassembled on a serving platter, in the shape of the bird with head, wings, legs, feet, and body.

Suan la tang
Hot-and-sour soup

4 dried shiitake
6¹/₂ oz (180 g) canned bamboo shoots
2 blocks tofu
4¹/₂ oz (120 g) lean pork
3 cups (750 ml) chicken broth
2¹/₂ Tsp light soy sauce
1 Tsp salt (or to taste)
5 Tsp vinegar
¹/₄ Tsp pepper
5 Tsp cornstarch, mixed with 2¹/₂ Tbsp cold water
1 egg, lightly beaten
1¹/₂ Tsp sesame oil
1 green onion (scallion,) minced

Rinse the mushrooms and soak for 30 minutes in hot water.
Meanwhile, drain the bamboo shoots and slice thinly lengthwise. Slice the tofu into narrow strips and finely chop the pork.
When the mushrooms are soft, strain them, trim away the hard stems, and finely slice the caps.
Place the mushrooms, bamboo shoots, and pork in a saucepan, add chicken broth, soy sauce, and salt and gently heat until boiling. Reduce the heat, and simmer for 3 minutes. Add tofu, vinegar, and pepper. Bring back to the boil, pour in the cornstarch mixture and stir until the soup has thickened.
Slowly beat in the beaten egg. Ladle the soup into individual bowls, drizzle sesame oil into each bowl, and sprinkle with green onions (scallions).

酸辣湯

竹藤湯

Zhu teng tang – Steamed pigeon soup

Suan la tang – Hot-and-sour soup

71

Peranakan

The Peranakan or Straits Chinese live mainly in Singapore, as well as in Malaysia, where there are large communities in the states of Mallacca and Penang. The inhabitants are the descendants of mixed marriages between Chinese men and Malaysian women and, just as their language is indubitably Malay with some Chinese words, their cuisine has evolved into a distinct blend of Malaysian and Chinese elements. Pork, which is normally taboo in the predominantly Islamic cuisine of Malaysia, is thus combined with Malaysian spices, roots, herbs, and coconut milk. Soups, vegetables, meats, and poultry dishes are prepared in the Chinese way, but are accompanied by chopped chili peppers and shrimp paste. Among the Peranakan specialities are a pork stew in a sauce based on soy sauce, soup with chopped pork, shrimp and bamboo shoot dumplings, and *ayam buah keluak*, a recipe for chicken which features the seeds of the Indonesian pangi tree (*buah keluak*).

Ayam buah keluak
Chicken with pangi tree seeds
Serves 4-6

1 x 3lb 5oz (1.5 kg) oven-ready chicken, cut into serving pieces
20 *buah keluak (pangi tree seeds)*
3¹/₂ oz (50 g) lean ground pork
2 Tbsp sugar
1 piece galangal root, (³/₄ oz (20 g)), minced
1 piece fresh turmeric root (1¹/₄ in(3 cm)), peeled and chopped (or substitute 1 Tsp turmeric)
6 candlenuts, chopped
10 fresh red chili peppers, sliced into rings
7 oz (200 g) shallots, peeled and chopped
1 Tsp shrimp paste
Juice of 8 Tbsp tamarind pulp and 4 cups (1 l) Water
1 stem lemongrass, chopped
1 Tsp salt
6 Tbsp oil

Thoroughly scrub the *buah keluak* and soak in water for 24 hours, changing the water frequently. Slice off the broad end of the seed and remove the kernel with a fork. Save the shells. Mash the kernels with the fork, add the pork, 2 teaspoons of sugar, and a little salt, and knead well. Fill the shells with the mixture and reserve. Heat the oil in a saucepan and fry the galangal, turmeric, candlenuts, chili peppers, shallots, and shrimp paste until the flavors have fully developed and oil seeps out. Add the chicken pieces, *buah keluak*, lemongrass, the remaining sugar, and salt, and stir well. Then add the tamarind juice. Bring to the boil, reduce the heat, and simmer for 30 minutes.

Buah keluak

Because they contain toxins, the seeds of the pangi tree (*Pangium edule*), a native of Java and Bali, have to be carefully prepared before cooking. As well as scrubbing the ridged shell, the seeds should be soaked for at least 24 hours, and the soaking water discarded. When shopping for the seeds, make sure that they have a certain amount of weight; if they feel too light, they may either be empty or dried up. Discard any that smell stale or musty.

These seeds are a favorite ingredient in Peranakan and Eurasian cooking. They feature in the chicken dish, *ayam buah keluak*. However, whereas the Peranakans open, empty, and then refill the shells, Eurasians cook them as they are and remove the contents with forks from the dish as they eat it.

Eurasian food

The mixed marriages which have taken place between Asians and British, Portuguese, Dutch, and other Europeans who came to Singapore and Malaysia to be traders and colonizers, have resulted in yet another minority. As with the Peranakan, the union of different cultures is reflected in the food. The Eurasians have developed east-west dishes which unite European dishes with spices, chili peppers, herbs, soy, and other Asian sauces. A simple omelet is so much more exciting with the addition of fresh red chili peppers and onion rings. Even corned beef, served with roasted chili peppers and onions, elevates this humble food to new and unexpected heights. The Eurasians baste roast beef and pork with a barbecue sauce based on soy sauce, and serve meats with a chili sauce dip. To provide variety, Eurasian kitchens also produce chicken pies, stuffed cabbage, and roasts. *Devil* is a typical Eurasian dish which is traditionally served at Christmas.

Devil
Serves 8-10

1/2 cooked chicken (leftover), meat removed and cut into bite-sized pieces
1 1/4 lb/(500 g) cold roast pork (leftover Chinese pork), cut into bite-sized pieces
6–8 dried chili peppers
2 large onions, peeled and cut into thick slices
2 slices ginger root, very thinly sliced
4 medium-sized tomatoes, halved
4 medium-sized potatoes, peeled and halved
2 cups (500 ml) water
4 cabbage leaves, sliced into large strips
1 small cucumber, peeled, halved, seeds removed and cut into 1 1/2 in (4 cm) pieces
8 3/4 oz (250 g) cocktail frankfurters (to taste)
1 Tsp mustard powder
4 Tsp vinegar
salt
3 Tsp oil

Spice paste

8 shallots, peeled and chopped
2 garlic cloves, peeled and chopped
1 Tsp turmeric
2 stems lemongrass, chopped (or substitute 1 Tsp ground lemongrass)
1 piece galangal root, chopped (or substitute 1 Tsp powdered galangal)

Halve the dried chili peppers lengthwise and remove the seeds. Chop the chili peppers and soak in hot water for 30 minutes. This will make them easier to pound in the mortar. (We recommend wearing plastic gloves for this stage).

Heat a teaspoon of oil in a skillet and fry the chili paste until the full aroma has developed. Remove the paste from the skillet and save for later use. Sauté the sliced onions in a little oil in the wok or in the pan and set aside for later use. Thoroughly blend the ingredients for the spice paste with a pestle and mortar.

Heat the remaining oil in a wok or skillet, and fry the paste until the aromas develop. Add half the fried chili paste, onions, ginger, tomatoes, potatoes, and water. When the potatoes are half-cooked, add the cabbage, cucumber, chicken, roast pork, and small frankfurters (optional). As soon as everything is cooked through, season with powdered mustard, vinegar, salt, and the remainder of the chili paste.

The name of this Christmas dish hints at its spiciness, although our recipe is actually a mild version for beginners. This recipe usually calls for around 20 chili peppers. For an even hotter Christmas, cook it the day before. Leaving the Devil to rest for 24 hours and then re-heating it brings out the full devilishness of the dish. This is why it is never cooked in small amounts, there has to be enough to spice up the entire holiday period.

Chinese cooking utensils

竹蒸籠

炒鍋

Zhu zheng long: These bamboo baskets are available in various sizes. They are placed on an inset which fits inside a saucepan or wok of boiling water. Several baskets are stacked one on top of the other before the lid is put on, and the steam which flows straight from one level to the next cooks several dishes at the same time. This cooking method is practical and energy-saving.

Originally, the Chinese all-purpose pan or wok was made of cast iron, but today it is more likely to be stainless steel or aluminum. Its rounded bottom makes it an ideal vessel for cooking Chinese food. A wok is extremely versatile as it can be used for boiling, braising, stir-frying, deep-frying, and, with the addition of an inset and a lid, for steaming. Before using a new wok for the first time, wash it thoroughly with hot water and detergent. Then pour some oil into the wok and distribute it evenly over the internal surface. Discard the excess and wipe with kitchen paper.

大菜刀

Da dao: A cleaver or a broad-bladed chopping knife is an absolute essential for Chinese cooking. It is used by skillful chefs for slicing vegetables into dainty strips, cutting wafer-thin slices of meat, or even chopping up bones. The heavy, wide blade is used for crushing garlic or ginger and it is also ideal for conveying chopped ingredients to the wok or saucepan.

漏勺

刀

Dao: In addition to the chopping knife, there are occasions when a large kitchen knife comes in handy, although this is rare. Asian kitchens tend to make do with remarkably few utensils. Most Chinese are accustomed to cooking in relatively small spaces.

Lou shao: Strainers and ladles made of brass wire mesh with bamboo handles (which do not conduct heat) are simple but effective tools when you want to lift food out of hot oil or boiling water.

鍋蒸鍋

Gang zheng long: Gang zheng long: A metal steamer with one or two steaming pans which can be placed directly on the hob. The bottom pan holds the water, and the food is contained in the steaming pans which fit over it. It is important to ensure that not all the holes in the steaming pans are covered with food as this will block the steam and stop it from penetrating.

燉鍋

Dun tang: A double-boiler, consisting of a bottom pan or boiler, which is one-third filled with water, and a top part for the ingredients, which fits snugly on top of the boiler. This method of steaming is a particularly healthy and gentle way of cooking, as the moisture content of the food is preserved. Double-boilers are used for steaming soups, particularly those soups which contain medicinal herbs.

湯勺

平鏟

Wo chan and *shao zi:* Flat spatulas and scoops, made of metal with wooden handles, are suitable for use with woks and unglazed earthenware pots.

碪板

Zhen ban: These solid, heavy chopping boards which are actually slices of tree trunk. They are available in a variety of sizes.

筷子

Kuai zi: Wooden chopsticks of various lengths are also used for cooking. They are useful for gripping solid ingredients and whisking or blending liquids. An steamer inset is quickly improvised by arranging four chopsticks in a grid pattern in the bottom of a wok.

帶蓋碗

Weng: Lidded bowls come in many sizes. They have a variety of uses, from storage containers to soup tureens.

砂鍋

Sha bao: These china pots are glazed on the inside only, and are suitable for slow cooking, braising, and stewing.

75

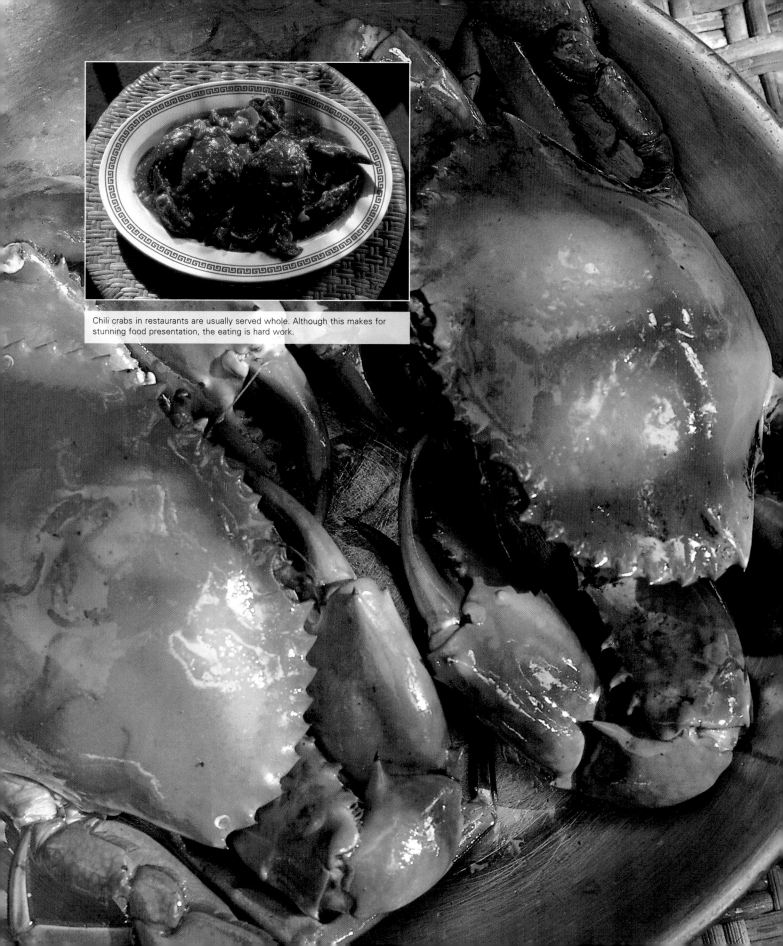

Chili crabs in restaurants are usually served whole. Although this makes for stunning food presentation, the eating is hard work.

魚菜 Fish cookery

It is said that the time to catch crabs is during the new moon, when they are at their best, whereas one should perhaps settle for something else during a full moon, as this is a period when it is not advisable to eat crabs. Connoisseurs value the females for their roe and the fat beneath the shell. Mangrove crabs, blue crabs, and stone crabs are all available, but gourmets can barely wait for fall when the Chinese crabs, a freshwater variety with hairy claws, arrive in Singapore.

Crabs should be bought live if at all possible though in some countries (the UK for instance) they are rarely sold this way. The more they wriggle about at the fishmongers the better. Fresh crabs are almost odorless and their shells should exhibit a slight sheen. Before cooking, crabs must be thoroughly scrubbed. The next step is rather more daunting. In Singapore, crabs are killed by inserting a skewer deep inside the mouth opening. Another way of killing them is to plunge them headfirst into boiling water, thereby destroying the nervous system in seconds. They should not be left in the hot water for too long as otherwise they will start to cook.

La jiao pang xie
Chili crabs

2 large crabs
oil for frying
4 garlic cloves, peeled and chopped
1 large onion, cut into quarters
2 cups (500 ml) water
3 Tbsp tomato sauce
2 Tbsp chili sauce
2 Tsp sugar
1 Tsp salt
2 Tsp cornstarch, mixed with 3 Tbsp water
1 egg, lightly beaten

Spice paste

4–6 fresh red chili peppers
4 dried chili peppers, seeds discarded and soaked in warm water (to taste)
6 shallots
4 slices ginger root
1 Tbsp dried shrimp, soaked in warm water

After killing the crabs as described previously, chop them into quarters, and then crack open their shells with the blunt end of the chopping knife.

Pound the ingredients for the spice paste with a pestle in a mortar. Heat the oil, and fry the crabs over medium heat for 2 minutes. Remove the crabs and drain. Discard most of the oil, but leave 2 tablespoons in the wok. Increase the heat and sauté the garlic and onions until translucent. Add the spice mixture and fry until the flavors have developed fully. Add the crabs and water and stir. Add the tomatoes and chili sauce, sugar, and salt, and stir thoroughly. Then pour in the cornstarch-and-water mixture and slowly stir in the beaten egg.

Serve hot with thick slices of French bread to mop up the sauce. Chili crabs are often on a seafood menu. Instead of crabs, use 14 oz (400 g) jumbo shrimp.

Zheng jin mu lu
Steamed sea bass
Serves 4-6

1 sea bass (about 1lb 9oz (700–750 g)), whole with the head
3 green onions (scallions)
3–4 slices ginger root, about 1/16 in (2 mm) thick
5 Tbsp oil
1 Tbsp grated ginger root
1 Tsp rice wine
4 Tbsp light soy sauce
1 Tbsp sugar
1 Tsp sesame oil
pepper

Garnish

1 Tbsp green onions (scallions) minced
2 stems coriander (cilantro) leaves, stems broken into small pieces

Thoroughly clean the fish and pat dry with kitchen paper. Make three diagonal slashes on each side. Bring the water in the steamer to the boil. Arrange the green onions (scallions) on the bottom of the steamer inset, add the ginger, and place the sea bass on top of the onions and ginger. Cover the pan and steam for 8-10 minutes or until the fish feels firm when pressed gently with the back of a fork.

Arrange the fish on a serving platter and remove the green onions (scallions) and ginger.

Shortly before the fish is ready, heat the oil in a pan and sauté the grated ginger. Add wine, soy sauce, and sugar, and stir until all the sugar has dissolved. Season this sauce with sesame oil and a pinch of pepper, and pour it over the fish immediately. Serve hot, garnished with chopped green onions and fresh coriander.

Left: The crabs may be cooked in advance by deep-frying them for 2 minutest.

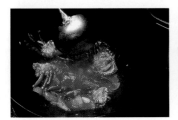

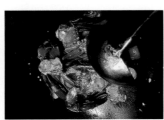

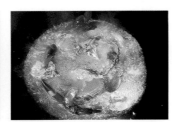
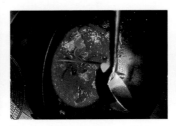

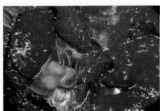

Fry the garlic, onions, and coarsely chopped spices.

Add the prepared crab portions and turn frequently in the hot oil.

When the crab pieces are a golden-brown, add 2 cups (500 ml) of water.

A teaspoon of salt and 2 teaspoons of sugar provide the sauce with a contrast of flavors.

Stir the correct amount of tomatoes and chili sauce into the liquid.

Bring to the boil and thicken with cornstarch.

The sauce should have stopped bubbling when you stir in the egg

The finished dish will be coated in an aromatic, creamy sauce.

Zui xia
Drunken shrimp

12 large, live shrimp
2 Tbsp sticky rice wine *(hua diao ju)*
2 cups (500 ml) chicken broth

Rinse the shrimp thoroughly and keep the heads on. Place shrimp in a deep bowl and add the wine. Cover the bowl and shake to marinate the shrimp evenly. When the shrimp cease to move, place them in the boiling broth until they are pink. However, the real reason for failing to prepare this dish will most likely be that it is almost impossible to get hold of live shrimp outside Southeast Asia, unless you live near a shrimp fishery.

Zheng xia
Steamed shrimp

1¼ lb (500 g) uncooked jumbo shrimp
½ Tsp salt
3 green onions (scallions), halved
8 thin slices ginger root
2 Tbsp Chinese rice wine

Remove the feelers of the shrimp but keep the shells and heads on. Rinse thoroughly and drain. Pour water in a steamer and bring to the boil. Arrange one half of the green onions and 4 slices of ginger in a deep dish, arrange the shrimp over the top, and sprinkle with salt. Scatter the remaining green onions and sliced ginger over the shrimp. When the water has reached a rolling boil, stand the shrimp in the steamer, and steam on high for 10-15 minutes. Remove the shrimp out of the steamer and drizzle with wine. Serve hot.

Yan ju xia
Deep fried salted shrimp

17½ oz (500 g) jumbo shrimp, head and tail left on (preferably thin-shelled shrimp)
1½ Tsp salt
oil for frying

Rinse the shrimp and pat dry. Sprinkle with salt, and leave for 30 minutes.
Heat the oil in the wok. Reduce heat to medium, and place the shrimp in the wok. Deep fry for 5-6 minutes and serve immediately.

Chao xia
Fried shrimp

1¼ lb (500 g) medium-sized shrimp, washed and drained, head and tail left on
½ Tsp salt
2 garlic cloves, peeled and finely chopped
2 slices ginger root, finely chopped
1 Tbsp Water
1 Tsp dark Soy sauce
2 fresh red chili peppers, sliced diagonally into rings (if the seeds are removed, the taste will be milder)
3 Tbsp oil

Sprinkle the shrimp with salt. Heat the oil, add the ginger and garlic, and fry until lightly colored. Add the shrimp and stir until they are pink. Add a tablespoon of water, then the soy sauce, and stir. Scatter chili rings over the top and serve immediately.

Place the rinsed, undamaged shrimp in a deep bowl and cover it with a lid.

Shrimp don't exactly like the idea of swimming in wine, but this is what happens to them.

This is why the bowl should always be firmly covered with a lid.

When the shrimp have stopped moving, drop them into the boiling broth.

魚翅 Shark fins and other exotica

Shark fins are valued for their nutritional value, but thanks to their high price, they are even more esteemed as a status symbol. Preparing shark fins for cooking is a demanding and time-consuming task. The sun-dried fins have to be soaked for several days, and carefully cleaned before use. Nowadays, semi-prepared shark fins are available in the shops for around US$140.00 per kilogram (2.2 lb) (as compared to US$800.00 per kilogram for untreated shark fins). Semi-prepared fins need only be soaked for half an hour, then cleaned, boiled, rinsed under a faucet, and cooked for a further two hours. The gristly parts of the fins look a little like upholstery needles after preparation.

The best known shark fin dish is probably the rich soup served at Chinese banquets. Because the shark fins are so costly, the main function of this soup is to convince guests of the host's material success. Since the preparation of the soup is an inordinately difficult and time-consuming task, it is best eaten in restaurants. Almost as famous as shark fin soup, is *fu yong*, a shark fin and crab meat omelet.

Abalone *(Haliotis asinina)*, also known as ormer or sea-ear because of its shape, is a gastropod which lives in warm waters throughout the world. Due to overfishing it is almost an endangered species and thus a great delicacy. Abalone can grow up to 4 in (10 cm) in length, and takes between five and ten years to mature. This mollusk, with its beautiful shell lined with dark mother-of-pearl, is rich in protein, phosphorus, iodine, and calcium. It is reputedl to be beneficial for the liver, kidneys, and eyes. Abalone is sold fresh, frozen, canned, or dried. Fresh abalone will fetch around US$107 per 2.2 lb (1 kg) in Singapore and must be steamed for 1-2 hours. Canned abalone is precooked so it is ready for immediate use. Abalone is added to pork-based soups, braised with vegetables and mushrooms, roasted, or marinated in lemon juice and sesame oil.

Medium-sized Australian shark fins are about 4-6 in (10-15 cm) long. Japan, Indonesia, and the USA are also suppliers of shark fins.

Dried abalone from Japan costs approximately US$2000 per 2.2 lb (1 kg.) It needs soaking in warm water overnight and is then steamed for 3-4 hours.

Rolls of dried fish maw are available in food stores. The fish maw (fish belly) is cut into sheets and then laid out to dry. The sheets are cut into strips and either added to soup or stir-fried.

Chicken feet reputedly strengthen the tendons. The Chinese esteem them for their gelatinous texture in stews made with fermented black beans and in bean and abalone soup.

燕窩

You just have to climb high enough

Birds' nests

If you can spare US$600 for 3½oz (100 g) of best quality swallows' nests, you will probably not be averse to spending money on your well-being; and if your health doesn't profit, at least your ego will. Like shark fin soup, swallows' nest soup serves mainly as a status symbol. The extortionate prices paid by wealthy Chinese in order to enjoy a pleasure which appears somewhat dubious to western palates, is the reason why men in China, Thailand, Indonesia, or in the famed Niah caves of Sarawak, Eastern Malaysia, seem so willing to risk life and limb by climbing to dizzy heights to reach the nests of the swiftlet *Collocalia fuciphaga*, a subspecies of the swallow family which uses down and saliva to cement its

Nest-gathering can be simplified by encouraging the birds to nest in suitable, empty houses.

Swiftlet nests consist mainly of pre-digested protein. The best quality nests are pale in color, but the most sought after have a red tinge.

In a few days of hard work in the caves, peasants can gather enough birds' nests to feed their families for an entire year.

Women are given the laborious task of cleaning the nests.

Packaged swiftlet nests ready for export.

The nests are boiled three times to clean them.

A restaurant presentation of birds' nest soup.

edible, milk-white nests. The birds live in colonies and attach their nests to the barely accessible cave walls or, as on Java in Indonesia, to timber beams in the attics of abandoned houses. The birds must not be disturbed while they are rearing their chicks, or they will not return to build new nests. The nests which will end up as soup ingredients are only gathered after the young have learned to fly and the nests have been abandoned.

Before they can be cooked, the nests must be soaked overnight in cold water. When the nests are soft, they expand in volume. The water is frequently replaced, and the threads carefully rinsed away. Tweezers are used to remove tiny feathers.

The clean birds' nests are steamed to produce an unusual soup which may be flavored with chopped chicken or pork. As an alternative, the nests may also be steamed with rock candy to make a sweet dish. The soup is said to be an effective tonic, and those who can afford to pay for it will enjoy its pleasures and beneficial effects on a weekly basis.

Soup-ready swallows' nests have undergone several time-consuming, labor-intensive cleansing processes and dramatically changed their appearance.

砂鍋煲豬角

Ingredients for *jiu shou bao fu bao*: (clockwise from top) dried tangerine peel, whole nutmeg, oyster sauce, Szechwan pepper, garlic, chili peppers, pig's feet, cinnamon, cloves (right), dried abalone (left), dried frog (right), licorice (left), and star anise.

砂 小
鍋 局
魚 菜

Cooking in unglazed pots

The outer surface of Chinese earthenware pots is coarse, sandy, and porous, but on the inside, the pots are sealed and smoothly glazed. These pots are used to cook food slowly and gently at moderate heat, gradually allowing excess liquid to escape. This preserves the food's flavor as it cannot evaporate as readily as it would in an open wok when the oil is not at a sufficiently high temperature. Furthermore, the earthenware pots can be taken from the hob straight to the table, so the food is served whilst still steaming hot.

Brand new earthenware pots must be "broken in" before they are used, and there is some controversy surrounding the best method for doing this. Some people recommend that the pots be soaked in water for 24 hours, after which water should be boiled in them and then left to cool down. Others prefer to soak the pots for no longer than two or three hours and then to cook rice or gruel in them. Yet a third school of thought disagrees utterly and advocates instead filling the pots with water which has been used to wash rice and leaving them for three days before they are ready to be used for the first time. There is only one thing they all agree on, and that is that a Chinese earthenware pot must never be placed in an oven as this will cause it to crack.

Sha bao ju sun ke
Fish cooked in a earthenware pot
(Illustration below)

1 medium-sized freshwater fish
oil for frying
3 garlic cloves,peeled and minced
4 Tbsp soy sauce
2 green onions (scallions), only the lower 4 1/2 in (12 cm)
4 slices ginger root, about 1/16 in (2 mm) thin
2 pieces green onion (scallion), sliced into 2 1/2 in (6 cm)) strips, and coriander (cilantro) leaves
1½ cups (375 ml) chicken and pork broth

Slit the fish lengthwise along the belly and gut it. Deep-fry it for 5 minutes, then discard most of the oil. Add chopped garlic, soy sauce, green onions, and sliced ginger to the oil. Cover and leave to simmer for 5 minutes. Then add minced green onions, coriander, and broth and simmer gently until nearly all the liquid has been absorbed.

Sha bao fan
Rice cooked in an earthenware pot

1 chicken breast
2 Chinese wind-dried sausages
4 dried shiitake, washed and soaked
2 Tbsp oil and 1 shallot, sliced
1 Tbsp sesame oil
1 piece ginger root (1 1/2 in (4 cm)), peeled and grated
2 Tbsp dark soy sauce
1/2 Tsp pepper
1/4 Tsp salt (to taste)
1 lb (450 g) rice

Slice the boneless chicken breast into bite-sized portions and cut the sausages into thin diagonal slices. Prepare the mushrooms by first discarding the hard stems and then slicing the caps very finely.
Fry a sliced shallot in some oil in order to draw out the flavor. Discard the shallot when brown and leave the oil to cool.Add a little water to the grated ginger and press to obtain 2 tablespoons of ginger juice.

Combine the chicken, sausage, and mushrooms with the sesame and cooking oils, soy sauce, pepper, salt, and ginger water and leave to marinate for about 30 minutes.
Cook the rice in the pot over moderate heat (there should be sufficient water to cover the uncooked rice by ¾ in (2 cm)). After 5 minutes, add the marinated ingredients and cook slowly until the water has been absorbed and the rice is cooked (approximately 30 minutes).

Jiu shou bao fu bao
Pig's foot and abalone cooked in a earthenware pot
(Illustration on page opposite)

1 pig's foot
4 Tbsp oyster sauce
oil for frying
2 fresh red chili peppers, finely chopped
2 garlic cloves, peeled and finely chopped
1 Tsp Szechuan pepper
2 pieces cinnamon stick
6 whole cloves
2 pieces star anise
1 piece dried tangerine peel
4 licorice roots (Glycyrrhiza – kum chou)
1 small dried frog, rinsed
1 spice nut (chao guo)
1 cooked canned abalone
coriander (cilantro) leaves

Rinse the pig's foot, rub it with 2 tablespoons of oyster sauce, and then deep-fry until brown.
In the earthenware pot, fry the chopped chili peppers and garlic, using only a minimum of oil. Place the pig's foot in the pot and add sufficient water to cover. Then add the rest of the oyster sauce and all the other ingredients except the abalone. Simmer over low heat for 1½ hours, or until the pig's foot is tender. When the pig's foot is almost cooked through, remove a ladle full of sauce and heat in a separate pan. Add the sliced abalone to the earthenware pot and spoon the heated sauce over the top. Cover and leave to cook until done. Bone the pig's foot and garnish with fresh coriander leaves.

For *sha bao ju sun ke*, heat oil in an earthenware cooking pot.

Deep-fry the fish after it has been gutted and "butterflied".

Use a ladle to discard most of the oil, then add soy sauce and garlic

Add green onions and ginger and cover. Leave to braise for a little while.

Scatter finely chopped green onions and leaf coriander over the fish.

Pour in the broth made of chicken or pork bones.

Allow to simmer until most of the liquid has evaporated.

The fish is cooked and served in the earthenware cooking pot.

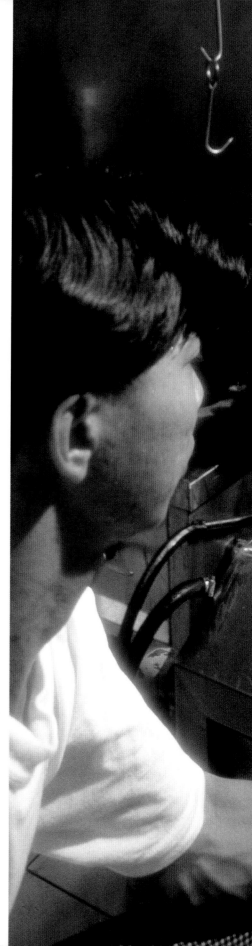

乳豬 Suckling pig

The piglets which are bred in the Chinese province of Hunan end their short lives as much sought after suckling pigs *(shao ru zhu)*, and are raised on a special diet based on cabbage. The piglets weigh around 6½ lb (3 kg) when they are three or four months old and ready for slaughter.

To eradicate the smell of pig, hot water that has been perfumed with sliced ginger must quickly be poured over the piglets. This procedure is repeated several times. After the meat has been thoroughly patted dry, the piglets are brushed with soy sauce and then evenly coated with a marinade of malt sugar, fermented red beancurd, Chinese wine, vinegar, light soy sauce, ginger juice, and sesame oil. This "lacquer" is applied at least twice more. The piglets have to be hung up after each application to ensure that they dry evenly all over. This process takes approximately six hours. When the skin is a golden-brown color, the piglets are ready to be barbecued over an open charcoal fire. While on the barbecue, the piglets are regularly brushed with the marinade. Occasionally the skin may be burned intentionally for a few seconds and then sprayed with a mixture of salt water and lime juice which makes the skin particularly crispy. A piglet will need to be barbecued for around 45 minutes before it is cooked through.

As with Peking duck, the most important aspect of a suckling pig is its crispy, tasty skin. Before the suckling pig is served, the skin is cut off, cut into small squares with a sharp knife, re-arranged over the piglet, and brought to the table with a syrupy dip of sweet bean sauce. In some restaurants the meat is removed as soon as the skin has been eaten, but in others the meat is sliced and served again as a separate dish.

Right: These suckling pigs barbecuing over an open charcoal fire are no older than four months, weigh 6½ lb (3 kg) on average and have been on a strict diet of cabbage for their entire short lives.

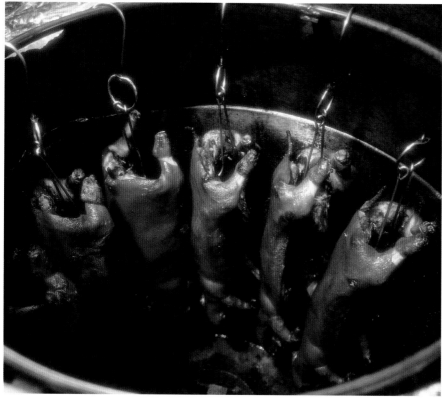

The suckling pigs have to be hung to dry after each "color application" because their skin is their main "selling point."

Even at this late stage, the suckling pigs are brushed with marinade and a mixture of salt water and lime juice.

The whole procedure serves to ensure that the skin is as crisp as possible. It is more valuable than the meat and is carefully peeled off the rest of the suckling pig.

Thanks to the chef's skill, no fat remains on the crispy skin which is cut into rectangles.

Finally, each crispy square of skin is put back where it came from to form a "suit of armor", and the suckling pig is ready to be served.

火鍋

Mongolian hotpots or steamboats

This dish originates in northern China where it is a particularly popular winter dish thanks to the small charcoal stove which would originally have been used to heat the pan. Although Chinese families like to assemble around the dining-table, the heat of the steamboat in winter would have been an added attraction. It is said that the first hotpot used only mutton, because it started life as a purely Muslim speciality.

The word steamboat seems to communicate some of the cosy, convivial atmosphere in which this dish is eaten, comparable perhaps to eating a fondue. Those restaurants which specialize in steamboats have tables with a central opening for the little gas stoves over which the steamboats are cooked.

These special cooking vessels are generally made of aluminum or stainless steel, and have a central funnel which is surrounded by a "moat" (faintly reminiscent of a bundt pan or tube pan) which is filled with a clear, rich chicken broth. Modern restaurants tend to be more innovative and will now offer the option of a spicy Thai soup called *tom yam*. The soup is served with a large selection of fresh, raw ingredients; thin slices of chicken, beef, pork, pig's liver, shrimp, squid, fish balls, shrimp balls, and squid balls, various types of tofu, different varieties of mushrooms, clams, cellophane noodles, many other types of noodle, lettuce, various Chinese greens, and a variety of herbs and spices.

For a steamboat, bring the broth to boiling point on the stove top before adding the food you wish to cook. It is best to keep to a particular sequence when adding the ingredients. Start with foods that will require longer cooking times, such as pork and chicken. Tofu and slices of filleted fish or fish steaks do not take long to cook and should be added later with the vegetables, which should also not be left in the broth for too long. The noodles are added at the end when the broth has become deliciously rich. Everyone at the table is issued with a ladle for the soup as well as a small brass basket with a wooden handle which is used to place the food in the hotpot and to retrieve it when cooked.

Diners will also be offered a raw egg which they may either whisk in their bowls to use as a dip for the cooked ingredients, or slip into the broth half-way through the meal to further enrich the broth. A selection of dipping sauces accompany the meal, such as light soy sauce with the optional extra of finely sliced red or green chili peppers, hot or sweet chili sauce, and mustard. The choice of dipping sauces is determined solely by preference.

The broth is sipped at the end of the meal, when it has absorbed all the flavor and goodness of the ingredients. Increasingly, steamboat is becoming a popular New Year's Eve dish because the whole family can gather around the hot pot, thus symbolizing unity and harmony.

To improvise a steamboat at home, you could use an electric saucepan, although it should not be too deep. A pan of hot chicken broth should also be kept near at hand in case the steamboat needs topping up as the broth reduces during cooking. However, it is impossible to recreate the atmosphere of the hotpot gathering.

Each participant has a brass "landing net" which is filled with an assortment of raw ingredients and then dipped into the broth until they are cooked.

Sliced fillet of fish is easily overcooked.

Shellfish are plucked from their shells and served in their own juices.

Plenty of vegetables such as sliced green onion should be provided.

Fresh and marinated mushrooms are included in the ingredients.

Undamaged, raw jumbo shrimp look impressive in the steamboat.

Yu cai jian is made by wrapping vegetables in fish paste.

Sea cucumber is a special delicacy.

Cubes of fresh tofu need very little cooking time in the broth.

Wo bing
Lotus paste pancakes
Serves 4-6

4 oz (110 g) all-purpose flour	
pinch of salt	
1 egg	
²/₃ cup (150 ml) water	
8 oz (230 g) lotus paste or red bean paste	

Sift the flour and salt into a bowl, make a well in the center, and drop the egg into it. Lightly beat the egg with a spoon whilst simultaneously working more of the flour into it and slowly adding water. Beat the batter until it is smooth, then leave to stand for 30 minutes.
Place a skillet over medium heat and brush with oil. Add enough batter for a large pancake and reduce heat. When the pancake begins to solidify, lay a fine rectangular layer of lotus paste onto the center and then flip the long sides over first, followed by the shorter sides toward the center to cover all of the lotus paste. Seal the seams with a little fresh batter, then flip the pancake over and fry the other side until it is golden-brown. After you have turned the pancake out of the pan, heat enough oil to deep-fry the pancake.
Cut the golden, deep-fried pancake lengthwise through the center and then five times at right angles, sprinkle with toasted sesame seeds, and serve immediately.

To make your own lotus paste, soak lotus seeds for 2-3 hours and use a toothpick to remove the green germ at the center which has a bitter taste. Boil the seeds until they start to disintegrate, drain, purée, and push through a sieve. Stir-fry the paste in a little oil until it is dry. Add sugar to taste and stir until it has fully dissolved and then continue stirring for a further 30 minutes without stopping. Leave to cool.
You should be able to find lotus paste in Chinese supermarkets.

The rectangles of lotus paste should be prepared in advance by rolling out a small amount of paste between two sheets of kitchen paper and storing in the refrigerator.

藕泥餡餅

Brush oil inside a large skillet.

Pour sufficient batter into the skillet to flow in a thin film over the base.

Position the lotus paste in the center of the pancake.

Seal the seams of the folded pancake with batter.

⏚ Desserts
㨤

The Chinese version of dessert is not as frivolous as its counterpart in the West, where we have something sweet at the end of a meal just for the pleasure of it. Chinese desserts are always health-promoting in one way or another, like the bird's nests steamed with candy. Walnuts improve memory, and many other nuts and seeds are favored ingredients in desserts. On hot days, cold desserts may replace entire meals. Over the years, the Chinese in Singapore have learned to enjoy foreign desserts like the Malaysian pudding made of sweet potatoes, yams, and coconut milk and *ice kacang*, a bowl of boiled red beans, corn kernels, and multi-colored cubes of jelly, covered with crushed ice to form a cone, topped with colored syrup and condensed milk. These icebergs have to be negotiated with a spoon and seem popular at any time of day, not just at the end of a meal.

Zhi ma hu
Black sesame cream

8 Tsp (40 g) rice
3/4 cup (100 g) black sesame seeds
5 cups (1 1/4 l) water
3/4 cup (200 g) sugar

Soak the rice for an hour, then drain.
Clean the sesame seeds and discard any grains of sand. Wash, drain, and dry. This can be done a day in advance. Roast the sesame seeds in a dry skillet or in the oven for 5-10 minutes. In a food processor, grind the roasted sesame seeds and rice with some of the water you have reserved, until the paste is smooth. Push the mixture through a sieve into a saucepan. Add sugar and the remaining water. Simmer at low heat, stirring all the time until the paste thickens. Serve in individual bowls.

Yin guo yu ni
Yam paste with ginkgo nuts

2 medium-sized yams (yuca), well cleaned, peeled and sliced
15 ginkgo nuts, shelled, soaked in warm water and peeled (or use canned ginkgo nuts)
7 oz (200 g) sugar
1 shallot, peeled and sliced into thin rings
3 Tbsp oil

Steam the sliced yams and then mash while still warm. Boil the ginkgo nuts (the seeds of *Ginkgo biloba*) until done and drain (the canned fruits have already been cooked, they only need draining before use.) Place the nuts in a skillet, add 1 tablespoon of sugar, and fry, stirring constantly until all the sugar has melted and the nuts are coated with the molten sugar. Set aside.
Heat the oil and fry the sliced shallots until they are brown to flavor the oil. Discard the shallots.
Fry the mashed yam in the oil and add the remaining sugar whilst stirring continuously. The paste has to be smooth and gleaming. Add the ginkgo nuts and stir.

Longyan dou fu
Almond-flavored jelly and longan fruits or fruit salad

1/8 oz (7 g) agar-agar sheets (or use unflavored gelatin)
5 cups (1 1/2 l) water
7 oz (200 g) sugar
3/8 l fresh milk
1 Tsp almond extract
1 can longans or fruit cocktail

Cut each sheet of agar-agar into three pieces, rinse, soak for 30 minutes, and drain. Simmer in a small saucepan over moderate heat until the agar-agar has dissolved (if using unflavored gelatin, prepare it according to the manufacturer's instructions).
Add the sugar and bring to the boil. Stir in the milk and almond extract and remove from the heat. Strain the mixture through a sieve into a shallow bowl, making a layer of jelly approximately ¾ in (2 cm) thick. Leave to cool and refrigerate. When it has set, cut the jelly into cubes or diamonds. Arrange in a serving bowl or individual sundae glasses, and arrange the longan fruits or fruit cocktail over the top.

Hong dou tang
Sweet red bean porridge

10 1/2 oz (300 g) red beans, cleaned, washed and soaked for 1 hour
3 cups (3/4 l) water
1 piece dried tangerine peel
1/2 cup (120 g) sugar

Coconut cream

7 oz (200 g) grated coconut (about 1/2 coconut)
1/2 cup (125 ml) water
pinch of salt

Place the soaked beans into a deep saucepan with fresh water and tangerine peel and bring to the boil. Reduce the heat and simmer until the beans are soft. Add the sugar to the beans, stir, and return the bean mixture to the boil.
Mix the grated coconut with water and press through cheesecloth to obtain coconut milk. Put the milk and salt in a pan and bring to boiling point. Leave to cool. To serve, place red bean paste in individual bowls an pour 1 tablespoon of coconut cream over the top.

He tao hu
Sweet walnut soup

7 oz (200 g) shelled walnuts
2 1/4 oz (60 g) dried Chinese red dates
2 cups (500 ml) water
3 1/2 oz (100 g) brown sugar
4 cups (1 l) Water
3 Tbsp cornstarch, mixed with 3 Tbsp water

Boil the walnuts for about 10 minutes, or until they are soft. Drain thoroughly and use a toothpick to remove the walnut skins while they are still warm.
Soak the dates in warm water and pit them.
Grind the walnuts and dates with 2 cups (500 ml) water in the blender until the mixture is smooth.
Put brown sugar and 4 cups (1 liter) of water in a shallow saucepan, add the walnut and date mixture, stir and slowly bring to the boil. Add the cornstarch-and-water mixture and bring back to the boil, stirring continuously to bind the liquid. To serve, pour into individual bowls.

The Chinese believe that walnuts have the power to improve mental ability. One look at a walnut should explain the connection.

Deep-fry the pancake in hot oil until it has become golden-brown.

Remove the pancake from the oil and leave to drain.

Use a sharp knife to cut the pancake into narrow strips.

Scatter toasted sesame seeds over the top and serve while still warm.

新年 New Year

The preparations for this important event start between fourteen days and one month before the actual day. The house must be spic and span and is thoroughly cleaned, walls are painted, curtains washed. Everything must look as new for the New Year. Hectic shopping expeditions to buy food, plants, and red paper scrolls inscribed with proverbs wishing good luck and prosperity reach their highpoint on New Year's Eve. Small red parcels (*hong bao*) containing money are prepared for giving to children, to unmarried women and men and to grandparents. All these gifts must be given in pairs, so there must never be one solitary note or a single coin inside one of these red parcels!

On New Year's Eve, the whole family gets together for a meal which is sure to promise much luck and happiness and which must contain several or all of the following ingredients: chicken, shrimp, fish, fish swim-bladders, sea cucumber, mushrooms, shark fins, abalone, seaweed, pressed duck, and wind-dried sausages.

New Year's Day is the time for visiting friends and relations. Two tangerines are exchanged and red parcels are handed over. Red, pink, and orange are lucky colors, black is taboo. Visitors are offered tasty tidbits served on an octagonal tray.

Life on New Year's Day is not all that simple. No word signifying bad luck may be uttered, no sharp objects may be picked up. As a result, all the meals for this day must be cooked the day before. As a rule, the food is vegetarian, consisting of cabbage, mushrooms, pieces of tofu, seaweed, and cellophane noodles. At all costs, nothing must be dropped or broken. Cleaning the floor on this day would mean that all the good luck was being wiped away. All of these taboos are supposed to ensure that the New Year brings nothing but luck and prosperity to the Chinese.

The New Year festivities last for fifteen days, and visits continue to be made during this period. On the third day, however, no one goes visiting, as this is supposed to be the day on which someone is most likely to pick a quarrel. On the second or fourth day it is okay to make a business deal, but never on the potentially unlucky third day! Since noise drives away all that is evil or unlucky, lion dancers are particularly sought after during the fifteen-day celebrations. Dance troops visit hotels, private homes, and businesses, in which the *hong bao* dangle down from above. Accompanied by cymbals and drums, the dancers jump around, demonstrating their skill and agility, and building pyramids to haul in the *hong bao*.

The seventh day of the New Year is everyone's birthday. A salad of raw fish (*yusheng*) is eaten on that day. The salad contains paper-thin slices of raw fish (wolf-fish or salmon), finely grated vegetables, candied melon and limes, red and white pickled ginger, pomelo, sesame seeds, jellyfish, and peanuts which are all tossed in a dressing of oil, plum sauce, pepper, and ground cinnamon. The Chinese use their chopsticks, to toss a salad high in the air and shout *"lo hei"*, the wish for luck and prosperity.

Below: Weeks before the great day, the streets begin to fill up with booths offering traditional New Year dishes.

Right: An abundant choice of dried sausages and pressed duck for the family feast.

Air-dried and glazed pork sausages. Their outer layer is called wax, but is not in fact made of wax.

Some air-dried, "waxed" sausages also contain liver.

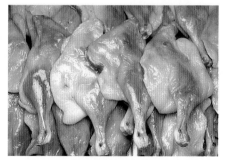

Partially boned and pressed duck portions are a brilliant success on New Year's.

A large variety of glazed and candied fruits and nuts is on offer.

Bottle gourds with lucky stickers are given as gifts and used to decorate the home..

Special New Year's cakes made of glutinous rice and sugar are colored red, of course

Red and gold good luck wishes for health, happiness, and prosperity can be written to order.

Steamed lunar New Year cakes will appear on every table this time of year.

A little snack of broiled "sweetmeat", sugar-glazed dried pork

The first full moon makes its appearance on the fifteenth and last day of the festival. In the past, this was the day when young girls would throw oranges into the sea and pray for wealthy and handsome husbands whilst many thousands of dollars worth of fire-crackers would be exploded. Nowadays, families are more likely to settle down to a good meal, while young couples go out to enjoy themselves.

The Return of the Gods

After midnight of the 24th day of the 12th lunar month, the gods must be sent back to heaven. The Kitchen God is accorded very special treatment as he is the one who has heard the house gossip throughout the year and who gathers information for the Jade Emperor. The Kitchen God is therefore sent on his way with a large farewell feast of vegetarian delicacies and sweetmeats of all kinds created to sweeten his tongue; sticky dishes designed to make it more difficult for him to pass on his reports, and wine to affect his judgement. Business people pray to the god of Wealth, offering him food which will greet him after his voyage to heaven in the New Year. He can appear in many guises: as warrior, minister, citizen, businessman, or hero.

The Jade Emperor rules the heavens and is highly revered since all the other gods defer to him. On his birthday on the ninth day of the first lunar month, a table is laid with food, golden smoking paper, and paper palaces. The offerings include fried pork, large roosters which have been specially se-lected for their size and large cockscombs, as well as large ducks, specially bred for this occasion. There must also be plenty of fruit, including tangerines, as well as special moon cakes, cooked seafood, birthday buns shaped like peaches for longevity, a vege-tarian "pig" made of peanuts, as well as other vegetarian offerings, wine and sugar cane, because the names for these sound like "thanksgiving" in the Fujian dialect. The fruit must be decorated with red paper strips for luck. After each member of the family has prayed at the altar, it can be cleared and the food can be eaten.

Golden and red decorations and innumerable types of garlands are sold in the streets, because every house has to be cheerfully decorated for the festivities to enable good luck to move in at the New Year.

柚子 Pomelo

The pomelo, also known as the shaddock, is the largest member of the citrus family. Depending on the particular variety, the peel will vary in color from green to yellow-green. The flesh may be yellow-green or pink. The shape is rounded at the bottom, tapering slightly at the stem end, though some pomelos are completely round, like a giant grapefruit.

The best way to select the fruit is by weighing it in the hand. The heavier it is, the juicier it will be. To open the fruit, make a cross in the thick peel and pull it off bit by bit. The wooly white membrane which remains attached to the fruit can be peeled off using a fruit knife. The fruit itself consists of segments which are covered by a tough, bitter skin which should be removed before eating.

Cantonese housewives braise the fresh thick peel in a rich brown sauce. As the peel is very porous it easily absorbs the sauce's flavor. To prepare this dish, first boil the peel in water to eliminate its bitterness. Then soak the peel in cold water and thoroughly squeeze the water out. Cook the finely sliced peel in a little fat with dried shrimp, chicken broth, oyster sauce, and sesame oil. Instead of shrimp you can use pork. Pomelo peel prepared in this way is said to taste even better than chicken. Thinly sliced pomelo peel can also be dried in the sun and burnt in slow burners, so that the smoke repels mosquitoes and midges. Even the pomelo blossom is used in China to flavor tea in the same way as jasmine.

The pomelo plays an important role in Chinese festivals, especially on New Year's Day, because its Chinese name *luk yao* sounds like the word for abundance, thereby hinting at an abundance of good fortune. The roundness of its shape promises abundance and prosperity. By eating the fruit in company or giving it away as a gift, you are expressing the wish that everything it represents comes true.

The pomelo is also one of the gifts offered to the gods because it is believed to have magical powers. Believers wash themselves in water scented with fragrant pomelo peel to protect themselves from evil spirits. Pomelos are in season around the turn of the year.

Always weigh a pomelo in the palm of the hand before buying it — the heavier the fruit, the juicier it will be.

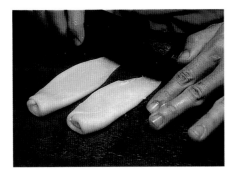

To make *lian rong shao bing*, roll lard dough inside a piece of ordinary dough. They will appear as thin layers when the dough is rolled out.

When the strips are rolled up, the different types of dough will separate into additional layers. The dough is then rolled out and rolled up again.

Finally, using your hands, shape the dough into a flat loaf. When baked, this dough will produce something akin to puff pastry.

蓮籽豆包

Store-bought buns are stamped with red good luck symbols, rather than glazed with egg yolk.

Fill the small flattened pastry loaves with sweet lotus paste and mold the dough around the top of the paste to seal it in.

Roll the filled dough balls several times by hand on the cookie sheet, press down lightly, and sprinkle with a few sesame seeds.

The symbol for double good fortune completes the auspicious exercise. However, if you make these buns yourself you will have to make do with egg yolk.

食象散意長勺菜肴

Symbolic Foods

The Chinese do not eat merely to satisfy hunger, they do so to maintain health and cure ailments, and in the hope that it will help them achieve success, wealth, many sons, and a good life. The Chinese believe their fate to be influenced by auspicious and inauspicious omens which are plentiful in daily life, and which are actively pursued and manipulated. For instance, the number 8 is a positive symbol as it sounds like the word for success, the number 4, on the other hand, is negative because it sounds like the word for death. So the number 8 is sought out as often as possible, be it in a house number or a car license plate. Red and yellow are lucky colors which is why they predominate in the Chinese New Year festivities the main objective of which is to ensure good luck for the forthcoming year. Red dates or golden yellow tangerines simply have to be good luck symbols. *Ho see*, the Cantonese word for oyster, sounds like good deeds and well-being, which is why oysters are eaten on New Year's Day, as are the *bao yu*, the abalone, for success and affluence, or *luk yao*, the pomelo for abundance. And a small good luck bun filled with lotus paste for breakfast can do no harm…

Lian rong shao bing
Chinese bun filled with lotus paste
For 20 rolls

2 cups (250 g) all-purpose flour	
1/2 cup (125 g) lard	
1/2 cup (125 ml) Water	
1 Tbsp sugar	
1lb 5oz (600 g) lotus paste (recipe p. 90)	
1 egg yolk	
1 Tbsp sesame seeds	

Lard dough

1 1/2 cups (180 g) all-purpose flour	
1/2 cup (125 g) lard	

Sift the flour into a bowl, add the lard, and knead well. Gradually add the water and sugar, and continue kneading until the dough is smooth and pliable. Leave to rest for 30 minutes. Preheat the oven to 350°F (180°C). Knead the ingredients for the lard dough. Divide both doughs into 20 pieces each. Roll one piece of lard dough inside one piece of flour dough, roll out thinly, roll up, and roll out again, then roll up one more time. Shape each piece into a ball. Make a depression in the center and place a little lotus paste in it. Wrap the dough around the paste and shape into round cookies. Brush with egg yolk, sprinkle with sesame seeds, and bake 15 minutes on the center shelf.

Seaweed *(facai)* sounds like prosperity, as in "gongxi facai", the greeting exchanged between friends and relatives on meeting.

Dried fish maw *(yu piao)* expands when used as an ingredient in soup. If you eat *yu piao*, your luck may stretch in the same way.

Red dates *(hong zao)* are not only red, they are also sweet and can bring you luck and sweeten your life at the same time.

The golden color of the pumpkin make it a good luck symbol promising growing prosperity.

The word for fish *(yu)* sounds similar to the word for wealth. Eating fish frequently can therefore help create, secure, or increase your wealth.

The Cantonese word for sea cucumber *(hoy sum)* sounds like luck or joy and, since it expands in water, it represents the swelling of joy.

Melon seeds *(gua zi)*, of which there are so many inside each fruit, symbolize an abundance of descendants..

If you give someone two tangerines on New Year's Day, you wish abundant wealth on them, as the word for tangerine *(kam)* sounds like the word for gold.

Chinese Festivals

中國傳統節日

The Chinese like to combine their festivals with special dishes which relate to the season in which the festival falls. Apart from the Chinese New Year, the greatest events in the Singaporean festival calendar are the Dragon Boat Festival, the Festival of the Hungry Spirits, and the Mid-fall Festival.

Dragon Boat Festival

The Dragon Boat Festival is celebrated on the 5th day of the 5th lunar month, in other words, around the beginning of June. One of the stories about the origin of this festival tells the tale of government minister Qu Yuan. An intrigue perpetrated by a group of corrupt civil servants led to his dishonor and banishment, which caused the disheartened minister to wander through the land writing poetry. One day, however, his misery seemed so great that he drowned himself. Some fishermen who saw him immediately rowed out to look for him. When they couldn't find him, they threw rice into the river to appease his spirit. The rice grew into triangular, pyramid-shaped dumplings called *zong*. The fishermen's search for the poet is commemorated by the Dragon Boat Festival. The bows of the boats are shaped like dragon's heads, and the rowers move their oars to the beat of drums. Dragons and noise are believed to ward off the river monster who could threaten the spirit of the dead poet. Today, dragon boat races take place every year at the beginning of the festival and *zong* are eaten to commemorate the death of the minister-poet.

These pyramid-shaped dumplings owe their shape to the way the two bamboo leaves in which they are cooked are arranged and folded. The dumplings consist either of plain glutinous rice, or are also available with sweet or savory fillings. For plain dumplings, glutinous rice is soaked in water to which soda ash has been added. This turns the rice yellow and gives it its unmistakable flavor. The cooked dumplings are dunked in sugar or honey. Sweet fillings consist of bean or lotus paste. The savory fillings can include pork with chestnuts, or mushrooms and shrimp fried with shallots, garlic, and herbs. Vegetarians eat *zong* filled with mushrooms and black beans. The luxury version of *zong* will contain a salted egg yolk. It takes quite a lot of practice to fold the bamboo leaves just right.

Festival of the hungry spirits

This festival occurs in the seventh lunar month and the festivities last for a whole month. The gates of Purgatory are opened to release the spirits of all those lost souls wandering the Earth. They need to be pacified and comforted by means of generous gifts of prepared meals, fruit, flowers, and the burning of enormous candles, incense, and joss-sticks. As this is a most inauspicious time, no one would ever dream of getting married during the period of this particular festival.

Along the streets, long tables are spread with mountains of food offerings. Stages are erected in the street and classical Chinese opera is performed, although in some places the opera performances have been superseded by pop concerts given by Chinese singing stars. It is almost as though even the spirits wanted to keep up with the times! Since the food offerings and events are sponsored by local stores and businesses who are well aware of the power of advertising, and make sure the living participants know who has been so generous, it can be assumed that the interests of the living have a rather higher profile than those of the dead. Most of the food offerings are later distributed among all the spectators and participants.

Not only is there plenty to eat, but the air is full of the fragrance of the countless incense sticks lit to appease the spirits.

When the gates open to allow entry to the hungry and neglected spirits, they find everything the heart desires.

To make glutinous rice in the wok, fry a little garlic, then add the rice.

Sprinkle with a spice mixture which includes five-spice powder.

Mix all the spices into the rice, stirring well to ensure even distribution.

Add a generous splash of soy sauce to the frying rice

Continue stirring until the rice is evenly coated with the sauce.

Place the cooked rice in a bowl-shaped basket and leave to cool.

Soak the brittle, dried bamboo leaves for 3-4 hours.

Lay two bamboo leaves over each other to form a conical shape.

Fill the parcel with pork, mushrooms, shrimp, and chestnuts

Cover with rice, fold the parcel, and tie it up with a bow

Whole bundles of these little packages are steamed for 1½ hours.

Zong are available in many different flavors, both sweet and savory.

Mid-fall Festival (Moon Cake festival)

This festival, which is celebrated by processions of children carrying paper lanterns, falls on the 15th day of the 8th lunar month. This is when the moon is at its fullest and brightest. Moon-shaped moon cakes are either bought as gifts or eaten. According to legend, these moon cakes were invented to conceal news of a revolt planned against the brutal rule of the Mongols. Moon cakes are sliced into the tiniest slivers and washed down with plenty of China tea.

The dough, which may have any of a variety of fillings, is shaped in special cookie molds, and is brushed with egg yolk before baking. Traditional fillings include sweet black bean or lotus paste, with the optional addition of a salted egg yolk, and a mixture of nuts and pickled melon. Modern recipes experiment with durian or yam. In addition to the baked cakes there is also a steamed white cake, made of wheat dough wrapped in rice paper which is called "snowy skin."

月餅

餐館 Restaurant

To enjoy a restaurant meal to the full, you need a party of at least four people, because the greater the number of dishes you can taste and share, the better. Contrary to western dining etiquette, it is not customary for each guest to order a dish for himself in a Chinese restaurant. When ordering, it is important to ensure that the dishes are balanced with respect to tastes and textures. The first dishes should be light, perhaps a cold appetizer or a soup, followed by poultry, meat, fish, and vegetables. If the meal is not accompanied by plain boiled white rice, it should be concluded with noodles, fried rice, or a different rice dish. The selection of dishes should also reflect a variety of cooking methods.

For special occasions, such as birthdays and weddings, eight to ten dishes are ordered for each table of ten guests. Even more may be ordered if the host can afford it. To emphasize their social status, the wealthy may like to add suckling pig, shark fins, and abalone to the regular dishes. Peach-shaped pastry dumplings and noodles are a must for birthday celebrations as they are a symbol of longevity. For obvious reasons, the noodles

Before the meal

A Chinese meal starts with sweet-and-sour pickled vegetables, boiled peanuts, or sweetened walnuts.

Sweet-and-sour pickles also include carrots, radishes, turnips, and cucumbers. The carrots and radishes are sliced crosswise or lengthwise, pickled cucumbers are only ever sliced across. They are sprinkled with salt and left for about 30 minutes. The resulting brine is rinsed off, surplus water may be squeezed from the vegetables. They are now softer and crunchier than before. The vegetables are then placed in a solution of vinegar and water and left for at least 6 hours. Another appetizer consists of large peanuts boiled in their skins in water to which a little salt and five-spice powder have been added. Walnuts are boiled in a sugar and malt solution, they are then drained and fried.

must not be cut. Drinks served during such a meal will include tea, beer, brandy on the rocks or brandy with ginger ale. During the course of the dinner party, the loud and unrelenting cry of *"Yam seng"* may fill the room. This means something along the lines of "here today, gone tomorrow!" This has been known to develop into a sort of competition, with each table competing to be the loudest (and the most incessant!)

Chinese dinners do not start punctually, and it can be an hour before all the food has been brought out, since guests tend not to arrive until long after the time specified on their invitations. The reason for this is that, by arriving later, the guests avoid being thought of as greedy.

The meal is served course by course. In some restaurants, there is waiter or waitress service, in others guests help themselves. After the last course, hot towels are handed out and shortly after that the guests leave the restaurant. Any social chit-chat takes place before or during the meals. Chinese do not like to linger at table once the food has been cleared away.

Whether there are many guests or a group of a few close friends, there is always an excuse for a banquet of many courses at a restaurant (see right).

冷盤

Leng pan: An appetizer platter includes deep-fried vegetarian "goose" of tofu skins, jellyfish, jumbo shrimp on lettuce, roast duck, and shark fin omelet.

蟹肉魚翅

Xie rou yu chi: To make shark fin soup, the shark fins are cooked in a broth with crab, pork, chicken, and Yunnan ham.

炸雞

Zha ji: Crispy portions of deep-fried chicken are arranged on a serving platter and served with dry toasted salt.

醬蒸尼羅

Jiang zheng ni luo hong: Red tilapia (a freshwater fish), steamed in fermented soybean sauce and garnished with green onions.

醉蝦

Zui xia: Drunken shrimp are marinated in rice wine whilst alive, before being cooked in a vegetable broth.

北菇爬樹

Bei gu pa shi shu: Black mushrooms are shiitake braised in a brown sauce with Chinese greens, garlic, and green onions.

炸冞貝芋頭

Yu rong zha dai zi: Scallops wrapped in puréed yam and deep-fried until golden-brown are best served with a sweet-and-sour sauce.

干燒伊麵

Gan shao yi mian: Yee fu noodles, stir fried with chives and paddi-straw mushrooms (paddi-straw mushrooms are grown on beds of rice straw).

壽桃

Shao bao: No birthday or wedding banquet is ever complete without these little peach-shaped buns symbolizing longevity.

A Chinese table setting

A place setting in a Chinese restaurant will include a platter for meat, fish, and vegetable dishes, a porcelain bowl with a spoon for soup and rice, a smaller bowl for soy sauce and/or sliced chili peppers, chopsticks, a serving spoon, and a tea cup. The plate is positioned in the center, and the bowl and spoon at the top of the place setting, to the left of the plate. The small sauce bowl stands to the right of the rice bowl, chopsticks and serving spoon rest on a small bar to the right of the plate, the tea cup is on the right, next to the chopsticks.

Chopstick etiquette

Never spear food with your chopsticks. Waving chopsticks in the air whilst talking is also regarded as bad manners (unless for the express purpose of inviting someone to partake of the meal), and chopsticks must never be allowed be put into the mouth while eating and they should not be allowed to touch the lips. It is not acceptable to stick chopsticks into a rice bowl, like incense sticks in an urn. Dropping one's chopsticks is a sign that unavoidable misfortune is on its way. However, chopsticks may be tapped on the table in order to reposition them.

Vegetable artefacts as elegant as carved ivory

Food art

The presentation of food has been elevated to an art form in some Chinese restaurants. This includes the intricate carving of vegetables into flowers, such as tulips and chrysanthemums, or figurines. It may also involve the arrangement of ingredients for a cold dish to form a gently rolling landscape. Root vegetables carved in the shape of figurines serve as table centerpieces, but they have to be more than merely beautiful. Like Shu, who stands surrounded by the peach-shaped buns, they must symbolize longevity, or many descendants like Fu, or wealth as promised by Lu. The winter melons used as soup terrines are carved with Chinese pictograms, symbols for good luck and success. And the salutations are reusable —these carved vegetable figures may bring their magic to several banquets before they need to be replaced

A carrot is transformed into a bird — with talent, a great deal of practice, and the right tools.

Even an experienced vegetable carver will spend at least two hours carving this exquisite figure on an oblong winter melon.

This intricate lotus flower made of yam may become the centerpiece for an appetizer.

As ephemeral as these works of art appear, many can be re-used several times to adorn a buffet.

This highly ornamented water-melon is appropriately adorned with the Chinese character for wealth.

中國酒 Wine

Chinese wines are made of rice, wheat, or millet rather than grapes, and are sometimes flavored with rose or chrysanthemum petals. They are generally drunk at room temperature, sometimes they are heated but never chilled. The wines vary greatly in their alcoholic content and some feature unusual ingredients. Some have to be sipped by the spoonful and are never drunk by the glass. Chinese wines are not only drinks, they may be used as ritual offerings and as tonics. As medicines they help to relieve a variety of ailments, such as rheumatism, strengthen vital organs such as the kidneys or the liver, promoting physical and mental vitality and longevity, fortifying the blood, stimulating the circulation, and warming the reproductive organs of women in labor.

1 *Yao jiu:* Various medicinal ingredients are steeped in rice wine for six months or more to produce this herbal tonic. The ingredients include the fungus *Cordyceps sinensis*, ginseng, boxthorn fruits, knotgrass, and the broths made from the roots of Solomon's seal and longwort. A weekly dose of 4 tsp (20 ml) will help maintain kidneys, eyes, hair, circulation, and complexion in good condition.

2 *Kao liang jiu:* This wine is made of millet and can be traced back to Confucius' family, which is as good as saying that it has been around for a very long time. It is a clear drink like gin, but with an alcohol content of 55-60%, it is considerably stronger.

3 *Shao hsing chia fen jiu:* This wine is made from glutinous rice and comes from Shao Hsing in southern China. The recipe is very ancient and is said to have once contained millet as well, but the tyrannical emperor Chun Chee Wong, better known for building the Great Wall, issued an order that the millet be replaced with more glutinous rice. The wine is served warm and is suitable for cooking

4 *Mei kuei lu:* The history of this rose petal wine dates back 300 years to the Ming dynasty. The best rose wine comes from Tianjin. To make rose

藥酒　　高粱酒　　紹興加飯酒　　玫瑰酒

wine, rose petals are added to millet wine before fermentation and distillation. This clear wine is drunk on its own or in cocktails, and is also used to flavor preserved meats, steamed fish, or chicken

5 *Xi han gu jiu:* This herbal wine is enriched by the addition of eight restorative ingredients. They are the seeds of the Tree of Life and of a type of pine, boxthorn fruits, the root stocks of Solomon's Seal, the flowers of a type of bellflower, as well as geckos, staghorn, and dogs' testicles. This elixir of life becomes stronger the longer it is kept, and is a cure for senility, poor eyesight and hearing, and helps maintain a youthful appearance. Bottles of this wine have been found in tombs dating from the Han Dynasty (206 BC-260AD).

6 *Zhu ye qing jiu:* Young bamboo shoots are added to rice wine to produce a slightly bitter drink with a

pleasing aroma. It is served at room temperature or even cooler, never too warm. Bamboo rice wine goes very nicely with fish

7 *Shao hsing hua diao ju:* This rice wine is suitable for use in cooking and similar to *shao hsing chia fen jiu* (3). Also sold under the name *huan jiu,* yellow wine, this wine is drunk warm. Wine-makers sometimes replace some of the rice with wheat.

8 *She jiu:* Snakes, including cobras, are laid in rice wine for at least six months. They are first gutted and the poison glands removed. Small amounts of snake wine are taken against the cold and are said to be beneficial against rheumatism.

Barkeeper Ngiam Tong Boon, who originally came from Hainan, invented the Singapore Sling in the Raffles Hotel in 1915.

Tiger

Nobody in Singapore would bat an eyelid if you asked for a "Tiger." Tiger Beer is a name which appears on almost every street corner in Singapore. The British were rather partial to the beer and promoted its sale. It is widely available throughout the Asian Pacific, where numerous breweries produce this beer. Fraser & Neave Ltd, a regional company, and the Dutch firm of Heineken founded the Malaysian Breweries, a joint enterprise which began brewing Tiger Beer in 1931. The beer, which was first brewed in Singapore, was similar to Heineken. The name Tiger Beer was chosen because tigers are a symbol of strength to the Chinese. This "Tiger" is now available in fifty countries worldwide.

Raffles Hotel first opened in 1887. For over a century, eminent socialites, businessmen, and famous personalities came to stay and spread the hotel's reputation. It closed in 1989 for a two-year refurbishment program to restore it to its former glory.

Singapore Sling

You haven't been to Singapore if you haven't had a Singapore Sling at the Raffles Hotel, birthplace of this famous cocktail.

This hotel, the most luxurious in southeast Asia, is named for Sir Stamford Raffles. It opened in 1887, by which time Raffles had already been dead for 61 years. Whilst scouting for a trading post on the route to China in 1819, Raffles dropped anchor at St John's Island and paid a visit to Singapore, then within the Sultan of Johore's sphere of influence. He decided it would be a good place for a free port. When he died at the age of 45, Raffles had only spent a total of 12 months in "his" Singapore but his presence can still be felt throughout the country. The intense red glow of the Singapore Sling has been present in the Long Bar at Raffles since 1915, when Hainanese barkeeper Ngiam Tong Boon invented the drink. Many famous personalities have been guests at Raffles Hotel over the years, including Somerset Maugham and Rudyard Kipling, and quite a few of these eminent guests probably had more than one Singapore Sling whilst sitting at the bar, undoubtedly the best place to do so. This is where the electric ceiling fans ensure cool air whilst you sip your drink and nibble fresh peanuts. The floor is often carpeted with peanut shells.

The unusual, pink color of the Singapore Sling is due to the fact that it was originally conceived as a drink for ladies. However, it is doubtful that all the 500 Slings served at Raffles on a typical day are destined for the "weaker" sex. Men have been known to travel halfway around the world for it, like the two gentlemen who flew on Concorde from London to Singapore in 1985, drank a few Slings, and then returned home the same afternoon!

Singapore Sling

2 Tbs (30 ml) gin
1 Tbs (15 ml) cherry brandy
8 Tbs (120 ml) pineapple juice
1 Tbs (15 ml) lime juice
1 1/2 Tsp (7.5 ml) Cointreau
1 1/2 Tsp (7.5 ml) D.O.M. Benedictine
2 Tsp (10 ml) grenadine
1 dash Angostura bitters
1 slice pineapple
1 cocktail cherry

Put all the liquids into a cocktail shaker with some crushed ice, shake, pour into a glass, and garnish with the pineapple and cherry.

Malaysia

Kalau tiada beras
Kerja tidak deras

A lack of rice makes
for slow work.

Malaysian proverb

The Cameron Highlands in the Ipoh
region, Western Malaysia

Preceding double page spread:
Malaysian women weave glutinous rice
pudding containers out of leaves

When two people of the same sex meet in Malaysia, they gently touch each other's hands and then their own breast with the fingertips. This is a gesture which means, "I hold your friendship in my heart."

The Malays are predominantly Moslems, whose daily life is determined by the Koran. This means that they are not allowed to eat pork or drink alcohol. Rice is the staple food which is served at every meal. Breakfast may consist of *nasi goreng*, fried rice, *nasi lemak*, coconut rice, *lontong*, pressed rice, or *bubur*, rice gruel. Any of these may be served with sweetened tea or coffee with the optional addition of condensed milk.

For lunch and supper, rice is served with four or five fried or braised dishes, accompanied by tidbits, chilies, and sambal. Malaysian dishes are seasoned with shallots, curry spices, garlic, chili peppers, and shrimp paste as well as with galingale, candlenut, coconut milk, tamarind, lemongrass, or palm sugar.

The Malays are a hospitable people and unexpected visitors are always welcome to share a meal. Bowls are filled with food and are available to all. Although the use of knives and forks is finding acceptance, many Malaysians still eat with the fingers of their right hands. Therefore, there are always finger bowls and jugs of water within reach so that anyone can wash their hands before and after meals. Eating together is an important element in social life, although it is still usual for men in traditional households to be served their meals by the women of the household who eat when the men have finished. However, these structures are beginning to break down and there have been changes. Eating is therefore no longer a domestic "ritual" as it was at the beginning of the century, when Malaysian food was only ever prepared in the home. Nowadays, Malaysian food can be found in restaurants and on street stalls. It is even possible to get Chinese or Thai specialities which have been adapted to suit Moslem rules of food preparation.

Beverages

Street stalls everywhere offer a multitude of cold drinks. These are bright pink, yellow, green, caramel-colored, or milky white and are a constant source of temptation in the humid and hot climate of Malaysia. Some are more or less unadulterated juices from tropical fruits such as limes, guavas, water melons, starfruits (carambolas), or sugar cane. Usually served with ice and with the occasional addition of a few tablespoonfuls of pandanus leaf syrup, these drinks could lead one to believe that you have never tasted anything more refreshing.

Furthermore, there are some interesting mixed drinks waiting to be tasted. For example, *katira*, which is also drunk during Ramadan, is made of condensed milk, rose-water, and *biji selaseh*, the seeds of a type of basil which swell when they are soaked in water. These seeds are also found in *air selaseh*, a boiled concoction of pandanus leaves, cloves, cardamom, sugar, and water. *Air jagung* is made of fresh chopped corn, mixed in the blender with water and pandanus syrup. *Air asam*, a pleasing sweet- and-sour drink made with water in which the white parts of tamarind has been boiled, and flavored with a dash of pandanus syrup. *Cendol* is a nourishing drink of coconut milk sweetened with palm sugar syrup, and swimming with tiny green "tears" of gram flour.

For those who prefer something hot to drink, because hot drinks are said to be more effective thirst-quenchers, there is *mata kucing* tea, a fruit tea made with brown sugar, fresh ginger, pandanus leaves, and the dried pulp of the *mata kucing longan*, a cherry-sized, brown fruit containing a brown pit and a tough skin. Tea and coffee are also available for sale on the street, already mixed with sugar and condensed milk. A type of herb tea is made by boiling one or two pandanus leaves in the water for the tea.

1 Fresh lime juice: The juice of large green limes, syrup, water, and ice
2 Fresh watermelon juice
3 Fresh starfruit juice
4 Banana Delight: 2 ripe bananas, 2 Tbs (30 ml) fresh orange juice, 2 Tbs (30 ml) pineapple juice, 4 tsp (20 ml) mango juice and 2 tsp (10 ml) grenadine
5 Coconut water: Open the top of a young coconut and drink the sweet water with a straw. The soft flesh can be scraped out with a spoon. This refreshment should not be indulged in too frequently as it is said to weaken the constitution.

Tea bushes thrive high above the sea

Tea Plantation

The Cameron Highlands lie approximately 5000 ft (1500 m) above sea level in the State of Pahang in the Malay peninsula. They were named for the British surveyor William Cameron who discovered the untouched plateau with its myriad of mountain streams for the British colonial rulers, to whom this paradise was a welcome retreat from the tropical heat of the coast. It was another Englishman, J. A. Russel, who realized that this upland climate was ideal for growing tea, a brilliant money-making scheme for Malaya. A. B. Milne of Ceylon (now Sri Lanka), a tea-planter, and Russel were jointly granted a land concession in the Cameron Highlands and established the Boh Plantations in 1929. Tea plant by tea plant, the plantations were hewn out of the virgin jungle. Tree felling and planting were performed by hand, by Tamil hands to be precise, as the British had hired labor in India to assist in the development of the uplands. Many of the Indians who live in this region today are descendants of that labor force. Mules were the only assistance provided for this clearing work. Today the plantation covers about 3,000 acres, yielding 8.8 million pounds (4 million kg) of tea is produced, 50% of Malaysia's domestic consumption. Boh tea is also exported to other countries such as the United States and Japan.

The tea grown in this region is an India tea of the Assam variety (*Camellia assamica*). It was originally a purely tropical plant, barely able to tolerate temperate climates. More robust plants have since been created by repeated crossings with *Camellis sinensis*, a tea bush which is actually frost-resistant. The bushes are grown from seed in the plantation's nursery. First the seeds are soaked in water, which is also the first stage of quality control. Any seed that floats to the surface is discarded. The top grade seeds are then spread out on damp linen sacks where they are left to germinate. As soon as the seeds crack open it is time to plant the seedlings in sandy loam soil. In many other places, tea bushes are not grown from seed as described above but from cuttings. The young plants are transplanted to the fields when they have reached a height of around 16 inches (40 cm). There are about 5,000 bushes to the acre, planted done in parallel rows at a distance of up to 40 inches (1 metre) between each plant. After six months the tea bushes need regular pruning until they are around four years old and ready for picking. This ensures that they grow into bushes about 40 inches (1 metre) high with a thick network of branches. If this drastic pruning were not performed the bushes would grow into trees up to 66 feet (20 meters) in height. Generally, only the young shoots consisting of a bud and two leaves are harvested. The bushes are picked as often as possible. In the Indonesian lowlands, where tea is also grown, this can be up to 30 times a year. Since plucking the leaves weakens the plants, they need to be given plenty of care and attention.

1 Even today, tea is picked by hand.
2 It takes a long time to fill a basket with the two leaves and a bud, and many baskets are needed, ...
3 ... if the poorly paid pickers are to earn a living.

4 The top three leaves on a young shoot provide the highest grade of tea.
5 The tips of the young tea shoots are harvested by the basketful and then packed.
6 The fresh green leaves are taken to the factory where they are turned into crumbly, dry, black tea leaves.

The tea plantations of the Cameron Highlands in Western Malaysia have been carved out of the virgin forest.

This immense carpet of green tea is constantly combed for young shoots, ready for plucking.

Coconuts

To this day, coconuts, the fruit of the coco palm (*Cocos nucifera*), are picked by hand. If a tree is not too tall, a long pole with a blade attached to one end can be used to cut down the nuts — although, they are not really nuts at all but stone fruit. Taller trees are climbed by skilled, nimble-footed men who pick the fruit. Alternatively, there is a species of wild monkeys (*beruk*) that can be trained to fetch the coconuts from the trees. Only males are selected for this task, and their three-month training period begins when they are six months old. A monkey on a long leash is taken to a tree to pick coconuts. His trainer gives the command and the monkey begins his ascent. As the monkey climbs higher, more of the leash is let out. Occasionally, the monkey may take a rest on the way up, causing the trainer to repeat his order more forcibly. When the animal has reached the crown, his trainer utters a different order and tugs on the leash. The monkey selects a coconut and twists it so that it falls to the ground. He continues in this way until his trainer tells him to come down.

Coconuts consist of a thick outer husk which can vary in hue from green to greenish-yellow to brownish-orange. Under the skin there is a fibrous mass. Only after the skin and fiber have been removed does the hard dark-brown shell of the nut itself become apparent. This shell has to be cracked open to reveal the white flesh.

Coconuts take twelve months to ripen fully. At eight months, the liquid or coconut water (not to be confused with the milk) in the young fruit is sweet and refreshing and the white flesh is still soft and sticky. This kind of coconut is served with its top cut away to provide an opening from which to drink the water and through which a spoon can be inserted to scrape out the flesh. The Chinese avoid drinking too much coconut water as it disturbs the balance of Yin and Yang. Ripe coconuts contain less water and the flesh which has hardened is suitable for grating. Sometimes, ripe coconuts contain the beginnings of a germinating sprout which can range in size from that of an onion to that of an orange. The germ is edible and is very sweet.

The specially trained monkeys have to be kept on a long leash while they work.

The monkey's skill and the help of gravity, ensure that the coconuts are soon picked.

The white coconut flesh is laid out to dry in the sun, reducing the liquid content from 50% to 5%. This dried flesh, called copra, is taken to the oil-mill for processing.

From a botanical point of view, the fibrous layer beneath the leathery outer skin is comparable with the flesh of any other fruit, but it is unequaled in its versatility and is thus a very valuable commodity.

The coco palm and the coconut have many uses. When the white flesh has been removed, the hard, dark-brown shell can be used to make bowls, ladles, spoons, and other household goods.

Coco-palm leaves are dried to serve as roofing thatch (*attap*). The young yellow leaves can be used to weave little boxes for rice cakes (*ketupat*), as well as hats, baskets, and mats. The older leaves are useful for wrapping food before broiling or barbecuing (*otak-otak*). The sharp spines on the leaves are strong enough to serve as kabob (*satay*) skewers and are even used as broomsticks bristles and brushes.

The durable and elastic fibers of the dried outer shell of the nut make good stuffing for mattresses and are used to make brushes, brooms, and mats as well as kindling. They can also be turned into coconut fiber cords. These fibers, known as coir, are resistant to salt water and so in the past they were the standard material of which ropes and ship's tackle were made.

Finally, the coco palm provides timber which is an important construction material and is even suitable for making furniture

Copra

The dried white flesh of the coconut contains up to 70% fat and is pressed in oil-mills to obtain coconut oil. In its unrefined state, coconut oil is somewhat pungent and therefore unsuitable for use in cooking. It makes good lamp oil and acts as a raw material for soap, cosmetics, and candles. Before it can be used as a hair oil, jasmine and other flower extracts are added to the coconut oil to hide its strong odor. The residue from the oil-pressing makes a nourishing feed for cows and chickens.

Refined and deodorized coconut fat (cocoa butter or coconut cream) makes good shortening for frying and roasting, and is used by the confectionery industry to make glazes. Since its setting point lies at between 64°F and 77°F (18°C and 25°C), it is usually solid at room temperature in the West, whereas it is more likely to be liquid in the tropics where it originates. To make coconut cream at home, gently simmer thick coconut milk until the liquid turns to oil. The crumbly residue which is left behind can be stored and used as a garnish.

To open the outer shell of the fruit, ram it against a pointed stake firmly anchored in the ground.

A well-aimed blow against a hand-held nut is sufficient to split it open.

A sharp serrated scraper is another good tool for removing the fresh coconut flesh from the shell.

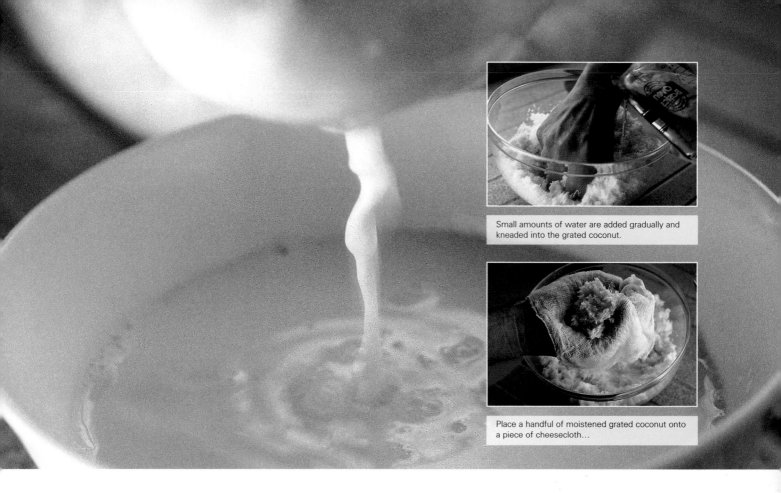

Small amounts of water are added gradually and kneaded into the grated coconut.

Place a handful of moistened grated coconut onto a piece of cheesecloth…

Coconut milk

Coconut milk is obtained by squeezing grated coconut, with or without the addition of water. It should not be confused with the coconut water found inside fresh coconuts. For the thicker version, frequently referred to as No.1 milk in recipe books, press the freshly grated coconut through a piece of cheesecloth. If the quantity of liquid thus obtained is insufficient, add some water to the grated coconut and squeeze out the liquid by hand once or twice, and then press one last time through the cheesecloth.

To make thinner, or No.2, milk, add 1 cup (250 ml) of water to the grated coconut and knead by hand. Repeat this process a few times before straining the excess liquid into a bowl and pressing the grated coconut through cheesecloth. Thanks presumably to years of practice, southeast Asian house-wives are extremely skilled at pressing grated coconut and can even make it with their bare hands.

When both thick and thin milk are called for in a recipe, the thin milk is always used first. Thick milk is added right at the end of the cooking time and should only be brought to the boil once, and used immediately before the dish is ready to serve.

A thick layer of cream forms on top of coconut milk if it is left to stand. This is often what cookbooks mean by coconut cream.

Various coconut grating tools are available in Malaysian stores, from a simple grater for home use to special wooden benches on which the person grating sits astride, half a coconut held in both hands, whilst passing the coconut in a circular motion, over the metal grating attachment fixed to one end. Food processors have also proven effective. In Asian countries, where coconut milk forms part of the staple diet. Of course, freshly grated coconut can be bought in any oriental (Thai or East Indian) food store.

If fresh coconuts are not available, dried grated coconut is a viable alternative. However, it must be soaked for at least 30 minutes in double its volume of hot water before pressing can begin. However, coconut milk is now available in powder form and it can also be bought canned. Both forms have to be diluted with water in accordance with the manufacturer's instructions. Be sure to buy unsweetened canned coconut, it is often imported from Thailand.

… and press until the grated coconut is almost dry.

The reward for all this hard work is coconut milk, a vital ingredient in southeast Asian cooking.

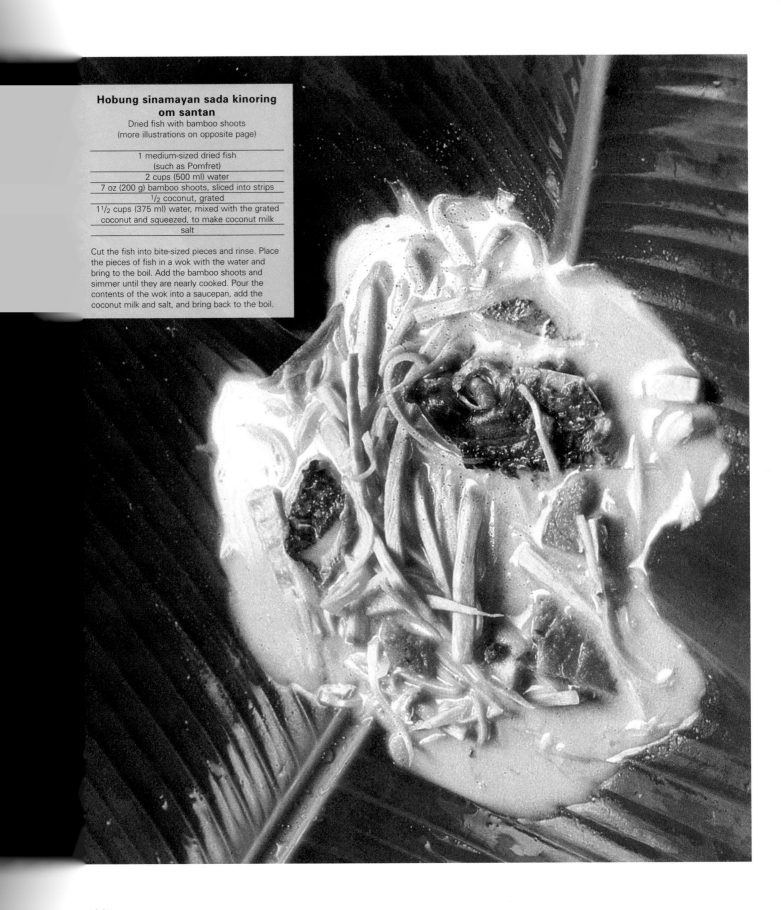

Hobung sinamayan sada kinoring om santan
Dried fish with bamboo shoots
(more illustrations on opposite page)

1 medium-sized dried fish (such as Pomfret)
2 cups (500 ml) water
7 oz (200 g) bamboo shoots, sliced into strips
1/2 coconut, grated
1 1/2 cups (375 ml) water, mixed with the grated coconut and squeezed, to make coconut milk
salt

Cut the fish into bite-sized pieces and rinse. Place the pieces of fish in a wok with the water and bring to the boil. Add the bamboo shoots and simmer until they are nearly cooked. Pour the contents of the wok into a saucepan, add the coconut milk and salt, and bring back to the boil.

Sambal kelapa
Coconut -*sambal*

2 fresh red chili peppers, cut into 3–4 pieces, seeds discarded
5 shallots, peeled and chopped
1/4 coconut, grated (about 4 oz (100 g) grated coconut, brown skin removed)
juice of 1 tsp tamarind pulp mixed with 2 Tbs water
salt
sugar

Pound the chilies in a mortar then add the shallots. When these have reached the same consistency as the chilies, add the grated coconut and a pinch of salt, and pound until you have a smooth paste.
Place the chili-and-coconut paste in a bowl, add tamarind juice, sugar, and salt, and stir well.

This *sambal* stimulates the appetite and is one of many dishes served during a meal. Even if you have a food processor, it is worth taking the time and effort to pound the ingredients with a pestle and mortar as this makes for a much more intense flavor.

Coconut cream for fillings

4 oz (120 g) palm sugar (gula melaka), grated or broken into pieces
4 Tbs (60 g) brown sugar
1/2 cup (125 ml) water
2 pandanus leaves, tied in a knot
1/3 coconut, grated (about 2/3 cup (150 g))
1 pinch salt

Place the palm sugar, brown sugar, water, and knotted pandanus leaves in a saucepan and simmer at medium heat until all the sugar has dissolved. Stir occasionally. Remove the leaves and strain the syrup through a sieve. Return the syrup to the pan and add the grated coconut and salt. Simmer at low heat, stirring continuously, until the mixture takes on a thick, moist consistency.

This mixture is used to fill pancakes.
The palm sugar can be replaced with raw brown sugar, but note that raw brown sugar is sweeter and therefore less is required.

Tahi minyak
Coconut crumbs

1 coconut grated
2 cups (500 ml) water

Combine grated coconut and water and press out the milk. Bring the milk to the boil in a saucepan.
Reduce the heat to medium and leave to simmer.
Reduce the heat further when the milk begins to separate into oil and coconut crumbs. Stir until the crumbs have turned brown. Remove the coconut crumbs, cool and store in an airtight container. Use as a garnish.

The oil can be brushed on meat or fish before broiling. The whole process takes 1-1 1/2 hours.

The ingredients for *hobung sinamayan sada kinoring om santan* are dried fish, grated coconut, and bamboo shoots.

Cut the fish into bite-sized pieces.

Simmer the fish and bamboo shoots in water.

Place in a saucepan and cook in the coconut milk.

Serunding daging
Spicy chopped beef

1 1/4 lb (500 g) lean beef
1 Tbs ground coriander (cilantro)
Juice of 1 Tbs tamarind pulp and 1/2 cup (125 ml) water
1 coconut, grated
1 cup water, mixed with the grated coconut and squeezed, to dilute the milk
salt
1 Tbs sugar

Spice paste

10 dried chili peppers, split open, seeds discarded
10 shallots, peeled and chopped
2 garlic cloves, peeled and quartered
2 pieces ginger root, about 1/2 in (1 cm) thick

Trim all traces of fat from the beef, cut into large cubes and simmer it in water until tender. Drain and leave to cool. Finely chop the meat.
Pound the chilies with the shallots, garlic cloves, and ginger to a paste in a mortar with a pestle. (It is advisable to wear rubber or plastic gloves when working with chilies.)
Combine the chopped beef with the spice paste and ground coriander and place in a deep skillet or wok.. Add the tamarind juice, coconut milk, and salt. Bring to the boil and then add sugar. As soon as the mixture begins to take on a creamy consistency, start stirring continuously, simmering until the liquid has evaporated and the flavor has fully developed.
Serve with steamed rice or *ketupat* (pressed rice cake). Prepackaged *ketupak* is available in oriental stores and will keep for several days.

Sayur lodeh
Mixed vegetables in coconut sauce

7 oz (200 g) cabbage, sliced into 1 in(2 cm) pieces
200 g yam beans, sliced into strips
7 oz (200 g) beans, sliced into 1-inch (2 cm) pieces
6 1/2 Tbs (100 g) baby corn
4 slices thick tofu, sliced diagonally
1 turmeric leaf
2 bayleaves
1 piece lemongrass, lightly crushed
1 1/2 coconuts, grated (about 3 cups (700 g))
1 cup (250 ml) water mixed with the grated coconut and squeezed, to make thick coconut milk
2 pints (1 l) water combined with the grated coconut and squeezed, to make thin coconut milk
salt
4 Tbs oil

Spice paste

3 onion, peeled and chopped
3 garlic cloves, peeled and quartered
1 piece lemongrass root (1/2 in (1 cm)), thinly sliced
6 1/2 Tbs (100 g) dried shrimp, soaked
1 piece shrimp paste (blachan), 1 x 1 x 1/2 in (2 x 2 x 1 cm)
1 tsp turmeric

Use a pestle and mortar to pound the ingredients for the spice paste.
Heat the oil and fry the spice paste, turmeric leaf, bay leaves, and lemongrass. Add the thin coconut milk when the flavors have developed, bring to the boil, and simmer for 5 minutes. Add salt, cabbage, yam bean, beans, and corn. Cook for another 5 minutes, then stir in the tofu and rich coconut milk. Bring back to the boil and simmer until all the vegetables are cooked through.

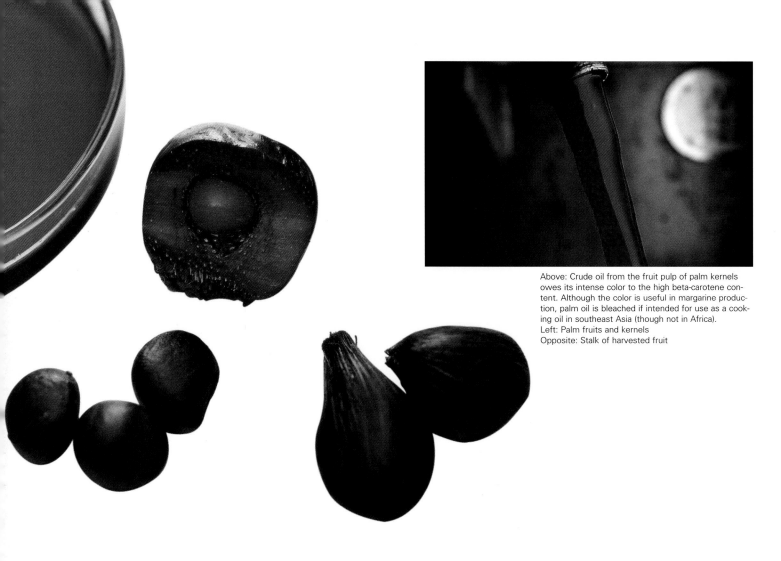

Above: Crude oil from the fruit pulp of palm kernels owes its intense color to the high beta-carotene content. Although the color is useful in margarine production, palm oil is bleached if intended for use as a cooking oil in southeast Asia (though not in Africa).
Left: Palm fruits and kernels
Opposite: Stalk of harvested fruit

Oil Palms

Malaysia owes its oil palms (*Elaeis guineensis*) to the British colonial rulers who brought them in from West Africa. In the old days, when the colonizers regarded the colonies as a kind of gigantic garden in which anything could be cultivated which generated profit seldom seems justifiable in the light of today's heavy emphasis on ecological issues. At the same time, however, oil palms are nowadays of enormous economic importance for Malaysia. They provide three commercially valuable commodities; palm oil from the pulp of the fruit, palm kernel oil from the pits or kernels, and briquettes, a waste product from palm kernel oil extraction. Briquettes contain residual fat and about 20% protein, so they are valuable animal fodder. Both

sorts of oil are used for the production of margarine, in the same way as coconut oil, and are important cooking and frying fats, as long as the palm fruits are subjected to further processing very quickly, even on the day they are harvested, since otherwise the enzyme which both contain separates the fat into glycerine and fatty acids. If the oil contains more than 5 percent of free fatty acids it becomes unsuitable for culinary purposes. It remains usable, however, for the soap and cosmetics industry. The special composition of palm kernel oil, which distinguishes it from palm oil, renders it particularly valuable for soap production since it produces a rich foam.

Oil palms are impressive trees, which can grow to a height of 199 feet (30 meters.) The slender trunk supports a head of as many as 30 plume-like leaves. The large and heavy fruit-bearing stalks (28 in (70 cm) long, 20 in (50 cm) wide and as much as

23 lb (50 kg) in weight) ripen from the third year onward in the angles of these leaves and bear as many as 2000 individual fruit the size of plums. The tree yields the best fruits from the twelfth year onwards, and fruits for about 25 years. Being a purely tropical plant, the oil palm requires an average temperature of 79°F (26°C) and cannot withstand it if the temperature drops below 40°F (15°C) or if there are periods of drought lasting longer than three months. It also needs a deep soil, rich in nutrients. If all these conditions are fulfilled, an oil palm will bear fruit all year round, which thanks to the fat content of the pulp and in the seed kernels makes it one of the tropical oil plants with the most prolific yields per acre. The fruits are harvested by cutting them down with a sickle attached to the end of a long bamboo pole. The blade is placed around the stem of the fruit-bearing stalk and wrenched downward.

The innumerable plum-sized stone-fruits which ripen on a single fruit-bearing stalk are separated from the bunch for further processing.

An oil matter

The harvested fruit-bearing stalks are first sterilized in steam to deactivate an enzyme which causes the undesirable separation into glycerine and free fatty acids. The individual fruits are then picked from the stalk. The bare fruit stalk is relegated to the compost heap and is recycled as fertilizer for the palms.

The next operation consists of mechanically breaking down the pulp of each fruit to release the oil. This reddish-orange colored crude oil is decanted for the purpose of further processing in the margarine and cooking oil industries.

The pressed fibrous briquette is subjected to two other mechanical operations during which the fruit fibers are separated from the pits. The pits or seeds are subsequently dried in a silo and are then sorted and opened to remove the kernels. The kernels are also subjected to a drying process before being packed in sacks for sale to producers of palm kernel oil. The crushed pulp residue of palm oil and seed husks are used as fuel for the drying furnaces. The kernel oil is extracted from the dried kernels in oil crushers. Even the residue from this process is a lucrative commodity, because it makes excellent animal fodder, so nothing made from palm fruits is wasted.

Gula melaka

Palm sugar is extracted from the flower-bearing stalks of the sugar palm (*Arenga pinnata*) and the attapalm (*Nypa fruticans*). These palms are cultivated specifically for their harvest of coveted sweet sap and therefore cannot be allowed to bear any fruit. Sap extraction usually starts when the tree is three to four years old. In order to prevent the opening of the upper petal of the flower-bearing stalk, it must first be tired firmly closed with suitable fiber. Then the flow of the sap to the flower-bud is stimulated by gently tapping it for several days with a stick, damaging the cell tissue. In addition, the flower-bearing stalk is very gradually bent downward. After a period of three to four weeks, the tip of the top petal is cut off and a container is placed beneath it to collect the sap. This is usually emptied once a day, though twice a day during the most productive phase. Every day, the surface has to be re-cut to allow the sap to ooze out unhampered.

In the tropical heat, the whitish sap starts to ferment within a few hours; this process is undesirable for palm sugar extraction purposes and attempts are made to delay the process by putting adding a little ground limestone, ground into a paste, at the bottom of the collector. Even so, the sap collected must be processed without delay. To this end, it is first strained through a sieve before being boiled for four to five hours in huge iron vats until the liquid thickens. A small piece of coconut kernel is always added to the vats apparently prevents it boiling over. To test whether the sap has boiled for long enough, a drop of it is slipped into water. If it solidifies, the syrup, which is now thick and orange-brown, is poured into another vat, and stirred for approximately 20 minutes with a wooden paddle until it starts to crystallize. The thick liquid is now poured into vertical bamboo canes which are carefully lifted out of the mixture after approximately 15 minutes, when the syrup will have solidified and retained this sugar cylinder shape on the table. The sugar is so hard that when required for use it must be grated or chopped into pieces. Palm sugar is known as *gula melaka* in Malaysia and Singapore, *gula jawa* in Indonesia, and *jaggery* in Sri Lanka. It adds a special flavor to cakes or puddings which other sugars do not have. If you cannot find palm sugar, use dark brown or muscovado sugar or Mexican piloncillo as substitutes.

Toddy

The sap of the sugar palm is only sweet as long as it is fresh. If it remains standing for a long time untreated, it starts to ferment and within around 24 hours is converted to *toddy* (palm wine). When this natural palm wine is distilled, a brandy is produced which is known as *tuak* in Indonesia and *arrack* in Sri Lanka. Palm wine was very popular among plantation workers and rubber collectors in Malaysia. However, Moslem religious law strictly prohibits the consumption of alcohol so the making of palm wine or palm brandy is currently prohibited in Malaysia. *Arrack* is sold in non-moslem parts of Southeast Asia, such as some Islands in Indonesia and in Singapore.

Sago gula melaka
Sago pudding

1 cup (250 g) sago, rinsed and drained

Coconut sauce
1 coconut, grated, about 1 lb (450 g); brown husk first removed
2 cups (500 ml) water, boiled and cooled
salt

Palm sugar syrup
300 g palm sugar, grated or broken into pieces
1¼ cups (375 ml) water

Boil water in a deep saucepan. Add sago and stir. It is ready when the sago starts to turn transparent. Rinse sago in a large wire sieve under running water from the faucet to flush out surplus starch. Fill one large or four small bowls or gelatin molds with sago and refrigerate until chilled.
Combine the grated coconut with the boiled and cooled water to saturate it , then press it through a sieve. Add a little salt and stir. Reserve the liquid.
To make the syrup, simmer the palm sugar and water in a saucepan over a low heat until sugar dissolves, stirring occasionally. Strain the mixture through a sieve into a pitcher.
To serve the pudding, unmold it onto a flat serving platter or individual dishes and hand the coconut sauce and palm sugar syrup separately so that everyone can pour their own sauce and syrup over their pudding according to individual taste.
This pudding complements a spicy curry entrée.

The sugar palm sap which has been collected is boiled for 4-5 hours in huge iron vats.
Main picture: When the palm sugar sets in the bamboo canes, the volume shrinks.

The upper petal of the flower-bearing stalk is firmly bound shut to prevent the bud opening.

The flower-bearing stalk is bent gradually downward and the tip is cut off so that the sap can ooze out unhampered.

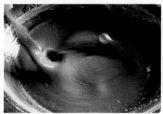

The sap is boiled until it becomes a thick orange-brown mass which is then stirred until it crystallizes.

The mixture is poured into bamboo canes where it cools and turns so hard that you have to then grate or chop it.

Jackfruit grows directly from the trunk — a branch would not be strong enough to support it anyway!

In actual fact, it is a deceptive package — only 30% of the pseudocarp (false fruit) is edible.

The edible parts are well protected beneath a thick husk and a fleshy fibrous layer.

In the street markets, jackfruits are sold from which the seeds have already been removed.

Nangka

Reaching the edible parts of the gigantic jackfruit (or jakfruit) involves a certain amount of unpleasantness; for one thing there is the rotten smell emitted by the wart-like knobbly shell, and then there is the sticky sap which oozes out when you cut it open, in which case it is best to rub a generous amount of oil into your hands and knife blades to protect yourself from it. The yellow seed pods at the core are sweet in flavor and their flesh is crunchy. They contain a relatively large seed which is edible when cooked, with a flavor similar to that of potatoes. It is often an ingredient in curry dishes. Fully ripe jackfruits can be eaten raw, and are delicious when the cavity left when the seed is removed is filled with vanilla ice cream. The unripe fruits can be encountered in many southeast Asian dishes as a cooked vegetable.

The evergreen jackfruit tree (*Artocarpus heterophyllus*) is native to India and Sumatra can grow to 65 ft (20 m) in height. The fruits grow on the trunk of the tree. Stories are told of jackfruit which weighed more than 120 lb (55 kg) and measured 36 x 20 in (90 x 50 cm) when harvested! However, only about 30% of the pseudocarp (false fruit) is edible.

Nangka lemak
Jackfruit in coconut milk

1¹/₄ lb (500 g) unripe jackfruit
1 coconut, grated
3 cups (750 ml) water
4 oz (120 g) salted dried fish, soaked and drained, (dried cod or stockfish can be substituted)
(200 g) shrimp, peeled
salt to taste

Spice paste

6 shallots, peeled and chopped
2 dried chili peppers, soaked, seeds discarded
1 thin slice fresh turmeric or ¹/₄ tsp turmeric
¹/₂ tsp black peppercorns

Peel jackfruit and cut into slices (rub oil into hands and knife beforehand). Stir 1 cup (250 ml) water into grated coconut to saturate the coconut flesh and obtain a thick milk. Reserve the milk, then repeat the operation with 2 cups (500 ml) water to obtain a thin milk. Place shallots, chili peppers, saffron, and peppercorns in a mortar and crush them with a pestle.

Parboil jackfruit in lightly salted water and drain. In a saucepan, combine the salt fish, shrimp, spicy paste, and thin coconut milk in a saucepan and bring to the boil again, stirring intermittently. Pour in the thick milk, bring to the boil once again, and cook for 10 minutes, stirring constantly. Serve with rice.

129

Queen with body odor

Durian

Duri means "thorn" in Malay, and that is exactly what it is — a thorny fruit in the literal sense. You can smell it long before you can see it. It is the queen of fruits to southeast Asians, yet hardly anyone in the West can bring themselves to share this appreciation, because durian has such a penetrating, fetid odor that hotels display notices banning durians in hotel elevators because the odor lingers for days afterward! Nor are they allowed to be transported in rented cars. No way should durians thus be stored in the refrigerator unless they are thoroughly wrapped, because otherwise everything in the refrigerator will absorb the stench.

The selection of durian fruits is almost a ritual. Connoisseurs examine the rind, assess the color, shake the fruit to see whether the seeds are loose — an indication of ripeness — take a deep breath, and then decide. Consumption of the durian becomes a social event. Normally a single fruit is not enough; purchasers buy several

The Durian is probably the only fruit which is actually banned from some places. The warning notice is richly deserved!

The stench of the Durian has been described as a mixture of onion, strong cheese, rotten eggs, and rotting meat, all soaked in turpentine!

at a time, and when they are cut open, all the enthusiasts' mouths start to water. They try each fruit and compare the respective flavors in detail. It is regarded as inappropriate to drink alcohol after the consumption of durian. Instead, an empty fruit shell is filled with drinking-water, a pinch of salt is added and the durian-eaters drink from the shell. According to the Chinese interpretation of a balanced diet, the drinking of salt water after eating durian or mangosteen neutralizes the heat of the fruits. Durian is eaten with the fingers; there is only one way to get rid of the strong odor which appears to penetrate the skin immediately and that is to hold a piece of empty durian shell under the faucet and allow the water to run along the hard green shell and onto the hands. Soap is completely ineffectual in eliminating the odor!

Durians are mostly eaten raw as a fruit, but the flesh is also used in desserts to which coconut milk is added. It is also used as flavoring in cakes, cookies, ice creams and soufflés. Durian flesh is boiled with sugar to form a thick dark brown paste which is shaped into rolls. These rolls are called durian cakes or durian paste in Singapore, Malaysia, and Thailand. They are served

To open the tough durian, you must find the weak spot in its shell.

Insert the knife at this spot and break the shell open.

Once it starts to break open, the thick thorny shell easily comes apart and reveals the rich fruit pulp.

It is the soft cream-colored seed casing which triggers the tastebuds and is the subject of such controversy.

sliced, and are nibbled as a snack in between meals.

Tempoyak is a product native to Malaysia and is made from ripe durian. It is a slightly salted durian paste which is stored for a week in wide-mouthed, sealed, air-tight jars. When it is ready, the semi-solid mass smells like vinegar. *Tempoyak* is used to season certain vegetable dishes or is mixed with chili peppers to make a dip. It could be described as an acquired taste.

In western Malaysia, durian (*Durio zibethinus*) thrives in Jahore, Perak, Kuantan, Pahang, and Kelantan. The tree requires a moist, hot climate, moderate rainfall, and cannot withstand any long periods of drought. The soil should always be well-drained and loamy. Durian trees bear fruit once or twice a year. The fruit yield increases in line with the age of the trees, so that a ten-year-old tree can produce as many as two hundred ripe fruits which grow directly out of the trunk, since no branch would be strong enough to hold them. Moreover, durians are not harvested — they fall to the ground when they are ripe. So think twice about standing under a durian tree when the fruits are ripe!

Pengat durian
Durian in coconut milk and palm sugar sauce

1 medium durian, not too ripe, seeds and pulp only
1 coconut, grated (white flesh only)
3 cups (750 ml) water, combined with grated coconut
6 oz (180 g) palm sugar, grated or chopped into pieces
2 pandanus leaves, tied into a small knot

Boil the durian seeds with the pulp in a little water. Add coconut milk, palm sugar, and pandanus leaves. Bring to the boil over a moderate heat to dissolve the sugar, stirring occasionally. When cooked through, remove the mixture from the heat and discard the pandanus leaves. Serve as a dessert or snack in individual bowls. Durian seeds are edible when cooked.

Kuah durian
Durian sauce

1 coconut, grated (white part only)
1/2 l (500 ml) water, combined with the grated coconut
6 oz (180 g) palm sugar
2 Tbs rice flour, mixed with 2 tsp water
4 oz (120 g) durian pulp

Simmer the coconut milk in a saucepan with the palm sugar over a moderate heat to dissolve the sugar. Strain the mixture through a sieve, return to the saucepan and, combine with the diluted rice flour, stirring continuously. When the sauce comes to the boil, add durian pulp to taste.
This sauce is an ideal complement to pancakes.

Pineapple

Those who consider themselves connoisseurs of fresh pineapples should try them sometime with a dip made from dark soy sauce and fresh red chili pepper rings. In Malaysia, fresh pineapple is prepared for eating by rubbing salt into after it is peeled; the salt is then rinsed off again before the pineapple is cut into slices. This minimizes the searing acid taste on the tongue. The Malaysians boil diced pineapple with sugar to make a thick stewed fruit purée for use as a pie filling, jam, and candied fruits. These are items which also appeal to the tastebuds of westerners. Pineapple is equally worth trying cooked with fish or in shrimp curries with tamarind sauce. Pineapple combines very well with steamed fish in a sweet-sour sauce and is also a tasty ingredient in vegetable salads.

Pineapples cultivated in Malaysia

Gandol: This is a cross between *mas merah* and Smooth Cayenne. It is normally cultivated for canning purposes. The plant grows to medium height and the leaves have small thorns pointing in the direction of the tip of the leaf. The cylindrical fruit weighs approx. 2½ lb (1 kg) and is visibly flaky. The flesh is transparent and golden in color.

Mas merah: The cylindrical fruit weighs around 5 lb (2 kg) when ripe. This variety has thornless leaves. The flesh is firm, fibrous, transparent, and golden in color. It is highly suitable for canning.

Sarawak: The large fleshy fruit achieves a weight of 5-10 lb (2-4 kg). The leaves have a red stripe down the center and the tips of the leaves are thorny. The flesh of the fruit is yellow with a bluish tinge and very sweet. This variety is cultivated for eating fresh, since its porous flesh makes it unsuitable for canning.

Smooth Cayenne: This variety, which is similar to Sarawak, was originally bred in Australia.

The pineapple is a bromeliad, so the flower-head grows from the center. The seed-pods ripen into berries which fuse to form a pseudocarp (false fruit).

A pineapple is ripe enough for harvesting if one of the inner leaves of the crown pulls out easily.

Cultivation in the open-air instead of in hothouses takes up to 22 months, more than double the time taken in hothouses, but is more economical.

Right: before canning, the pineapple cubes travel beneath another line of water sprinklers so that any remains of the shell are washed away.

The *gandol* variety has clearly defined scales, which are a sign of that the fruit has a good flavor.

In this canning factory, the fruit is still cut into chunks or slices by hand.

Canning is not entirely automated, female factory slice and sort the fruit.

These tidy layers of pineapple rings in cans are a very familiar sight in East and West.

Traditional baking

Cakes and pastries (*kueh*) are not eaten in Malaysia (or in Indonesia) at a specific time of day or on specific occasions as they are in the West. Many pastries, cakes, and cookies are savory rather than sweet and are not always oven-baked but may also be steamed, in the Chinese tradition. Sweet, rich pastries and cakes and stewed and steamed baked goods are served for breakfast, as a dessert, or simply as a snack in between meals.

Of course, the basic ingredients in pastries and cakes is flour. Wheat flour is seldom used in Malaysia, it is replaced by flour from tropical starchy grains and roots, such as sticky rice, rice, sweet potatoes, manioc, or

A new slant on cake-baking. This Malay woman is sitting cross-legged on the floor and has everything she needs spread out around her.

sago palm. Cakes and pastries are usually sweetened with *gula melaka*, the sweet sap tapped from the flower-bearing stalks of the sugar palm, or with dark brown raw sugar. The liquid used is coconut milk which adds fat to the pastry dough at the same time. Pandanus leaves provide a subtle flavor similar to that of vanilla as well as an appetizing color. The Malays have a long way to go before they reach saturation point in terms of artificial colorings, so gaudy, commercial food colorings are extremely popular.

Many cakes are wrapped in banana skins to complete the cooking process. Some of steamed cakes are wrapped with great skill to make square, triangular or cone-shaped parcels. Skewers made from the central rib of the coconut palm frond hold the parcels in shape and prevent them from opening during cooking. These cakes are mostly steamed, boiled, or and deep-fried in oil, and only occasionally baked in the oven. A waffle-like cookie is made which is dried out between heated iron plates like a waffle iron.

The dough for *kueh denderam* is rolled out on a floured surface until it is approximately ¼ in (1 cm) thick.

A cookie-cutter is then used to cut shapes and rings in the dough.

Deep-fried in plenty of hot fat the cakes still rise.

Kueh denderam look a little like and also taste remotely like gingerbread.

This delicious cake known as *kueh bakar manis* is cooked on the stovetop in a traditional pot. A wood fire provides the heat source from below, and charcoal is heaped on the tin lid as a heat source from above.

Kueh denderam

To make deep-fried rice-flour cakes, use rice flour with cane sugar or dark corn syrup and coconut milk and work it into a smooth dough. Roll dough out to a thickness of about ¼ in (1 cm) in thickness and use a pastry-cutter to carve out clover-leaf cake shapes the size of side-plates. Then make holes in the dough with a long stick. These cakes are fried in hot oil and have taste a little like gingerbread.

Kueh bakar manis

To make Baked Cake, beat together sugar, eggs, coconut milk, and flour. Season with ground cinnamon, fennel, and star anise. The sap of mashed pandanus leaves adds flavor and color to the cakes. The cake mixture is poured into a mold and cooked in a Dutch oven with heat above and below the pot, in the way Dutch ovens were traditionally used in the United States.

Rempeyek

Rice Flour Chips with Peanuts can be eaten at almost any time of the day or night. To bake them, you need a special instrument in the shape of five flat metal dishes (imagine something like the lids of cans) arranged in a circle, and welded in the middle to a long, vertical metal prong, which is used to hold this five-part chip-mold. *Rempeyek* is made from a thin liquid batter of rice flour, eggs, and coconut milk, seasoned with ground dried anchovies, coriander, cumin, and fennel seeds, and salt. The whole contraption is first dipped briefly into hot oil, removed, and a few nuts are placed in each of the metal dishes. Then a thin layer of batter is poured over them. The contraption is then lowered into a wok containing hot oil. The batter sets in a matter of minutes and the chips can be removed from the molds. They continue to cook, however, in the hot oil and roasted until they are golden-brown in color. Then they are scooped out and left to drain well.

Rempeyek, rice flour chips with peanuts, and their ingredients.

Kueh bakar manis – baked cake

The ingredients for *krepik bawang*, onion chips, and the finished product

Krepik bawang

For these spicy onion chips use wheat flour mixed with curry powder, ground anchovies, onions, and salt in a bowl. The mixture is then divided in two and one half is colored with chili powder. A little water is added to each portion and each is kneaded into a smooth dough. Each lump of dough is rolled out into strips. One yellow strip is placed on top of a red strip, then both layers are rolled up tightly together and thin slices are cut from them. This is how to get two-tone chips; all that is left to do is to deep-fry them briefly in oil.

Kueh sepit

The name of delicate wafers, made from a batter of coconut milk, flour, eggs, and sugar, flavored with ground fennel seeds, star anise, and cinnamon, is Love Letters. The thin liquid batter is baked between two iron hot-plates and then rolled around a wooden rolling pin while it is still warm. This must be done quickly, if it takes too long, the thin sheet of dough becomes brittle and breaks in the attempt.

Dodol

This pudding, made from sticky rice, coconut milk, palm sugar, brown and white granulated sugar, and pandanus leaves, is cooked in a deep skillet for nine hours, stirring constantly, until all the ingredients have combined to form a sticky, brown, shiny smooth mass like taffy. It is then left to cool and poured into containers woven from the leaves of a tree which is related to the pandanus (screwpine). The leaves are cut

Kueh sepit, Love Letters are "written" here on a beautiful old waffle-iron. The thin, liquid batter is seasoned with fennel, anise, and cinnamon.

The ingredients for *dodol*, the thick mass (rear), and the finished product (center)

into very thin strips for this purpose, then soaked and drained. They are then woven into little boxes of different shapes. When *dodol* is made at home, small quantities are cooked and stirred for no longer than two hours. This very sweet, rich dessert resembles similar to Mexican *cajeta* and is eaten in the same way. It can be served as a snack, or spread on toast like Egg Jam. When sold commercially it is wrapped in individual foil or plastic containers.

Kueh baulu

The mixture for these Small Baked Cupcakes consists of flour, sugar, eggs, and vanilla extract, with yellow food coloring added if liked. It is then poured into small molds and baked in a Dutch oven, over a fire and under the heat of glowing charcoal as described above for *kueh bakar mani*.

Epok-epok

The dough for these Malaysian pasties is a mixture of wheat flour, salt, margarine, and water stirred together. The filling consists of ground dried anchovies, toasted grated coconut, ground lemongrass, and garlic, seasoned with chili powder and sugar. The dough is rolled out thinly and placed in a hinged plastic mold. A small quantity of the filling is placed in the center and the hinged mold is closed. The pastry is thus trimmed and crimped at the edges. The result is a perfectly shaped pastry parcel which needs only to be deep-fried. The larger models are called curry pockets. They are filled with potatoes, onions, and then beef, chicken, or lamb.

Kueh baulu – small baked cupcakes

Epok-epok: roll out the dough as thinly as possible and place the mold underneath a corner of it.

Spoon a little of the filling onto the dough in the mold.

Close the hinged mold and press firmly together.

The result is a perfectly shaped *epok-epok* pasty which is deep-fried in oil.

Krepik pisang

Deep-fried banana chips are produced from unripe plantains or cooking bananas (*pisang tanduk*), and require the simplest possible preparation. Cook, peel, and slice the bananas and then deep-fry them. A variation of this is to dip the slices into sugar syrup before deep-frying.

Mangkok kueh

Steamed Rice Cakes take a long time to make. Mix cooked, cooled rice with yeast and let it stand overnight. Then work sugar, rice flour, and water into the rice until you have a smooth consistency and let it stand for another six hours before adding baking soda. You can leave the mixture white or divided it into portions and add food coloring. It is then poured into individual molds and steamed. Once steamed, the cakes are light and spongy. Eat them with sugar-cane and grated coconut for breakfast or in between meals as a snack.

Putu piring

For these Steamed Rice Cakes with Palm Sugar Filling, spoon coarse-grained ground rice into a mold, place a spoonful of chopped palm sugar in the center, and pile rice flour on top. Press a small piece of pandanus leaf into the cake in such a way that it can be removed before the cake is eaten. Drop the raw soft dough balls onto pieces of cheesecloth, and place these parcels into the funnel-shaped bottom parts of the special rice-cake molds which have been arranged inside a steamer. Cover the molds with lids and let the cakes cook as the steam rises up from below into the molds. When they are ready, remove them and serve them hot with freshly grated coconut.

Mangkok kueh – steamed (colored) rice cakes

For *putu piring* first fill the lid of the mold with coarse-grained rice flour.

Then press a piece of palm sugar in the center.

Apply a second layer of rice flour.

Shape each rice flour cake with the aid of the bottom part of the mold.

Drop into cheesecloths, then place the soft dough balls in the molds.

The steaming hot *putu piring* are served with grated coconut.

The molds for *putu piring* consist of a funnel-shaped bottom part and cone-shaped lids. The steam rises up through the opening in the bottom of the funnel.

Eating out

Coffee Shops

Coffee, tea, and other hot or cold drinks are served in these traditional eateries with a simple breakfast of toast, boiled egg, and cakes. Nowadays, more and more space in coffee shops is being leased out to sellers of noodle, gruel, and rice dishes. The atmosphere is relaxed, the service is swift and businesslike. Fans cool the air, there is no air-conditioning here. You order your food at the stalls, sit down wherever there is a free table and the waiter comes to take the drink order. In some coffee shops you pay as soon as the food has been brought; in other places you pay the check after eating. For drinks you can call the waiter and pay him. No tip is expected.

Hawker Centers

First you grab a free table and sit down. At peak times it is a case of survival of the fittest! You make a mental note of your table number (if applicable). One of you guards the table while the others look at what is on offer at the surrounding stalls. Once you have decided what you want, you give the seller at the stall your order and include your table number. You pay when waiters have brought the food you ordered to your table. You can buy as many dishes from different sellers as you like, but each stall must be paid separately. Sellers seem to have a photographic memory, because they find you wherever you are sitting, even at Hawker Centers where the tables are not numbered.

Food courts offer a rich selection of meals which consist of an entrée such as noodles, rice with broiled Chinese pork or roast duck. You have the choice of Chinese, Malay, or Indian cuisine. There is also always a stall with an abundant supply of soft drinks. Hawker Centers are informal eateries with simple tables and stools and they are frequently located near big markets.

Food Courts

These are sophisticated versions of the Hawker Centers. You eat in air-conditioned surroundings and sit on comfortable chairs or benches. The atmosphere here is more formal and even familiar to westerners used to food courts in shopping malls, but some people may prefer them to the rustic charm of the Hawker Centers. Food is ordered in the same way as in the Hawker Centers. The Food Courts are sometimes self-service.

Restaurants

Restaurants range from the basic, whose menu selection is limited to elegant restaurants with extensive menus. Waiters wait on tables and take orders as in the West. Diners can also consult the waiter for his recommendation if they cannot decide what they want to eat. These restaurants frequently offer local dishes.

Left: Hawker Centres are busy places at all hours of the day, and there are constant comings and goings. The atmosphere is very informal, but the stools are not that comfortable.

Above. a wide selection of foods is on offer at Hawker Centres which includes both simply prepared as well as very sophisticated fast foods.

One of many dishes

Soups

Soups are almost always one of the courses of a main meal but they occupy a different place in a Malay meal as compared to a Chinese meal or a meal served in the West. In Malaysia, soups and entrées are served together and soup is drunk during the course of the meal (a fact which has an impact on the quantities of the ingredients). Often a few spoons of soup are added to rice to make it softer and easier to eat. A basic distinction is made between light soups which are served on hot days and richer soups which are more suitable for cold days. Clear, light soups include *sayur bening* (vegetable soup), *lauk pindang* (fish soup with garlic, galangal, onion rings, and lemongrass) and *lauk asam* (tamarind paste soup with fish or vegetables). The recipes are safe or also exciting variations on a theme of coarsely ground dried anchovies, shallots, fresh chili peppers, a little dried shrimp paste, and fish or vegetables. The fuller richer soups like *sop ayam* (chicken soup), *sop ekor lembu* (oxtail soup) or *sop kambing* (lamb soup) owe their flavors to spices like coriander, fennel, cumin, pepper, star anise, and cinnamon. These soups are garnished with roasted onion rings, garlic, chopped green onions, and coriander (cilantro) leaves.

Lauk pindang
Fish soup

4 fish steaks, cut from saltwater white fish, such as red snapper, redfish, or cod
1 garlic clove, peeled and quartered
1 thin slice galangal
5 cups (1 1/4 l) water
4 shallots, peeled and sliced into rings
1 stem lemongrass, lightly crushed
2 dried tamarind slices
salt
1 onion, sliced into rings

Place the garlic and galangal root in a mortar and grind to a paste. Set a saucepan of water on the stove and add shallot rings, lemongrass, dried tamarind, and salt. When the water boils, add the onion rings and fish steaks to the soup. Bring rapidly back to the boil, then reduce the heat and simmer the fish until done. As soon as the fish is cooked, remove it from soup, cut it into bite-sized pieces, and serve it in individual bowls. Pour over the broth over the fish and serve immediately.

Sayur bening
Vegetable soup

10 1/2 oz (300g) cabbage, shredded
3 Tbs dried anchovies, halved, heads discarded
6 shallots, peeled and quartered
1–2 fresh red chili peppers, cleaned
2 pints (1 l) water
salt

Rinse the anchovies and coarsely mash them in a mortar. Repeat the process with the shallot pieces and chili peppers. Set a saucepan of water on the stove and stir in the spicy paste. As soon as the water boils, add salt and the cabbage strips to the hot water. Bring back to the boil and cook for a short while. Instead of cabbage you can use any other vegetable in season.

Sop ekor lembu
Oxtail soup

(600 g) oxtail, cut through at the cartilage but not chopped
1 onion, peeled and sliced into rings
1 cinnamon stick
1 tsp coriander seeds
1/2 tsp cumin seeds
2 pints(1 l) water (or enough to cover the oxtail in the pot)
4 potatoes, peeled and quartered
salt

Garnish
fried onions rings
2 green onions (scallions) sliced into rings

Thoroughly clean the pieces of oxtail. Add them to saucepan with onion, cinnamon stick, coriander seeds, and cumin seeds. Add cold water, set on the stove, and bring to the boil. As soon as the soup boils, remove the scum produced by the meat with a slotted spoon and reduce the heat. Let the soup simmer on low heat until the pieces of oxtail are soft but the meat is not falling off the bones. Add the potato pieces to the soup, salt, bring the soup back rapidly to the boil and reduce the heat again. When potatoes are cooked and the meat is tender, remove the pieces of oxtail from the broth. Bone the meat and divide it into portions. Arrange it in individual bowls. Fill the bowls with broth and garnish with the onion rings and green onions (scallions).

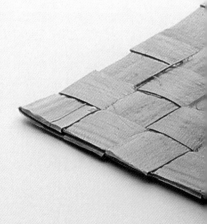

Sop ayam
Chicken soup

2 small chicken breasts or 2 large legs (about 14 oz (400 g)
3 Tbs oil
1 small onion, peeled and sliced into thin rings
1 piece cinnamon stick, 2 in (4 cm) long
4 cardamom seeds
4 cloves
5 cups (1¼ l) water
2 stems lemongrass (bottom parts), lightly crushed
½ oz (10 g) cellophane noodles, soaked, drained, and chopped
2 potatoes, boiled, peeled and sliced into pieces

Marinade

1 slice ginger root, ¼ in (5 mm) thick
2 garlic cloves, peeled and quartered
1 tsp ground coriander (cilantro)
½ tsp ground cumin
½ tsp turmeric
½ tsp freshly ground pepper
½ cup water

Garnish

3 shallots, sliced into rings and fried
1 green onion (scallion), minced
2 coriander (cilantro) stems, leaves minced

Mash the ginger and garlic in a mortar then mix to a paste with the coriander, cumin, turmeric, pepper, and water. Rub it into the chicken flesh and marinade for 15 minutes. Heat oil and fry onion rings, cinnamon, cardamom, and cloves. When onions have browned, add the marinated chicken and fry briefly until the flavors are released. Add the lemongrass, then cover with the water, and bring to the boil. Reduce the heat and let the soup simmer until the chicken is cooked. Remove the chicken meat, leave to cool, then cut into thin slices.

Add the cellophane noodles to the soup and bring to the boil. Serve the small pieces of chicken and sliced potato in individual bowls, pour the hot soup over them, and garnish with fried onion rings, minced green onions (scallions), and fresh coriander (cilantro) sprigs or leaves.

Sop ayam – Chicken soup

A one-pot dish

Noodles

Wheat noodles and rice noodles are appreciated as being complete meals in themselves. In this connection "in themselves" is almost a misnomer, since the variety of flavorings which can be served in several individual bowls for the purposes of a rice meal, are served up in one bowl here. At least that is the way it appears, when you see the number of ingredients. Fried noodle dishes are cooked with all kinds of vegetables, as well as with tofu, squid, shrimp, or beef, and garnishes can include fresh red or green chili peppers sliced into rings, grated cucumbers, green onions (scallions), garlic chives (*allium tuberosum*), fried onion rings, herbs, and halved or quartered limes. If the noodles are served with sauces, a distinction is made between sauces based on tamarind which are light, sweet-and-sour, and spicy, and very rich sauces based on coconut milk.

Mee goreng
Spicy stir-fried wheat noodles

1¼ lb (500 g) fresh yellow wheat noodles (*mee*), cut into short pieces
(300 g) shrimp, peeled (heads reserved for soup base)
½ cup (125 ml) water
6 Tbs oil
2 garlic cloves, peeled and chopped
1 Tbs dark soy sauce
8 oz (250 g) squid, cleaned, peeled, and sliced into pieces
10½ oz (300 g) *choi-sum*, leaves removed from the stems and sliced into 2 in (4 cm) pieces
7 oz (200 g) beansprouts, roots trimmed
salt

Spice paste

10 dried chili peppers, soaked, seeds discarded
2 fresh red chili peppers, seeds discarded
1 onion, peeled and chopped

Season the shrimp heads with salt and leave to marinate for 10-15 minutes. Rinse, grind them in a blender with ½ cup (125 ml) water, then strain through a sieve. Reserve the mixture. Place dried and fresh chili peppers and onion in a mortar and mash. Heat oil in wok, add the garlic and lightly brown, then add the spice paste and fry until the flavors are released. Add the ground shrimp heads, stir in soy sauce, then add the squid and peeled shrimp and mix well. Add first the stems then the leaves of *choi-sum* and stir well.
Rinse noodles briefly, add to the wok, and stir-fry for 5 minutes, then mix in the beansprouts and season with salt. Serve as soon as the beansprouts are cooked through.

Kwei teow goreng
Stir-fried rice noodles with beef

18 oz (800 g) fresh rice noodles (*kwei teow*)
8 oz (250 g) fillet of beef, sliced into strips
1 cup (200 g) beansprouts, roots trimmed
8 oz (250 g) shrimp, peeled
2 cups (200 g) water spinach, chopped
1½ Tbs dark soy sauce
5 Tbs oil

Spice paste

8 dried chili peppers, soaked, seeds discarded
4 fresh red chili peppers, seeds discarded
1 onion, peeled and chopped
1 garlic clove, peeled and quartered

Mash the chili peppers, onion, and garlic in a mortar. Heat the oil in wok and fry this spicy paste until the flavors are released. Add the beef and stir. Add the soy sauce and shrimp to wok and cook for a few minutes. Add noodles and stir well. Stir-fry the water spinach and beansprouts until the vegetables are cooked through but still slightly crunchy.

Tip: When stir-frying noodles, they must be stir-fried for 1-2 minutes after the addition of each ingredient.

Mee rebus
Fresh wheat noodles in rich sauce

1 lb (500 g) fresh yellow wheat noodles (*mee*)
7 oz (200 g) beansprouts, roots trimmed
2 Tbs ground coriander
1 Tbs soybean paste (*tauceo*)
5 pints (1½ liters) chicken broth
1 large sweet potato, boiled, peeled and mashed
2 tomatoes, sliced into rounds
4 Tbs oil

Spice paste

12 dried chili peppers, soaked, seeds discarded
8 shallots, peeled and chopped
2 garlic cloves, peeled and quartered
6 thin slices galangal root

Garnish

2 hard-boiled eggs, quartered
2 blocks firm tofu, sliced into strips, sprinkled with a little salt, fried until golden-brown
3½ oz (100 g) Chinese garlic chives, minced
6 shallots, sliced into rings and fried 4 fresh green chilies, sliced into rings
2 small limes, halved

Place chilies, shallots, garlic cloves, and galangal root in a mortar and grind to a fine paste with a pestle. Heat the oil in a saucepan and fry the spicy paste in it until the flavors are released. Add ground coriander and tofu. Fry for two minutes. Place mashed sweet potato in a bowl, add a little chicken broth, and stir until you have a smooth purée. Add this and the remaining broth to the fried ingredients. Stir well, and continue to stir while bringing to the boil. Season with salt. The sauce should be of a creamy consistency. When almost ready, add the tomatoes. Blanch first the beansprouts then the noodles for 1-2 minutes in boiling water and drain. Serve noodles and beansprouts in individual bowls, ladle the sauce over them, and garnish them. Serve the limes on the side, so that diners can squeeze lime juice into their soup just before eating.

Momofuku's Stroke of Genius

Instant noodles can now be found in practically every Asian household. They were invented by a Japanese from Osaka, Momofuku Ando, and have become a world-wide hit. Although relatively new in the West, they have been around in southeast Asia since 1958, and new varieties are constantly being launched on the market. Instant noodle meals in plastic cups (pot noodles) are also obtainable here just like in the West. All you need to do is add boiling water and wait a few minutes. Asian tourists who fear they will not be able to adapt to Western cuisine bring plentiful supplies of instant pot noodles in their luggage, just in case.

Penang laksa
Rice noodles in sharp spicy sauce

1½ lbs (600 g) wolf-fish (*ikan parang*), steamed, flesh flaked
5 cups (1½ l) water
Liquid from 6 Tbs tamarind paste mixed with 1 cup (250 ml) water
2 dried tamarind slices
6 stems knotgrass (*daun kesum*), leaves thinly sliced
2 Tbs sugar
1 tsp salt
(800 g) fresh or dried thick rice noodles (*beehoon kasar*)

Spice paste

14 dried chili peppers, minced, soaked, seeds discarded
1 piece shrimp paste (*blachan*),1,5 x 1,5 x 1 cm
2 stalks lemongrass (only lower parts), sliced into thin strips
2 slices galangal, about ⅛ inch (4 mm) thick
4 Tbsp (120 g) shallots, peeled and chopped

Garnish

½ small pineapple, cut into pieces or strips
1 cucumber, peeled and thinly sliced
6 Chinese cabbage leaves, shredded
3 fresh red chili peppers, sliced into rings, seeds discarded
3 mint stalks, leaves chopped, stalks discarded
3 tsp shrimp paste (*petis*), diluted in a little warm water

Place chili peppers, shrimp paste, lemongrass, galangal, and shallots in a mortar, and grind to a paste. Set a saucepan of water on the stove and add the spice paste, tamarind juice, tamarind slices, and knotgrass and bring to the boil. Reduce the temperature and simmer for 20 minutes.
In the meantime, soak the dried noodles for 15 minutes, blanch, and drain until they are dry. Fresh noodles do not need soaking.
Add the chopped fish, sugar, and salt to the mixture and let it stand for 10 minutes. Remove the tamarind slices before serving.
Serve the noodles in individual bowls, arrange the garnish over them, ladle the hot sauce over the top, and put 1 teaspoon of *petis* (diluted shrimp paste) in each bowl.

Petis is a thick, dark paste of a syrupy consistency, made of fermented dried shrimp, and is a staple in southeast Asian cuisine. It has a very strong flavor.

Herbs and Spices

Bunga cengkih: cloves *(Syzygium aromaticum),* shown here as buds on the tree (Indonesian: *bunga cengkeh;* Chinese: *ding xiang*)

Kucai: garlic chive (*Allium tuberosum*) offers an interesting combination of chive and garlic flavors (Chinese: *jiu cai*).

Daun bawang: green onions (scallions) *(Allium fistulosum)* are similar to the varieties obtainable in the West (Chinese: *cong*).

Bunga kantan – bud of the red ginger plant (*Phaemeria speciosa*) for salads and curries (Indonesian: *honje, palang*; Chinese: *xiang hua*)

Daun selaseh – Basil (*Ocimum basilicum*) is used in curries (Indonesian: *daun kemangi*)

Daun kari – Curry leaves (*Murraya koenigii*; Chinese: *gah li ye*); salam leaves (*daun salam*) are used in Indonesian cuisine instead

Cecur: lily rootl (*Kaempferia galanga*) similar in flavor to ginger (Indonesian: *kencur*; Chinese: *sha jiang*)

Lada kering: soak dried chilies first in warm water; they are milder if the seeds are removed (Indonesian.: *cabai/cabe kering*; Chinese: *la jiao gan*).

Lada merah/lada hijau: fresh chili peppers; long ones are hotter than round ones (Indonesian: *cabai/cabe merah/hijau*; Chinese: *hong/qing la jiao*).

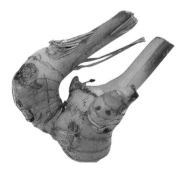

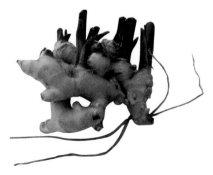

Lengkuas: galangal (galingale) root (*Alpinia galanga,* syn. *Galanga major*); ginger-like, but used more sparingly (Indosian: *laos*; Chinese: *lan jiang*)

Halia tua: corm of the ginger root (*Zingiber officinale*) has a stronger flavor than galangal (Indonesian: *jahe tua*; Chinese: *jiang*).

Halia muda: young ginger root, also called stem ginger (*Zingiber officinale*; Indonesian: *jahe muda*; Chinese: *nen jiang*).

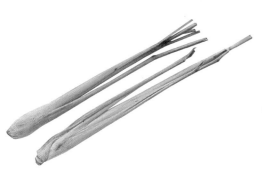

Serai: lemongrass (*Cymbopogon citratus*) 4-6 in (10-15 cm) (Indonesian: *sereh*; Chinese: *xiang mao*) has a bulbous root and lemony flavor; use only the lower part, near the stem.

Daun limau purut: Kaffir lime leaves (*Citrus hystrix*) give a citrus flavour to curries or broiled foods (Hindi: *daun jeruk purut*; Chinese: *suan gan ye*).

Daun kesum: knotgrass, Vietnamese coriander *(Polygonum odoratum)*; sharp peppery herb used in rich coconut sauces (Chinese: *ku wo ye*)

Asam keping – dried tamarind slices *(Tamarindus indicus)*, leavening agent for soups and sauces (indon.: *asam gelugur*; chin.: *a shen pian*)

Limau kesturi – Limes *(Citrus aurantiifolia)* with thin green skin; the juice is used (indon.: *jeruk nipis*; chin.: *suan gan*)

Buah keras: candlenut (*Aleurites moluccana*) for binding and enriching sauces (Indonesian: *kemiri*; Chinese: *ma jia la*)

Daun seladeri: celeriac (*Apium graveolens*; Indonesian: *daun seledri*; Chinese: *qin cai*)

Daun pandan: Pandanus leaves (*Pandanus odorus/ tectorius*) emit rose and vanilla scents; the green sap is used as coloring (Chinese: *xiang lan ye*).

Kunyit basah: fresh tumeric (*Curcuma domestica*) gives curries their bright yellow color (Chinese: *huang jiang*).

Daun kunyit: tumeric (*Curcuma domestica*) leaf is used in curries or for wrapping up fish for broiling (Chinese: *huang jiang ye*).

Daun ketumbar: coriander (cilantro) leaf (*Coriandrum sativum*; Chinese: *yan sui ye*)

147

Salads

Malay salads are served as a part of a menu with other dishes or as a snack in between meals. The latter applies particularly to salads which are made from raw vegetables or from a combination of fruits and vegetables. In terms of its function as a food, a salad tends to have all the characteristics of an appetizer. Conversely, salads made from cooked vegetables can be a substitute for a meal consisting of several courses. Oil-and-vinegar dressings, like vinaigrette, are unknown in Malaysia. Salad dressings here usually consist of a spicy triple clash of sweet, sour, and sharp flavors, in which lime tamarind juice replaces the vinegar. Richer dressings are enriched with coconut milk and/or ground peanuts.

Kerabu timun
Cucumber salad

2 cucumbers, sliced into strips
2 Tbs grated coconut, toasted without oil
3 Tbs dried shrimp, soaked in water
6 fresh red chili peppers, seeds discarded
1 Tbs grated dried shrimp, pan-fried without oil
1 red ginger bud, sliced into thin slices
1 Tbs dark brown sugar
salt
2 limes, juice squeezed

Finely crush the toasted grated coconut with the dried prawns in a mortar. Add chilies and blend with the other ingredients; do the same with the roasted dried shrimp paste.
Place the cucumber and paste in a bowl and sprinkle with the sliced red ginger bud. In a second bowl, stir the sugar and salt into lime juice. The salad should not be prepared until just before it is to be served.
This salad would be served as an appetizer, consisting of several dishes. *Kerabu* is the Malay name for this sort of composition of raw or cooked vegetables in a dressing made from grated coconut, chili peppers, dried shrimp, and lime juice.

Jengganan
Salad of cooked vegetables for 2-4 people

3 pieces firm tofu, quartered into triangles
2 packets tempeh (fermented soybean paste)
5 oz (150 g) beansprouts, roots trimmed
3½ oz (100 g) green beans, sliced into 1 in (2 cm) pieces
10½ oz (300 g) water spinach, sliced into in 2 in (4 cm) pieces
5 oz (150 g) cabbage, shredded
oil for frying

Heat the oil in a wok then stir-fry tofu until slightly brown. Drain and reserve.
Stir-fry the tempeh, drain it and leave to cool; cut it into bite-sized pieces. Fill a deep saucepan with water and bring it to the boil; add 1 teaspoon salt.
Blanch each of the following vegetables separately: beansprouts, green beans, water spinach, and cabbage. Rinse the vegetables in cold water and drain them.
To serve, arrange the vegetables on a serving platter with the stir-fried tempeh and tofu. Pour the dressing over them just before serving.
Serve with spicy peanut sauce (*sambal jengganan*). See recipe on page 165.

The quantities indicated are enough for a complete meal for two people or a side-dish for four people.

Gadoh-gadoh – salad made from cooked and raw vegetables

Kerabu timun – cucumber salad

Gadoh-gadoh
Salad from cooked and raw vegetables
For 4 or 6 people

5 oz (150 g) cabbage, sliced and blanched
7 oz (200 g) beansprouts, roots trimmed, blanched and drained
5 oz (150 g) water spinach, cut into in 2 in (6 cm) pieces and cooked until tender
5 oz (150 g) green beans, sliced into 2 in (5 cm) pieces and boiled until tender
3 pieces firm tofu, fried until golden brown and sliced into 9 pieces
2 packets tempeh (fermented soybean paste), shallow-fried and sliced into bite-sized pieces
4 potatoes, boiled, peeled and thickly sliced
3 hard-boiled eggs, cut into slices or pieces
2 cucumbers, cut into pieces
1 small yam bean, sliced into pieces
6–8 shrimp crackers

Dressing

20 fresh red chili peppers, seeds discarded
1 piece shrimp paste (blachan) 1 x 1 x 1/4 in (3 x 3 x 1 cm)
2 Tbs oil
2/3 coconut, grated (about 9 oz (300 g))
3 cups (750 ml) water, mixed with the grated coconut, and squeezed to make milk
7 oz (200 g) roasted peanuts, finely ground
juice of 1 Tbs tamarind pulp mixed with 1/2 cup (125 ml) water
1 Tbs palm sugar (or 1 tsp dark brown sugar)
salt

Crush the chili peppers in a mortar, add the piece of shrimp paste, grind, and blend with chili peppers. Fry the paste in hot oil until the flavors are released. Add a little coconut milk and ground peanuts and stir until you have a smooth mixture. Add the remaining coconut milk, tamarind juice, sugar, and salt and bring slowly to the boil. Season with sugar and salt to taste. You can serve the different vegetables either together on a large platter or separately in individual bowls. In both cases, spoon a little of the dressing over the each salad and garnish with shrimp crackers (break up large crackers into 2 or 3 pieces).

Gadoh-gadoh means "clash", which presumably refers to the variety of different vegetables which go into the creation of this dish. The quantities indicated are enough for an entrée for four people or a side-dish for six people.

Rojak
Fruit and vegetable salad

1 cucumber, halved lengthwise and cut into rounds 1/4 in (5 mm) thick
1/2 pineapple, sliced into 1/4 in (5 mm) chunks
1 small yam bean, sliced into 1/4 in (5 mm) chunks
1 starfruit (carambola), sliced into segments, each segment sliced into pieces
1 unripe mango, peeled and sliced into pieces
1 guava, sliced into pieces
1 bud of the red ginger plant, thinly sliced (to taste)

Dressing

3 Tbs black shrimp paste
10 fresh red chili peppers, seeds discarded
1 Tbs dried shrimp paste, toasted in a dry skillet
2 Tbs sugar
6 limes, juice squeezed

Place all the chopped vegetables and fruits in a large salad bowl.
Place the chilies in a mortar and mash to a paste, add the toasted shrimp paste and blend with the chilies. Place this paste containing the black shrimp paste, sugar and lime juice into a bowl and stir. Do not mix the dressing with fruit and vegetables until you are about to serve the salad.
The bud of the red ginger plant gives the salad a particularly delicious flavor.

Rojak – fruit and vegetable salad

Rarities and baby vegetables

Water-spinach

Water-spinach (*Ipomoea aquatica*) is a leaf vegetable native to the tropics which can be encountered in two different varieties. One has a hollow stem and large heart-shaped leaves so that it grows and flourishes in water and spreads over the surface like waterweed. When buying this variety, look for firm stems with green leaves. The second type also needs plenty of water to help it grow, but grows on land rather than in the water. The leaves are darker and thinner. As vegetables, there is hardly anything to choose between the two varieties. Both have a high vitamin C content and a slightly laxative effect. The pretty, bell-shaped white, pink, or red flowers are rarely seen even in the plant's natural environment. Water-spinach is related to the sweet potato and to morning glory.

It is not advisable to store water spinach for any length of time, as the leaves will turn yellow within a few days, and the stems will lose their firmness. As with most other leaf vegetables, water spinach shrinks when cooked and a large bunch of fresh leaves will lose two-thirds of its bulk.

Before cooking, water spinach must be carefully washed and cleaned and the tough tips of the stalks trimmed away. The leaves are separated from the thick stalks, since they do not take the same amount of time to cook. The mild flavor is similar to that of spinach as eaten in the West. Water spinach is blanched and added to salads and soups. It is particularly popular when stir-fried with a strongly-flavored paste of dried chili peppers and dried shrimp.

Kangkong goreng blacan
Stir-fried water spinach with shrimp paste

(600 g) water spinach, leaves removed from thick stalks, stalks sliced into 2¹/₂ in (6 cm) pieces
2 Tbs dried shrimp, soaked and drained
salt to taste
4 Tbs oil

Spice paste
8 dried chili peppers, soaked, seeds discarded
8 shallots, peeled and chopped
2 garlic cloves, peeled and quartered
1 piece *blacan* (shrimp paste), 1 x 1 x ¹/₂ in (2 x 2 x 1 cm)

Mash chili peppers, shallots, garlic cloves, and shrimp paste in a mortar. Heat oil in wok, add spicy paste with salt and fry until the flavors are released. Fry dried shrimp in it for 1 minute. Add vegetable stalks and stir-fry for about. 1 minute, then add leaves. Continue stirring until the vegetable is covered by the spices and is just cooked.

Opposite: The variety of leafy vegetables on offer on even the most modest vegetable pushcart includes both types of water-spinach (front left), asparagus beans (center), lemongrass (front right) and drumsticks, the fruit of the horseradish tree (far left). In the top row, from the left, there are green onions (scallions), banana leaves, and banana blossoms.

Below: A flourishing vegetable patch. A turmeric plant is in the foreground.

Kangkong goreng blacan – fried water spinach with shrimp paste

Stink beans

From the distance they look like giant pea pods, but they are in fact the attractive fruit-bearing stalks of a semi-wild vegetable tree (*Parkia speciosa*), which grow to a height of up to 83 feet (25 m). The twisted pods of the stink beans (*petai* in Malay) grow to 14–20 in (35-50 cm) long and dangle from the treetops. Each pod may contain as many as eighteen beans. To process the vegetable, the pods are broken or cut into pieces, the beans are scraped out and then cooked whole or halved. They can be nibbled raw, dipped into *sambal blacan*. The raw beans apparently have a very positive effect on diabetics. The beans are also sold roasted and salted. Recipes for cooked stink beans often contain shrimp or dried anchovies as well as *sambal*. Consumption of *petai* leaves has a similar impact on the body to that of garlic and asparagus, in that it produces an unpleasant odor. Bad breath can be avoided, however, if raw cucumber is eaten with the beans.

The sight of vegetables growing on trees may be a surprise to people from the West.

Stink beans are rarely cultivated in large patches; they often grow in freely accessible places so you only need to be a good climber if you want to pick them.

Stink beans (*petai*) can be bought at local markets. The pods are tied in large bunches. The beans are either eaten raw, roasted, or stewed with fish.

Beansprouts

Malaysian schoolchildren, like many others, study seed germination and growth by watching beansprouts. In their first science lessons, they soak the seeds in water for two to three hours until the husks split. The beansprouts are then placed on damp absorbent cotton under glass, so that the children can follow the progress of the seedlings. The tiny beans are now transferred to a dark place. Within the next 24 hours, a root appears, a miniature stalk emerges, and the husk falls off. In a few days, the beansprouts will be long enough to use. During this period, the children need do nothing more than make sure that the absorbent cotton does not dry out. What young schoolchildren learned in their first natural history lessons used to be a lifesaver for Asian students studying abroad. In the days when beansprouts were not readily available outside the Asian community, many new arrivals were able to grow this inexpensive and nutritious food on the window-sills in their dorms.

Most commercially available beansprouts are grown from mung beans (*Vigna radiata*), and occasionally from soybeans (*Glycine max*). While the high nutritional value of fresh shoots, emerging from undamaged, untreated seeds has only been appreciated relatively recently in the West, they are an old stand-by in Oriental medicine. For the Chinese, the importance of the fresh shoots has been understood for thousands of years, particularly in those regions with a harsh climate. A handful of sprouts consumed at regular intervals prevents scurvy, a disease caused by vitamin C deficiency.

Beansprouts are not used in Chinese and Malaysian cooking merely for their nutritional value, they are also important for their texture. Their firm crispiness is enhanced by serving them alongside contrasting ingredients. Beansprouts are often used in soups and noodle dishes; Malaysian cooks are always careful never to overcook the tender shoots, they should still be *al dente*.

The top layer of green leaves are trimmed away before the shoots are sent to market.

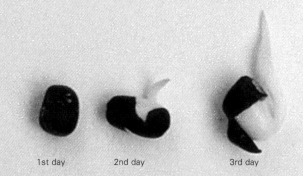

1st day   2nd day   3rd day

5th day   6th day

Black soybeans shortly after germination.

The shoots are watered at regular intervals.

By the fourth day, the young shoots are almost ready for eating.

Top quality beansprouts are clean, short, firm, and unbruised.

Taugeh goreng kucai
Fried Beansprouts with Chives

3½ cups (400 g) beansprouts, washed, dried, roots removed
1 tbsp oil
2 garlic cloves, peeled and chopped
3 bunches chives, cut into 1 in (3 cm) lengths
salt
2 fresh red chili peppers, sliced into rings, seeds discarded

Heat the oil in a wok or skillet and lightly brown the garlic. Add the beansprouts, chives, and salt. Stir-fry over high heat for 1 minute. Mix in the chili peppers and then serve with rice. Green onions (scallions) may be used instead of chives.
As an alternative, fry a little salt fish, shred with two forks, and sprinkle over the vegetables.

Taugeh masak kerang
Fried Beansprouts with Baby Clams

3½ cups (400 g) beansprouts, washed, dried, roots removed
2 cups (500 g) baby clams, washed, cooked, opened and flesh removed from the shells
2 tbsp oil
2 garlic cloves, peeled and chopped
2 fresh red chili peppers, sliced lengthwise in narrow strips, seeds discarded
2 celery ribs, cut into 2 in (5 cm) lengths
salt

Heat the oil in a wok or skillet and brown the garlic and chili pepper strips until the aromas develop. Add the beansprouts and celery and stir-fry over high heat, taking care that the beansprouts do not become mushy. Add the baby clams and salt. and fry for another minute, stirring well. Serve immediately.
If fresh baby clams are not available, use mussels in season.

Tahu goreng
Fried Tofu with Beansprouts
For 2 or 4 people

4 blocks firm tofu
1 cucumber, halved and cubed or thinly sliced
1¼ cups (300 g) beansprouts, washed, dried, roots removed
Sauce
1 fresh red chili pepper, seeds discarded
2 fresh green chili peppers, seeds discarded
1 garlic clove, peeled and quartered
1 x ½ in (1 cm) piece palm sugar, or 1 tsp dark brown sugar
⅓ cup (80 g) finely ground roasted peanuts
2 tsp soy sauce
2 tsp wine vinegar
½ cup (125 ml) boiled and cooled water

Fry the tofu until it is golden brown on all sides. Leave to cool and then cut each block into nine pieces. To make the sauce, crush the chili peppers and garlic in a mortar with a pestle. Add the crushed palm sugar, ground peanuts, soy sauce, vinegar, and water to the paste and mix well.
Arrange the fried tofu with the cucumber and beansprouts on a serving platter, then pour some of the sauce over it. Serve the rest of the sauce separately in a bowl.
This dish can be served as an entrée, in which case the above quantities will suffice for 2 people. If, like the other recipes, it is part of a larger menu, then the quantities given will be sufficient for 4 people.

Taugeh goreng kucai – Fried beansprouts with garlic chives.

Tahu goreng – Fried tofu with beansprouts.

Bihun goreng
Fried Rice Noodles

1 lb 5 oz (600 g) dried rice (cellophane) noodles, weighed without the packaging
1¹/₃ cups (150 g shrimp) peeled
2 cups (500 g) beansprouts, washed, drained, roots trimmed
2 tbsp oil
¹/₂ cup (125 ml) water or broth
salt

Spice Paste

6 dried chili peppers, soaked, chopped, seeds discarded
2 garlic cloves, peeled and sliced

Garnish

1 piece firm tofu (about a scant cup)
2 hard-cooked eggs, quartered
1 bunch chives, chopped into 1 in (2 cm) lengths
2 tbsp fried onion rings
2 limes, halved

Pat the tofu dry and then fry until golden brown. Drain and leave to cool. Cut into equal-sized cubes. Crush the chili peppers and garlic in a mortar with a pestle. Heat the oil in a skillet and then fry the paste, until the aromas develop. Add the water or broth and stir well. Mix in the shrimp and salt. Bring the mixture to the boil, then add the rice noodles, followed by the beansprouts. Simmer for 5 minutes. Divide into portions. Mix the garnish ingredients and sprinkle them over the dish. Immediately before serving, squeeze the limes and pour the juice over the dish.

Urap taugeh
Fried Beansprouts with Grated Coconut

2 cups (450 g) beansprouts, washed, drained and roots trimmed
¹/₃ coconut, grated (about 1¹/₃ cups)
¹/₂ tsp salt
juice of 2 limes

Spice Paste

8 dried chili peppers, soaked, chopped, seeds discarded
6 shallots, peeled and chopped
20 dried shrimp, soaked, drained and patted dry

Crush the dried chili peppers, shallots, and dried shrimp into a paste in a mortar with a pestle. Combine the grated coconut, salt and paste and fry in a heavy skillet over a low heat, stirring constantly. Continue stirring until the aromas develop. Add the beansprouts to the coconut mixture and stir well for 1-2 minutes. Remove the skillet from the heat and drizzle the lime juice over the vegetables. No oil is used in this dish.

Urap taugeh – Fried beansprouts with grated coconut

Eggplant

The skin of the southeast Asian eggplant (Malay: *terong*) is not as tough as its American counterpart. Asian eggplant may be round, pear-shaped or elongated. Most are a dark to pale violet in color, but some are a pale green. White eggplant are unusual.
Malaysian cuisine uses eggplant mainly in curry dishes, with a tamarind sauce or with a sambal. The Chinese use the elongated green and violet eggplant in stir-fried dishes or stews. One popular way of serving eggplant is to cut the vegetable diagonally into thick slices. Each slice is split inside to make a pocket. This can be filled with ground fish or ground pork.
When choosing eggplant, look for firm flesh and a shiny skin. After halving the vegetable lengthwise or slicing it, soak it in salted water. This helps to prevent discoloration and also helps to draw out some of the bitterness. Before cooking, rinse, drain, and pat dry.

Kari ikan dengan terong
Fish curry with eggplant

1 lb 5 oz (600 g) fish (bonito or king mackerel), sliced into strips or steaks
3 Asian eggplant, sliced lengthwise, each half sliced into three pieces
4 tbsp oil
10 shallots, peeled and sliced into rings
2 garlic cloves, peeled and sliced
2 thin slices ginger root
2 tbsp curry powder for fish curry, mixed to a paste with a few drops of water
1 sprig curry leaves
1/2 coconut, grated (about 1 1/2 cups (200 g))
2 cups (500 ml) water, mixed with the coconut, milk squeezed out
Juice of 2 tbsp tamarind paste mixed with 1 cup (125 ml) water
salt

Heat the oil in a skillet and fry the shallots, garlic, and ginger, until they are soft. Add the curry paste and leaves, stir well and fry for one minute.
Pour in the coconut milk, tamarind juice and salt and bring to the boil. Add the eggplant slices, reduce the temperature, and leave to simmer for five minutes. Finally, add the fish and leave to cook gently until the eggplant is soft. Serve hot.

Terong asam
Eggplant with tamarind juice

14 oz (400 g) eggplant
4 tbsp oil
1 slice galangal, lightly crushed
1 onion, peeled and quartered
2 tbsp (30 g) dried shrimp, soaked and chopped
1/2 coconut, grated (about 1 cup/200 g)
1 cup (250 ml) water, mixed with the coconut, milk squeezed out
1 tsp sugar
salt
juice of 2 tbsp tamarind paste mixed with 1 cup/ 1/4 l water
7 oz (200 g) shrimp, heads removed, peeled

Spice Paste
12 dried chili peppers, soaked, seeds discarded
1 garlic clove, peeled and quartered
1 piece shrimp paste (blacan), 1 x 1 x 1/2 in (2 x 2 x 1 cm)
2 candlenuts

Halve the eggplant lengthwise and then cut each half into 3–4 pieces. Soak in salted water. Meanwhile, crush the chili peppers, garlic, shrimp paste, and candlenuts in a mortar with a pestle. Rinse the eggplant and leave to dry. Heat the oil in a skillet and fry the paste, galingale, and onions, until the aromas develop. Add the shrimp and fry. Stir in the eggplant, coconut milk, sugar, and salt. Braise over medium heat, stirring occasionally. When the eggplant is cooked, add the tamarind juice and fresh shrimp. As soon as the shrimp is cooked through, remove from the heat, and serve.

Sambal terong
Eggplant sambal for fish, poultry, or meat

7 oz (200 g) eggplant
1/2 tsp turmeric
3–4 tbsp oil
4 fresh green chili peppers, minced, seeds discarded
1 onion, peeled and minced
1 1/2 tsp sugar
salt
4 tbsp lime juice

Wash the eggplant and slice it, though not too thinly. Rub with the turmeric. Heat the oil and brown the eggplant slices. Combine the chili peppers, onions, sugar, salt, and lime juice in a bowl, then add the fried eggplant slices.

Terong belado
Eggplant in a spicy sauce

1 lb (500 g) Asian eggplant, sliced lengthwise
4 fresh red chili peppers, seeds discarded
4 fresh green chili peppers, seeds discarded
1 onion, peeled and chopped
2 tbsp oil
salt
juice of 4 limes

Fry the eggplant until half-cooked. Leave to drain and reserve. Crush the chili peppers and onions in a mortar with a pestle. Heat the oil in a skillet and fry the chili paste and salt, until the aromas develop. Stir in the lime juice, add the eggplant, and mix well.

Terong asam – eggplant with tamarind juice

Sambal terong – eggplant sambal for fish, poultry, or meat

Bitter gourd

Peria, the Malay name for bitter gourd or bitter melon *(Momordica charantia)* is a popular vegetable in southeast Asia. In Malaysia, it is fried with chili peppers and spices, braised with coconut sauce, or eaten raw in salads. Wafer-thin slices of *peria* are eaten with a dressing of fried grated coconut and grated dried shrimp.

The deeply furrowed fruit of this climbing plant derives its name, not surprisingly, from its bitter flesh. This bitterness needs to be drawn out before it is eaten. When buying, choose firm fruit, as this tends to be less ripe and less bitter. Before cooking, peel the skin, halve the fruit, and remove the seeds and white parts. Slice or dice the flesh, sprinkle with salt, and set aside for about 20 minutes. Rinse off the salt and squeeze out the flesh. This will reduce the bitterness.

Peria goreng udang
Bitter Gourd with Shrimp

1 large bitter gourd, about 14 oz (400 g)
1¼ cups (300 g) shrimp, heads removed, peeled
3 tbsp oil
salt
1 cup (100 g) grated coconut
1 cup (250 ml) water, mixed with the coconut, milk squeezed out

Spice Paste
8 dried chili peppers, soaked, seeds discarded
1 onion, peeled and chopped
1 garlic clove, peeled and quartered

Peel the bitter gourd, halve it, and remove the seeds and white parts. Cut the flesh into thin slices. Sprinkle both sides with salt and then set aside for 20 minutes. In the meantime, crush the chili peppers, onion, and garlic into a smooth paste in a mortar with a pestle. Rinse the salt off the bitter gourd slices and squeeze the flesh.

Heat the oil in a skillet, add the grated ingredients and salt, and fry until the aromas begin to develop. Now add the shrimp and stir-fry briefly. Add the coconut milk. Bring the mixture to the boil. When the sauce thickens, add the bitter gourd slices, stir well and simmer over medium heat until the liquid has almost evaporated.

Hinava
Marinated Raw Fish with Bitter Gourd

7 oz (200 g) bonito or king mackerel
Juice of 5–6 limes (more may be needed)
1 small bitter gourd, peeled, halved, seeds and white parts discarded
7 shallots, peeled and sliced into thin rings
1 piece ginger root (¼ in (1.5 cm) thick), shredded
2 fresh red chili peppers, halved, seeds discarded, sliced into thin strips
salt
1 *bambangan* pit, grated

Fillet the fish and cut into thin slices. Fill a bowl with lime juice, add the fish, and leave to marinate until the flesh is slightly translucent (there should be enough juice to barely cover the fish.)

Cut the bitter gourd into wafer-thin slices. Squeeze the fish to remove any excess lime juice. Mix the bitter gourd, shallot rings, ginger, and chili pepper strips with the fish. Season with salt and sprinkle over the grated *bambagan* pit. Knead the mixture by hand, until the fish looks as if it has been ground. Serve with rice.

The *Bambagan* fruit is a member of the mango family, and is native to Borneo. The grated pit is used as a raising agent as well as a preservative for easily perishable foods.

1 Fillet the fresh fish and skin it.
2 Squeeze a generous quantity of lime juice into a bowl
3 Halve fresh red chili peppers lengthwise and remove the hot seeds

4 Peel the bitter gourd, remove the seeds and white parts, then slice the flesh thinly
5 Squeeze the marinated fish to remove excess lime juice
6 Finely chop or grate the rest of the ingredients and mix them with the dried fish

Hinava, a speciality of the Kadazan in Sabah, eastern Malaysia, is served country-style on a green leaf

Ingredients for *hinava:* fresh fish, bitter gourd, limes, shallots, and chili peppers (the other spices are not shown).

Tuberous Roots

Manioc

Manioc (*Manihot esculenta;* Malay: *ubi kayu*) originated in Brazil, reaching Indonesia via Africa as a by-product of the Portuguese slave-trade in the late 18th century.

In order that the roots of this shrub with its woody stems can develop maximum starch content, the plant needs certain temperature, light, and rainfall levels — and these are only achieved in tropical climates. There are bitter and sweet varieties of manioc; neither should be eaten raw, as the tuber contains prussic acid which is poisonous. The acid evaporates when the root is cooked. When manioc is farmed, the tubers are ready for harvesting in about six months. Manioc leaves are also edible and are used in curries. The young shoots are stewed and served with *sambal blachan.* Young manioc tubers are boiled or steamed and eaten with sugar or grated coconut. Grated manioc root is used in cakes and puddings. It can also be cut into chips and fried.

Fresh manioc does not keep well, but, as it is a valuable source of starch and a staple, ways have been found to preserve it. The peeled tubers are cooked into a mush, which is dried and then ground or soaked in water, so that the starch is washed. This substance, known as tapioca, has many culinary uses.

The tuberous manioc root plays an important part in the diet; the leaves are steamed and eaten as a vegetable.

The older tubers are tough and are only of value for their starch content. They are usually made into tapioca.

Yam (Yucca)

In southeast Asia, the water yam or Asian yam (*Dioscorea alata*; Malay: *ubi keladi*) is probably the most important of the 250 different types of yam (yucca). This climbing plant is grown up stakes, as it is only by exposure to light that the tuber will develop fully. Unlike the production of manioc and sweet potatoes, the cultivation of yams is labor-intensive and consequently expensive. For this reason, these yams are not easy to find outside southeast Asia. The underground roots need a dry period to settle in. After about 10 months, the above-ground growth dies back and the tubers can be dug up (a back-breaking task). The number of tubers and their size depends on the variety. Some produce slender, horizontal, underground side roots, which can be peeled and used as a vegetable. Yam roots are cooked or steamed in sweet, substantial dishes. For the popular regional dessert, *bubur cha cha*, yams are diced and boiled in coconut milk with sweet potatoes. There is no danger in eating the cultivated yam, but there are wild varieties which contain the poisonous alkaloid dioscorin, although the toxicity evaporates when the yam is cooked. Other yam varieties contain a steroid, which is a source of cortisone, hydrocortisone, and progesterone though they are mainly the wild, central American varieties that have a high proportion of this steroid.

The yam (yucca) is a starchy root vegetable like the potato. When cooked, it has a similar floury texture.

The underground side-shoots of the yam plant are also edible. They are peeled and cooked like vegetables.

Sweet potatoes

Although natives of South America, sweet potatoes have found their way into all the tropical and sub-tropical zones of the earth, areas they would otherwise never have reached. Today, China is responsible for about eighty percent of world production. Roots form at the nodes on the creeping shoots and then disappear down into the soil, where the sweet tubers take about four months to develop. Sweet potatoes (*Ipomoea batatas*; Mal.: *ubi keledek*) are boiled or steamed and then mashed. They may also be made into cakes, cut into slices, dipped in batter and fried. The harvest begins as soon as the leaves of the year-old plant begin to die back. The young leaves and shoots are also eaten as vegetables. The sweet potato is not related to the potato.

Sweet potato tubers are ready only four months after planting.

Sauces and dips

Malaysian sauces and dips are invariably hot, as chili is always one of the main ingredients — nor is it used sparingly! Varying quantities of the following are usually included: *blacan*, the savory paste made from shrimp , black shrimp paste, shallots, ginger, galangal root, and garlic. Vinegar, tamarind juice, lime juice, dark soya sauce and/or water may be used to dilute the sauce. The sweetener which is essential to the sauce is made from sugar cane or palm sugar (*gula melaka*). Ground, roasted peanuts are important for consistency, as they give the sauce body and nutritional value. The sauces described here all have keeping qualities. As long as they are kept in a sealed glass jar, such as a Mason jar, in the refrigerator, they will last for a week. These sauce are served in tiny saucers and food is dipped into them as it is eaten. This is the origin of tomato ketchup, so popular in the West.

Sambal cuka
Vinegar and chili dip

10 fresh red chili peppers
1 piece ginger root, $1/2$ in (1 cm) thick
2 garlic cloves, peeled and quartered
2 Tbs vinegar
1 Tbs sugar
1 tsp salt

Crush the chilies in a mortar with a pestle to make a smooth paste. Add the ginger and garlic and grind well. Stir vinegar, salt, and sugar into the paste. This dip goes well with seafood or boiled and steamed poultry.

Sambal asam
Tamarind and chili dip

10 dried chili peppers, soaked, seeds discarded
1 piece shrimp paste (*blacan*), 1 x 1 x $1/2$ in (2 x 2 x 1 cm), dry-roasted in a skillet
Juice of 1 tsp tamarind pulp, diluted in $1/2$ cup (125 ml) water
2 tsp sugar
$1/4$ tsp salt

Crush the chilies in a mortar with a pestle and then add the shrimp paste. Grind the chilies into the paste. Combine the water and tamarind pulp, strain through a sieve, and collect the liquid. In a bowl, combine the chili and shrimp paste with the tamarind juice. Stir in salt and sugar. This dip makes a good accompaniment for fried fish and boiled vegetables.

Sambal chili kecap
Chili dip with black sauce

8 fresh red chili peppers, seeds discarded
1 piece shrimp paste (*blacan*), $1/2$ in x $1/2$ in x $1/2$ in (1 x 1 x 1 cm), toasted in a dry skillet
4 shallots, peeled and chopped
2 garlic cloves, peeled and quartered
5 Tbs dark soy sauce
1 Tbs dark brown sugar
Juice of 4 limes

Crush the chilies in a mortar with a pestle. Add the fried shrimp paste, then the shallots and garlic. Mix everything together well, rubbing evenly. In a bowl, blend the soy sauce, sugar, and lime juice into a smooth paste. Serve this dip with broiled or fried fish.

Sambal chili kecap – Chili dip with black sauce

Sambal cuka – Vinegar and chili dip

Sambal asam – Tamarind and chili dip

Sambal jengganan
Spicy peanut sauce

15 dried chili peppers, soaked, well drained, and seeds discarded
2 Tbs oil
2 garlic cloves, peeled
1 Tbs tamarind pulp
1 piece shrimp paste (blacan), $1/2 \times 1/2 \times 1/2$ in (1 x 1 x 1 cm)
2 cups (500 ml) boiled water, cooled
3 Tbs dark brown sugar
$1/4$ tsp salt
1 cup (200 g) roasted peanuts, coarsely chopped

Heat the oil and fry the chili peppers for about 30 seconds. Remove and set aside. Heat the oil again and fry the garlic cloves whole until light brown. Set aside. Fry the tamarind pulp for 1 minute and set aside. Cook the shrimp paste in a little oil until the aromas develop and then set aside. Place the fried tamarind pulp in the boiled water. Press it through a sieve and catch the liquid in a bowl. Crush the chili peppers, shrimp paste, and garlic in a mortar with a pestle. Mix together the paste, tamarind juice, sugar, and salt in a bowl and then add to the ground peanuts. Stir well. The sauce should be thick and syrupy.

Sambal satay
Peanut sauce for satays

20 dried chili peppers, soaked, well drained, and seeds discarded
1 stem lemongrass, lower part sliced into pieces
3 thin slices galangal
2 garlic cloves, peeled and quartered
1 Tbs coriander seeds, dry-roasted in a skillet
1 tsp caraway seed, dry-roasted in a skillet
Juice from 3 tsp tamarind pulp dissolved in 2 cups (500 ml) water
4 Tbs oil
1 cup (200 g) roasted peanuts, coarsely chopped
3 Tbs brown sugar
$1/2$ tsp salt

Crush the chili peppers in a mortar with a pestle, adding the lemongrass, galangal, garlic, coriander, and caraway seeds. Continue until the mixture has an even consistency. Stir the tamarind pulp into the water, strain through a sieve, and catch the liquid. Heat the oil in a skillet and fry the crushed ingredients, until the aromas develop and the oil separates. Add the ground peanuts, tamarind juice, sugar, and salt. Mix together well and bring to the boil, stirring occasionally. Reduce the temperature and simmer, until the sauce is syrupy and the oil rises to the surface. This sauce is suitable as a dip with barbecued chicken, beef or lamb (satay).

Sambal jengganan – Spicy peanut sauce

Sambal satay – Peanut sauce for *satay*

Satay

Satay consists of small wooden skewers threaded with chunks of meat. These kabobs are popular in Singapore, Malaysia, and Indonesia, where they are often served as snacks. The recipes for the marinade and the peanut sauce vary from region to region. Satay is an example of how Malaysian cuisine was greatly influenced by the Arabs who went there to trade from the Middle East. In Malaysia and Singapore, traveling peddlars used to roam the streets selling satay. These fast-food salesmen later set up permanent stalls by the roadside. Most are easy to find, you just make for the source of the appetizing aromas wafting through the air as the meat cooks over charcoal. Order the first portion and, while you are eating that, the trader will carry on cooking so that he can keep you supplied until you have had enough. He will calculate the bill by adding up the used skewers. While you are eating, it is always entertaining to watch him, as he prepares the satay with dexterous, rapid movements and at the same time fans the flames, which suddenly shoot up as tiny drops of oil catch fire. A satay seller's working day starts long before the traders open up their stands and light their charcoal burners. They must slice up the beef, lamb, and tripe (menudo) into tiny pieces, remove and chop up the flesh from chickens and then marinate it all for several hours in a special spice mixture, usually made according to a closely-guarded, secret recipe. The central ribs of coconut palm leaves are often used as skewers. The final preparatory stage involves threading the marinated meat on to the skewers, brushing them with an oil-and- sugar mixture and then grilling them on the charcoal grill. Basting continues while they are cooking. This prevents the meat from drying out and gives the meat a glazed look. Satay is often served with ketupat (pressed rice), cucumber, raw onions, and a little bowl of peanut sauce. Shrimp satay is now becoming fashionable and the Chinese make satay with pork, an idea that they have borrowed from Malays who are not moslems.

Ingredients for a satay:
1 Sugar
2 Salt
3 Fresh tumeric
4 Minced ginger
5 Root ginger
6 Garlic
7 Peanuts
8 Peeled garlic
9 Peeled tumeric
10 Beef satay
11 Lemongrass
12 Onion
13 Fresh chili peppers

Marinated and grilled meat kabobs, shown here made from beef and chicken, make perfect snacks.

Mackerel packages?

Otak-otak

If you are not tempted by the *satay* stand, walk around the corner and the inviting aroma emanating from an *otak-otak* cart may prove more interesting. The broiled fish packages on sale here are much appreciated by the Malays and many others, just as much as meat kabobs. Fillets of Spanish mackerel or finger fish are minced and ground and then blended into a smooth paste with grated spices, including lemongrass, galangal, fresh chili peppers, turmeric, shallots, minced kaffir lime leaves, and curry powder for fish curries. Toasted coconut flakes and thick coconut cream (which rises to the surface of rich coconut milk) lend a special flavor and give the fish paste the necessary elasticity and smoothness. Some of the paste is then spread on to narrow strips of coconut leaf, a second leaf strip is added as a wrapping, and toothpicks are inserted at each end to hold the little package together. The fish packages must now be baked in the oven or grilled over charcoal until the leaves are lightly charred. This fish paste is not just used for *otak-otak*, it is also served with rice or, supplemented with cucumber slices, as a delicately-flavored sandwich filling, though of course, bread sandwiches are a relatively modern introduction in Malaysia. For *otak-otak*, the narrow strips of coconut palm that are used for the wrapping are cut from the middle section of the leaf. They are very stiff and need to be soaked for a while before use. In Singapore, ready-cut leaf strips are imported from Malaysia. *Otak-otak* is also available as a steamed dish. For this version, the fish are cut into thin slices, which are then coated with the spice mixture and wrapped in banana leaves, instead of coconut leaves.

Ask a Malay what coconut leaves are used for and the most likely response will be as the wrapper for *otak-otak*, as these little fish packages are a popular snack.

A little raw fish paste is spread on to a piece of palm leaf.

Cocktail sticks are used for securing the little package.

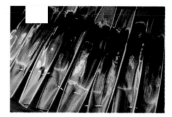

Otak-otak production is teamwork, one group fills, the other packs.

The little packages made from two strips of leaf are ready for the grill.

The charcoal and charred palm leaves give the *otak-otak* a distinctive aroma.

When the packages are ready, they must be chargrilled at high temperature.

Blacan

As the tide comes in, the tiny shrimp are washed straight into the net.

The paste is first kneaded by hand and then shaped in a mold.

In the seas off the Strait of Malacca and the island of Penang fishermen are often seen wading in deep water in search of *geragau*, tiny shrimp , which appear at certain times of the year and are then caught at high tide. The fishermen use a special triangular, fine-meshed net spread over two crossed stakes. When the nets are full they are brought ashore, and the larger shrimp, little fish, and other items are thrown back. The shrimp that remain are rinsed in sea water and left on the beach to dry. They are then mixed with salt and left to dry in the sun for a further five to eight hours, before they are crushed to a paste in a wooden trough. Special machines in modern production plants now do this job. The paste is then left to dry in the troughs for one or two weeks and crushed again from time to time. This process is repeated several times, as the interim drying process helps to prevent spoiling. When the paste is ready, it is pressed into round or rectangular shapes, but left in the sun once more before being packed. Each separate shape used to be wrapped in tiny mats of woven coconut leaves, but now paper is usually used. The natural color of *blacan* is dark brown, but the paste is often sold dyed a deep pink or dark violet. Given the high salt content, the finished product has a long shelf-life. When left in the sun to dry out, the *blacan* will last even longer. *Blacan* is mainly used as a flavoring. Sometimes a little is ground with chili peppers, shallots, and other ingredients to make the basic flavoring for many Malaysian dishes. This same shrimp paste is popular elsewhere in southeast Asia. *Blacan* is called *trassi* in Indonesian and *kapi* in Thai.

Below: An important factor in the production of *blacan* is the repeated sun-drying. This process helps to increase the shelf-life of this otherwise rather perishable fish product.

The blacan cakes drying for the last time before packing.

Sambal blacan is sometimes described as the caviar of southeast Asia.

Above: Filling bottles with the prepared *cinkaluk* is a fairly stress-free task.

Blacan is the basis for a garnish called *sambal blacan* without which no Malaysian meal is complete. A small quantity of this sauce is stirred into steaming rice. It is prepared with a mortar and pestle. Wiping out the remainder with hot rice is as much fun as scraping the bottom of the cake mixing bowl!

Sambal blacan

1 piece *blacan*, ³/₄ x 1 x ¹/₂ in (2 x 2.5 x 1 cm)
8 fresh red chili peppers, each sliced into 3–4 pieces
salt
2 small limes, halved

Fry the *blacan* in a skillet until the aroma develops. Crush a few chili peppers with some salt in a mortar with a pestle. Gradually add the rest of the chili peppers and grind evenly. Finally, add the *blacan* and mix well with the chili peppers. The completed mixture should be neither too smooth nor too coarse. Serve with the lime halves. Squeeze the juice over the *sambal* just prior to eating.

Cinkaluk

The basis of *cinkaluk* is the same tiny species of shrimp that is used to make *blacan*. Like *blacan*, the production of *cinkaluk* remains a cottage industry near the fishing villages, although there is a tendency now for the work to be carried out in small production units. The main problem for factory owners, however, is the availability of the shrimp. Along the coast, many housewives make *cinkaluk* for their own use. Shrimp, salt, and cooked rice are all that is needed. The hand-picked shrimp are washed in seawater and then left to drain. When they are dry, plenty of salt and about 6 percent cooked rice is added. Large jugs are filled with the mixture. These are then covered and left for three to four weeks. A fermentation process takes place during this period. When the liquid is ready, it takes on a pinkish tinge. The rice and salt will have dissolved and the liquid will be much thinner. *Cinkaluk* is served as an appetizer with raw shallots, chili peppers, and a few squeezes of lime juice or eaten with rice, fish, and vegetable shoots. It is very, very salty, the taste is — to put it mildly — difficult to get used to. Like *blacan*, it has a rather pungent smell.

Before any further processing, it is carefully sorted by hand. The larger seafood and other items are put to one side.

The fermented *cinkaluk* is sold or stored at home in bottles).

Once the shrimp have reached a weight of 1 – 1½ oz (25-35 g), the fish farmers consider them ready for harvesting. The best are just over 12 in (30 cm) long.

Freshly caught tiger shrimp, easily recognized by their bright stripes, are popular all over the world.

Shrimp tails are classified according to size and weight: from U7 (less than 7 per pound (454 g)) to 91-110 (91-110 to the pound).

Breeding shrimp

Tiger shrimp (*Penaeus monodon*) are the the largest whip-tail shrimp . They are an an important form of seafood in southeast Asia, as they are prized both at home and abroad for their firm, aromatic flesh. Shrimp farming takes place throughout the year in Malaysia. It is a lucrative business with few risks as shrimp grow quickly, feeding off vegetable and animal matter. Bred in special pools, a generation of shrimp takes no more than three or four months to reach maturity. By then they will have attained an average weight of between 1 – 1½ oz (25 – 35 g) and are ready for market. They are caught in nets when the water is drained from the pond. If fish farmers wish to remove only a part of the stock, in order to select some of the larger examples and to leave the smaller ones to grow on, then special nets with easy-to-lift surrounds are used. Every time the water is drained completely, the workers take the opportunity to completely clean out the pond. Both freshwater and saltwater shrimp are bred in southeast Asia. The freshest shrimp are always steamed and served with a chili pepper and vinegar dip. Chinese recipes often add a little wine, green onions (scallions), and ginger during the steaming process. In Malaysia, both large and small shrimp are cooked in a hot sambal or tamarind sauce. Both are eaten with or without their shells and heads. As in China, Malaysian cuisine combines the smaller types of shrimp with noodles and vegetables, whereas the larger ones are usually grilled or broiled. In south-east Asia, shrimp are sold raw, either chilled or on a bed of crushed ice. When buying shrimp, whether raw or cooked, select specimens that are firm when pressed and have undamaged heads.

From time to time, all the water in the breeding ponds is drained, the whole population collected, and then the fish farm is given a thorough clean.

Crabs

In the West, crabs are often boiled. For some types of crab, the crabmeat is removed from the shell and claws, and sold in an almost unrecognizable form (mainly because it takes too long for live crabs to reach the fishmonger). In southeast Asia, crabs are usually sold live with the claws bound together or else they are boiled and the various parts sold separately. When buying live crabs, look for active specimens with undamaged legs and claws. The large meaty crabs from Sri Lanka are the most popular. Crab is usually eaten with the fingers. In restaurants that specialize in seafood, nutcracker-type implements are usually on hand to split open the claws, although the carapace is usually cracked before cooking. A simple, but effective, method of preparing fresh crabs is to steam them. To create a splendid meal, little more than a chili pepper and vinegar dip is required. Crabs can be broiled over charcoal, they can be cooked in a chili or similarly spicy sauce, or braised in a curry sauce. The flavor is greatly enhanced when crab is cooked with salted black beans.

Musk crab or coral crab

There is an unmistakable cross-shaped marking on the back of this crab's shell which is why it is called the "cross crab" in some languages. According to legend, a Jesuit priest by the name of Father Francis Xavier came to the Orient in the 16th century to spread the Gospel. He travelled to Goa in India, the Strait of Malacca in Malaysia and the Moluccan Islands in Indonesia. One day, Father Francis found himself in a sailing boat with two Portuguese aristocrats on the way from Ambon, when a storm blew up. It became so violent that the priest's companions gave up all hope of survival, but the priest stayed calm; he held the crucifix firmly in his hand and immersed it in the sea. The storm abated immediately, but the cross slipped out of his fingers and disappeared underwater. Some 24 hours later, the travelers landed on the island of Baramurah. When Francis and one of the men were walking along the beach, a crab emerged from the sea, holding the cross upright in one of its claws. It made its way over to Francis, who went down on his knee and took the cross, whereupon the crab returned to the sea. The overjoyed priest kissed the crucifix and prayed for a whole hour. This species of crab is found in large numbers in the Straits of Malacca and is often described as the Father Francis crab. Some people regard it as sacred and refuse to eat it. These crabs are at their most plentiful in June, around St Peter's Day. Fishermen take them home, and preserve them and keep them, or give them as gifts. That is when children hear the story of the crab and Father Peter for the first time.

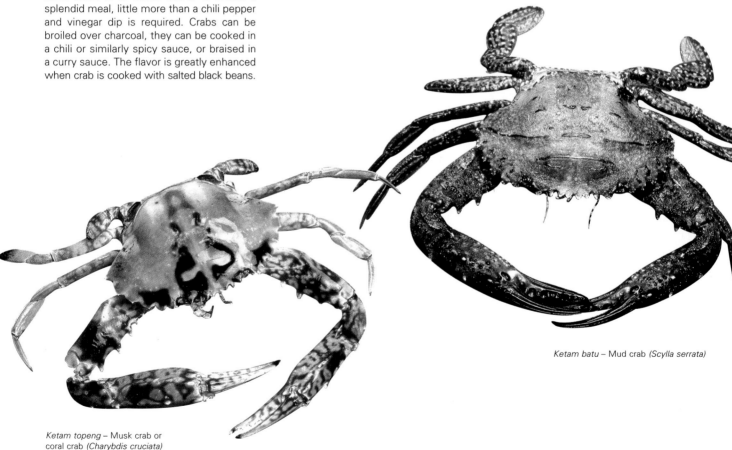

Ketam batu – Mud crab *(Scylla serrata)*

Ketam topeng – Musk crab or coral crab *(Charybdis cruciata)*

Mud crab

In culinary and commercial terms, this is the most important type of crab in southeast Asia, as it has a large proportion of flesh. The carapace of the male can reach a width of nearly 9 in (22 cm). They are quite fierce creatures and do not give up the fight for survival easily. At market stalls they are usually seen with their claws bound together.

Blue swimmer crab

This crab is found throughout the Indo-Pacific region, particularly on the sandy mud flats at river mouths. The males are bluish-gray with white spots, while the female is brown with white spots. This species sheds its outer shell and when it is soft-shelled, it can be eaten whole... and tastes delicious!

Ketam renjong – Blue swimmer crab
(*Portunus pelagicus*)

Ketam masak nanas
Crab curry

2 live crabs, weighing about 3¼ lb (1½ kg)
½ medium pineapple, not too ripe
2 Tbs ground coriander (cilantro)
1 Tbs chili powder
1 tsp turmeric
1 stem lemongrass, lightly crushed
⅔ coconut grated (about 1½ cups (350 g))
2⅓ cups (⅔ l) water, mixed with coconut and squeezed to extract the milk
5 Tbs oil
salt

Spice paste
10 shallots, peeled and chopped
4 garlic cloves, peeled and quartered
1 piece ginger root, 1 cm (½ in) dick
3½ oz (100 g) grated coconut, toasted in dry skillet

Clean the freshly killed crabs in running water and brush thoroughly. Cut off the claws and crack the shell. Crush the shallots, garlic cloves, root ginger, and toasted grated coconut to a paste in a mortar and pestle. Halve the pineapple lengthwise and then cut it into eight equal pieces. Heat the oil in a skillet and fry the spicy paste with the coriander, chili powder, turmeric, and lemongrass, until the aromas develop. Add the pieces of crab and mix them together with the spices. Pour in the coconut milk and bring to the boil. Stir in the pineapple chunks and leave the curry to simmer over a low heat until the pieces of crab are cooked.

Crabs are killed by placing them in boiling water head first, then holding them under water for at least 2 minutes, though not long enough to start cooking them, as the recipe calls for fresh crab. In many parts of the U.S., it is not possible to buy live crabs except in farmers' markets. It is against the law to dissect the crab while it is still alive. However, this recipe could also be made with cooked crab.

175

Shellfish

For many years now clams and mussels have been farmed in the coastal waters off Malaysia, usually at a depth of about (1.80m). Clams need about a year to mature. When they are ready, the fishermen sail out in their boats to the beds and, using long poles, drag baskets over the sand. When they reach the surface, the shellfish are shaken to remove the excess sand. Clams, mussels, and Manila clams are sold live in street markets, or at least that is the claim. A fresh bivalve will be slightly open, but the gap will close as soon as it is tapped on a table. If it does not close, then it is not fresh and must be discarded. The same applies to bivalves which do not open during cooking.

Below: *Kerang* – for some recipes the clams are shelled, for others they are cooked on the shell.

Sambal kepah
Spicy Manila clams

2½ cups (600 g) fresh Manila clams on the shell
salt
(½ cup) 125 ml water
1 Tbs oil
1 stem lemongrass, lightly crushed

Spice paste

3 fresh red chili peppers, seeds discarded
4 shallots, peeled and chopped
1 garlic clove, peeled and quartered

Wash the shells. Crush the chilies, shallots, and garlic in a mortar with a pestle. Heat the oil and fry the spice paste and salt until the aromas develop. Add the lemongrass and fry briefly. Pour in the water and add the clams. Stir well and cook over a medium heat, until the shells open.

Kerang masak papaya
Clams with papaya

2½ cups (600 g) small clams, shelled and washed
2 tsp dried anchovies, finely ground
4 shallots, peeled and finely chopped
½ tsp ground black pepper
1 unripe papaya (about.14 oz (400 g)), peeled and diced
3 cups (750 ml) water
1 stem lemongrass, lightly crushed
salt

Place all the ingredients in a saucepan and bring to the boil. Leave to simmer for 5 minutes.

The fishermen return from the shellfish beds with their catch.

If the journey has been worthwhile, then the boats will be full to the brim with clams and mussels.

Oblong baskets on the end of long poles are used to sweep the sea bed.

The fishing trip does not always live up to expectations. Often the journey is in vain.

A look inside a live mussel (*kupang*)

Siput: Razor clams are narrow and have growth rings like trees.

Gonggong: Whelks of the Strombus genus are not as tasty as clams. Whelks are hard to find in the U.S.

Kerang (left) and *kepah* (right), are two types of clam best served with a simple chili-and-vinegar dip.

Kupang masak asam
Sweet-and-sour mussels
Serves 2 or 4 people

2 (1 kg) mussels, washed and beards scraped, sorted
2 pieces tamarind, scraped
2 sprigs basil
1 piece lemongrass, lightly crushed
1 Tbs sugar
2 tsp salt
4 cups (1 l) water

Spice paste
4 fresh red chili peppers, seeds discarded
4 shallots, peeled and chopped
1 garlic clove, peeled and quartered

Crush the chili peppers, shallots, and garlic cloves to a paste in a mortar with a pestle. Place all the ingredients in a saucepan and bring to the boil, reduce the heat, and then leave the mussels to simmer. When the mussels have all opened, remove the saucepan from the heat. Discard any mussels which have not opened. Serve the mussels immediately in individual portions with some of the broth. This recipe can be cooked as an entrée like *sambal kepah* (see page 176) or as one course of a meal.

Above: *Kupang* — green-lipped mussels are cooked in their shells in soups, steamed, or braised in a *sambal* or bean sauce.

Gonggong masak ubi kledek
Littleneck clams in coconut sauce

2¼ lb (1 kg) littleneck clams, washed and cleaned, tips of necks trimmed
14 oz (400 g) sweet potato, cut into large cubes
10–15 dried shrimp, soaked and drained
4 Tbs dried beans, soaked overnight
1 coconut, grated (about 1¼ lb (500 g))
5 cups (1250 ml) water, mixed with the grated coconut, squeezed , milk retained
salt

Spice paste
1 fresh red chili pepper, seeds discarded
1 onion, peeled and chopped
5 garlic cloves, peeled and quartered
1 piece shrimp paste (*blacan*), 1 x 1 x ½ in (2 x 2 x 1 cm)
1 piece fresh turmeric root, ½ in (1 cm) thick, or substitute ½ tsp ground turmeric

Crush the chili pepper, onion, garlic clove, shrimp paste and turmeric to a smooth paste in a mortar and pestle. Drain the soaked beans. In a saucepan mix together the spicy paste with the coconut milk, sweet potatoes, beans, and the salt and leave to simmer over a moderate heat, until the beans only need a further 10 minutes. Add the clams and leave to simmer for the final 10 minutes.

The whelk is a shell shaped like a twisted horn. The meat is dark and rubbery. Since whelks are not sold commercially in the United States, littleneck clams have been substituted. Other clams could be used.

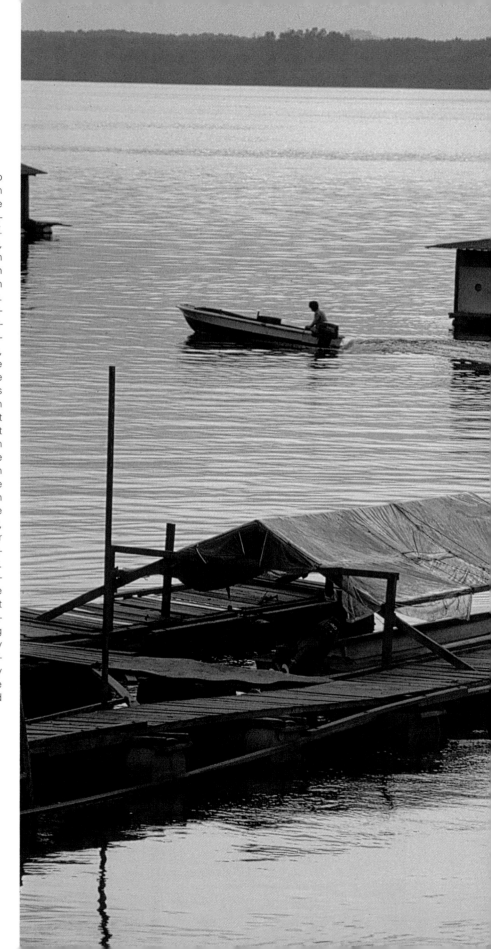

Kelong and pen

Kelong are large, ingenious traps used to catch sea fish. They are usually to be seen off the east and west coasts of the Malaysian peninsula and off the coast of Indonesia, where they are known as *batawei*. A *kelong* consists of at least three parts, which are connected to one another with narrow openings. The best place to position them is at the water's edge, so that the fish are washed into them on the incoming tide. The posts which mark out the traps are usually made of bamboo or *nibong* (*Oncosperma tigillaria*), materials that are resistant to salt water. To complete the traps, nets are rigged up between the posts. The rows of posts lead like fences directly to the trap entrance. The current drives the fishes forward, but in their attempts to swim around the "fence," they follow a route that leads them straight into the trap. In the last section of the trap, a net is spread out on the ground. The fishermen, who spend the night sitting in the comfort of the cabin above the *kelong*, pull the net in from time to time. The next morning, the catch from the *kelong* is brought ashore by boat. Some saltwater fish, such as sea bass, snapper, and grouper, are farmed in floating cages or pens. A platform must first be built of a saltwater-resistant wood, usually *nibong*. Strong wire-netting cages are then suspended from this platform, which must be anchored firmly to the sea bed. The best place for these pens is in a quiet bay or a lagoon, in which the current is not too strong and the difference between high and low tides is quite small, but nevertheless perceptible. The tides provide the necessary change of waters and also oxygenate the cages. It is important for fish excreta and food scraps to be washed away.

Pen, floating fish farms are usually found in quiet bays washed by tides which are perceptible but not too strong.

In the fishing villages of western Malaysia, most of the activity takes place in the morning and early evening, when the boats are leaving and returning.

Cabins on stilts, rising above the water, are overnight shelters for the fishermen who keep an eye on their *kelong*, which looks like a huge creel.

Tenggiri batang: bonito or Spanish mackerel (*Scombridae*; Indon.: *tenggiri*) grows to some 32–40 in (80–100 cm) in length. This firm, tasty fish is sliced into steaks and fried or braised in a tamarind or coconut sauce.

Pari nyiru (Mal., Indon.): sting ray (*Trygonidae*) this fish, which has soft, gristly bones can weigh between 18–22 lb (8–10 kg) when fully grown. It is usually broiled with herbs and spices, cooked in a hot tamarind sauce, or stir-fried with salted vegetables.

Selar kuning: yellow-band trevally (*Carangidae*; Indon.: *selar*); caught in large shoals off the east coast of western Malaysia, these fish, some 5 in (12 cm) in length, are usually fried or braised in a tamarind sauce.

1 *Udang merah ros:* (*Metapenaeus affinis*; Indon. *api-api*) is a farmed shrimp with firm flesh. It can be steamed, boiled, or stir-fried
2 *Udang minyak:* pink shrimp (*Parapenaeopsis hardwickii*) common in the Indo-Pacific region
3 *Udang merah ros:* smooth-backed shrimp (*Metapenaeus ensis*); now farmed to satisfy a booming export market.

Kerang (Mal., Indon.): cockle (*Cardiidae*)

Kepah: Smooth Venus (*Veneridae*; Indon.: *remis*)

Kurau (Indon.: *mal*): threadfin (*Polynemidae*); small examples are barely 12 in (30 cm) long, but they can grow to 50 in (120 cm). The flesh of this fish, which inhabits the waters off the west coast of Malaysia, is tasty and has many culinary uses. Heads of larger specimens are used in fish-head curry.

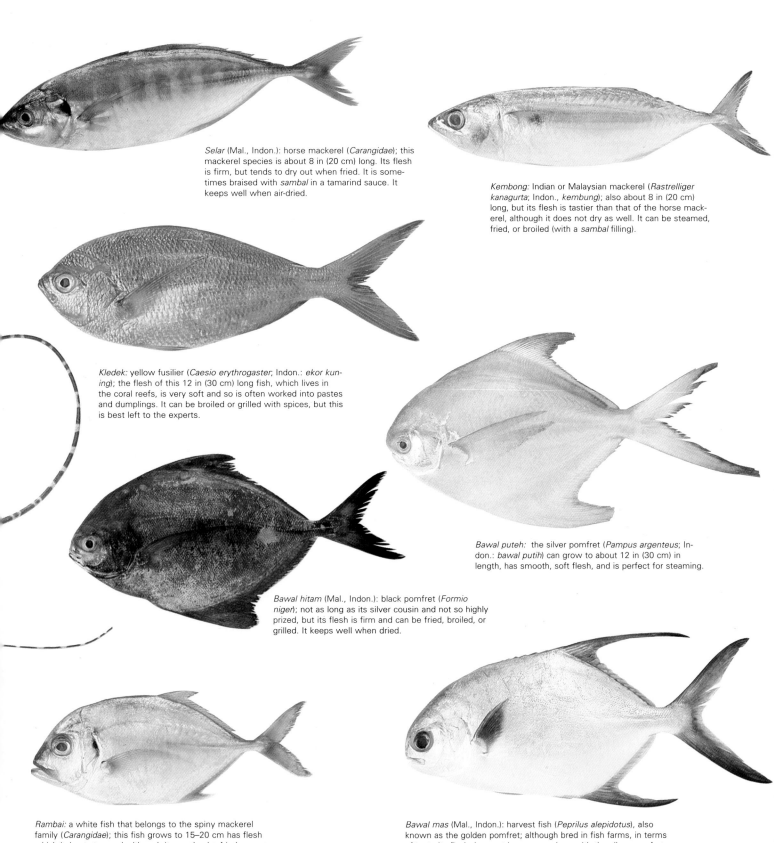

Selar (Mal., Indon.): horse mackerel (*Carangidae*); this mackerel species is about 8 in (20 cm) long. Its flesh is firm, but tends to dry out when fried. It is sometimes braised with *sambal* in a tamarind sauce. It keeps well when air-dried.

Kembong: Indian or Malaysian mackerel (*Rastrelliger kanagurta*; Indon., *kembung*); also about 8 in (20 cm) long, but its flesh is tastier than that of the horse mackerel, although it does not dry as well. It can be steamed, fried, or broiled (with a *sambal* filling).

Kledek: yellow fusilier (*Caesio erythrogaster*; Indon.: *ekor kuning*); the flesh of this 12 in (30 cm) long fish, which lives in the coral reefs, is very soft and so is often worked into pastes and dumplings. It can be broiled or grilled with spices, but this is best left to the experts.

Bawal puteh: the silver pomfret (*Pampus argenteus*; Indon.: *bawal putih*) can grow to about 12 in (30 cm) in length, has smooth, soft flesh, and is perfect for steaming.

Bawal hitam (Mal., Indon.): black pomfret (*Formio niger*); not as long as its silver cousin and not so highly prized, but its flesh is firm and can be fried, broiled, or grilled. It keeps well when dried.

Rambai: a white fish that belongs to the spiny mackerel family (*Carangidae*); this fish grows to 15–20 cm has flesh which is best steamed, although it can also be fried.

Bawal mas (Mal., Indon.): harvest fish (*Peprilus alepidotus*), also known as the golden pomfret; although bred in fish farms, in terms of taste its flesh does not bear comparison with the silver pomfret.

Dengkis: the rabbit fish (*Siganidae;* lindon.: *beronang lada*) boasts firm, tasty flesh, the underside being the most sought after. Although best fried, it can also be steamed.

Kunyit-kunyit (Mal., Indon.): the vitta snapper (*Lutianus vitta* is a member of the large snapper family, which is well represented in Malaysian waters. Nearly all snappers are edible. They are best fried or steamed, but can be prepared in other ways.

Kerapu: red grouper (*Epinephelus;* lndon.: *garoupa, kerapu*); groupers are found in all warm, tropical waters. The color serves as a camouflage and so it varies depending on where it happens to be. In culinary terms, the reddish-colored species is the more attractive. When fresh, *kerapu* are delicious served steamed or added to sweet-and-sour braised fish dishes.

Ikan sabelah (Mal., Indon.): flounder (*Psettodidae;* Thai.: *pla lin ma*); a flatfish imported from Thailand, used very much like cod in the West.

Belanak (Mal., Indon.): gray mullet (*Mugilidae*) is about 12 in (30 cm) long and feeds on tiny sea creatures filtered out of the mud. These can adversely affect the flavor.

Selayur: the scabbard fish (*Trichiuridae;* lndon.: *tajur, selayur*) grows to a length of 3-7 ft (1–2 m). It is often found in the coastal waters of the South China Sea. The front half provides the tastiest flesh. Fish steaks are either fried or broiled. Much prized by the Chinese.

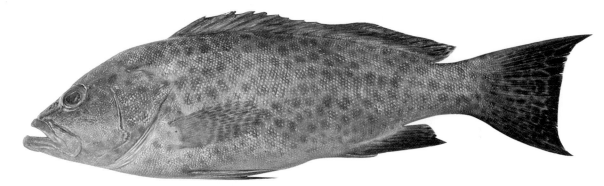

Barat-barat: trigger fish (*Aluteridae*; Indon.: *pakol*); about 20 in (50 cm) long when fully grown, it has a skin that is so firm and tough that it is removed before cooking. Whether steamed, grilled, or braised in a curry, it always tastes good.

Ikan merah: red snapper (*Lutianus argentimaculatus*; Indon.: *kakap merah*); a striking fish which can grow to a length of about 24 in (60 cm) and is probably the best known of the snapper family. It is eaten throughout the Chinese diaspora, and is also a popular Pacific fish. Its flesh is tasty, but, because of its big head and strong bones, there is often not enough of it.

Kerapu bunga (Mal., Indon.): brown grouper is usually steamed or fried, like the red grouper. The flesh is firm and tasty. The head is often used in Chinese soups.

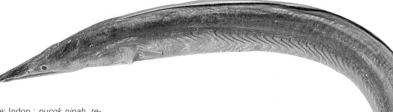

Belut kuning: yellow eel (*Muraenesocidae*; Indon.: *pucok nipah, re-mang*);this eel is 40–60 in (100 and 150 cm) long; the flesh is cut into slices and then steamed with salted black beans.

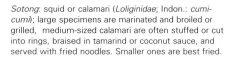

Sotong: squid or calamari (*Loliginidae*; Indon.: *cumi-cumi*); large specimens are marinated and broiled or grilled, medium-sized calamari are often stuffed or cut into rings, braised in tamarind or coconut sauce, and served with fried noodles. Smaller ones are best fried.

Anchovies, usually boiled and salted at sea, are left on the beach to dry.

When viewed at close quarters, anchovies reveal their sheen.

Small fry

Anchovies

The island of Pangkor lies more or less opposite Ipoh, off the west coast of the Malaysian peninsula. Its beaches are lined by attractive fishing villages on stilts visible from the ferry as it approaches from the mainland. The anchovy fishing boats set sail twice a day and the catch (called *ikan bilis* in Malay) are cooked on board in salted water. Anchovies spoil easily and are only sold fresh in the immediate vicinity. You are thus far more likely to find them, even in Malaysia, salted, canned, or packed in jars. The drying process, which usually takes place on the beach, does not always guarantee the quality of the anchovies, especially if there are insufficient opportunities for the night-time catch to cool properly. The drying process takes from five hours to one day.

Sambal ikan bilis kukus
Sambal with steamed anchovies

8 oz (250 g) steamed anchovies, heads removed
2 fresh red chili peppers, ground into a paste
¼ Tsp turmeric
3 Tbs oil
5 shallots, peeled and sliced into rings
½ Tsp dark soy sauce
Juice of 1 lime
1 Tbs water

Combine the chili paste and the turmeric. Add the anchovies and mix well. Heat 2 tbs of oil in a skillet and fry the anchovies until they are slightly crisp. Remove and set aside. Heat 1 Tbs of the oil, add the shallots, and sauté them until they are soft. Return the anchovies to the skillet and add the soy sauce, lime juice, and water. Combine well and cook until the liquid evaporates. Check the seasoning before adding more soy sauce, as anchovies already contain plenty of sauce. Serve with rice.

Ikan bilis goreng bawang
Fried anchovies with onion, chilies, and peanuts

3½ oz (100 g) dried anchovies, heads removed, rinsed and well dried
Oil for deep-frying
1 onion, peeled, halved and sliced
1¾ oz (50 g) roasted peanuts
1–2 fresh red chili peppers, seeds discarded, sliced into rings

Heat the oil in a frying pan and fry the anchovies until golden brown. Remove quickly and leave to drain. Heat 1 Tbs of oil and brown the onions. Return the anchovies to the pan, sprinkle with the peanuts, and mix well. Add the chili rings, stir, remove from the heat, and serve.

Ikan bilis goreng kacang
Fried anchovies with peanuts

3½ oz (100 g) dried anchovies, heads removed, washed and dried well
3½ oz (100 g) peanuts
oil for deep-frying
2 fresh red chili peppers, seeds discarded
2 garlic cloves, peeled and quartered
2 Tbs oil
2 Tsp brown sugar
Juice of 3 small limes

Fry the anchovies until they are brown. Leave to drain and set aside. Fry the peanuts over a medium heat, until they too are brown. Leave to drain and set aside. Grind the chili peppers with the garlic cloves in a mortar with a pestle. Heat 2 tbs of oil in a skillet and fry the paste until the aromas develop. Add the sugar and lime juice. As soon as the sauce starts to boil, return the fried anchovies and peanuts to the skillet. Stir the anchovies and nuts and then pour the sauce over them. These anchovy recipes should not be regarded as complete meals, but should be prepared as appetizers in a menu consisting of several courses. The quantities have been adjusted accordingly.

Ikan bilis fritters
Steamed and deep-fried fresh silver fish

1¼ cups (150 g) all-purpose flour
½ cup (80 g) rice flour
¼ Tsp salt
1¼ Tsp coriander, roasted and ground
¼ Tsp cumin, roasted and ground
1 small bunch coriander (cilantro) leaves, chopped
2 eggs
½ cup (125 ml) water
3½ oz (100 g) steamed silver fish
oil for deep-frying

In a bowl, combine the flour, rice flour, salt, crushed seeds, and chopped coriander leaves. Add the eggs and beat well. Gradually pour in the water and mix until the mixture has a thick pouring consistency. Stir in the silver fish. Heat the oil. Fry the mixture in the hot oil a spoonful at a time until golden brown. Leave to drain and serve with chili sauce.

Silver fish are barely ¾ in (2cm) in length and are a smaller variety of anchovy. They are available dried or pre-cooked in oriental stores.

Ikan bilis goreng bawang – Fried anchovies with onion, chili peppers, and peanuts

Freshwater fish

Where tin used to be mined in the state of Perak on the Malaysian peninsula, sea bass, catfish, and tilapia are farmed in the water that has filled the old workings and turned them into lakes. Tilapia is related to the catfish, and there are species which live in fresh and brackish water. It is farmed successfully in industrialized countries and in the Third World. In Malaysia and Indonesia, white tilapia from Egypt, which are found in the Red Sea and the Nile Delta, are bred rather than the otherwise more popular red tilapia. The fish is almost boneless and its white, flaky

When the tilapia are in the fattening pond, they are fed three times a day with a precise amount of food, so that they put on weight and are ready for market as rapidly as possible.

flesh can be steamed, fried, or and broiled. At the age of only three weeks, the tilapia fry are removed from the hatcheries to the breeding grounds, where they spend the next three months until they weigh about 7 oz (200 g). They are then kept for another three months in ponds where they are fattened up. When they reach 2–2½ lb (800 g–1 kg), they are ready to be sold. As many as 30,000 fish are kept in the ponds, which need additional oxygenation to maintain the water quality. The oxygenating machines have the added advantage of being useful for guiding the movements of the fish. When the growing tilapia need to be attracted into the fattening pond, the fish farmers switch off the oxygenating machine and open the entrance into the new tank. The stressed fish will happily swim into the new waters, since the oxygen levels are higher there. This may be rather unsporting, but it is highly effective.

White tilapia, a member of the large cichlid family

Ikan duri (Indon.: *ikan lele*): catfish from the sea are usually darker than fresh water catfish. These smaller, brownish-black fish without scales (there is an albino variety) and a slimy coating occur in the rivers and lakes of Thailand, Vietnam, Laos, Myanmar (Burma), and Cambodia. They vary in size between 10–32 in (25–80 cm). The Malaysians prefer to eat them with a spicy tamarind sauce.

Ikan siakap (Indon.: *kakap putih*): Some varieties of the bass family (*Moronidae*) are freshwater fish and these are farmed successfully in Malaysia. Their firm flesh is really tasty and can be prepared in a number of different ways. However, the sea bass is undoubtedly of better quality. Steaming will bring out the unique aroma of its flesh.

The songfish belongs to the carp family (*Cyprinidae*) and is 12–20 in (30– 50 cm) long. Despite its many bones, the flavor is greatly appreciated. The Chinese, for example, use it in fish head *beehoon*. As it releases a distinctly fishy aroma, it should be fried first, then added to a broth. Serve it with thin rice noodles. The Malaysians prefer to cook songfish in a spicy tamarind sauce.

The difference between Malaysian and Chinese cuisine

The Malaysians generally prefer to eat fish such as small horse mackerel, Indian mackerel, or pomfret. Fresh or dried anchovies are just as popular as Spanish mackerel and ray, or freshwater fish such as tilapia and catfish. Fish are generally fried, but their skins are often rubbed with spices or else they are stuffed with the same spice mixture before frying or broiling. The mixture usually consists of grated shallots, chili peppers, garlic, and nuts. Chopped fish chunks and steaks are also served in a spicy tamarind sauce. On the other hand, the Chinese prefer to cook larger fish such as sea bass, grouper, and snapper. Fish that is really fresh is simply steamed, so that its true flavor can be fully appreciated. Westerners are often a little disconcerted when the Chinese serve fish whole, heads included. Many Chinese like the bony parts of the fish, claiming that they are delicately flavored, smooth, and soft. Even the eyes are not rejected. On the contrary, the gelatinous texture of the eyes is much appreciated. Other ways of preparing fish are frying and braising. Slices of fish, plus vegetables and other ingredients, are stir-fried in a wok or else boiled in soups and served with noodles or rice gruel. Yellowtail or wolf herring tail is puréed, worked into a dough with cornstarch and salted water and then shaped into fishcakes or fishballs. These are then used in soups or served with noodles. Tofu or vegetables, such as eggplant, okra, and chili peppers, are sometimes added to the ground fish mixture.

A sharp, narrow knife is used to gut the songfish (*selar kuning*).

The cleaned stomach cavity is brushed with a prepared mixture of spices.

If the fish is to be fried, a curry mixture may also rubbed onto the skin.

The fish are then fried evenly on both sides at medium temperature.

A fishy speciality?

Fish head curry

It is now about 30 years since an Indian by the name of Gomez first created this dish in his small restaurant in Singapore's Tank Road. It was not really intended for his fellow Indians, who did not regard fish heads as anything special. It was much more in tune with the tastes of the many Singaporean Chinese, who regarded fish heads as delicacies. The Chinese in Singapore and Malaysia have also developed a particular liking for spicy foods and so a great number of factors came together. Not surprisingly, these fish curries have achieved great popularity in Singapore and Malaysia. Be prepared for an experience if you order a fish head curry in a restaurant. When the bowl full of steaming hot curry eventually appears on the table, there is no mistaking the fish head. Every diner receives a piece of banana leaf and a portion of rice. Then the fun starts. First of all the tender flesh of the fish cheeks is shared out, after that everything else that is soft is systematically removed, but the best parts, which are saved until last, are — the eyes and lips. The meal is only finished when all that remains are the bones of the skull. If you are trying this dish for the first time, you may prefer to opt for the "beginner's" version, using smaller heads. If you are adventurous enough to try this dish — and if your guests are similarly adventurous — be prepared for a pleasant surprise. Many newcomers cannot resist asking for a second helping!

Rub salt into the fish head and rinse thoroughly under running water

In a bowl, combine the onion, garlic, chili peppers, tomato, curry powder, leaves, and water

Stir in the raising agent, tamarind juice, and leave for a short time

Fry the second onion, the remaining curry leaves, and the seeds in the oil

Halve the larger okra, add to the spices, and fry all over

Now pour the contents of the bowl over the okra and bring to the boil

Just before the end of the cooking time, add the thick coconut milk which was prepared earlier.

Stir all the ingredients together and bring the curry back to the boil over a medium heat.

Place the fish head in the curry, spoon some of the lightly bubbling sauce over it, and simmer until done.

Fish-head curry

For 2 or 4 people
1 large fish head, about 2lb (900 g)
Juice of 2 Tbs Tamarind syrup and 3 cups water
6½ oz (100 g) grated coconut and ½ cup water
½ onion, peeled and sliced
1 garlic clove, peeled and sliced
1 fresh red chili pepper, sliced into 3–4 pieces, seeds discarded
1 fresh green chili pepper, sliced into 3–4 pieces, seeds discarded
1 tomato, quartered
2 sprigs curry leaves
4 Tbs curry powder for fish curry
salt
½ cup water
3 Tbs oil
1 onion, peeled and sliced into thin rings
2 Tsp whole mixed spices
8 okra pods

Rub salt into the fish head and wash thoroughly. Soak the tamarind pulp in water and then strain through a sieve. Retain the liquid and set aside. Mix the grated coconut with the water and then squeeze out the liquid to create a thick milk. Set aside. In a bowl, combine the sliced onion, the chopped red and green chili peppers, the quartered tomatoes, the leaves from on of the curry plant sprigs, salt, water, and tamarind juice. Leave to stand for a short time. Heat the oil in a saucepan and fry the thin onion rings, the curry leaves from the other sprig, and the whole mixed spices for 2 minutes, or until the aromas develop. Add the okra (larger pods halved) and fry. Pour in the curry mixture, cover, and bring to the boil. Add the coconut milk and bring back to the boil. Now place the fish head in the broth and leave until cooked. Serve with rice. Portions depend on the size and type of fish head. Without any other garnishes, the quantities given here should serve two people, with additional garnishes and rice they will serve four.

The whole spice mixtures are available from good supermarkets and oriental food stores, the mixtures will vary. Every region, often every family, has its own preferred mix, just as with curry powder and *garam masala*. However, cumin, black mustard seeds, fenugreek seeds, and peeled mung beans or navy beans are essential ingredients.

Daun kari: curry leaves; the fresh leaves of the orange rue (*Murraya koenigii*), a type of citrus, are important ingredients in not only Malaysian, but also Sri Lankan and south Indian curry dishes. The 1½–2 in (4–5cm) long, lance-shaped, dark green leaves have a distinctly hot, but slightly sharp flavor. They can be added to the mixture at the start of cooking, but the aroma only develops after about 5 minutes and so they are often added just prior to serving. Dried curry leaves, whose aroma is fainter, are sold ground into the commercially-available Madras curry powder. In Indonesia, the leaves of a closely related plant called *daun salam* are used.

Rice

Rice can be a surprisingly versatile basic food. Long-grain polished white rice from Thailand is prized in Singapore for its flavor. Malaysians, on the other hand, grow their own rice. It is boiled, steamed, fried, and cooked either on its own or with the addition of coconut milk, spices, and herbs. When it is shaped into rolls, molded into coconut-leaf baskets or into bamboo sticks, it is known as pressed rice. The best fried rice (*nasi goreng*) is made using leftover rice, or rice cooked some time earlier, as it is more grainy. In Kelantan, Northern Malaysia, freshly harvested brown rice is steamed with herbs and coconut milk. *Nasi kandar* is an Indian Moslem dish; the original version comes from Penang, the island off the west coast of Malaysia. It is traditionally sold in the street from booths. Hot boiled rice used to be kept in wooden barrels (today, plastic containers are used) and ladled out in a coconut shell used as a scoop. Accompaniments might include such delicacies as meat curry, fried fish, curried squid, or fishheads, to name but a few. Basmati rice (Pakistani long-grain rice) is more expensive than locally produced rice, and is thus usually reserved for festive occasions. It is the best choice for *biriani*, a substantial rice dish of Indian origin, made with clarified butter, milk, saffron, and other spices. Both white and black sticky rice, rice flour, and white sticky rice flour are essential for the preparation of cakes and desserts. Unpolished rice is more nutritious and so it is given to young children to help them to grow.

There is even more to rice than all this. If a family has experienced misfortune but the tide has turned again in its favor, a dish called *bubur merah bubur putih* (red gruel, white gruel) may well appear on the table. This is made from rice boiled with coconut milk, pandanus leaves, and salt. Palm sugar (*gula merah*; *merah*) is added to half the mixture (*merah* means red). This "red" rice is served together with the white as a symbol of the victory of good over evil. A prayer is uttered, and this rice is eaten as a purification ceremony, so that the evil powers to which the family members were exposed can no longer touch them.

The rice pot rests on two bamboo sticks, which are raised on bricks above the fire — rice cooking can be as simple as that.

Often, rice is cooked during the day in large quantities, which can then be used for various purposes as required.

For *nuba laya tenga* (rice in leaves) boiled rice is drained and then beaten to the consistency of a smooth paste.

A spoonful of this rice paste is placed in the center of a leaf (*daun isip*) and then folded into a package.

These packages are steamed to make little cakes, light or more substantial, which are eaten as snacks.

Above: Rice-growing is still a labor-intensive, arduous task, and the rice-farmer's relationship with his paddy-field remains a close one.

191

Nasi kuning
Yellow rice

1¾ cups (400 g) rice, rinsed and drained
1 piece ginger root, ½ in (1 cm) thick
2 garlic cloves, peeled and quartered
3 Tbs *ghee* (clarified butter) or butter
1 onion, peeled and sliced into thin rings
4 shallots, peeled and sliced into thin rings
1 piece cinnamon stick, 1¼ in(4 cm) lang
2 whole cloves
2 cardamon seeds
2 sections star anise
4 cups (1 l) water
3 Tbs condensed milk
salt

To color
saffron strands, dissolved in 2 Tsp water
or ½ Tsp yellow food coloring,
mixed with 2 Tsp water (or rosewater)

Garnish
fried onion rings

Pound the ginger and garlic to a paste in a mortar. Heat ghee or butter and fry the onion rings in it until golden-brown. Add the ginger and garlic paste, shallot rings, cinnamon, cloves, cardamon, and star anise; fry until the various flavors develop. Add the rice and cook until it is transparent. Add the water, milk, and salt, and stir well. Bring to the boil, reduce the heat, and let the rice simmer. When it is nearly dry, drizzle the colored water over it, cover, and cook until all the liquid has evaporated. When the rice is cooked, stir the food coloring into it with a spoon and mix well. Arrange on serving platter, garnish with fried onion rings, and serve with a meat curry.

Nasi kunyit
Rice with turmeric

1¾ cups (400 g) rice, rinsed and drained
1 piece fresh turmeric root, 2¼ in (6 cm) lang
1¼ cups (300 g) grated coconut (dark rind removed)
mixed with the same amount of water
¼ Tsp salt

Peel the fresh turmeric, grind it in a mortar, and tie it into a piece of cheesecloth. .
Drain the rice and let it soak for 3 hours in the water in which the cloth containing the turmeric has been hung, until the grains of rice have taken on the yellow color of the turmeric.
Mix the grated coconut with water and squeeze in a piece of cheesecloth to obtain thick coconut milk. This recipe calls for at least 1½ cups (350 ml) coconut milk. If necessary, add more water to the grated coconut and squeeze until you have the required quantity. Add salt to the milk.
Bring the water to the boil in a pressure cooker. Add the rice and steam for 30 minutes. Remove the rice from the pressure cooker, and stir the coconut milk into it. Steam for a further 10-15 minutes, or until all the liquid has been absorbed.

This dish is indispensable on particularly festive occasions such as weddings or circumcision ceremonies. To serve, fill a dish with the rice, pressing it down well, and unmold it onto a serving platter. Cut a circle out of a banana leaf and place it on the mound of rice. A few spoonfuls of shrimp *sambal* or a small quantity of a dry curry should be placed on top as a finishing touch. This rice is then served with bowls of various types of curry as side-dishes.

Nasi tomato
Tomato rice

1¾ cups (400 g) rice, rinsed and drained
1 garlic clove, peeled and quartered
1 slice ginger root, ⅛ in (3 mm) thick
1¼ Tbs *ghee* (clarified butter) or butter
1 onion, peeled, halved and thinly sliced
½ Tsp salt
2½ cups (600 ml) water
¾ cup (200 ml) tomato soup

Grind the ginger and garlic to a paste in the mortar. Heat ghee or butter and fry the onion in it until golden-brown. Then add the ginger and garlic paste and fry until the flavors develop. Add the rice and mix in well with the other ingredients. Mix the water with the tomato soup and add to the rice. Bring to the boil, reduce the heat, cover, and cook the rice until the liquid has been absorbed. Add salt and continue to cook over a very low heat, until the liquid has been absorbed and the rice is swollen. Serve with chicken or meat curry.

In Asia it is customary to wash rice before cooking it. Apart from the fact that it removes impurities, this practice also reduces the starch content. "New" rice is the term used for freshly harvested rice, which needs less water to cook in. "Old" rice, rice which has been stored for some time, needs more water. When cooked, "old" rice goes further than "new." Many Asian households now have an electric rice cooker. It is supposed to cook perfect rice, but most of these appliances also have a device for keeping the rice warm and the rice starts to taste stale. It is not advisable to cook rice in the microwave as this method does not bring out its full flavor.

Nasi goreng
Malayan-style fried rice
Serves 2 or 4

1 cup (225 g) rice, rinsed and drained
4 fresh red chili peppers, sliced into i 3–4 pieces, seeds discarded
4 shallots, peeled and chopped
1 garlic clove, peeled and quartered
⅓ cup(80 g) fresh green beans
¼ cup(60 g) dried anchovies, heads discarded, washed and drained
3 Tbs oil
1 Tsp salt

Boil the rice and allow to cool (it is preferable to cook it the day before it is required).
Grind the chili peppers, shallots, and garlic into a paste in a mortar. Cut the beans into small, pea-size pieces. Fry the dried anchovies in oil until lightly browned. Remove and drain. Add more oil to the skillet or wok and heat it. When hot,add the chili, shallot, and garlic paste and fry until the flavors have developed.
Then stir in the beans. When they are about half-cooked, after about 3 minutes, add the rice. Stir well to mix it in with the other ingredients. Add the fried anchovies, stir, and add salt if wished.

The quantities given will be enough for a meal for two people. The quantities of rice in all the recipes on these two pages have been geared to Asian tastes; Westerners may prefer a smaller portion of rice.

Nasi kuning – Yellow rice

Nasi lemak
Coconut rice

1¾ cups (400 g) rice, rinsed and drained
½ coconut, grated (about 2 cups (250 g))
4 cups (1 l) water, combined with the grated coconut, squeezed, milk reserved
½ Tsp salt
1 piece ginger root, ¾ in (2 cm) thick, peeled and lightly crushed
3 pandanus leaves, washed and tied in a knot

Mix ¼ litre water at a time with the grated coconut and squeeze it through a cloth in order to obtain 4 cups (1 litre) of coconut milk. Place the rice, coconut milk, and all other ingredients in a pan and bring to the boil. Then reduce the heat and let the rice simmer until it is cooked and all the liquid has been absorbed.

Ikan bilis sambal
Sambal of dried anchovies to serve with *nasi lemak*

3½ Tbs (50 g) dried anchovies
juice of 1 Tsp tamarind pulp and 3 Tbs water
4 Tbs oil
1 Tbs sugar
¼ Tsp salt

Spice paste
4 Tsp (20 g) dried chili peppers, soaked and sliced into pieces
2 onions, peeled and chopped
1 garlic clove, peeled and quartered

Remove the anchovy heads and halve each fish lengthwise. Drain and allow to dry well. (You may be able to buy anchovies prepared in this way in some oriental food stores.)
Mix the tamarind pulp with water and strain it, retaining the liquid.
Grind the dried chili peppers to a paste in a mortar with the onions and garlic.
Heat enough oil in a skillet or wok to fry the anchovies until they are golden-brown but not crisp. Drain and set aside.
Heat 4 tablespoons of oil, add the chili paste, and fry until the flavors have developed. Add tamarind juice, sugar, and salt and stir until the sugar has dissolved. Finally add the fried anchovies and cook for another 5 minutes. The sambal should have a firm consistency.

This is the original coconut rice which is so popular in Malaysia and Singapore at all times of day, for breakfast, lunch, or as a snack (of course the recipe for *ikan bilis sambal* will vary from one home to another, and each Malaysian homemaker has her own recipe.) The rice is also sold everywhere in small parcels from pushcarts in the street and in coffee shops. Each diner is given some rice, a *sambal* of dried anchovies, and a few slices of cucumber, all wrapped up in a banana leaf. *Nasi lemak* is now an acceptable dish to serve in polite society and is eaten at breakfast and lunch even in hotels, admittedly with a number of non-traditional additional ingredients, such as vegetables, chicken curry, *rendang* beef, fried anchovies with peanuts, or omelets. A Chinese variant found in Singapore may also include a slice of spam! The packages sold today in coffee shops and food markets contain a little fried fish, a piece of omelet, a few slices of cucumber, and some chili *sambal*.

Lontong – a stick of rice

One cup of rice (250 g) is enough for a *lontong* roll. The banana leaves are soaked in warm water to soften them. They are then dried, sliced into rectangles. These are used to line the lontong cylinders. The pieces must be exactly the same length as the cylinders, but should overlap the edges. The base and cover of the cylinders are lined in the same way. Wash the rice, drain it well, and spread it out on a tray to dry. Fill the lined, perforated metal cylinders, which are 8 x 2 in (20 x 6 cm) in size, with rice. Bring water to the boil in a deep pot, like an asparagus cooker. The pot should be slightly taller than the length of the cylinders. When the water boils, place the cylinders upright next to each other in the pan, and cook for 4 hours. The longer the rice is cooked, the longer it can be kept afterward. Remove the rolls from the cylinders and allow them to cool. They can be kept in the vegetable compartment of the refrigerator for several days.
Do not remove the lids until just before serving. Cut the rolls of rice into dice or slices and serve with a vegetable or curry dish which has been cooked in coconut sauce. Pour the hot food over the cold rice.
Pressed rice can also be prepared without special equipment. Wash 1¾ cups (400 g) rice, put it into a pan with 5 cups (1¼ l) water and a large pinch of salt, and cook, stirring occasionally, to a smooth purée consistency. When the liquid has nearly all evaporated, reduce the heat. Allow the rice to cool, transfer to a dish or bowl, and spread a damp cloth over it. Put a second dish or bowl on top, press down with a heavy weight and leave to stand for 3 hours. To serve, cut the rice into dice, repeatedly dipping the knife in cold water as you do so.

Before cooking, it is a good idea to sift through the rice, to search for small stones or other foreign bodies.

Then the rice should be thoroughly rinsed three or four times while being rubbed between the hands.

The cooking water should be no higher above the level of the rice than the first joint of the middle finger.

When the water has been completely absorbed, the volume of the rice will have doubled.

Loose rice cooked *al dente*, in a banana leaf bowl, ready to be served.

Lontong rice is cooked in perforated cylindrical metal molds which are lined with banana leaves. It should be cooked for at least 4 hours so that it can be kept for several days.

Ketupat

Ketupat boxes are woven from strips of young, pale green coconut palm leaves. The older, dark green leaves are too brittle and more difficult to work with. Most Malaysian women know how to weave these little leaf boxes, having learned the craft as children, but some men have also mastered it. With a little skill and practice it is possible to produce several hundred boxes a day.

To prepare *ketupat*, first wash the rice and then drain it well. The best way of drying it is to spread it out on a tray. Half-fill the leaf boxes with rice, leaving a small space inside so that the grains of rice have enough room for expansion. The opening is then closed by weaving a leaf over it.

The little boxes are then tied together in bundles of five or ten each, to make them easier to handle. The bundles of boxes are then lowered into a big pot of boiling water. The heat is reduced and the rice boxes are left to simmer for at least four hours. You must make sure that they are covered by water at all times. As with *lontong*, the longer the rice is cooked, the better it will keep. When it is ready, remove the bundles and let them cool. Pressed rice does not have to be eaten hot. *Ketupat* can be served with *satay* (kabobs) or meat and vegetable curries with plenty of sauce. If the rice is eaten with *satay*, the rice cubes are dipped in a spicy peanut sauce. The *ketupat* boxes are not opened until the rice is required. They are then cut in half vertically with a sharp knife and the two resulting blocks of rice are each cut into six pieces.

Ketupat can be kept in the boxes in a cool place for one or two days. If you want to keep it for longer, it should be placed in the refrigerator, but not in the coldest part, or it will harden. Before use, the rice in the leaf boxes just needs to be steamed briefly.

Experienced women can produce several hundred woven boxes a day, and it is fascinating to watch them at work.

First you cut thin strips from a leaf and remove every single leaf rib.

Lay the end of a strip over the palm of the right hand and hold in place with your thumb.

Then fold the strip round the fingers of the left hand and hold the roll in place.

Take a second strip and roll it in the same way using your right hand.

The difficult part is weaving the left-hand roll into the right-hand one.

The strips are woven together by folding them alternately over and under each other.

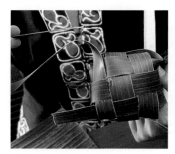

The *ketupat* box is closed up all round except for a small opening, through which it is stuffed with rice.

Half-fill each box with raw rice, close up, and place in boiling water.

Eating and fasting

Refraining from eating in order to observe the fast of Ramadan is one of the five pillars of Islam, the state religion of Malaysia. When they do eat, Moslems are allowed to consume only "pure" foods, which must conform to the dietary laws prescribed by their religion, which thus exercises a very direct influence on the everyday life of the faithful. A devout Moslem is not allowed to consume pork in any form. Also forbidden are blood, animals which have not been ritually slaughtered in the name of Allah, and alcohol in any form.

All meat, including poultry, must be slaughtered by severing the jugular vein in order to be pure (*hallal*), and thus permissible for eating. First the name of Allah must be called out when an animal is slaughtered. The death blow itself must be inflicted as quickly as possible with a carefully sharpened knife, in order to spare the animal unnecessary suffering. The throat, windpipe, and vein must be cut through without severing the spinal cord. All the blood must have been drained out before the head is separated from the body. This process is carried out for reasons of health, because blood is a breeding-ground for micro-organisms. The premature severing of the spinal cord can induce heart failure, which allows blood to stagnate in the blood vessels.

In areas with a predominantly Moslem population, *hallal* poultry and meat is available at the markets and supermarkets, where it is carefully labeled on the packaging.

Malaysians and Indians often eat lamb and mutton, unlike the Chinese, who find it rather too strong in flavor. Malaysians use it, as well as beef and goat meat, to make curry dishes, soups, and *satay* or cutlets. Spices are used liberally. In Malaysia, goats are often reared for their milk as well as for their meat.

Fresh lamb being sold at a booth in a large market mainly patronized by Moslems. In the city, the head of the household rarely slaughters meat himself, though this is still common in the countryside.

Dalca
Mutton with lentils
Serves 4-6

10½ oz(300 g) mutton ribs, fat trimmed away, cut into 2–3 pieces
3 Tbs curry powder for lamb curry
2 garlic cloves, peeled and quartered
2 slices ginger root, about ⅛ in(3 mm) thick
1 cinnamon stick, 1¼ in (3 cm) long
3 whole cloves
2 cardamon seeds
1 stem curry leaves (leaves only used)
⅔ coconut, grated (about 2½ cups (300 g)), to make 1 cup (250 ml) thick coconut milk
2 cups (500 ml) water, combined with grated coconut to make 2 cups (500 ml) thin coconut milk
⅔ cup (150 g) lentils (dal), washed and soaked for 15 minutes
10½ oz (300 g) potatoes, peeled and quartered
2 eggplant, halved lengthwise and each sliced into 1¼ in (3 cm) rounds
Juice from 2 Tbs tamarind pulp and 4 Tbs water
1 Tsp salt
2 tomatoes, halved
3 green chili peppers, sliced into pieces
3 Tbs oil
1 onion, peeled and sliced into thin rings
1 stem curry leaves

Grind the garlic cloves to a paste in a mortar with the root ginger. Put the mutton, curry powder, ginger, and garlic paste, cinnamon stick, cloves, cardamom, curry leaves, and thin coconut milk in a pan and bring to the boil over a moderate heat. Reduce the heat and let the ingredients simmer until the meat is nearly cooked. Add the lentils and potatoes. After 15 minutes, add the eggplant pieces to the pan and simmer for a further 5 minutes. Then add the thick coconut milk and tamarind juice, and season with salt to taste. Cook for 5 minutes. Add tomatoes and green chili peppers, cook for a few minutes, the remove from the heat.
Heat the oil in a skillet or wok and fry the onion rings and curry leaves until the onions are golden-brown. Add these with the oil to the cooked mutton, and immediately cover the pan with a tightly-fitting lid, in order to seal in the flavor. Allow to stand for a few minutes before serving.

To prepare dalca, you can use leg of mutton as an alternative to ribs. Mutton can be replaced by beef.

Kari kambing
Mutton curry
Serves 4-6

17½ oz (500 g) lean mutton or lamb, cut into slices
1 coconut, grated (about 2½ cups (300 g)), to make 1 cup (250 ml) thick coconut milk
3 cups (750 ml) water, combined with grated coconut to make 3 cups (750 ml) thin coconut milk
5 Tbs oil
1 piece cinnamon stick, 1¼ in (3 cm) long
3 cardamon seeds
4 whole cloves
2 segments star anise
5 Tbs curry powder for lamb
4 potatoes, peeled and quartered
2 tomatoes, halved
1 Tsp salt

Spice paste

8 shallots, peeled and minced
4 garlic cloves, peeled and quartered
3 slices ginger root each about ½ in (1 cm) thick
2 slices galangal root, each about ½ in(1 cm) thick

Squeeze 1 cup (250 ml) thick coconut milk out of the grated coconut and set aside. Add 1 cup (250 ml) water to the grated coconut and squeeze out. Repeat this process twice until you have produced 3 cups (750 ml) thin milk.
Heat the oil in a skillet, add the cinnamon, cardamom, cloves, and star anise segments, and fry gently for 1 minute. Add the spice paste and fry until the flavors develop, then add the sliced mutton, and stir well. Pour the thin coconut milk over the mixture and allow to simmer over a low heat until the meat is half-cooked, about 20 minutes. Add the potatoes and continue to simmer. When the potatoes are nearly cooked, about 15 minutes, add the tomatoes to the pan, then add the thick coconut milk, and season with salt to taste. Bring to the boil again, then remove the pan from the heat and serve the curry immediately with plenty of rice.

Kari kambing – Mutton curry

Sop kambing
Mutton soup
Serves 4-6

1 lb (500 g) mutton ribs, fat removed, sliced into pieces
4 Tbs oil
1 onion, peeled and chopped
3 garlic cloves, peeled and chopped
2 pieces ginger root, about ⅛ in(3 mm) thick
1 tomato, cut into cubes
¼ Tsp ground coriander
¼ Tsp ground cumin
¼ Tsp ground fennel seeds
1 piece cinnamon stick, 1¼ in (3 cm) long
3 cardamon seeds
3 whole cloves
5 cups (1¼ l) water
salt

Garnish

2 sprigs coriander leaves
3 shallots, sliced into rings and fried

Stir the powdered coriander, cumin, and fennel to a paste with a little water.
Heat the oil in a pan, add onions, garlic, ginger, and tomato and fry until the flavors have developed. Add the spice paste, cinnamon, cardamon, and cloves and fry for 1 minute. Fry the mutton gently, mix with the spices, then deglaze with water and season with salt. Bring to the boil, reduce the heat, and allow the ingredients to simmer until the meat is tender. Garnish with fried onion rings and coriander leaves and serve hot with French bread.

Kambing kecup
Mutton in soy sauce with onions and tomatoes
Serves 4-6

1 lb (500 g) lean mutton or lamb, cut into small cubes
1 Tsp freshly ground white pepper
salt
2 Tbs oil
1 onion, peeled and sliced into rings
2 Tomatoes sliced into rounds
1 piece cinnamon stick, 1¼ in (3 cm) long
1 Tbs dark soy sauce
1½ cups (375 ml) water

Season the mutton with salt and pepper and leave for 15 minutes.
Heat the oil in a heavy pan, add the cubed mutton and fry, turning frequently, to seal the surface. Add onion, tomatoes, cinnamon, and soy sauce and mix well. Add the water and allow to simmer over a low heat until the meat is tender. If all the liquid has evaporated before the meat is fully cooked, top up with a few tablespoons hot water. When the meat is tender, hardly any liquid should be left in the saucepan.

Rendang daging lembu
Beef braised in coconut milk
Serves 4-6

1lb 5oz (600 g) beef, sliced into strips
2 kaffir lime leaves
1 turmeric leaf
1 stem lemongrass, lightly crushed
1 piece of galangal root the size of a walnut, lightly crushed
4 Tbs ground coriander
1 Tsp cumin seed
2 Tsp sugar
salt
1 coconut, grated (2 Tbs reserved)
5 cups (1¼ l) water, combined with the grated coconut, squeezed to make thin coconut milk

Spice paste
10 dried chili peppers, soaked, seeds discarded
8 shallots, peeled and chopped
2 Tbs grated coconut, toasted

First make the spice paste. Grind the the dried chilies, shallots, and the toasted grated coconut (the 2 tablespoons are taken from the whole grated coconut). In a deep pan, mix the beef with the paste. Add all the other ingredients, pour on the coconut milk, and stir everything well. Bring to the boil, then reduce the heat and allow to simmer in an uncovered pan until the beef is tender, stirring from time to time. When most of the liquid has evaporated and the coconut fat begins to settle, remove the pan from the heat. Stir more frequently toward the end of the cooking time to prevent the food from sticking and burning. The mixture should be thick and fairly dry and this can take up to an hour.

Rendang is a popular dish in Singapore, Malaysia, and Indonesia. It is usually made with beef, but chicken or mutton are also used. The recipe varies from one region to another. *Rendang* is always served with rice or *ketupat* (pressed rice).

Semur
Beef stew
Serves 4-6

1lb 5oz (600 g) beef, cut into 1½ in(4 cm) cubes
2 slices ginger root
4 garlic cloves, peeled and quartered
2 Tbs oil
4 fresh red chili peppers, seeds discarded, ground to a paste
1 piece cinnamon stick, 1¼ in (3 cm) long
2 cardamon seeds
3 whole cloves
2 segments star anise
1 stem lemongrass, lightly crushed
1 piece of galangal root the size of a walnut, lightly crushed

1½ cups (375 ml) water
½ cup (125 ml) dark soy sauce
1 piece tamarind pulp, sliced
1 Tsp sugar
salt to taste

Grind the ginger and garlic to a paste in a mortar. Heat the oil in a pan and and fry the ginger and garlic paste in it until the flavors have developed. Gently fry the chili paste, then add all the other herbs and spices including the lemongrass and galangal and continue cooking. Deglaze the pan with water and add soy sauce, tamarind slices, and sugar. When the mixture comes to the boil, add the cubed beef, bring back to the boil, reduce the heat and simmer until the meat is tender. Season with salt to taste shortly before the end of the cooking time.

The dish known as *semur* in Malaysia and Indonesia is called *adobo* in the Philippines and soy sauce stew in China. Basically it consists of beef, chicken, or fish braised in soy sauce base, combined with other ingredients which vary from country to country. Malaysians and Indonesians add tamarind pulp and chili peppers, Filipinos add rice vinegar and peppercorns, and the Chinese spice it with star anise and five-spice powder. All use garlic, either ground to a paste or in whole cloves. The dish tastes even better when reheated (the addition of vinegar or tamarind pulp improves its keeping qualities).

Kurma
Mild beef curry
Serves 4-6

1lb 5oz (600 g) beef, cut into 1¼ in(3 cm) cubes
3 Tsp *ghee* (clarified butter or butterfat)
3 Tbs coriander seeds
1 Tsp cumin seeds
1 Tsp white peppercorns
1 Tsp poppyseeds
2 cardamon seeds
2 whole cloves
1 piece cinnamon stick, ¾ in (2 cm) long
1 coconut, grated (about 14 oz (400 g))
3 cups (750 ml) water, combined with the coconut, and squeezed, milk reserved
3 potatoes, peeled and quartered
salt
juice of 1 lime

Spice paste
2 pieces ginger root, about ½ in (1 cm) thick
6 shallots, peeled and chopped
4 garlic cloves, peeled and quartered

Grind the ginger, shallots and garlic in a mortar. Grind the coriander, cumin, pepper, and poppyseeds to a powder. Heat the ghee and fry all the spices in it. Gently fry the beef, deglaze with coconut milk, and allow to simmer. After 15 minutes, add the potatoes and salt. When the potatoes are cooked, the meat tender and the sauce thick, add the lime juice and serve.

Daging masak asam
Beef in tamarind sauce
Serves 4-6

17½ oz (500 g) beef, cut into ¼ in (5 mm) thick slices
4 Tbs oil
1 stem lemongrass, lightly crushed
1 piece of galangal root the size of a walnut, lightly crushed
Juice of 3 Tbs tamarind pulp and 2 cups (500 ml) water
1 Tsp salt

Spice paste
24 dried chili peppers drained, seeds discarded
12 shallots, peeled and chopped
2 garlic cloves, peeled and quartered
1piece fresh turmeric root, ⅝ in(1.5 cm) long

Grind the chilies, shallots, garlic cloves, and turmeric, heat the oil in a pan and fry the spice paste in it until the flavors develop. Gently fry the cubed beef, stir in lemongrass and galangal root, deglaze with tamarind juice, season with salt, and bring to the boil. Reduce the heat and simmer until the meat is tender and the sauce has thickened.

Sop kambing – Mutton soup

Rendang daging lembu – Beef braised in coconut milk

Hari Raya

The end of Ramadan, the month of fasting, is a time of celebration for Muslims.

The four weeks of Ramadan are a time of physical and spiritual purification, a time during which willpower and stamina are put to the test. The obligation to fast is imposed upon all believers, with the exception of children under seven and the sick or elderly. The fast begins at sunrise and no eating or drinking is permitted until sunset (smoking and speaking ill of others are also banned.) The daily fast ends with the consumption of one to three dates. A prayer should be said before eating, but if that is not possible, the prayer may be said after the meal.

Eating and drinking are permitted between sunset and sunrise, and while some families make use of this time for the consumption of particularly lavish and imaginative meals (the preparations for which keep the women of the family busy almost all day), others honor the principle of the fast, and during this period consume only the bare necessities for life in two meals, one in the evening and one at dawn.

The devout Moslem has a basic obligation to perform good deeds, and this is particularly true during Ramadan. A tithe is paid to the old, the widowed, and generally to anyone in need. During this time food markets appear in the streets, selling all kinds of raw and cooked foodstuffs as well as cakes and drinks, and part of the income derived from sales is devoted to charitable causes. The drinks offered include *air bandung* (syrup with milk), *air nenas* (pineapple juice), *air selaseh* (water flavored with spices, including basil seeds), and *mata kucing* tea (an infusion of dried longan fruits), or *katira* (a drink prepared from condensed milk, syrup, rosewater, and basil seeds).

On the eve of the festival of Hari Raya (*Hari Raya a'id el fitr*) the whole house is decorated, sometimes new drapes are hung, and all members of the family share in the activities. Whatever dishes can be prepared in advance are cooked during the evening, and everything else is freshly prepared the following morning.

Very early in the morning, before the men leave for the mosque, the young people must express their respect for their elders and ask their parents for forgiveness for any offense they have caused them. Then the men make their way to the mosque and the women, who pray at home, go to the kitchen. When the men return from prayer, the whole family sits down to a substantial brunch. Children are given presents of money in green wrappings, because green is the color of Islam. Yellow is the royal color, and black the ceremonial one. For the rest of the day, there are visits from friends and family members, who are pampered at all times of day with every type of dish, cakes and delicacies. Non-Moslem friends are also invited to take part in the festivities.

The visits and hospitality used to continue for thirty days, but today the visits take place only on the second and third days of the festival, and after that perhaps at weekends. With all these reciprocal visits, some basic ground rules are necessary. To make sure that no visitor arrives to find the family are themselves on a visit, on the first day of Hari Raya, the young people visit relatives and friends, while the older people stay at home to welcome them. On the second day, the older people visit first their relatives and then their friends.

A thirty-day festival was appropriate for the lifestyle of the days when people still lived in *kampongs* (villages). There were no fences or enclosures, and the sense of community was much stronger than it is today. People went in and out of their neighbors' homes in a totally informal manner. Dishes were often shared and exchanged, to a point where the tables groaned under the weight of all the bowls, dishes, and plates. Traditional dishes included *ketupat*, *lontong*, *lepat* (sticky rice cooked with black-eyed beans and wrapped in coconut leaves), *sayur lodeh*, *serunding*, *rendang*, *opor ayam*, *sambal goreng*, and *sambal udang*. These dishes were accompanied by drinks such as tea, coffee, diluted syrups, and soda pop.

The month of fasting ends with a festival at which one can eat to one's heart's content with a clear conscience. Essential on these occasions are the woven *ketupat* boxes containing cooked rice.

A few days before the festival, the rising excitement can be felt in the streets. Housewives are busy shopping, not only for food but also for new drapes and fabrics to decorate the home.

The original inhabitants

Orang Asli

Many centuries had to pass, countless prejudices overcome, and racial discrimination broken down before the Malaysians, advancing ever further inland from the coasts of the present-day western Malaysia, recognized the original inhabitants, leading a nomadic life in the jungle, for what they were, namely, people who wanted to live their own lives in seclusion, undisturbed, according to their traditional laws. The forest-dwellers lived on what their surroundings provided. They ate fruits, leaves, and young shoots. They knew which leaves possessed healing powers, and they hunted animal prey with bow and arrow or with blowpipes.

Up to the present day they remain divided into two groups, each consisting of several sub-groups. The main groups consist of the originally fully nomadic Semang and the semi-nomadic Senoi. The continual destruction of their living space on the one hand, and the increasing efforts of the Malaysian government on the other, have affected the living conditions of the Orang Asli, so that many of them have now given up the nomadic life altogether and have become settled, though they live far from the big cities. They have become farmers and cattle-breeders on a modest scale. Many have given up their original animistic religions and converted to Islam.

For those Orang Asli who have clung to their old religion, their environment remains populated by spirits, heavenly beings who must be propitiated by sacrifices and rituals, particularly if any of the innumerable taboos which regulate their daily life have been broken. The list of proscribed behavior is a long one, and ranges from incest through the torture of animals to over-noisy celebration and boisterous children's games. The chief guardian of taboos is the god Karai, who lives somewhere in the heavens. He sends the storms, and when lightning strikes he meets his wife, who lives within the earth. This kindly female earth goddess plays a decisive role in most creation myths. The earth, flanked by the sun and moon, already existed but she populated it with plants and living beings.

Today, the Orang Asli live in small villages; they keep chickens and goats and grow manioc. They attribute their existence to the earth goddess. They still eat the leaves,

For *lemang*, you need a banana leaf, sticky rice, coconut milk, and a bamboo cane which is closed at one end by a natural knot in the wood.

First the bamboo cane is lined along its whole length with the banana leaf.

Then the softened sticky rice is used to stuff the cane and is moistened with salted coconut milk.

The bamboo canes are subjected to the heat of burning charcoal for about two hours. The rice, when cooked, is removed from the pipe along with the leaf and cut into pieces.

shoots, and fruits which flourish in their environment. These include the coconut palm, which has a multiplicity of uses: the coconut water serves as a drink, the dried shell as fuel and the flesh of the coconut as food, or it can be used to produce coconut milk for cooking.

Now and again, a free-range chicken will appear on the menu; it will be slaughtered by slitting its throat and it is scalded with boiling water before it is plucked. The remaining small feathers will then be burnt off over an open fire. The rest of the preparation is very simple; the chicken is rubbed with some salt and grilled or stewed in coconut milk.

Small animals such as birds, bats, wild boar, and even monkeys are hunted for their meat. Some Orang Asli still use blowpipes for this purpose. These consist of two bamboo canes joined together, which are slid into a protective hollow bamboo pipe, some 6 ft 8 in (2 m) long to prevent warping. A cylindrical wooden mouthpiece is attached to contain the thin arrow, whose point has been dipped in the juice of *ipoh* leaves (*Antiaris toxicaria*). A hand-carved stopper made of root fiber is attached at the other end as a holder. The hunter exercises pressure by blowing through the mouthpiece, and this propels the arrow in a straight line out of the pipe and toward the hunted game. Once hit, the animal dies within a few minutes.

Right, above: Demonstration of a blowpipe
Right, below: A slaughtered chicken is scalded with boiling water to make plucking easier.

Basic presentday foods

Lemang: To cook sticky rice in bamboo, bamboo canes of the required thickness are cut into pieces 16 in (40 cm) long, in such a way that the growth knots of the bamboo form a natural seal. The cane is lined with young banana leaves and stuffed four-fifths full with softened sticky rice, and then salted coconut milk is poured onto the rice. Crushed banana leaves are used as a stopper at the other end. The bamboo canes are now placed over burning charcoal and left for a good two hours; they must be turned from time to time to ensure even cooking of the contents. As soon as cooking is completed, the rice is pulled out of the bamboo cane in a roll, and sliced up with a sharp knife.

Kueh lepat ubi: For this steamed manioc cake, grated tapioca flour is mixed with palm sugar, wrapped in a banana leaf, and steamed.

Quiver, arrows, and mouthpiece of a blowpipe

The smaller monkeys are also sought-after as game.

Many of the Orang Asli have now become settled in one place.

Preparing a chicken for cooking is quite a labor-intensive job.

Ayam masak merah
Chicken in red sauce
Serves 4-6

1 chicken, about 2 lb10 oz (1.2 kg), oven ready cut into serving pieces
½ cup (125 ml) oil
2 Tbs paste of freshly ground chili peppers (chili powder mixed with water can be substituted)
1 Tbs curry powder for chicken, mixed to paste with water
1 cinnamon stick, 1½ in (4 cm) long
3 cardamon seeds
3 whole cloves
3 star anise
2–3 bayleaves
1 15 oz (425 g) can tomato paste
1 cup (250 ml) water
1 Tbs sugar
salt

Spice paste
15 garlic cloves, peeled and quartered
1 piece root ginger, 2 in (5 cm) thick
3 onions, peeled and chopped

Grind the garlic, onions, and ginger in the mortar. Heat the oil in a pan and fry the spice paste until the flavors have developed. Add the chili paste, whole spices, soy, sauce, water, tamarind slices, and sugar. Stir well and bring to the boil. Add the chicken pieces and simmer until they are done. Add the tomatoes and chili peppers, and season to taste with salt.

Ayam gulai kecap
Chicken in soy sauce
Serves 4-6

1 chicken, about 2 lb10 oz (1.2 kg), oven ready cut into serving pieces
½ cup (125 ml) oil
2 Tbs paste of freshly ground chili peppers
1 cinnamon stick, 1½ in (4 cm) long
3 cardamon seeds
3 whole cloves
3 star anise
(250 ml) dark soy sauce
3 cups (750 ml) water
2 slices dried tamarind pulp
½ Tbs sugar
2 tomatoes, quartered
2 green chili peppers, halved lengthwise
2 red chili peppers, halved lengthwise
salt to taste

Spice paste
5 garlic cloves, peeled and quartered
2 onions, peeled and chopped
1 slice ginger root, 1 in (2 cm) thick

Grind the garlic, onions, and ginger in the mortar. Heat the oil in a pan and fry the spice paste until the flavors have developed. Add the chili paste, whole spices, soy sauce, water, tamarind slices, and sugar. Stir well and bring to the boil. Add the chicken pieces and simmer until they are done. Add the tomatoes and chili peppers and season to taste with salt.

Ayam sambal asam
Fried chicken with spices and tamarind
Serves 4-6

1 chicken, about 2 lb10 oz (1.2 kg), oven ready cut into serving pieces
5 Tbs oil
Juice from 2 Tsp tamarind pulp and 4 Tbs water
2 Tsp sugar
salt

Spice paste
15 dried chili peppers, soaked, seeds discarded
1 onion, peeled and chopped
1 stem lemongrass, lower 2 in (5 cm) sliced into pieces
2 slices ginger root, about ½ in (1 cm) thick

Grind the chili peppers, onion, lemongrass, and ginger in the mortar. Heat the oil in a deep skillet and fry the spice paste until the flavors have developed. Add tamarind juice, sugar, and salt. Braise until the mixture is almost dry. Add the chicken pieces, mix with the spices, and cook, uncovered, over a moderate heat until the chicken is tender, stirring occasionally.

Kari ayam – Chicken curry

Ayam masak merah – Chicken in red sauce

Ayam percik – Spicy broiled chicken

Kari ayam
Chicken curry
Serves 4-6

1 chicken, about 2 lb10 oz (1.2 kg), oven ready cut into serving pieces
⅛ l oil
6 Tbs curry powder for chicken
1 piece cinnamon stick, 1½ in (4 cm) long
3 cardamon seeds
2 whole cloves
1 star anise
2 Tbs grated coconut, toasted
1 coconut, grated (2 Tbs reserved)
1 cup (250 ml) water, combined with the grated coconut and squeezed, to make thick coconut milk
3 cups (750 ml) water, combined with the grated coconut and squeezed, to make thin coconut milk
4 potatoes, peeled and halved
2 tomatoes, halved

Spice paste
10 shallots, peeled and chopped
6 garlic cloves, peeled and quartered
1 piece ginger root, 1¼ in (3 cm) long

Grind the shallots, garlic, and ginger to a paste in a mortar.
Heat the oil in a deep skillet and fry the spice paste in it until the flavors have developed. Add the curry powder and all the spices, and fry gently. Add the chicken pieces and mix with the spices. Sprinkle the toasted coconut on top and stir in well. Deglaze with the thin coconut milk, season with salt, and add the potatoes. Bring to the boil, then reduce the heat and simmer over a moderate heat. When the chicken and potatoes are nearly done, pour the thick coconut milk over them, bring back to the boil, add the tomatoes, and serve.

Ayam percik
Spicy broiled chicken
Serves 4-6

1 chicken, about 3 lb 5 oz(1.5 kg), oven ready cut into serving pieces (or about the same weight of chicken drumsticks)
coarsely ground black pepper
salt
1 Tbs ground coriander
2 Tsp ground cumin
1 coconut, grated
2½ cups (600 ml) water,combined with the grated coconut and squeezed, to make thin coconut milk
1 Tsp salt
4 Tbs oil

Spice paste
18 shallots, peeled and minced
2 stems lemongrass, the lower 2 in(5 cm) sliced into pieces
1 piece of galangal root the size of a walnut, lightly crushed
4 candlenuts

Sprinkle the chicken pieces liberally with coarsely ground black pepper and with salt and leave for at least 30 minutes.
Grind shallots, lemongrass, galangal root, and candlenuts to a paste in the mortar. Add the ground cumin and coriander and stir in. Heat the oil in a deep skillet and fry the spice paste in it until the flavors have developed. Deglaze with coconut milk and season with salt. Simmer for about 10 minutes over a low heat. As soon as the sauce thickens and the oil begins to rise to the surface, remove the pan from the heat. Rub the chicken pieces dry with a cloth, cover with the sauce, place on a sheet of foil, and broil them. During cooking, brush the chicken pieces repeatedly with sauce.

Ayam masak putih
Chicken in white sauce
Serves 4-6

1 chicken, about 2 lb10 oz (1.2 kg), oven ready cut into serving pieces
salt
½ coconut, grated (about 2 cups (250 g)), brown skin discarded
1 cup (250 ml) water, combined with the grated coconut and squeezed, to make thick coconut milk
2 cups (500 ml) water, combined with the grated coconut and squeezed, to make thin coconut milk
4 Tbs oil
2 tomatoes, quartered
salt

Spice paste
1½ Tsp black peppercorns
1½ Tsp white peppercorns
6 shallots, peeled and chopped
1 piece root ginger, 1 in (2.5 cm) thick
1 piece galangal root, 1 in (2.5 cm) thick

Rub some salt into the chicken pieces and leave for at least 30 minutes.
Meanwhile, grind the black and white peppercorns in a mortar, then grind to a fine paste with the shallots, ginger, and galangal root.
Wipe the chicken pieces dry with a cloth.
Heat the oil in a deep skillet and sauté the spice paste in it until the flavors have developed. Season with salt and cook the chicken pieces all over in the pan for three minutes, while covering with the spices. Deglaze with the thin coconut milk. Bring to the boil, reduce the heat, add the tomatoes, and simmer over a low heat until the chicken pieces are almost cooked. Pour the thick coconut milk over the chicken and bring back to the boil before serving.

Living in the long-house

Sarawak

Eastern Malaysia consists of the states of Sarawak and Sabah on the island formerly known as Borneo. Between these two states lies the Sultanate of Brunei. The rest of the island, known as Kalimantan, belongs to Indonesia.

The largest group of original inhabitants of Sarawak are the Iban (Sea Dayaks), who make up about a third of the total population; the Bidayuh (Land Dayaks) represent slightly over 8 percent, the Melanau 5.8 percent and the Orang Ulu 5.5 percent of the population. The non-indigenous population consists of about 20 percent Malaysians and some 30 percent Chinese.

The Iban or Sea Dayak were farmers and lived in wooden long houses which were covered with leaves. They were — and in some cases still are — built on very tall stilts, to prevent enemies ramming their spears up through the floors. A staircase made from tree-trunks leads to an external veranda (*tanju*), which, like the second veranda inside the house (*ruai*) is reserved for socializing. Between these lies a guest veranda (*pantar*). The inner communal veranda leads to the transit veranda (*tempuan*), which opens onto the individual living space (*bilek*) of each family. Up to 60 families may inhabit one long-house.

The Iban women have a reputation as skilled weavers. They also work in the fields and look after the household. Their chores include cooking and making fermented drink made from sticky rice (*tuak*) which packs quite a punch.

The Bidayuh, or Land Dayaks build their long-houses against the sides of steep hills for protection against their enemies. They use bamboo as a building material, as well as for cooking vessels. Like the Iban today, they still make rice wine and toddy, fermented palm sugar juice. Rice is treated with great respect as it is the staple. The threshed rice is stored in granaries, which are built next to the long-houses and are very effective in protecting the crop from attacks by rodents.

The Melanau used to live near the sea, in houses built some 40 ft (12 m) above ground level, since attacks by pirates were not infrequent. Today, they mainly inhabit the central coastal region. Their staple food is sago rather than rice. The Melanau earn their livelihood from agriculture or fishing, depending on the season. One of their specialities is slices of raw fish, which are prepared with *asam paya*, a sour tropical fruit.

The Orang Ulu, who settled further up the coast, originate from Central Borneo and were famous for their metalworking skills. Their long-houses were built to last, and allowed them enough time to occupy themselves intensively with cultivating the land and developing a clever system for irrigating the rice fields. They have a marked artistic bent and create extremely beautiful beadwork. The women wear closely fitting beaded caps, which are a mark of their social status. The larger the beads and the more colorful the designs, the higher will be the rank or social class of the wearer.

Pottery

The Iban and Kelabit, who belong to the Orang Ulu group, produce clay pots for household use. These pots are hand-made, using the local black or brown clay. A sufficient quantity of clay is rolled into a thick cylinder, and a central hole carefully made in it from above with a thick wooden stick. Once the opening has been made, the pot is given further shape, first by hand and then by beating with a flat piece of wood. This procedure gets rid of any pockets of air still remaining in the clay, but also gives additional smoothness and uniform thickness to the walls of the pot. A pattern is carved into the other end of the wooden tool, and this is imprinted on the soft clay when the stick is used to beat the pot.

The pots are fired for about an hour over a wood fire, with the opening downward. Then they are subjected to a sort of tempering process. The bark of a particular tree is pounded in water until a red color is produced. The pots are placed in this solution in order to stop them from cracking. Alternatively, the outer surface may be treated with resin to provide additional protection against breakages. This pottery is part of the standard equipment of the kitchens (*dapor*) of a long-house. The long-houses vary slightly in design, but each family has its own kitchen, which is part of its private living space (*bilek*). The kitchen opens into the living and sleeping area and the floor is covered with mats. Cooking is performed over a wood fire. While preparing or cooking the food, the women usually sit or squat on the floor. Bowls and plates are lined with leaves, which are also used to wrap the food before or after cooking.

Very large pots are also used as containers for rice, for pickled fish or wild boar, or even for liquids such as rice wine.

The original inhabitants of Eastern Malaysia no longer live in long-houses but in idyllic settlements.

Tribal dances of the Iban have become popular in performance at tourist centers.

Making a typical pot begins with a clay cylinder.

A deep depression is formed in the cylinder with a wooden stick.

This depression is then worked further by hand.

With the opening downward, the pots are fired for about an hour.

It is predominantly the women who ensure that the traditional crafts are preserved.

Before the fish is wrapped in the banana leaves it is marinated for 30 minutes in the spice mixture.

Luang senunuh
Mackerel fried in banana leaves
(Orang Ulu)

4 small mackerel or Spanish mackerel, scales removed
4 young banana leaves, cut to fit the fish
turmeric leaves, cut into thin strips

Spice paste
ginger root
Garlic cloves, peeled and quartered
shallots, peeled and chopped

Grind the root ginger, garlic, and shallots, as many as you like, to a smooth paste in a mortar.

Slit the fish in the belly and gut them (remove the gall-bladder whole and discard it). Make two or three deep cuts on each side, coat with the spice paste, and leave for 30 minutes.

Place each fish on a piece of banana leaf, sprinkle with top some strips of turmeric leaf, and roll up the leaf. Secure the package with wooden skewers and grill over an open fire. If using this recipe at home on a barbecue, wrap the fish in other edible leaves if banana leaves are not available, and use a metal grilling rack.

The recipes on the next few pages are for regional dishes, and are reproduced as cooked by the native inhabitants. We have dispensed with specific quantities for the sake of authenticity. None of the women who kindly allowed us to peep into their cooking pots measured ingredients with scales or measuring cups.

The fish packages gains a special flavor from the finely sliced turmeric leaves.

The fish are cooked well wrapped in banana leaves, so they are not directly exposed to heat.

The ingredients: *daun singkeh*, manioc leaves, lemongrass, chicken, shallots, garlic, ginger, turmeric leaves, and coconut shoots.

Marinate the chicken pieces for 30 minutes in salt, turmeric leaves, and lemongrass.

Manok pansoh
Chicken cooked in bamboo
(Iban)

1 small, oven-ready chicken
salt
turmeric leaves, thinly sliced
lemongrass, the lower part of the stem finely sliced
manioc leaves
garlic cloves
shallots
ginger root
tepus (coconut palm shoots)
daun singkeh

Bone the chicken and cut the meat in bite-size pieces. Marinate the chicken pieces for at least 30 minutes with salt, turmeric leaves, and sliced lemongrass. Meanwhile, coarsely chop the manioc leaves, mix with salt, and pound.

To make this dish, you will need a piece of bamboo as thick as your arm, and cut so that the knot at one end forms a natural stopper. This bamboo cane is now stuffed up to about 4 in (10 cm) from the rim with layers of pounded manioc leaves, strips of turmeric leaves, marinated chicken pieces, chopped garlic cloves, chopped shallots, slices of ginger, and strips of chopped *tepus* (coconut shoots). The remaining space is then stuffed with *daun singkeh*, the edible leaves of a plant growing in the jungle. The bamboo cane is then cooked over an open fire. This is a slow and careful process which can take from 30 to 60 minutes. When the dish is cooked, the contents of the bamboo cane are shaken out onto a banana leaf.

Stuff the bamboo cane with the layered ingredients and finish with *daun singkeh*.

The contents of the bamboo cane are cooked slowly and carefully over an open fire.

Within 30–60 minutes the food is cooked and the dish can be served on a banana leaf.

Sabah

This region, which covers an area about twice the size of Connecticut, is only very sparsely populated; according to statistics, there are no more than six people per square mile. The original inhabitants of Sabah (formerly North Borneo, eastern Malaysia) are divided into the Kadazan (previously known as the Dusun), the Murut and the Bajau, as well as a few more very small tribes.

The rice-growing Dusun, the most advanced of the communities, settled chiefly in the western plains. The Moslem Bajau and several of the smaller tribes considered piracy to be the most lucrative source of income, and at one time terrorized sailing ships in the Peninsular waters. In keeping with their profession, they spread out along the coastal strips. Once the days of piracy were over, they took to fishing, rice cultivation, and livestock rearing. The Murut, who inhabited the interior of the country, lived as farmers and hunters. Each tribe has its own language, customs, and beliefs; however, tribal culture appears to be in decline.

The Kadazan represent the largest native group in Sabah.
Background: controlling the temperature, using lung power and a bamboo pipe.

The trimming of vegetables and other preparations for the meal are preformed while seated on the floor.

The art of cleaning the dishes in as little water as possible, but just as much as is necessary, is one which is learned the hard way when each drop of water has to be carried to the kitchen from afar.

Sago Delight
Fried sago worms
(*Kadazan*)

fresh live sago worms
oil
root ginger
shallots, peeled and minced
salt

The sago worms must first be thoroughly cleaned and carefully drained.

Peel the ginger root and shred it very finely. Heat the oil in a wok and sauté the shredded ginger-root together with the minced shallot until both release their aromas and the shallots are transparent. Season to taste with salt.

Tip the live sago worms into the hot oil and stir-fry for 5 minutes, or until soft. Serve at once. The heads of the worms, which do not soften even when cooked, should be pulled off and discarded before eating.

Anyone who finds this dish distasteful and suddenly discovers to their amazement that he or she has lost their appetite should perhaps think back to that shrimp cocktail consumed on New Year's Eve, or to the one dozen fresh (live!) oysters consumed on last year's vacation in Europe. Moreover, it is entirely conceivable that a jungle-dwelling Malay would recoil in horror if you offered him or her, say, a greasy cheeseburger or a chicken-fried steak with mashed potatoes.

Not exactly what one would call a still life! A lively, squirming mass of unwashed sago worms surrounds the shallots.

It is advisable to clean the sago worms very thoroughly, a process not made any easier by their distinctive anatomy.

Stir-fried sago worms with ginger, shallots, and just a pinch of salt.

Ingredients for the salad of palm sprouts and dried
shrimps in lime juice

Nomsom tuhau

Salad of palm shoots and dried shrimps
(Kadazan)

dried shrimp
fresh palm shoots
lime juice

Soak the dried shrimps in water to cover. In the meantime, cut off the fleshy tips of the palm shoots and
peel the stalks like asparagus. Slightly flatten the palm
sprouts with the back of a knife, then slice thinly and
place in a bowl. Drain the shrimps and add to the bowl
with the palm shoots. Drizzle with some lime juice and
knead well with your hand.

Cut off the fleshy tips of the palm shoots, then peel
the stalks like asparagus

First beat the palm shoots several times gently with
the back of a knife, then slice very thinly

Mix the finely sliced palm shoots with the soaked
shrimps and the lime juice

Many green plants found growing in the pristine jungle can be teamed with shallots and shrimp to make appetizing vegetable dishes.

The finely chopped, stir-fried vegetable has reduced dramatically in volume.

Lombiding sinayan kinoring giban
Stir-fried leafy vegetables
(Kadazan)

freshly sliced leaf vegetables
dried shrimp
oil
shallots, peeled and
sliced into rings

The "jungle vegetable" normally used in this dish flourishes along the riverbanks. Since leaf vegetables shrink considerably in volume when cooked, generous portions should be allowed per person.
Soak the dried shrimp in water. In the meantime, strip the leaves of the vegetable from the stalks and cut the stalks into small pieces.
Thoroughly drain the soaked shrimp.
Heat the oil in a wok. Add the shallots, cut into rings, add the shrimps, and sauté briefly. Next, add the stalks to the wok, followed shortly thereafter by the leaves, stirring constantly. Serve as a vegetable side-dish.

These traditional dishes are usually served in simple wooden or clay bowls which are lined with a fresh banana leaf. This not only looks attractive, but also serves to keep the bowls cleaner, so that less water is needed for cleaning them afterward. The banana leaf serves, so to speak, as the kitchen paper of the jungle, which ironically is being deforested for the cellulose requirements of the industrialized nations. The dishes were once exclusively hand-made, and in some cases, the old crafts have been revived and the tribes are once more making their own tableware. Some tribes have long been famous for their crafts.

Pakis
Stir-fried fiddleheads
(Kadazan)

freshly sliced fiddlehead fern
dried shrimp
oil
shallots, peeled and
sliced into rings

Like the leafy vegetable in the recipe opposite, there is a local edible fiddlehead fern which also grows along riverbanks.
Soak the dried shrimp in water. Meanwhile, wash the fern, strip the leaves from the stems and chop the fiddleheads into small pieces.
Thoroughly drain the soaked shrimps.
Heat a little oil in a wok; sweat the shallot rings until transparent and sauté the shrimp. Add the finely chopped fiddleheads and stir-fry them, followed by the more tender leaves, which should also be stir-fried briefly. Take care not to overcook the ferns. They are served as a vegetable side-dish.

Dried shrimp keep very well even in hot weather, which makes them an ideal ingredient in a hot climate. Moreover, they are strongly flavored enough to serve as a seasoning rather than a main ingredient in these vegetable dishes. This is proved by the fact that not even salt or chilies are added to them. Dried shrimp is a highly versatile seasoning ingredient for both hot and cold dishes. Even when used in cold dishes, they will still require pre-soaking in hot water.

Shallots and dried shrimps also go well with the fern.

Stir-fried for just a few minutes in a little oil, the vegetable dish is ready.

The pancake is made exclusively from grated coconut, sago flour, and water.

First the shredded coconut is roasted without any additional oil, until it is quite dry.

Pinompoh
Sago-flour pancake
(Kadazan)

¼ coconut, grated, brown skin discarded
Sago flour (about the same amount as the coconut)
water

Toast the grated coconut in a dry wok until completely dry. Add the sago flour, mix with the toasted coconut, and continue to cook for a few minutes. Just before the mixture starts to color, gradually stir in just enough water to bind the mixture. Mix the ingredients very carefully, press the mixture flat with a broad-bladed knife, and cook, covered, over moderate heat for about 10 minutes, or until the pancake is set and firm.
This pancake, which is nourishing and filling, is served for breakfast or as a snack with a cup of coffee.

These recipes—which are, of course, only a small sampling of the regional cooking of several East Malaysian tribes, some of whom still live in the traditional way—clearly demonstrate that even today, these native peoples could be self-sufficient, living deep in the jungle. Some of the tribes are familiar with the plants in their environment, and know which ones are edible, which ones are not, and which are of medicinal use, although more and more of this knowledge is dying with the village elders. Since there are no written records from the past, no-one can tell how much valuable information has already been lost.

Sago palm

The sago palm (*Metroxylon sagu*) grows wild in marshy coastal areas, but it is also cultivated. Since it is a tropical plant, it needs constant, high temperatures, high atmospheric humidity, and plenty of sunlight. The starch which makes the sago palm such a useful plant is stored in the trunk of the tree. Just before the palm begins to flower, which it does only once at the end of its 15-year life cycle, the stem becomes engorged with starchy matter. The tree is felled, and the stem is either sold to a processing company, or the (mostly native) owners keep the tree and process the starch themselves. To do this, the stem is split open and the starchy white part, which can be up to 32 in (80 cm) thick, is removed. The extracted starch is processed into fine sago flour, which in some cases is made into sago pearls. For this, the raw sago is pressed through sieves of a particular mesh, and the tiny drops are allowed to fall onto hot, shaking plates with the result that the drying starch is rolled into round grains.
Before the introduction of modern processing methods, the white part was shredded by hand and made into a fine paste, which was then soaked in wooden vats. The starch which settled on the bottom of the vat was then dried and ground. If sago palms are felled and left to lie on the ground for some time, certain beetles lay their eggs in them. These eggs hatch into larvae which are very protein-rich and are highly esteemed as food by the natives.

The dry, shredded coconut is mixed with about the same quantity of sago flour.

Once both ingredients are well mixed, the water is added drop by drop and stirred into the batter, and the wok is covered.

Indonesia

Asam digunung garam dilaut bertemu dalam belanga.

Even the tamarind from the mountains and the salt from the sea are able to meet in the pot.

Right: Paddy field on Bali

Preceding pages: Roadside stop — bananas from the plantations, before they are transported to local markets

Indonesia consists of over 13,000 islands, barely half of which are inhabited. Java, Sumatra, Kalimantan, part of the former Borneo, Sulawesi, and the western part of New Guinea (Irian Jaya) are the larger islands whose culture predominates. The rest of the archipelago is split up into chains of smaller and smaller islands. The group of islands known as Indonesia extends north and south of the equator, along a volcanic belt to which the Indonesian soil owes its high fertility. This, together with the warm, humid climate and high rainfall, provides the ideal conditions for the cultivation of every type of fruit and vegetable, including rice. In the cooler climate of the hill country, tea, coffee, and spice plants flourish.

The valuable spices native to Indonesia were a magnet for merchant seamen and settlers, including the Portuguese, Dutch, Arabs, Indians, and Chinese, all of whom have influenced the culture, religion, and eating habits of the islanders. Thus, the Indonesia of today is a country of great contrasts. The population of Java and Sumatra is predominantly Moslem. In northern Sumatra, where the Batak live, Christianity is the dominant religion, and the inhabitants of Bali practice a form of Hinduism in which Hindu cosmology is intermingled with the elements of a native religion and mythology, a sort of pantheism in which the world is seen to be filled with a host of spirits and demons.

In Indonesia, rice is eaten three times a day with hot and spicy dishes whose preparation is very time-consuming, but is seldom a problem in the traditional multi-generational household. The women usually cook enough food to be able to welcome unexpected guests in the appropriate fashion, and here as elsewhere, a hearty appetite is taken as a compliment to the cooking. Family members and guests sit cross-legged on the mat-covered floor, and an assortment of poultry, meat, fish, and vegetable dishes is served with soup, rice, and *sambals*. As in Malaysia, people eat with the fingers of their right hand. Water, fruit juices, sweetened tea without milk, or strong black coffee are the usual drinks. Rice wine may be offered, if the family's religion permits.

The tip of the riceberg

Nasi tumpeng

Whenever there is something to celebrate, be it a private, business, or public occasion such as the birth of a child, the founding of a company, or a good harvest, a festive *nasi tumpeng* (rice cone) is the natural accompaniment. The centerpiece of the dish is a cone of rice which has been boiled or steamed in coconut milk, and colored yellow with turmeric. Small cone-shaped woven bamboo baskets can be bought for steaming the rice, and these simplify the molding process. In these tropical latitudes, however, housewives also make use of banana leaves, which they twist into cones like ice-cream cones and into which the cooked rice is tightly packed. A shallow bowl is lined with a banana leaf, the rice cone is placed in the center, and accompaniments appropriate to the occasion in question, which conform to a strict set of rules, are arranged around the cone. These side-dishes must represent the forms of life in the various elements. These are: walking on the earth (beef), flying in the air (fowl), swimming in the water (fish), rooted in the earth (vegetables). At a funeral banquet, two *tumpeng* cones placed side by side symbolize the completion of the life cycle.

The most important person at the table, perhaps the guest of honor, cuts off the tip of the cone and serves it respectfully to an older, revered individual. In the meantime, the remaining guests help themselves to the following types of dish:

- *telur dadar:* fried omelet cut into strips (1),
- *sambal goreng kentang:* spicy fried diced potato (2),
- *ayam goreng:* roast chicken (3, 6),
- *pergedel goreng:* potato cakes (4),
- *sambal goreng tempe:* crisp-fried marinated strips of *tempeh* (fermented beancurd) (5),
- *timun acar:* pickled cucumbers or
- *krupuk udang:* shrimp crackers.

Gudeg

Gudeg, rice with green jackfruit cooked in a sweet sauce and served with other dishes, is a dish from central Java. The town of Yogyakarta has the reputation of serving the best *gude*g, not only in its restaurants, but also at its road-side stands. Some jackfruit, a portion of chicken, an egg, half a piece of tofu and a *sambal* with crispy water-buffalo crackling are served with rice as a complete meal on a plate. For a take-out, the meal is packed into a small woven basket lined with a banana leaf. Those trying *gudeg* for the first time may be surprised by its sweetness.

To prepare *gudeg,* remove the jackfruit's thick peel and cut the flesh into cubes. Boil the cubes in salted water for about one hour. Drain and set aside to cool. Meanwhile, hardboil and peel the eggs.

Prepare a sauce by grinding shallots, garlic cloves, candlenuts (*kemiri*), coriander, galangal root (*laos*) and bayleaf to a paste in a mortar. Then mix this paste with palm sugar and co-conut milk. Simmer the cubed jackfruit and strips of meat from the boned chicken in this sauce over a low heat. After the sauce has simmered for 45–60 minutes, it will be of the right consistency, and the jackfruit and chicken will be done. Add the peeled hardboiled eggs to the sauce and simmer for five minutes or until the eggs are heated through. One of the side-dishes served with *gudeg* is *tahu goreng bacem* which consists of tofu (called *tahu* in Indonesian) cooked with spices, then fried. To make it, cut pieces of tofu in half on the diagonal, then cook in a mixture of minced shallots, garlic, coriander, palm sugar, galangal root, bayleaf, and water, un-til nearly all of the liquid has evaporated. Then fry the tofu.

For *sambal goreng krecek*, crunchy water-buffalo crackling with sambal, the water-buffalo rind is first deep-fried until crisp, before being served with a cooked condiment made from diced shal-lots, garlic, chili peppers, chopped kaffir lime leaves, and a little coconut milk.

At 25 days old, the rice shoots are lifted from the seed bed and transplanted.

After a ceremony is performed to placate the goddess and the field is prepared, planting can begin.

After three months of carefully monitored growth, the rice should be fully ripe and the crop satisfactory.

The flooded fields are plowed up by water-buffalo, since the goddess cannot do everything herself.

The stalks are cut by hand using a special rice sickle.

The ashes of the threshed straw later find their way back onto the fields as fertilizer.

The freshly harvested rice (paddy) must dry in the sun for one to three days before being husked.

Rice goddess

Rice is synonymous with life and is sacred; for this reason, the cultivation of the cereal from shoots to ripened grain is firmly entrenched in the religious and social life of the farming community.

Balinese rice farmers have organized themselves into cooperatives or *subaks* who share an irrigation system. Not only is the maintenance of dykes and canals settled in the *subaks*, but the best days for planting, harvesting, sacrificing, and praying are also determined. Each *subak* has a small temple in the paddy-fields in which religious ceremonies are held. The temple must not be neglected, since it is the abode of the Rice Goddess when she dwells on Earth; the rest of the time she is embodied in the rice grain. Before the first irrigation of the fields, some *subaks* hold solemn processions to the famous Pura Ulun Danu temple on the banks of Lake Bratan, in order to pray for a never-failing supply of water.

As the feminine aspect of rice, Dewi Sri is the most important deity of the Balinese rice-growers. Since the coexistence of a feminine and masculine aspect is crucial for balance in all things, the farmers revere Dewi Nini as the masculine complement to Dewi Sri. Rice-straw figures of this god are prepared and distributed all around at harvest-time.

An auspicious day is chosen for the start of the new rice cycle and for plowing up the dry fields and scattering them with stubble from the old rice plants. Once this day is determined, a sacrifice is first performed, prayers are said, and the soil is sprinkled with holy water. Nor must the evil spirits be forgotten. In order to placate them, rice is strewn on the ground and moistened with palm wine. Only then can the work begin. As soon as the soil is prepared, the fields are flooded and plowed up by water-buffalo. Part of the irrigated area serves as a seed bed; a further sacrifice is offered and the seeds, which have been soaked and germinated, are entrusted to the earth.

After about 25 days, the rice shoots can be transplanted. Once the most favorable day has been established, the fields are manured and flooded once again. A group of workers pull the seedlings from the seed bed, lay them in bundles in bamboo bowls, and distribute them in the fields. Before the planting of the seedlings begins, a ceremonial planting must take place: once the offerings have been made and the prayers

White rice: this description applies only to the milled grain from which the outer bran layer has been removed.

Glutinous rice: The high starch content of this type of rice means that the cooked grains stick together making it ideal for eating with chopsticks.

Red rice: The red seed coat of this variety remains intact, since the grains are not milled.

Nasi goreng, fried rice, is the great favorite of Indonesian cooking, which comes in many variations.

intoned, nine of the seedlings are placed in the earth next to the offerings, one in the center and eight at the points of the compass. Only after all this is the paddy-field ready for planting.

In the first month of growth, small offerings are made; in the second, the goddess is honored out in the fields with a larger offering of rice, flowers, holy water, and rice wine. The rice begins to ripen.

At the end of the third month, harvesting begins. The fields are now dry, since irrigation is suspended two weeks before the harvest. Just before harvesting, the farmers once more pay homage to Dewi Sri in the fields, with offerings of woven coconut-palm leaves.

The loveliest celebration in the fields is a harvest thanksgiving festival. For days in advance, the women prepare offerings of rice cakes, fruit, and flowers, which they then bring in solemn processions to the temple.

Nasi goreng simply means fried rice. This dish, which is probably Chinese in origin, is served at both breakfast and lunch; every family has its own recipe. Perhaps the best-known variation is served with an omelet cut into thin strips.

Nasi goreng
Fried rice

8 oz (225 g) rice
2 eggs
1 onion, minced
1 garlic clove, crushed
2–3 fresh red chili peppers, sliced into rings
1 Tsp shrimp paste (*trassi*), softened
4 Tbsp oil
2 chicken breasts, thinly sliced
8 oz (250 g) peeled shrimp
½ Tsp chili pepper
¼ Tsp turmeric
1 Tbsp light soy sauce
2 Tsp tomato paste
salt to taste

Garnish

omelet sliced into strips
fried onion rings
cucumber and tomato slices
Shrimp crackers (*krupuk*)

Preparation: Cook the rice and leave it to cool. Lightly beat the eggs with salt. Make an omelet and leave to cool, then roll it up and slice it into narrow strips. Heat the oil and add the onion, garlic, shrimp paste, and chili peppers. When the ingredients give off their aroma, add the boned chicken breasts and shrimp, and sauté for 2 minutes. Stir in the chili powder and turmeric. Add the soy sauce, tomato paste, and salt, and stir. Tip in the cooked rice and stir-fry until hot. Serve, garnished with the omelet strips, fried onion rings, shrimp crackers, sliced cucumber, and tomato.

Nasi Padang

"Boiled rice, Padang-style" is a rather dull description of the cooking of the Minangkabau people in West Sumatra and their capital, Padang. In fact, their cuisine enjoys such a high reputation that a *rumah makan Padang* (Padang eating house) is now to be found in most towns in Java and Sumatra. The food is simple, the selection lavish, with often more than thirty dishes to choose from — not from a printed menu, but by having a look at the dishes which are brought to your table. Rice is always served as an accompaniment. If you are expecting a hot meal, however, you are in for a disappointment. All food is served at room temperature, as is often the case in the tropics. In Padang restaurants in Singapore, where Public Health Department regulations are stringent, the whole panoply of dishes can only be admired from behind glass and the waiter only brings to your table the food you have ordered.

• The basic flavoring is usually provided by a spice paste made from shallots, garlic, and turmeric, to which various seasonings are added. When cooking with coconut milk, thin coconut milk is added first, then the dish is rounded out with the thick milk.

Ayam gulai — Chicken curry in coconut sauce: Cook toasted, grated coconut with spice paste, coriander, cumin, chili powder, candlenuts, and ginger in thin coconut milk. Add lemongrass, cloves, and a cinnamon stick; cook the chicken in this sauce. Add thick coconut milk.

Ayam goreng pop — White fried chicken: Marinate chicken pieces in coconut water, garlic, lime juice, and vinegar for two hours, then shallow-fry at a low temperature. Skin before serving.

Cumi-cumi sambal — Squid with stink-beans: Cook in a sauce made of coconut milk, chili powder, turmeric, garlic, shallots, and stink-beans, add cooked squid pieces, and simmer.

Cumi-cumi gulai — Squid in coconut sauce: Cook the squid in water with chilies, turmeric leaf, pounded shallots, and turmeric root. Add coconut milk and basil, and reduce.

Gulai kikil — Beef curry in coconut sauce: Cook and slice brisket. Roast spice paste, pounded chilies, candlenuts, coriander, pepper, lemongrass, galangal, and salam leaf. Pour in coconut milk and add the cooked beef.

Gulai limpa — Ox liver curry: Roast spice paste and pounded chilies, coriander seeds, pepper, and candlenuts with lemongrass and galangal. Add coconut milk and cook the liver in this sauce.

Paru goreng — Fried beef lung: Cut cooked lung into slices, dry-marinate in salt, turmeric, and ground coriander seeds, and fry.

Gulai hati sapi — Ox-heart in curry sauce: Boil spice paste, pounded chilies, coriander seeds, pepper, and candlenuts in coconut milk. Slice the heart and cook it in the sauce.

Sambal kentang dengan tempe – Deep-fried potato chips and *tempeh* pieces: After deep-frying, coat in caramelized cane sugar mixed with chili powder.

Tumis bayem — Braised spinach with carrots: Roast shallots and garlic, add tomatoes and soy sauce. Add carrots, then spinach, and braise in the sauce.

Tumis daun singkong — Braised cassava greens: Roast shallots and garlic, add tomatoes and soy sauce, then braise the cassava greens in this sauce.

Lalapan – Raw vegetables with *sambal kemiri* dip: Roast peanuts, candlenuts, and chilies, and pound to a paste; stir in salt, sugar, water, and vinegar.

Ayam panggang — Grilled chicken: Roast the spice paste with pounded ginger, galangal, candlenuts, coriander, and cumin; add pepper, salt, kaffir lime leaves, and lemongrass. Add chicken quarters, pour in coconut milk. Brush the cooked chicken with oil and grill.

Sop ayam — Chicken soup: Simmer chicken pieces until half-done Roast pounded shallots, garlic, pepper, nutmeg, and whole cloves and add to boiling broth together with potatoes, carrots, and coriander stems. Garnish with boiled quail's eggs and roasted onions.

Sambal hati telur puyu – Quail's eggs with chicken hearts: Combine thick coconut milk with pounded chilies, turmeric root, and shallots. Cook until reduced, add fried chicken hearts, boiled quail's eggs, and stink-beans, and garnish with chili strips.

Kari kambing — Mutton curry: Roast shallots, garlic, cinnamon, cloves, and cardamom; grind to a paste with pounded chilies, coriander seeds, and cumin. Add coconut milk and cook the meat in this sauce.

Pindang baung — Fish in tamarind sauce: Marinate fish fillets in lime juice and salt for 10 minutes, then cook in a court-bouillon of water, shallots, garlic, chilies, turmeric root, galangal, lemongrass, and tamarind. Add tomatoes.

Ikan pecel lele — Catfish, rubbed with garlic and fried, served with chili and shrimp paste *sambals*.

Ikan asin pari — Fried dried fish: Before frying, soak the fish in hot water.

Ikan mas goreng — Fried carp: Marinate the fish in lime juice and salt for 15 minutes: rinse, pat dry, and fry. To make the *sambal*, stir lime juice, chili and shallot rings together with dark soy sauce.

Ikan mas dengan rebung — Carp with bamboo shoots in coconut sauce: Bring coconut milk to the boil with shallot rings, garlic, pounded chilies, turmeric root, ginger, galangal, lemongrass, salam leaf, and salt. Marinate the fish in lime juice and salt for 10 minutes, then cook in the sauce until the sauce thickens and turns creamy. Lastly, add the cooked bamboo shoots.

The other starchy accompaniment

Noodles

The Indonesians have the Chinese to thank not only for their fried rice, but for their noodles as well. The inhabitants of the Thousand Islands have, however, adapted Chinese noodle dishes to suit their own tastes, and in certain cases their dietary laws. Whatever motives might have lead to the omission, pork, which is preferred by the Chinese, is seldom found in Indonesian noodle dishes, chicken or beef being used instead. Shrimp, vegetables, and soy sauce seem to be equally popular additions every-where, whilst recipes with tomatoes and candlenuts can be looked on rather as pe-culiar to Indonesia. Noodles are served cooked in various ways. They can be either simmered in broth, used as a precooked soup garnish, or fried after parboiling.

Laksa ayam

Rice cellophane noodles with chicken in coconut sauce

1 lb (500 g) chicken pieces
8 oz (250 g) shrimp
½ coconut, grated (about 2 cups (250 g))
3 cups (750 ml) water, mixed with the grated coconut, squeezed, thin milk reserved
3 Tbsp oil
4 shallots, peeled and chopped
3 garlic cloves, peeled and quartered
4 candlenuts
½ Tsp ground coriander
salt
1 salam leaf
1 stem lemongrass, lightly crushed
7 oz (200 g) dried rice cellophane noodles (bihun), soaked in warm water and drained
2 hardboiled eggs, sliced

Garnish

1 Tbsp fried onion rings
a few sprigs of basil

Place the chicken pieces in a pot with cold water to cover. Bring to the boil, reduce the heat, and simmer gently until the chicken is cooked. Remove the chicken and leave to cool, then strip the meat from the bones and cut it into bite-sized pieces. Reserve the broth. Boil and shell the shrimp. Soak the grated coconut in water and squeeze dry. Pound the shallots, garlic cloves, and candlenuts to a paste in a mortar.
Heat the oil and fry the spice paste, salam leaf, and lemongrass until their fragrances are released. Deglaze with the chicken broth, then add the shrimp and chicken meat. Add the coconut milk and bring to the boil over moderate heat, stirring occasionally.
To serve, place a portion of rice thread noodles in each bowl, top with slices of hardboiled egg, moisten with several spoonfuls of the *laksa ayam,* and garnish with fried onion rings and basil.

Bakmie goreng

Fried noodles

1 lb (500 g) egg noodles
7 oz (200 g) beansprouts
3 garlic cloves, peeled and quartered
4 candlenuts
4 Tbsp oil
10 shallots, peeled and sliced into thin rings
7 oz (200 g) beef, cut into small dice
5¼ oz (150 g) shrimp, peeled
4 cabbage leaves, coarsely chopped
2 carrots, cleaned and thinly sliced
4 tomatoes, blanched, peeled, seeds discarded, diced
5 Tsp dark soy sauce
5 green onions (scallions), chopped
salt to taste

Garnish

one sprig fresh coriander (cilantro)
fried onion rings

Cook the noodles for 5 minutes in boiling water. Strain, refresh under cold water, and drain. Wash and drain the beansprouts, removing the roots.
Pound the garlic and candlenuts to a paste in a mortar. Heat the oil in a wok and stir-fry the shallots for 1 minute. Stir in the spice paste and add the cubed beef. Stir-fry the meat to seal, then immediately add the shrimp to the wok and stir fry until they turn pale pink. Add the carrots and cabbage and stir-fry until the vegetables are half-cooked.
Add the noodles, followed by the beansprouts; mix and stir-fry for 4 minutes. Add the diced tomatoes, soy sauce, and green onions, stir-frying until everything is thoroughly combined and the noodles are hot. Season to taste with salt if necessary.
Serve garnished with coriander leaves (cilantro) and fried onion rings.

Laksa ayam — Rice thread noodles with chicken in coconut sauce

Bakmie goreng — Fried noodles

Mee soto
Noodles with chicken in a piquant soup

17½ oz (500 g) chicken pieces	
6 cups (1½ l) water	
2 Tsp coriander seeds	
½ Tsp cumin seeds	
½ Tsp ground fennel seeds	
salt	
10½ oz (300 g) beansprouts, roots trimmed	
1lb 5oz (600 g) fresh wheat flour noodles	

Spice paste

8 shallots, peeled and chopped
4 candlenuts
1 slice galangal root
1 stem lemongrass, lower part only, sliced into thin strips
1 Tsp white peppercorns

Garnish

fried onion rings
chopped chives
chopped coriander (cilantro) leaves
fried potato cakes
(see next recipe)

Sauce

3–4 fresh red chili peppers, chopped
1–2 Tbsp dark soy sauce

Pound the shallots, candlenuts, galangal root, lemongrass and peppercorns to a paste in a mortar. Place the chicken pieces in a large pot with the 1½ l water, the spice paste, the coriander seeds, cumin, ground fennel seeds and salt and bring to the boil. Lift out the chicken pieces and reserve the broth.

Fry the chicken pieces for 20-25 minutes until they are lightly browned all over. Cool, then strip the meat from the bones and cut into thin slices. Blanch the beansprouts in boiling water, strain, reserving the water, and drain the sprouts. Bring the water to the boil once more, boil the noodles for 5 minutes, then remove and drain them. Reheat the broth yet again.
To serve, spoon the noodles into soup bowls, top with the beansprouts and the pieces of chicken, and ladle the hot broth into the bowls . Garnish with fried onion rings, chopped green onions (scallions) and coriander (cilantro) leaves, and add a potato cake. Hand the chili sauce separately.

Pergedel goreng
Fried potato cake

17½ oz (500 g) boiled potatoes
6 shallots, peeled and sliced into thin rings
4 green onions (scallions), peeled and chopped
salt
pepper
1–2 eggs, beaten
oil for frying

Mash the potatoes in a bowl. Sauté the shallots until golden brown, cool slightly and add with the green onions (scallions) to the mashed potatoes. Season with salt and pepper and knead well. Using a tablespoon, scoop out a little of the mixture and form into small, round cakes. Dip both sides of each cake in beaten egg and fry.
If the potato cakes are intended as a garnish, as with *mee soto*, the quantities given here may be reduced and the mixture made into smaller chips about the size of a silver dollar.

Mee soto — Noodles with chicken in a spicy soup

Indonesian Aromatics

Adas: Fennel leaves, flowers and seeds

Asam: Tamarind: the dried fruit pulp of the seed pod of this tropical tree is used as an acidulant. It is sold in blocks. To use, soften a small amount in hot water and squeeze out well, using the strained liquid to flavor foods. Tamarind has a slightly laxative effect.

Bawang putih: Garlic

Bunga cengkeh: Cloves

Cabe hijau, cabe merah: Green and red chili peppers.

Daun bawang: Green onions (scallions).

Daun jeruk purut: Kaffir lime leaves, available dried, frozen, and fresh. The dried leaves should be soaked.

Daun kemangi: Basil (the Asian type)

Daun ketumbar: Coriander leaves (cilantro).

Daun pandan: Pandanus leaves, screwpine leaves; the narrow, lance-shaped leaves of the screwpine are used chiefly in desserts to impart their green color and vanilla-like scent and flavor.

Daun salam: Salam leaves, Indonesian bayleaves. These are aromatic, and should be used sparingly (curry leaves may be substituted; Despite their English name, bayleaves are no real substitute).

Jahe: Ginger

Jinten: Cumin, an important ingredient of curry powders.

Kayu manis: Cinnamon

Kemiri: Candlenut, a variety of nut similar in appearance to the macadamia nut; unlike the latter though, it cannot be eaten raw, as it contains toxic substances which break down during cooking. Candlenut kernels are hard and very oily, and are used, pounded, in small quantities to thicken sauces in curries and braised dishes. The flavor they impart to foods is unmistakable. The nearest equivalents are almonds, macadamias, or Brazil nuts, but these are not the same. Shelled, prepackaged *kemiri* can be bought in Asian food stores.

Kencur: (*Kaempferia galanga,* syn. *Galanga minor*). A spicy root related to galangal

Kunyit: Turmeric. The rhizomes are used fresh like ginger, but they are also available dried and ground. Turmeric, an important ingredient in curry powder, imparts a bright yellow color to foods — a quality that the spice retains for much longer than its flavor. (In these recipes, we specify whether the fresh root or the dried powder is to be used.)

Laos: Galangal root (*Alpinia galanga,* syn *galanga major*), also spelled galingale; strong in flavor, this spice should be used sparingly.

Pala: Nutmeg

Sereh: Lemongrass; this shrub owes its flavoring ability to the volatile citronella oil it contains. It is primarily the bulb-like fleshy ends of the stalks which are used.

Once the beans have been soaked, skinned, halved, boiled, mixed with the yeast culture and the tubes filled with them, the microorganisms take over the rest of the tempeh-making process.

Now the tempeh-maker can relax, and need only make sure that over the next 48 hours the tubes are stored at the proper temperature of 80–85°F (25–30°C), preferably on wooden shelves.

Protected by the plastic, but with sufficient oxygen and in pleasant warmth, the microorganisms convert the loose bean kernels into the compact, camembert-like tempeh. The finished product retains the appearance of the soybeans and develops a pleasantly nutty aroma and flavor.

Tempeh

Whereas tofu (*tahu* in Indonesian) is manufactured from puréed soybeans and has a smooth, homogeneous consistency, for tempeh the beans are halved and remain visible in section in the finished product, although their texture is transformed. Indonesians consume more tempeh than tofu. Tempeh not only contains more protein than tofu, but also has more vitamins, and — with its nutty flavor — unequivocally more taste, as well as more calories (though it is still low in calories). Nevertheless, this soy product was saddled with a dubious reputation for quite some time, even though it indisputably helped to fill the bellies of those who could not afford meat. Ever since nutritional awareness has conferred status to poor man's food, however, tempeh is back in the people's good graces, and packets of tempeh wrapped decoratively in banana or teak leaves are once more a common sight in Indonesian markets.

Like tofu, tempeh, which is reminiscent of brie or camembert in appearance, can be prepared in any number of ways: marinated in powders or liquids, deep-fried, pan-fried, or pre-fried, then cooked in a spicy-hot coconut sauce; served with a dip, or added to a vegetable salad.

Tempeh is made at home and commercially manufactured. The washed soybeans are soaked until they swell and their skins loosen. The skins are then removed, and the beans halved, by hand or machine. Next, the soybeans are boiled for about an hour before they are strained, spread out on large boards, and sprinkled with a powdered culture of the yeast *Rhizopus oligosporus*. The beans are then left for 25 minutes before they are transferred to plastic tubes which are perforated to ensure sufficient air circulation. These require a constant temperature of 80-85°F (25-30°C) in order for the microorganisms to become fully active. Within 48 hours, the yeast turns the individual bean halves into a compact protein package (containing more vitamins than the original product.) The tubes are cut into portion-sized pieces and wrapped in leaves to be sold at the market. Nowadays the leaves serve a merely decorative purpose, but they hark back to the times when they were the only wrapping used during the fermentation process.

Tempe goreng
Fried tempeh

14 oz (400 g) tempeh
Juice from ¾ oz (20 g) tamarind pulp and ½ cup (125 ml) water
2 shallots, peeled and chopped
2 garlic cloves, peeled and quartered
salt
pepper
oil for frying

Cut the tempeh into slices 1 in (2 cm) thick. Soften the tamarind pulp in water and strain it through a sieve. Pound the shallots and garlic to a paste in a mortar and add to the tamarind juice. Season with salt and pepper and mix well. Marinate the tempeh slices in this mixture for about 45 minutes, turning them several times. Heat the oil for frying. Gently pat dry the marinated tempeh slices and deep-fry a few at a time until golden brown.

Background: Tempeh portions wrapped in banana leaves, ready to be sold.

Spices

Vanilla

Vanilla (*Vanilla planifolia*), a climbing plant and member of the orchid family, flourishes in damp, hot climates, such as those of the southeast coast of Mexico and Central America, the Caribbean, as well as in Indonesia, and southeast Asia. Each of its yellowish-green flowers opens for just a few hours on a single morning, and since they are only visited by humming-birds and certain insects, pollination is something of a lottery even under favorable conditions but becomes impossible if the plants are merely transplanted from the New World in ignorance of the local conditions. Thus, although the cuttings brought by the Dutch to Java in 1819 thrived, they never fruited. It was only with the discovery of artificial pollination in 1841 that vanilla pods could be grown in Java from 1846, thus ending the Mexican monopoly.

The beanlike pods form a month after pollination and continue growing for five to seven months. They are harvested before they open, and for a week they dried in the sun during the day and hermetically packed at night to make them "sweat." The fermentation thus triggered causes the pods to darken and lose moisture, while remaining supple, and causes the vanillin glycoside contained in the pods to split into glucose and vanillin, this giving the pods their characteristic aroma and flavor.

A long "sweat therapy" is needed to transform the odorless fruit into the aromatic vanilla pod.

Rich yields like these are only achieved through artificial pollination, a technique only developed in 1841.

In the wild, a cinnamon tree can grow to a height of up to70 feet (20 metres). The leaves also smell of cinnamon oil.

Once every six to seven years, the cassia tree is pruned to just above ground and the bark is peeled.

Cinnamon

The barks of two different evergreen trees are sold under this name: that of the cinnamon tree (*Cinnamomum zeylanicum*) which grows wild in Sri Lanka, and that of the Saigon cinnamon or cassia tree (*Cinnamomum cassia*), in introduced into Sumatra, among other places. In cultivation, both are trimmed into bushes. To obtain the valuable cinnamon sticks, the bark is peeled by one longitudinal and several transverse cuts from two-year-old felled saplings; the following day, it is stripped of the outer layers of bark. The inner layer is so thin that it usually rolls up from both long sides, unlike the somewhat thicker cassia bark, which is not split and rolls up from one side only. The tannins contained in the outer layers produce the slightly pungent flavor which makes cassia better suited to savory dishes, whilst the delicate flavor of cinnamon bark is set off to better advantage in sweet dishes.

A potion containing two cassia buds which have grown next to each other is meant to bring good luck to Indonesian brides.

Bark peelings telescoped into one other to form quills. Leftover and broken pieces are ground to a powder.

Nutmeg and mace

The nutmeg tree (*Myristica fragrans*) is indigenous to the Moluccas, the group of islands stretching from Morotai in the north, the Aru islands in the east and Wetar in the west, hence their other name, the Spice Islands. It is also grown elsewhere in Indonesia and in the Caribbean. The nutmeg is a slow-growing tree, and although it can reach a height of 70 ft (20 m), it is kept shorter on plantations. A first, modest crop may be expected in the seventh year, the size of which then increases year on year, then remains constant for a long while, until the tree shows signs of exhaustion at the age of seventy. The evergreen nutmeg produces small yellow flowers which ripen over six months into plum-like fruits. These are made into preserves in Indonesia and candied or preserved in syrup in Malaysia. Since the tree blooms almost uninterruptedly, both fruits and flowers can be found simultaneously on its branches. When the fruit is ripe, it bursts open, revealing the dark-brown seed which is protected by a red reticular seed casing, itself edible, and known as mace. The wooden seed casing is cracked open to reveal a shiny brown kernel — the nutmeg. After the harvest, first the fruit flesh, then the seed casing is removed from the seed. The seed and the seed casing are dried separately in the sun. By the time the drying process is completed, after three to six weeks, the kernels will have lost about one-quarter of their weight and will rattle around in their hard shells, which are then removed. Both nutmeg and mace are steam-distilled in order to preserve their volatile oils, and are sold whole or ground. Despite the measures taken to preserve their volatile oils, these are easily lost, and it is thus advisable only to grate or grind nutmeg and mace when they are needed, as both soon lose their potency. These two spices lend their unmistakable flavors not only to a variety of meat and vegetable dishes, but to baked goods and candies, and they have a special place in the cuisine of many countries.

Nutmeg and mace are not restricted just to culinary uses. The cosmetics and pharmaceutical industries have long valued the properties and active ingredients of both.

The fruit of *Myristica fragrans*, which harbors two important Indonesian exports, is either candied or made into preserves in its native land.

The nutmeg tree grows slowly, but reaches an imposing height and an advanced age.

Although fruits ripen constantly on a nutmeg tree, they are only harvested two to three times a year.

Pepper

Pepper *(Piper nigrum)*, one of the oldest known seasonings, was once also one of the most valuable, and to this day, remains one of the world's most important spices. Over half of the total annual yield comes from India and Indonesia. This tropical climbing vine is presumed to be indigenous to the forests of southern India. Cultivation of the plant reached Indonesia along with the Indians. Pepper was the first tropical spice to reach Europe via the Arab trade routes, where it soon developed a fixed trading value and was not infrequently named as a method of payment, in ransom demands and in dowry lists. By the end of the 15th century, the Portuguese succeeded in cutting out the Arab and Italian middlemen. In the 16th century, they established and controlled the Spice Route, from which they were ousted by the Dutch in the 17th century; they, in turn, were forced to give way to the English in the 18th century. Under favorable conditions, the Sumatran pepper trees will begin fruiting after three to seven years, and will continue to do so for a period of up to 20 years. Depending on the stage at which they are harvested and the manner in which they are processed, they are eventually sold as black, white, or green peppercorns. The berry-like fruits of the plant are ripe for harvesting about nine months after flowering.

For black peppercorns, the fruits are picked when fully developed, but still green and unripe. They are piled up and left to ferment for a few days, then dried for 24–48 hours in the sun, until they are dark brown and wrinkled. Black Lampung (southern Sumatra) is very hot, black Sarawak (Malaysia) is rather mild. The best black pepper, tellicherry, comes from the northern Malabar Coast of India.

For white peppercorns, the fruits are only harvested once they begin to turn red, and are then placed in sacks and left to soak in water for about eight days so that the outer covering can be rubbed off (the best way to accomplish this is to walk around on top of the sacks). The peppercorns are then washed and dried in the sun. Muntok, the best white pepper, is exported from the island of Bangka off the southeast coast of Sumatra, and is stronger than the mild white Sarawak pepper. White pepper is generally milder than black. Black peppercorns which are skinned by machine yield white pepper of an inferior quality.

Green peppercorns are fresh peppercorns which have been preserved in brine or freeze-dried.

An overwhelming proportion of the fruits thus harvested are processed into black peppercorns. The market share of green peppercorns preserved in brine is small.

White pepper is made from reddish, skinned fruits which ripen for longer. Lacking the weight and flavorings of the outer covering, white pepper has a lower yield and is milder than black pepper.

A single cluster bears up to 50 fruits per annum for around 15 years. What look like berries are actually stone fruits with an outer skin and kernel. When they are harvested and left to dry in the sun, they shrink and change color:. 220 lb (100 kg) of fresh fruits will yield 77 lb (35 kg) of black peppercorns.

Cloves

The evergreen clove tree (*Syzygium aromaticum*) belongs to the myrtle family and can reach a height of 40 ft (12 m). It starts to flower at between six and eight years old. Clove trees produce carmine-red flowers twice yearly or rather, they would do so if they were allowed to, but a cultivated clove tree is rarely seen in bloom, since the most of the volatile oils responsible for the flavor and aroma of the spice is present in the unopened buds which are just beginning to turn pink. This, therefore, is when the harvest takes place. The buds are picked by hand so that the branches of the tree are not damaged unnecessarily. The pickers bring basketfuls of stalks and leaves back to their homes, where, in a second step, they detach the buds by hitting the twigs against the palms of their hands. The yield is spread out to dry for a couple of days, then sorted, cleaned, and packed.

Like pepper, cloves have been an object of desire since ancient times. The court officials of the Han dynasty (206 BC – 220 AD) were already aware of their advantages, chewing cloves to perfume their breath before an audience with the emperor, who would then approach them graciously instead of drawing back in disgust. The antiseptic effect of the eugenol contained in clove buds promotes oral hygiene is known to dentists and toothpaste manufacturers to this day.

The demand for buds of these trees which were indigenous to the Moluccas did not bring unmitigated good fortune to the Indonesians. The Portuguese and the Dutch, who were vying for the monopoly on cloves, were greedy and unscrupulous. In order to retain control and to drive prices higher, the Dutch decreed that clove trees were henceforth only to be cultivated on the island of Amboina, and systematically felled any clove trees growing elsewhere in the Moluccas. What brought profit to the Dutch, plunged the Indonesians into despair. For generations they had planted a clove tree as a tree of life for each newborn child, and the fate of the tree was thought to be an omen for the life of the child.

Today, clove trees are also cultivated in Indonesia on Sumatra, in the hilly regions of Bali and in the north of Sulawesi, but the yields do not even meet their own demand, thanks to the Indonesian preference for the locally produced, clove-scented cigarettes known as *kretek*.

Kretek

The name of this Javanese speciality is onomatopoeic, since it mimics the crackling sound made when the smoker drags on it. *Kretek* is a cigarette whose tobacco is mixed with cloves in a ratio of 2:1. Each drag imparts an unmistakably sweet taste to the smoker, together with a pleasantly cool sensation. The popularity of clove cigarettes makes them a profitable business. *Kretek* manufacturers can be found on Java in Kudus, Surabaya, Malang, and Kediri.

To prepare the cloves for mixing with tobacco, they are first steeped in large concrete basins of water to which fruit flavoring is added. They are then spread out in the sun to dry. While they are still somewhat damp, they are chopped up by machine and mixed with different varieties of Javanese tobacco.

1 In this factory, *kretek* are still manufactured predominantly by hand — by women, as a glance in this crowded hall shows.
2 Rolling a cigarette requires few moves: first, the cigarette paper (originally, a corn leaf) is placed in the frame.
3 Next, the special mixture of two parts tobacco to one part cloves (with slight variations depending upon brand, of course) is placed on the paper and the cigarette is rolled.

4 Excess tobacco is cut away cleanly at the edges and collected. During the course of a day, a fair quantity mounts up.
5 Getting a grip on it: the cigarettes, now tidily trimmed, are tied together in handy bundles of 50.
6 Tied securely with a revenue seal, one bundle of *kretek* cigarettes after another rolls off the production line.

Tobacco from Sumatra

In 1863, Jacobus Nienhuys, the son of a tobacco broker, set sail from Amsterdam to the East Indies, as the archipelago was then known. He established himself as a tobacco planter near Medan. Others followed in his footsteps and established other plantations which were run for Dutch companies. The area in northeastern Sumatra has proved ideal for the cultivation of tobacco. There is sufficient warmth, the moderate precipitation levels on the northeast coast are just right, and the fertile volcanic soil is permeable (the lower mountain slopes of central and eastern Java offer similarly favorable conditions). The tobacco is planted in March, and only two months later the first leaves are ripe for harvesting. They are picked from the bottom upward, at regular intervals, depending on the degree of ripeness.

The best leaves grow close to the ground, and each plant has four to six leaves of this quality. The next six to eight leaves above these are of average quality, and further up, about six to eight leaves of the last category are picked. But even these are of such high quality that they are suitable for use as the wrapper leaves of cigars. There is only one tobacco harvest per year; the rest of the time, sugar cane grows on the same spot. The green tobacco leaves are dried in overlapping layers over smoke. For this purpose, they are strung out on lines and hung for 15–18 days. The smoke ("fire") cure begins on the sixth day. After the drying is over, the leaves are packed in bales and left for about 70 days to ferment. They are then sorted, first by color and quality (at the same time, the rolled leaves are smoothed out and laid in bundles), then by size. This work is often performed by women.

The bundles of sorted leaves, gathered together in bales, are now stored in damp rooms to ripen further. Tobacco is a valuable commodity, and the leaves must not be allowed to become too dry; if they were to break during processing, all the labor invested in them thus far would have been in vain. They are thus constantly tested for suppleness, and on particularly hot days they are sprayed for up to 90 minutes with a fine water vapor. Dust and dirt are also shaken off the leaves. Precautions go even further, however: the leaves are stacked in baskets or chests, pressed into bales, sewn up, weighed, labeled, numbered, and any pests they may harbor are smoked out.

Only now are the export goods ready for dispatch.

Classification of tobacco leaves

BH = *baik hijau* (good, green)
BK = *baik kuning* (good, yellow)
BI = *baik impit* (good, moist)

Damaged or substandard leaves are summarized in a second group:
PH = *pecah hijau* (broken, green)
PK = *pecah kuning* (broken, yellow)
PI = *pecah impit* (broken, moist)
PB = *pecah besar* (broken, big)

Step 1: The tobacco leaves are sorted by color and quality.

During this process, leaves of similar color and quality are smoothed by hand.

Before the next stage, leaves of similar color and quality are stacked by hand.

In the second stage, leaves of similar color and quality are sorted according to size.

The leaves thus sorted are now gathered together to ripen in bales of 15-30 leaves.

Prestige goes up in smoke

Cigars

Like the sorting of tobacco leaves, the rolling of cigars is usually women's work. A good number of factories on Java produce cigars (called *cerutu* in Indonesian, hence the English name "cheroot") geared to the individual requirements of different markets. The preferences of different customers vary substantially. For the European market, for example, the filler consists of a mixture of Javanese, Brazilian, and Cuban tobacco. Manufacturers from the United States send their own mixture for the filler to Java, already appropriately pre-cut according to variety, where it is then wrapped entirely to their specifications. Nothing but Brazilian tobacco is used as the filler for cigars which are meant to make the pulses of Philippine smokers race faster.

A cigar consists of a filler, binder leaf, and wrapper leaf. The light wrapper leaves come from the north of Sumatra, where favorable growing conditions encourage good-quality leaves to flourish. For the binder, a tough, dark leaf of lesser quality is generally chosen.

In the first step, the midrib of the tobacco leaf is removed. To do this, an operative wraps the leaf around her hand and quickly and skillfully pulls out the rib with the other hand. She smooths the two halves and sorts them into piles. Using templates of the required shapes for the various cigar formats, the binder leaves are then cut to size from the two halves. The scraps of tobacco accumulating from this process are included in the filler for Coronas and Double Coronas.

The wrapper leaves are soaked briefly in water, then dried for 90 minutes in a sheltered spot. This treatment gives them back precisely enough moisture to allow them to be easily wrapped. They must be soft and supple, while having a certain degree of firmness.

To roll the cigar, filler leaves are placed in the rolling device, the half-leaf to be used for the binder is spread out flat and the cigar is rolled by pressing down the lever. During this activity, the weight of the cigars is checked at 30-minute intervals. For the worker, this is not only a check to see whether she is still using the correct quantity for the filler; variations in weight also allow conclusions to be drawn as to the filler's moisture content.

The newly rolled, still unfinished objects must spend an hour in special corrugated boxes in a press before their edges are roughly tidied and they are turned by hand and pressed yet again. The cigar is now quite handsome looking.

The "bunches", as the pressed cigars are called at this stage, are now wrapped by hand in their tailor-made wrapper leaves. Many brands are only rolled over at the mouth-end and remain open at the lighting end. (The trim is not wasted, it ends up back in the filler.)

The finished, wrapped cigars are kept for a minimum of three weeks in the dry store to allow the mixed tobacco to ferment. They then make their way to a cold room. After this they spend two days in a fumigation tank, where the last insect that might have infested the tobacco gives up the ghost. Only then are they kitted out in cigar bands and transferred to their handmade boxes, preferably made of cedar wood, in order to continue to discourage undesirable lodgers.

Three months may elapse from the deribbing of the binder leaf to the packing of the finished rolled cigars into their stylish, handmade boxes.

Opposite page, below: a cigar box leaving this cigar factory in Java is 95% handmade, and together with its contents constitutes a luxury article.

The cigars are twice subjected briefly to appropriate pressure in order to stabilize their shape.

The cigars, so far consisting only of filler and binder, are fitted into special molded boxes.

The binder, which has been cut to size, is wrapped around the filler in the rolling device.

Considerable skill is required to roll a "bunch" perfectly in its wrapper leaf, which has been cut to size.

The rolled-over mouth end of the cigar is first carefully trimmed with the scissors...

... and then fixed in place with a tapioca-based plant adhesive.

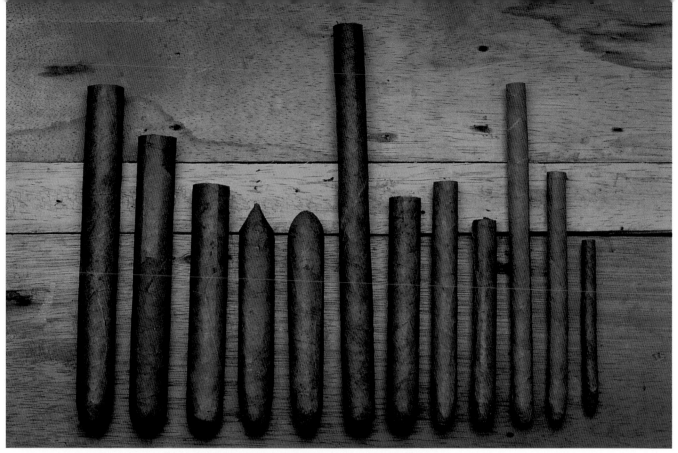

| Churchill | | Rothschild | | Delicados | | Corona | | Senoritas | | Slim Special |
| | Super Rothschild | | Senator Boheme | | Double Corona | | Panatela | | Panatela fina | | Borobudur (Cigarillo) |

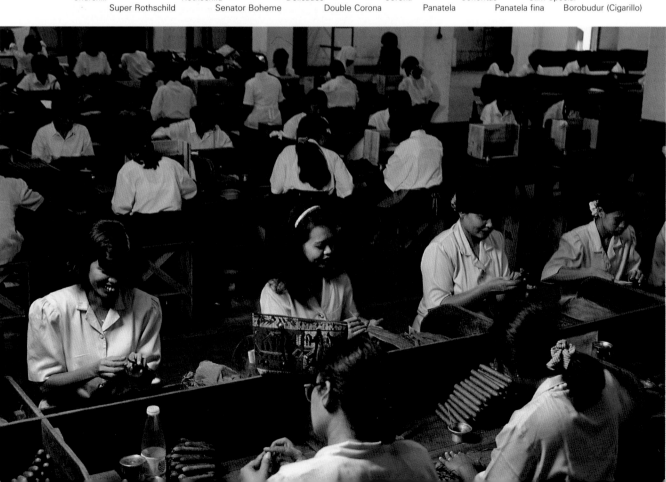

Coffee

At the beginning of the 18th century, when the Dutch were experimenting with the first coffee plants on Java, they chose the Arabica variety. Their success proved they had made a good choice, since increased cultivation and production flourished until all the plants were hit by disease in 1869. It was not until around the turn of the century that growers risked a second attempt with the Robusta strain. This variety also flourishes at fairly low altitudes (1,000–2,000 ft (300–600 m)) and is very popular in Indonesia. Coffee is not a major export, however, because on the world market the demand for Arabica is greater. In fact, Arabica has made a comeback and this time it is being grown at higher altitudes (2,000–4,000 ft (600-1200 metres)) which means that although it actually grows more slowly, it is of better quality and fetches higher prices.

In plantations, coffee trees are cultivated as bushes and cut back when they reach a height of 7 ft (2 m). If the trees were allowed to grow freely, they would reach a height of up to 40 ft (10 m). The small white blossoms, which generally all open briefly at the same time, ripen in eight to twelve months into dark red coffee berries. The two seeds — the coffee beans — are well protected by flesh and two layers of seed coating. The coffee berries are first soaked and then pass through a cylindrical crushing machine in which they are opened up and the seeds released. After two days' fermentation, the seeds go through a washing process to cleanse them of fruity sediment, after which they dry in the sun until the shell hardens. A husking machine removes this dry shell from the gray-green raw coffee. The familiar characteristics and aroma of coffee beans first become apparent as a result of the roasting process, often carried out by the actual importer himself.

Apart from this moistening process, small farmers practice a drying process. They pound coffee berries in mortars, dry this pulp in the sun and winnow the beans from their outer husks, like wheat is winnowed from chaff.

Indonesians like their coffee black, strong, and sweet. They do not filter it, but brew the coffee powder with hot water, stir it briefly, and drink it as soon as it has settled.

If a coffee bush is planted on an individual scale, the the simplest way to have a cup of coffee is to start by pounding fresh coffee berries in a mortar.

Coffee berries are roughly the size of small grapes and are bright red when ripe.

Crushed coffee berries dried in the sun are winnowed like grain.

Freshly roasted Robusta beans, the Indonesians' favorite coffee

Indonesian coffee drinks

Kopi bubuk: Freshly roasted, ground coffee. Sometimes it is mixed with corn which is boiled, roasted, and then ground together with the coffee beans.

Kopi jahe: Ginger coffee. A piece of crushed ginger root is mixed with sugar and heated. When it is boiling, ground coffee is stirred in and allowed to draw for 5 minutes. The ginger is removed before serving.

Kopi luak: Luak is a Javanese species of the civet cat, which is especially partial to fully ripened coffee berries, probably because of their sweet flesh. The hard seeds are excreted by them undigested. The beans then simply need to be collected and roasted immediately.

Kopi telur: Egg yolk beaten with sugar has hot coffee poured onto it. This is a breakfast drink in Sumatra.

Mandheling Coffee: A pungent, aromatic coffee from Sumatra.

Toraja Coffee: A very strong, pungent coffee from Sulawesi.

Characteristics of Indonesian teas

(Tips: young, bright leaf tips. Flowery: particularly flowery aroma. Orange Pekoe: delicate leaves immediately below the leafbuds. Pekoe: the next leaf below the bud. Additive: wood)

Leaf
OP sup: Orange Pekoe Superior; very tippy, often small cup
OP: Orange Pekoe; principal leaf grade of Java teas; often long, wiry leaf, no tips

Broken
FBOP: Flowery Broken Orange Pekoe; really coarse Broken with few tips
BOP coarse: Broken Orange Pekoe coarse; Indonesian synonym for Pekoe
BOP: Broken Orange Pekoe; principal broken grade of Java teas
BP/BOP 2: Broken Pekoe/Broken Orange Pekoe 2; very black tea often with an additive

Fannings
PF: Pekoe Fannings (syn. Broken Orange Pekoe Fannings): principal grade in Indonesia; black leaf, even grain, no tips, with scarcely any additive

The labor of a tea picker is tiring and badly paid.

The freshly picked leaves are first put into large tubs and left to wither.

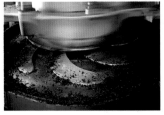

The withered leaves are shredded, sometimes by machine, and curled.

During fermentation, the juice extracted from the cells in the leaves oxidizes.

The tea turns black in the final hot air drying process.

Tea

Indonesia to-day produces almost 5.5 percent of annual world tea production and shares fifth place with Turkey on the list of tea-producing countries (Sri Lanka, whose tea has kept its old name of Ceylon tea, occupies fourth place). In northern Sumatra and Java, at altitudes of 3,000–6,000 ft (900–1,800 m), the tea grown is predominantly Assam. In western Java, tea is also sometimes grown on mountain slopes with fairly low temperatures. The plantations in these regions produce excellent export quality black tea. Unlike the tea on Sumatra, which owes its consistent, though not exceptional, quality to the fact that the island lies on the equator and consequently has a constant climate throughout the year, the quality of Javanese tea can vary due to the vagaries of the weather. The significantly highest quality is picked at the end of the dry season in September. Approximately 80 percent of Indonesian production is intended for export. Apart from the yield of some low-lying tea gardens on Java which produce green tea, the Indonesian crop consists mainly of black tea. The traditional methods continue to be used assisted by some machinery, although not the CTC (Crushing, Tearing, Curling) machine.

In this way fresh green leaves are turned into crumbly black tea, which must wither, curl, ferment, and dry. In the space of 17-20 hours, 9 lb (4 kg) of fresh leaves shrink to 2¼ lb (1 kg) of black tea.

During the withering process, the leaves lose around a third of their moisture in order to achieve the correct qualities for the subsequent curling. In Sumatra's most modern tea factories, the leaves are tipped into large withering tubs with wire-mesh covers. High-performance fans provide adequate air circulation. If necessary, the fan temperature can be increased and the direction of the air stream can be changed. This makes it possible to reduce the withering time by anything from a third to a half, so that the leaves move on to the next production phase after eight to twelve hours.

The aim of curling is to destroy the structure of the leaves so that the cell moisture can be released. This used to be done by hand but nowadays there are machines which can process the leaves almost as carefully. As soon as the first cells are destroyed, fermentation begins. This is an enzyme-supported change which occurs in the cell moisture upon contact with air.

In a special cup fitted with a lid, 8 fl oz (250 ml) boiling water is poured onto a 1-teaspoon (5 g) sample.

After five minutes, the tea is poured into a bowl and the leaf is tipped into the lid for testing.

Each individual infusion is examined for color and aroma.

Flavor and caffeine content also tell the taster a great deal about how the tea has been processed.

The leaf chaff is graded by sifting. What falls through the sieve is sent to the fermentation area and the rest must spend a further 30 minutes in the curling machine. It is at this stage, not during picking, that leaf grading is performed. Longer curling produces larger quantities of smaller leaf grades.

On the other hand, fermentation affects the taste of the tea. Spread out in thin layers, the curled leaves spend about 110 minutes in almost 100 percent humidity at a temperature of 95–104°F (35–40°C). This is when the aroma develops, the caffeine content increases, and three-quarters of the tannic acid is broken down (which is why black tea tastes less bitter and more fragrant than green tea which is unfermented.) The expert tea-taster recognizes from the smell and coppery color of the leaf when it has fermented sufficiently, so that the process must be stopped. The enzyme, previously so useful, is then deactivated and practically all the moisture from the leaves is drawn out in large hot-air dryers. As the moisture dries out of the cells the leaf particles turn black.

In a subsequent grading process during which the "raw tea" is strained through a series of sieves, the leaves are graded. The categories are, broadly speaking, Leaf, Broken, Fannings, and Dust. Leaf teas have only a very small market share (and with the introduction of machines into the traditional production process, their quality is somewhat impaired). Fannings and Dust are mainly used in teabags. The leaf grade refers only to the size of the leaf particle and not the quality of the tea.

Quality control is the province of the tea tasters. They pour exactly the same amount of boiling water, namely one cup or 8 fl oz (250 ml) onto exactly the same amount of tea, namely 1 teaspoon (5 g). The tea is then left to brew for exactly five minutes in special white china cups which have lids to fit them. The tea is then poured off into white china bowls and the wet leaves are tipped into the upturned cover of the cup. Of each type to be tasted there is now a sample of the dry and wet leaf and the actual infusion. The color of the wet leaf indicates whether fermentation was halted at the proper time and whether the air in the drying oven was at the right temperature. A dark copper color is indicative of careful processing, but a greenish tinge is a sign of insufficient fermentation. A bitter taste along with a dull, indeterminate color is a sign that the leaf contains too much moisture and has thus not been correctly dried.

Fermentation and drying develop the aroma, remove some of the bitter substances, and turn the creamy white color of the beans to chocolate brown.

Background picture: The pods are opened and the seeds fermented. The next stage in the process, making the cocoa powder, is generally performed in the country to which the cocoa is exported.

The bitter aftertaste

Cocoa

It is said that Christopher Columbus shipped the first cocoa plants from the Americas to Spain. The Spaniards then introduced them to the Philippines, whence they found their way to Java and thence to Sumatra. The cocoa beans were originally prized for the preparation of a hot drink that became a status symbol. At the Spanish court there must have been recipes for hot cocoa made with more than 20 different ingredients, including spices such as nutmeg, pepper, cloves— in fact anything that was rare and expensive. The mass-market and gourmet varieties grown in Indonesia are variations of the Forastero (mass market cocoa) from South America and Criollo (fine grade cocoa) from Mexico. To flourish fully, the plants need high precipitation, an average annual temperature of 80.6°F (27°C), consistently high humidity, and shade. The first beans can be harvested two years after planting. It takes six months from flowering for the bean to ripen fully. A cocoa pod contains on average 50 seeds, arranged in five rows lengthwise along the fruit. All that has to be done is to open them neatly and remove the seeds with their moist, creamy-white shells. For processing, the beans are collected in wooden fermenting crates. During the six-step fermentation, the beans must be turned between three and six times. This is why the boxes are laid out in tiers, because they can be more easily restacked. As soon as fermentation is sufficiently advanced, the beans are hot-air dried until they contain no more than about 7 percent of their original moisture. They are then graded and packed for shipping.

Cocoa can only grow in the tropics, but it satisfies a demand which emanates predominantly from what might be loosely described as industrialized countries. It is these countries which also control the trade in the fluctuating market and dictate its prices. Farmers in the cocoa-growing countries run the risk of losses on the harvests, but are forced to sell their cocoa beans at knockdown prices. Cocoa is a speculative commodity — in good years, a harvest has been sold 16 times over before it is ever turned into chocolate.

Wooden fermentation crates with perforated bases allow air to circulate and enable any build-up of water from condensation to drain away.

The beans are still too pale. A few more days in the fermentation crates are required before the internal chemical processes are complete.

The hot air blown through the beans from below draws out their moisture and completes the fermentation process.

The dried and graded cocoa beans are ready for shipment. The majority of Indonesia's production goes to Germany and the USA.

Cooking according to taste

Bika ambon

These flat palm-wine cakes are a speciality in the northern part of Sumatra, where there are shops which seem to prepare and sell nothing else all day long, something which the queue of evidently patient customers waiting from morning till night seems to bear out.

The first step in preparing *bika ambon* is to bring coconut milk to the boil for a short time with a substantial quantity of pandanus leaves and a pinch of salt. This gives the milk an interesting color and lends the cake an agreeable and lasting aroma. The leaves are left to infuse in the cooling milk and are only removed when the milk is used in the next cooking stage. Meanwhile eggs and sugar are whisked together and beaten to a sticky paste with tapioca flour. Enough of the cooled coconut milk is then added to form a thick dough. A generous dash of lightly fermented palm-wine is used as a raising agent. (Yeast can be substituted for the palm wine.)

The dough must then rest for about six hours, before being poured into square molds and baked golden-brown in a low oven. At the end of the baking time, the cook can help the browning process by increasing the heat or by broiling the cakes under a grill. During cooking, countless bubbles appear on the surface; when cooked, the texture is as porous as a sponge.

Originally the cake was baked in a charcoal fired oven which only gives off moderate heat. As soon as it was cooked through to the top, it was covered with a flat cookie sheet heaped with glowing charcoal so that it could be browned from the top.

Jajan pasar

Almost everywhere people can succumb to the temptation of nibbling at one or other of these colorful little morsels, a cross between a cookie and a candy. In addition to rice and sticky rice, used in whole grains or ground, their base is manioc starch, sweet potatoes, taro, or beans (wheat flour for baking was not used until the Dutch introduced it). The liquid is nearly always coconut milk and the usual sweetening agent is palm sugar. The little cookies are baked, but may also be steamed, boiled, and steeped in syrup.

But, not all *jajan pasar* are sweet. Quite often they have a hot, savory filling.

In Jakarta there's a wholesale bakery which sells *jajan pasar* and every other kind of cake and cookie imaginable. It is only open from midnight to daybreak and every possible bakery item is on sale here, even Western-style elaborately frosted cakes and candies. There is a constant flow of people, because this is where the great army of street vendors buy their stocks for the day.

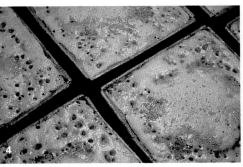
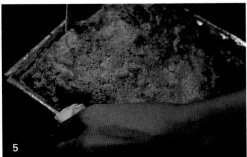

1 Thin coconut milk made from squeezed grated coconut mixed with water is brought to the boil with a substantial quantity of pandanus leaves and a little salt.
2 The milk is allowed to boil briskly for a moment, then it is removed from the stove, left to cool, and the leaves are discarded, having done their job.
3 The soft, thick batter is made from beaten eggs, sugar, tapioca, coconut milk, and palm wine. It is sprinkled with flour and must then prove for six hours.

4 It is then poured into square molds and baked at a low temperature. During this process, countless bubbles rise to the surface.
5 When baking is complete, the surface is golden-brown. When the cake is sliced it can be seen to be as porous as a sponge.
6 The cake leaves the store in a collapsible box, but it may not reach home in one piece!

From midnight to dawn anything can be bought in this wholesale bakery and candy store in Jakarta , from tiny delicate exotic cookies to kitsch, western-style frosted fantasy cakes.

Jajan pasar: these cookies, mostly sweet, can be found on any street corner

Klepon: Boiled sticky rice flour dumpling filled with palm sugar and rolled in grated coconut

Kue talam: Steamed layer cake consisting of one layer of ground rice with brown sugar and another of ground rice with coconut milk

Lepet: Sticky rice and black beans both boiled and wrapped in a coconut palm leaf, tied with seaweed.

Dadar enten: a green pancake made of wheat flour, coconut milk, and egg mixed with palm sugar and filled with coconut

Semar mendem: has the same filling as *lemper* (below left), but wrapped in a wheat flour-and-egg pancake

Kue lapis: steamed layer cake made of ground rice and tapioca with coconut milk

Kue lapis: jellyroll made of ground rice.

Kue bunga: two-color ground rice cake molded into an elegant flower shape

Lemper ayam: steamed sticky rice wrapped in a banana leaf with a spicy filling of chopped chicken

Getuk lindri: a steamed colored manioc flour, sprinkled with a little grated coconut

Kue lopes: steamed sticky rice wrapped inside a triangular palm leaf and boiled. It is served with palm sugar syrup

Serabi: creamy white or pandanus green pancake made of wheat flour, ground rice, egg and coconut milk simmered in a small earthenware pot with a lid - served with palm sugar or syrup

Roti kaya: green colored bread with "egg jam", made of egg, sugar, and coconut milk

Spekkoek: A cookie of Dutch origin consisting of at least 12 thin layers spiced with ground cinnamon, cloves, and nutmeg and baked in layers

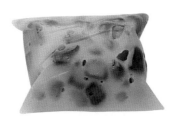

Pacar cina: Ground green beans boiled with sugar and coconut milk and mixed with pieces of colored bean; the thickened paste is wrapped into small packages for setting

Nagasari: A thickened paste made of ground green bean seeds boiled in coconut milk is garnished with a piece of ripe banana and wrapped in a banana leaf to set (an alternative recipe uses ground rice or corn and the garnish can be changed)

Putu ayu: Two-colored ground rice cake dyed with the juice of pandanus leaves

Wajik: Sticky rice boiled with palm sugar in various colors and shapes
Ongol-ongol (center): ground sago boiled with palm sugar

249

The salak palm tree has no trunk. The high crown rises to a height of up to 20 ft (5 m) above what looks like a short stem where the old leaves drop from the palm branches.

The fruit from the salak palm divides into three segments if the outer "snakeskin" is broken. Each contains a seed which, though inedible, makes a wonderful toy.

Right: On the "tree" the fruit still has a prickly skin that looks pretty fierce although this impression is deceptive. What look like prickles can, actually, easily be grated.

Salak

Snakeskin fruit (*Zalacca edulis*) are very popular in Indonesia and Malaysia. Because they are so perishable, they are hardly ever exported. The best varieties, whose fruits have a pleasant bittersweet flavor are *salak pondoh* in central Java and the larger *bali salak*. *Salak condet* from Jakarta taste very sour, even when fully ripe. The flesh is crisp and dry, with a rather faint aroma of apples. The ripe fruit can be eaten raw in fruit salads or prepared as a dessert. Unripe *salak* are cooked or preserved in vinegar. In their native country, they are available all year round but elsewhere, they can only be found in specialist food stores from February through April.

The salak-palm flourishes in damp soil in low-lying areas with constant precipitation. The central rib of the palm-leaf is covered with spines which makes it difficult to harvest the fruit in the center of the plants just above the ground.

Children use the pits to make a toy. They bore two holes in the pits and thread them onto a piece of string. When they pull the string tight, the seeds make a whizzing sound.

The salak-palm fruit is not the only part of the plant which is used. An extract made from the catkin-like flowers, has been discovered by the drinks industry.

Inside the hollow "trunk" of the banana shrub the flower grows upward.

Only the female (non-pollinated) flowers turn into fruit.

Even for sale locally, bananas are harvested green and ripen later in the stores.

Bananas

From the botanical point of view, the banana plant is a shrub. It fruits only once (a bunch of bananas consists of about 15 hands, each of which has 15-17 "fingers"). Once the fruit has ripened, all the parts of the plant above the ground die off. However, new shoots have already spread from the rhizome in the ground.

These days, bananas are cultivated practically anywhere they can grow, but their real home is in southeast Asia. The Spanish and Portuguese were the first to bring them to the Caribbean. In Indonesia and Malaysia, banana-growing is mainly the prerogative of small farmers who supply the domestic market, although Malaysia has an export trade with Singapore.

Bananas fall into two distinct categories – those for eating raw and those for cooking. Of the 30 varieties which flourish in Indonesia, only 14 are actively cultivated (see below). The most popular are *pisang ambon putih* and *pisang ambon lumut*. Even bananas for the domestic market are harvested green, because once fully ripe, they turn floury or rot. Bananas are eaten fresh and dried; they are steamed, boiled, baked, and deep-fried in rice-flour batter. *Jantong pisang*, male banana flowers are eaten as a vegetable. The leaves are used to wrap fish and rice cakes for steaming or for eating while traveling; they are used as disposable plates and as lining for dishes (the leaves become more supple when they are soaked in hot water). Chicken-pox scars are supposed to disappear if the inside of the skin of *pisang susu* is rubbed over them often enough.

Indonesian varieties

Giant Cavendish: 6–9 in (15–22 cm) long, thick skin, ripens to yellow; fine, cream-colored flesh, sweet, and very aromatic.

Pisang Ambon lumut (1): (Mal.: *p. masak hijau*) 6–8 in (15–20 cm) long; bright green to greenish fruit; ripening to yellow; fine, cream-colored flesh, fairly firm, sweet, and aromatic.

Pisang Ambon putih (3): (Mal.: *p. ambun*) 6–8 in (15-20 cm) long, smooth skin, ripens yellow; cream-colored flesh, fairly firm, lightly aromatic, sweet; good taste; stores well.

Pisang asam: Cooking banana
Pisang kepok: (Mal.: *p. nipah*) cooking banana; 4–6 in (10–15 cm); thick skin; ripens to yellow; cream-colored flesh.

Pisang klutuk: (Mal.: *p. hatu*) "stone banana", full of hard seeds; boiled unripe in the skin.

Pisang mas (5): 3–5 in (8-12 cm) long; think skin; ripens to golden-yellow; firm, bright-orange flesh, sweet, aromatic.

Pisang nangka (4): 7–10 in (18–24 cm); long, pointed and curved; thick skin; ripens to bright green, fine, cream- colored flesh; keeps and stores well.

Pisang raja: Dessert and cooking banana; 6–8 in (15–20 cm), large and curved with a thick coarse skin; ripens orange yellow; bright orange flesh; very sweet but coarse consistency.

Pisang raja sereh (2): (Mal.: *p. rastali*) 4-6 in (10 –15 cm); popular eating banana; very think skin; ripens yellow (dark brown patches when fully ripe); soft, white flesh.

Pisang seribu: Ornamental banana plant.

Pisang susu (6): 2–3 in (5-8 cm); bright yellow skin and flesh; very sweet; is similar to the pisang mas; belongs to the Ambon group.

Pisang tanduk (7): Cooking banana; 10–14 in (25-35 cm), 2-2½ in (6-6.5 cm) thick; ripens yellow, fine but firm, bright orange flesh; when cooked, very sweet; stores well and is used for the commercial market.

Pisang udang: ›Shrimp banana; red cooking banana.

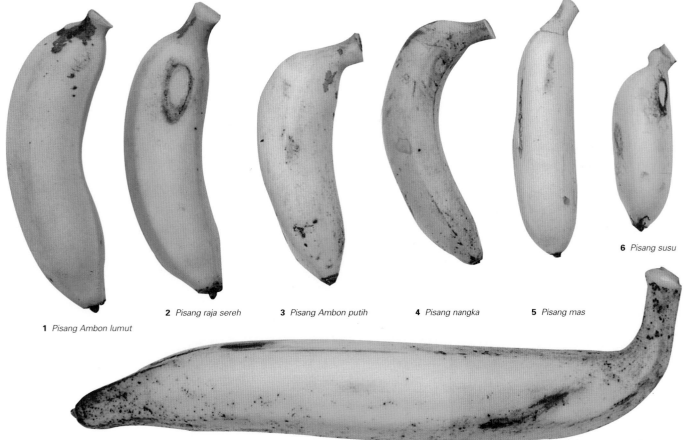

6 *Pisang susu*

2 *Pisang raja sereh*　　**3** *Pisang Ambon putih*　　**4** *Pisang nangka*　　**5** *Pisang mas*

1 *Pisang Ambon lumut*

7 *Pisang tanduk*

Indigenous and introduced

Fruits

The constantly overflowing baskets of fruit are what give Indonesian markets so much of their fascination. Fruit is comparatively good value and is an important source of nutrition. Climatic conditions are so favorable that many varieties do not ripen just once between May and August but a second time at the end of the year. Many fruits, such as bananas and papayas, can even be harvested all year round. If there is any seasonal variation, it is relatively unimportant on the Indonesian archipelago with its significant climatic differences.

Apocat
The avocado (*Persea americana*) originates from Mexico and is grown iat altitude here. In Indonesia, avocados are puréed and eaten sweet, with sugar and water, or they are blended with other fruits into *es campur*.

Tamarillo
The tamarillo or tree tomato (*Cyphomandra betacea*), which grows in the dark and originated in the Peruvian Andes, actually doesn't need a tropical climate. When the fruit is completely ripe (March – May) it is eaten raw, by cutting it lengthwise and scooping out the sour flesh, but more often it is stewed with sugar.

Kluwek/Keluwek
The large pits in this fruit of the *Pangium edule* tree contain toxic substances and must be carefully prepared in advance before they can be further processed: They must be pre-boiled and/or allowed to soak for about 12 hours in several changes of water. Just before they are used in a dish called *rawon*, the shells are crushed, the soft black kernels pounded in a mortar and blended with chili peppers, shallots, and other herbs and spices. The finished sauce is very dark and is something of an acquired taste.

Asam kranji
The tamarind (*Tamarinda indica*) came to southeast Asia from India, although its home is in East Africa. The cinnamon-colored pods, which ripen on tall trees, contain a sticky, dry, very tart fruit pulp; the pits are used as spices. The fruit pulp is softened in water and squeezed. The tamarind juice thus produced imparts an acid flavor to food. Candies are made from tamarind pulp mixed with sugar and the shoots and leaves are eaten raw, dipped in *sambal*. In traditional medicine, tamarind leaves are mixed with turmeric and used to alleviate the pain of burns. Overripe fruit can be used to clean copper and brass.

Jambu meté
The cashew tree (*Anarcadium occidentale*) comes from eastern Brazil and the West Indies. What looks like a pear is actually the soft, fleshy, widening stalk of the fruit. The actual fruit, the cashew nut, is underneath. The "cashew apple" is also edible and can be used to make preserves. The young leaves are eaten in salads in western Java and served with rice and *sambal*.

Kemiri
The candlenut is native to Australia. The fruit grows in a bunch and has a very thick shell. Inside the single white, oily kernel is pounded and is mixed with other herbs for cooking. Candlenuts are similar to macadamias, although they are not true substitutes. Toxic substances in candlenuts make them unsuitable for eating raw.

Delima merah
Under the leathery skin of the pomegranate (*Punica granatum*), which originated from Persia, there are bitter white parts, interspersed with seeds inside juicy sacs called arils.The pomegranate is valued for its pink juice. The thoughness of the skin means the fruit can be kept for such a long time. On Bali, the seeds and skin are ingredients in traditional medicines.

Jambu biji
The guava (*Psidium guajava*) originates from central America; various varieties are grown in Indonesia. Unripe fruit is cut up and eaten in salads; the soft flesh of the ripe fruit is eaten raw or liquidized and drunk as a juice. The numerous seeds inside are edible but hard and difficult to digest and the leaves are used for medicinal purposes.

Kedondong

The sweet balsam plum, also called the golden apple (*Spondias dulcis*), is of Polynesian origin. It resembles the mango and, like it, must be peeled. Like the mango, too, the large pit in the middle is coated with a fibrous layer which binds the seed to the flesh of the fruit. The sharp aroma of the fruit which is harvested before it is fully ripe gives a distinctive taste in salads.

Sirsak

The prickly annona (*Annona muricata*) does not belong to the durian family, although its other local name, *durian balanda*, which probably comes from the thorns covering the dark green skin, might give this impression. It comes from tropical America. The flesh of the pear or kidney-shaped fruit is fibrous, a little spongy and juicy although it contains a lot of black seeds. It tastes bittersweet and is sharper than the scaly annona. Only the juice is used.

Asam selong

The pitanga or Surinam cherry (*Eugenia uniflora*) comes from Brazil, reaching Indonesia via India and the East Indies. When fully ripe, the eight-furrowed fruit is a deep red. The flesh is juicy and soft with a slightly bitter smell when fully ripe. Otherwise, the taste is unpleasantly sharp. The fruit has a particularly high Vitamin C content.

Srikaya biasa

The scaly annona (*Annona squamosa*) is a native of the West Indies. The scaly skin of some varieties can take on a distinct greenish-blue coloring which turns lighter when the fruit is fully ripe. The flesh is bittersweet, white, creamy and full of black seeds with black seeds. Scaly annona are enjoyed both for eating as a dessert and drinking as a juice.

Duku/Langsat

The langsat (*Lansium domesticum*). a relative of the lychee, grows in large bunches on the tree. It is round, about the size of a walnut and has a tough brownish-yellow shell (which is burned to keep mosquitoes away). When the fruit is squeezed at the top end, the shell splits open and the fruit can easily be removed. The fruit has five or six segments and tastes bittersweet. Larger segments contain very bitter seeds.

Mangga

Various varieties of mango (*Mangifera indica*) are cultivated in Indonesia: *Mangga manalagi* is sold in eastern and central Java. Its flesh is yellowish and sweet and resembles the *mangga indramayu* which is grown in western Java. The skin of the *mangga gedong*, the "papaya mango" is yellow–orange and its flesh is reddish when fully ripe. It is very sweet and, along with the equally sweet and fragrant *mangga arumanis*, is reckoned to be the best. The season lasts from six to nine weeks in May and June. The trees blossom in December or January and throughout the four-month dry season, the fruit grows to maturity. In regions further to the south, there is a second season at the end of the year, before the monsoon. The hard wood of the mango tree is resistant to gnawing insects which makes it ideal for boat-building.

Jambu bol

The Java apple (*Syzgium samarangense*) is the fruit of a tree related to the clove tree. Apart from this green variety, a brilliant red one is also grown which very closely resembles the Malay apple (also called the otaheite apple). The bright, crispy moist flesh of the fruit calls to mind many apples grown for their juice rather than their flavor. Java apples are ideal for eating raw.

255

Melinjo

The *melinjo* or gnetum tree (*Gnetum gnemon*) reaches a height of up to 70 ft (20 m) in the wild. When the small oval fruit opens, it presents a really wonderful spectacle — in fact it is appreciated at least as much for its appearance as for its flavor. The fruit is ripe when the skin becomes brilliant orange. The color eventually becomes more intense and turns red, making the fruit even more beautiful but the fruit is now overripe. The fruit contains a pit which resembles an acorn.

The fruit and leaves of gnetum tree are edible and are to be found, for example, in *sayur asam*, a tart vegetable soup, which derives its sharp flavor from a sizeable quantity of tamarind juice. Peanuts make an acceptable, although not wholly satisfactory, substitute for *buah melinjo* and lemon juice can be used to give *sayur asam* its sour taste.

Generally, the melinjo seeds are worked into small patties with a slightly bitter but pleasant taste. They are added to drinks and used as garnish, in rather the same way as shrimp crackers are added to *gado-gado*, sprinkled over rice, or else quite simply dipped in a *sambal*. There is also a sweet variety, coated in palm sugar syrup, which is eaten between meals.

Emping melinjo

To prepare these snacks, the seeds are first quickly toasted in a hot sand-filled wok before being split and the white kernel being removed. The kernel is then put onto a hard surface and beaten wafer-thin. A second kernel is then beaten flat in the same way, then a third, then a fourth — about six kernels are needed before the *emping* has reached the required size. This thin patty must now be eased off the work surface and placed onto a bamboo rack to air-dry or sun-dry. It is only then that it is firm enough to package. *Emping* can be bought raw or fried, in which case they take on the uneven shape of shrimp crackers. They are sold ready-made in stores as well as home-cooked. A person with enough skill and practice can make up to 6½ lb (3 kg) of *emping* in a day.

Emping melinjo are served both raw and fried in oil.

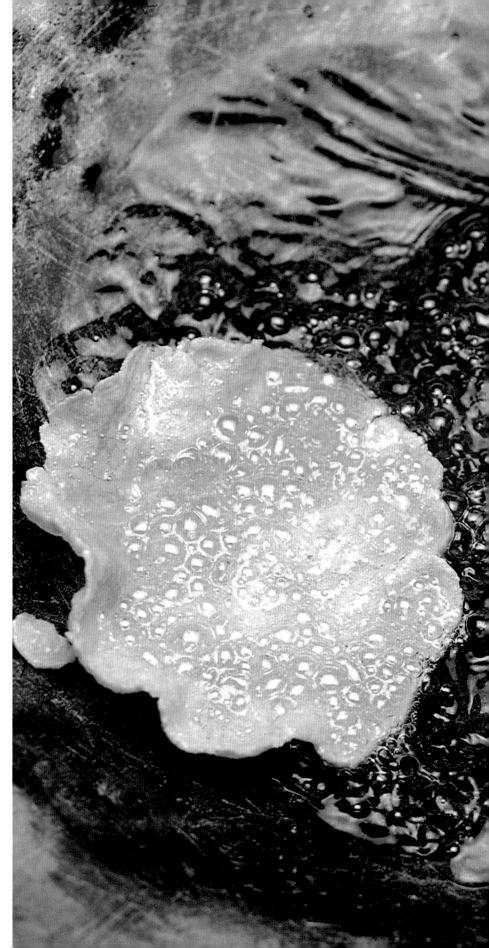

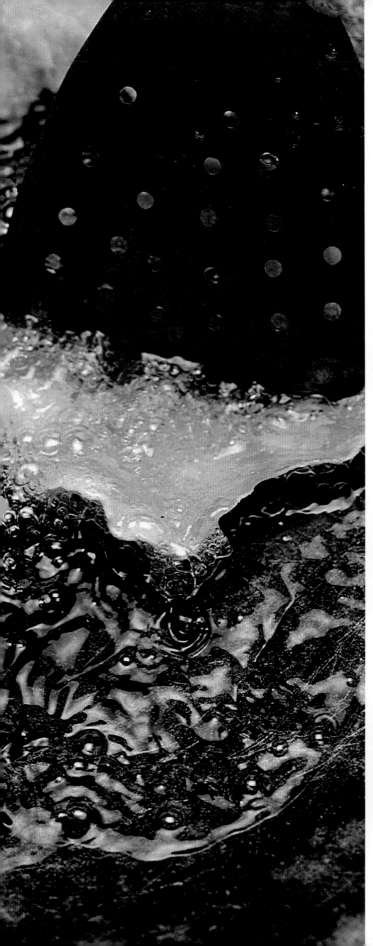

By the time the *melinjo* fruit has turned scarlet, the kernels are overripe.

To run a home-based *emping melinjo* business, scarcely any space and only a few utensils are required.

First of all, the seeds are toasted in hot sand for not more than two minutes.

They are stirred with a skimmer, removed, and hulled.

A wooden hammer is used to beat the kernels flat on an iron plate.

Four to six flattened kernels are made into a round *emping melinjo*.

The patties are still very fragile and must be removed from the base with care.

After they are dried on a bamboo rack, they can be fried or packed right away.

Kripik singkong

The manioc tubers are thinly peeled and cut into strips, thin slices, or matchsticks. They are rinsed in water, dried, and then deep-fried in hot oil in a wok. They are then drained and salted. Spicy manioc chips are then made in a further operation, either dipped in a thick mixture of cooked, shredded chili peppers, sugar, and salt, or else the cook goes to the trouble of brushing each individual chip with chili paste.

Miniature side-dishes

Snacks

Before the Indonesians were confronted with popcorn and other snacks from the West, they only had sweet, tangy, or dried fruit (*manisan*) or various varieties of chips or crackers. Fortunately, the variety of such preserved foods, because, when all is said and done, that it was they are, has not become less interesting. The need to preserve some of this abundance of fruit and vegetables, which in this climate grow in lavish profusion but perish just as quickly, probably contributed to the many varieties of preserved foods available. The widest possible variety of fruits are dried either with or without chili peppers and herbs, salted or coated with syrup. Preserved in large glass jars and clearly visible, *manisan* are a constant temptation practically everywhere.

Another form of preserving is frying, which creates a second wide range of popular snacks consisting of various sorts of chips (*kripig*). Manioc, sweet potatoes, nuts, water-buffalo hide, fish skin — the range is

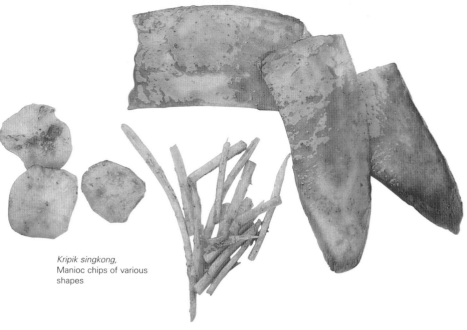

Kripik singkong,
Manioc chips of various shapes

almost endless, as long as the strips can be cut thin enough and fried rapidly in oil. Then there are crackers made of a sponge mixture or with ground rice or other flour blends (*rempeyek*) and the wafer-thin flatly beaten *emping* such as *emping melinjo* and the ever-popular *krupuk udang* or *krupuk ikan* (shrimp and fish crackers).

Some of these chips and crackers are used as side dishes. These include *rendang* (braised beef). Others are served as crackers with a bowl of *sambal*.

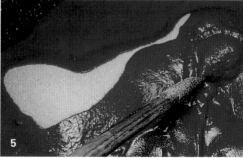

1 Here are some examples of *kripik*, manioc chips. First, the tubers are peeled.
2 They are then sliced, either in strips, thin slices, or matchsticks.
3 Then they are fried in batches for a few minutes in sizzling hot oil to remove their moisture.

4 When they begin to turn color, the *kripik* are removed from the oil and allowed to dry. After that they are salted.
5 If that doesn't offer enough promise of tastebud tingle, anyone choosing *kripik* can then have them dipped in chili paste.
6 Another way of making them more fiery, is to brush each one by hand with a sort of spicy glaze.

Manisan

Salak manis: snakeskin fruit pickled in boiling syrup

Bangkwang: Yam beans, pickled in boiling syrup and seasoned with chili

Sayur asin sawi: Sarepta mustard mixed with salt is used like *bangkwang* in vegetable salads.

Salak pedas: snakeskin fruit pickled in boiling syrup and seasoned with chili powder

Lobi-lobi: Batako plums (*Flacourtia inermis*) pickled in boiling syrup

Mangga manis: mango pieces pickled in boiling syrup

Jambu bangkok: pale guava pieces pickled in boiling syrup

Angur Bogor: grapes pickled in boiling syrup

Asam jawa manis: dried sugared tamarind pods

Belimbing: candied fruit from the cucumber tree (these are members of the starfruit (carambola) family, but the flavor is sourer)

Buah ligo: Lightly candied sweet-and-sour snake-berries (*Antidesma bunius: Bignay*)

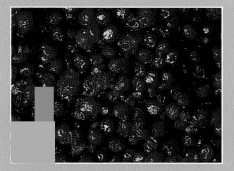

Ceremai: candied and dyed Otaheite berries (*Grosella*), a sour fruit with a pit.

Malaka: candied and dyed fruit of the *myrobalan* tree; when raw, they are just as sour as *ceremai.*

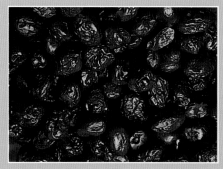

Simanalagi: small sour and salty picked mangoes (a special variety of *kalimantan*)

Mangga asin: salted and dried mango pieces

Mangga asam: sour, dried mango pieces

Mangga manis: sugared dried mango pieces

Pala manis: candied nutmeg (the flesh of the fruit is obtained at the time of harvesting the nutmeg and its blossom)

Pala manis: dried, sugared nutmeg fruit

Pala: dried fruit of the quartered nutmeg

261

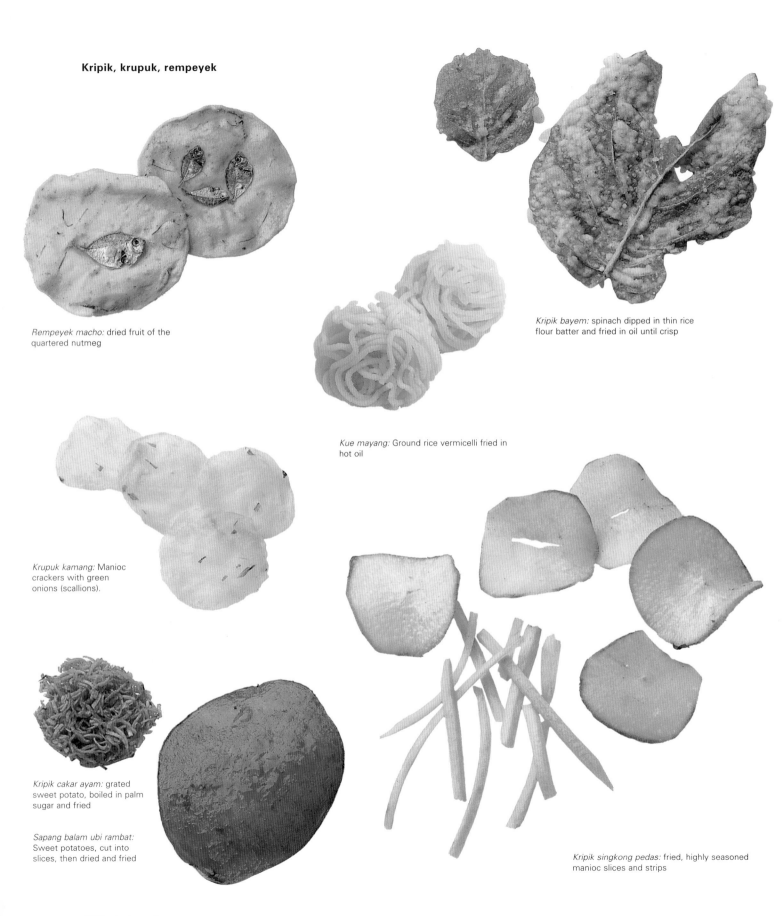

Kripik, krupuk, rempeyek

Rempeyek macho: dried fruit of the quartered nutmeg

Kripik bayem: spinach dipped in thin rice flour batter and fried in oil until crisp

Kue mayang: Ground rice vermicelli fried in hot oil

Krupuk kamang: Manioc crackers with green onions (scallions).

Kripik cakar ayam: grated sweet potato, boiled in palm sugar and fried

Sapang balam ubi rambat: Sweet potatoes, cut into slices, then dried and fried

Kripik singkong pedas: fried, highly seasoned manioc slices and strips

Kripik pisang: ripe bananas sliced lengthwise, dried and fried.

Pisang sale Ambon: a ripe banana halved lengthwise and fried.

Pisang sale siam: dried banana purée.

Usus ayam: cleaned chicken chitterlings, cut into pieces and halved down the middle before being dried and fried.

Krupuk kulit sapi: ox hide cut into strips, dried and fried

Kripik urat: water buffalo tendons cut into strips, dried and fried.

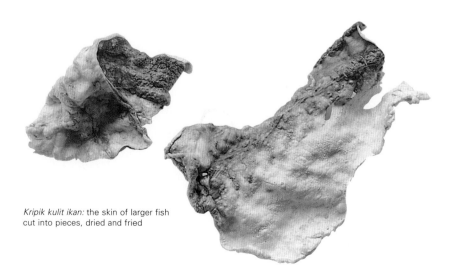

Krupuk kulit jangat: dried and fried water buffalo hide

Kripik kulit ikan: the skin of larger fish cut into pieces, dried and fried

263

Cobek and *ulek-ulek* for grinding spices

Spoons and ladles made of coconut shells with wooden handles

Parut kelapa, the grating board for grating fresh coconut

The modern aluminum version of the *dandang* for steaming rice

In the kitchen

Living conditions on the Indonesian archipelago are very varied and the difference between the large towns and the remoter parts of the small islands seem to be not just worlds but light-years apart. In places where electricity or gas cannot be taken for granted, a glance into a kitchen can easily give the impression that the clock has been turned back to a distant past. This means that the kitchen is equipped as a thoroughly functional unit containing only those items of equipment that are strictly necessary for preparing the various dishes. The food is either cooked on charcoal stoves or, if possible, in the open air on a brick stove using wood as fuel. An important tool here is a plaited bamboo strip fan *(kipas)* which is used to get the fire going. The oven is basically no more than a rectangular metal box (which, strictly speaking, describes every oven, no matter what progress has been made over the years in the way it actually works). Heat is provided from above and below like the old Dutch ovens, by two bowls of glowing charcoal, one above the metal box, the other below it. This works very well indeed, as long as a very watchful eye is kept on the food being cooked, because it is not easy to maintain a constant level of heat over a lengthy period of time when using this method. But since cooking is regarded as a sociable event, there are always willing helpers around, one or other of whom will take the time to check the oven.

Of course, a refrigerator is not a standard item, but it can almost be dispensed with if the necessary produce can be bought fresh at market every day or else fetched from the yard. Many houses have a rice storage area in which a large quantity of rice can be kept.Many families still grind their rice into flour by hand, using an impressive stone mortar and long, thick wooden pestle.

One of the most indispensable pots is the aluminum rice steamer. The rice is first cooked — but only just — in any old pot at all. Once it has absorbed the correct quantity of moisture, it is then transferred to the steamer *(dandang)* and cooked until done. The traditional steamer, a dual-coned vessel with a funnel in the center, is made of copper. It must be filled with boiling water to just the halfway mark. A plaited bamboo basket *(kukusan)* is suspended in the top part of the steamer and, with a lid placed on top, the al dente rice is left to cook through. Next to the steamer, the most widely used cooking utensil is the wok *(wajan)*, whose smooth, overall curve ensures an even distribution of heat.

When the words "pound in a mortar" are used in a recipe, this should not conjure up the traditional pharmacy equipment. The Indonesian mortar is a wide, smooth stone bowl *(cobek)* used typically with a wooden or stone pestle *(ulek-ulek)*. In it, ingredients are not so much ground as crushed, because the pestle is held in the hand and gently moved up and down. It seems apparently effortless, although it does require a bit of practice. Crushing is an integral part of the initial preparation of spice ingredients such as chili peppers, shallots, garlic, peanuts, grated coconut, candlenuts or, indeed, anything that can be made into a paste. You may prefer to use an electric grinder and the result will certainly be satisfactory, but the paste will not be quite like one that is ground in the mortar (and purists maintain that it is just this difference that tells them apart when choosing between the two). If the *cobek is new*, wipe it out with stale bread or grated coconut so as to remove any loose little stones.

The one item that is ever-present in the Indonesian kitchen is a coconut-grater *(palut kelapa)*. In its simplest form, it consists of a wooden board covered with small nails. The most expensive model is so large the person doing the grating can sit astride it and use her own weight to stabilize the grater fixed at one end of this "bench" so that the coconut can be moved with both hands.

Many of the spoons, ladles, and sieves used are made of coconut shells to which wooden or bamboo handles are attached. They are simple, economical, and useful, even if they do not last very long. Covers for food are also woven from bamboo. A range of jugs, bowls, and dishes of various types and sizes completes the basic equipment in a traditional Indonesian kitchen. There are not even any chairs or stools as women squat by the fire to do their cooking.

Sambal

A *sambal* is a dip for raw or cooked vegetables, roast, broiled and grilled chicken, fish and other dishes. It is also added to rice to give that extra little dimension to the food. If a dish is not spicy enough for the Indonesian palate, a *sambal* can correct this defect easily and individually. Generally, it contains a generous quantity of chili peppers as well as the other flavorings.

Only if the *sambal* ingredients are ground together in the mortar—the Indonesian stone version (*cobek*), of course, which has the shape flat rounded bowl with a specially shaped pestle, the *ulek-ulek*—will they have that unique consistency which characterizes sambal and affects its taste. A *sambal* need not always be fiery hot, Sambal *kacang*, for instance, is a peanut sauce which is also used as a dressing for the colorful *gado-gado* vegetable salad, popular throughout Southeast Asia, and it is relatively mild and sweet. However, most Indonesian sauces contain chili peppers.

Sambal ulek
Chili paste

1 cup (250 g) fresh red chili peppers
1 Tsp salt
1 Tsp vinegar
1/4 Tsp sugar
1 Tsp oil
1 Tbs hot water

Cook the chilies until soft. Drain them and pound them in the mortar with all the other ingredients to a smooth paste. Let this cool and pour it into an airtight container. If stored in the refrigerator, the chili paste will keep for a week. This paste can be used as a substitute for fresh chilies in many recipes.

Sambal soto
Sambal for Soups

6 fresh red chili peppers
10 bird's eye chili peppers
1 garlic clove, peeled and quartered
3 candlenuts
1/2 Tsp salt
sugar
Juice of 3 limes
3 Tbs water, boiled and cooled

Cook the chili peppers till soft. Toast the garlic and nuts in a dry skillet. Pound these ingredients to a smooth paste in the mortar. Season with salt and sugar. Stir in the water and lime juice. This *sambal* is a side-dish which is served with *soto ayam* (chicken soup) or *soto daging* (beef broth).

Sambal ayam goreng kalasan
Sambal for roast chicken

10 fresh red chili peppers
1 Tomato
6 shallots, peeled and chopped
5 Tbs oil
2 Tbs water
3 Tsp palm sugar (*gula java,* or use dark brown sugar)
1/2 Tsp salt

Cook the chili peppers and tomatoes until soft. Drain and pound them with the shallots. Heat the oil and fry the paste. Add sugar, salt and water. Cook over a low heat until the oil has been absorbed. A dip for *ayam goreng Kalasan* — Kalasan roast chicken.

As a rule of thumb, the thinner the chili pod, the stronger the fiery taste

Ingredients for a simple *sambal*: chili peppers, garlic, sugar, salt, vinegar and water

Above: A very adequate range of commercially produced *sambals* are available so they do not have to be made at home.

Sambal bajak
Cooked chili and tomato *sambal* (central Java)

10 fresh red chili peppers sliced into rings
1 Tbs shrimp paste *(trassi)*
2 Tbs palm sugar *(gula jawa,* or use dark brown sugar)
1/2 Tsp salt
5 Tbs oil
2 Tomatoes, skinned and finely chopped
1 salam leaf
1 stem lemongrass, lightly crushed
1 x 1/2 in (1 cm)) piece galangal root , lightly crushed
Juice of 2 Tbs tamarind pulp and 2 Tbs water

Pound the chili peppers to a paste in a mortar with shrimp paste and palm sugar. Heat the oil and fry the ground ingredients in it. Add the chopped tomatoes, the tamarind juice, the salam leaf, lemongrass, and ginger root and braise over a low heat, stirring continuously until the mixture is cooked.
Serve with rice and roasts

Be very careful when handling hot chili peppers. Do not rub or touch your own eyes or anyone else's and avoid contact with any mucous membrane. It is best to wear disposable plastic gloves. The seeds are the hottest part.

Sambal trassi
Shrimp and chili *sambal*

10 fresh red chili peppers sliced into rings
3 birdseye chili peppers, sliced into rings
2 Tomatoes
1 Tbs shrimp paste *(trassi),* toasted in a dry skillet
1 Tsp salt
1 Tbs palm sugar
Juice of 6 limes

Pound the chilies, tomatoes, and shrimp paste in a mortar. Add salt, sugar, and lime juice and blend well. Serve as a side-dish or dip.

Sambal lado
Sambal with dried anchovies (western Sumatra)

10 fresh green chilies
5 shallots
8 Tbs small dried anchovies, rinsed, drained, gutted and heads removed
1 Tsp salt (to taste)
Juice of 2 limes

Cook the chili peppers and shallots until soft and allow to dry. Fry dried anchovies in a dry skillet. Pound the chili peppers and shallots coarsely. Mix with the fried anchovies, salt, and lemon juice. Serve with a cooked vegetable.
The anchovies can be replaced by 2 tomatoes. Cook the chili peppers with the tomatoes and shallots until the liquid evaporates, then grind the mixture coarsely. Season with salt, mix with fish or chicken, and then stir-fry the ingredients in a little oil. Service with rice.

The chili peppers and garlic cloves are ground together in a grinder or food processor. Sugar, salt, vinegar, and water are blended in.

The ground ingredients (the photo was taken before the liquids were added) are then cooked a little longer. The consistency should not be too smooth.

Soup

A soup *(soto)* with fish, poultry, or variety meats may be eaten as a one-course meal or served as one of a series of dishes. Vegetable and fish soups tend to be served as part of a meal. These are clear broths, some more substantial than others, and which owe their specific flavors largely to various combinations of chili peppers, shallots, garlic, herbs, and lemongrass.. Occasionally they are colored with fresh turmeric. The rice which is the mandatory accompaniment to every meal is often flavored by being moistened with a little soup or several spoonfuls of sauce (for this reason alone, the series of dishes will always contain one or two which have a dipping sauce).

Sop bayem
Spinach soup

1¼ lb (500 g) spinach leaves, washed and coarsely chopped
5¼ oz (150 g) sweet potato, peeled and cubed
4 cups (1 l) water
2 shallots, sliced into rings
1 garlic clove , thinly sliced
1 green chili pepper, sliced into rings, seeds discarded
1 salam leaf
salt

Bring the water to the boil with the shallots, garlic, chili pepper, and salam leaf. Add the sweet potatoes, bring to the boil, reduce the temperature, cover, and boil for 10 minutes over a low heat.
Add the spinach, season with salt, and simmer for a few minutes over a low heat until it wilts. Serve hot.

In this recipe, leaf spinach may also be replaced by water spinach.

Soto daging
Beef soup

1¼ lb (500 g) lean beef, preferably shoulder or brisket
8 cups (2 l) water
1 Tsp freshly ground black pepper
1 piece cinnamon stick, 2 in (5 cm) long
3 whole cloves
¼ Tsp freshly grated nutmeg
6 shallots, peeled and chopped
2 garlic cloves, peeled and quartered
2 Tbs oil
1 Tsp dark soy sauce
salt to taste

Garnish

2 stems fresh coriander (cilantro), finely chopped
fried onion rings
Juice of 2 limes

Put the meat in a pan with the cold water, pepper, the cinnamon stick, cloves, and nutmeg. Bring the water to the boil, reduce the heat, and let the meat simmer until tender. Remove the meat, dice it, and reserve it. Crush the shallots and garlic cloves using a pestle and mortar. Heat the oil, fry the paste in it, and then add it, together with the soy sauce, to the meat broth. Add the meat and bring the soup back to the boil. Add salt to taste, and then simmer for 2-3 minutes. To serve, pour the soup into a bowl, season with lime juice, and garnish with chopped coriander and fried onion rings.

Soto ayam – Chicken soup

Sop bayem – Spinach soup

Soto ayam
Chicken soup
Serves 4-6

1 oven-ready chicken (about 1 kg (2½ lb)	
6 cups (1½ l) water	
salt and pepper	
3 Tbs oil	
½ Tsp freshly ground black pepper	
¼ Tsp turmeric	
3½ oz (100 g) cellophane noodles	
3½ oz (100 g) beansprouts, roots trimmed	

Spice paste
8 shallots, peeled and chopped	
2 garlic cloves, peeled and quartered	
2 candlenuts	

Garnish
1 green onion (scallion), chopped	
2 stems fresh coriander (cilantro), finely chopped	
fried onion rings	

Place the chicken in a pan filled with cold water and season with salt and pepper. Bring to the boil and then simmer until the meat is cooked. Remove the chicken, strain the broth, and set aside. Bone the chicken and cut the meat into narrow strips.
Soak the cellophane noodles briefly in hot water and then drain. Blanch the beansprouts in boiling water and drain them.
Crush the shallots, garlic cloves, and candlenuts using a pestle and mortar. Heat the oil in a skillet and fry the paste in it, along with pepper and turmeric. Stir the mixture into the chicken broth, bring to the boil, and simmer for 2 minutes.
To serve, place a portion of cellophane noodles, beansprouts, and chicken in a soup bowl, pour the hot broth over them, and garnish with chopped green onions, coriander leaves, and fried onion rings.

Sop ikan pedas
Spicy fish soup

1¼ lb (500 g) fish steaks (catfish, bream, redfish)	
Juice of 1 lime	
3 Tbs oil	
1 stem lemongrass, lightly crushed	
1 slice galangal root ½ in (1 cm) thick, lightly crushed	
1 salam leaf	
4 cups (1 l) water	
salt	
6–8 *belimbing wuluh*, sliced lengthwise	

Spice paste
5 shallots, peeled and chopped	
2 chili peppers, sliced into rings	
2 garlic cloves, peeled and quartered	
1 slice ginger root, ½ in (1 cm) thick	
1 slice turmeric root, ½ in (1 cm) thick	

Marinate the fish steaks in lime juice for 10-15 minutes.
Meanwhile, crush the shallots, chili peppers, garlic cloves, ginger, and fresh turmeric to a paste using a pestle and mortar.
Heat the oil in a pan, add the spice paste, lemongrass, galangal root, and salam leaf and fry until the aromas start to develop. Add the water. Bring the liquid to the boil and reduce the heat. Add the marinated fish and season with salt to taste. Five minutes before the fish is cooked, add the *belimbing wuluh* and leave to simmer.

Although it is called a soup, this dish is not eaten with a spoon, but is used as a sauce to moisten rice.

Belimbing wuluh

Bilimbi (*Averrhoa bilimbi*) is a close relative of the carambola or starfruit. The yellow-green or green stemmed fruits grow up to 3 in (7 cm) long, and look not unlike a pickled gherkin. When cooked in a dish, they impart a pleasantly acidic taste. Like many similar acidic fruits, they are enjoyed as *manisan*, preserved in syrup or candied, as well as pickled by being tossed in salt, dried in the sun, and then preserved in brine.
Traditional Malay medicine has yet more preferred uses for Bilimbi. A solution made of grated fruit and salt, spread over the face, is said to cure acne; a paste of the leaves helps against itching, and the fruit juice reduces fever. The juice also serves to remove stains from fabric and from the skin.

Sop ikan pedas – Spicy fish soup

Fish

As would be expected in a country consisting of so many islands, fish is a major source of protein in the diet of most of the Indonesian population. On everyday menus, it appears more frequently than meat. In general, whole fish are cooked in preference to pieces of larger fish. Dried fish is eaten when fresh fish is unavailable. Fish is either fried with a mixture of aromatic spices, or fried plain and served with a *sambal*. It can be garnished or stuffed with herbs and barbecued on a charcoal grill, when it is sometimes first wrapped in banana leaves. Filleted and diced fish can be wrapped in banana leaves, then steamed with spices, herbs, and young vegetables. Fish is stewed in coconut milk, tamarind juice, or in a thick spicy sauce containing some or all of the following ingredients: shallots, garlic, candlenuts, coriander seeds, chili peppers, salam leaf, tamarind paste, ginger, lemongrass, galangal root, turmeric, and lime juice.

Only where the fishing grounds are sheltered from seasonal storms by large land masses do the fishermen bring in catches the whole year round; in regions exposed to the open sea, the boats are beached during the rainy season, from November through April. But even in the high season, no fisherman would ever venture out at full moon since, as any child knows, the catch will not be worth the trouble.

In the sea between East Java and Bali, the catch consists mainly of sardines, of which *lemuru*, the Indonesian oil sardine *(Sardinella longiceps)*, is the best known. Mackerel, coral fish, small sharks, and tuna also swim into the nets. Most sardines caught end up in cans, and many are sold to Japan.

Fishing in Indonesia

By the sandbanks and in the calm waters beyond the coastal regions, fishing yields can be extremely profitable. Indonesian fishermen also venture onto the high seas. The numerous rivers, marshes, and lakes offer a wide variety of freshwater fish. Not

The Bugi, an ethnic group in the southwest of the Celebes (Sulawesi), are well-known throughout Indonesia for their colorful boats.

By contrast, a *jukung*, an outrigger, 20 ft (5 m) long but only 20 in (50 cm) wide, appears almost fragile.

Between fishing trips, the fishermen gather seaweed, which is dried, ground to a powder, and sold as agar agar. A local recipe involves processing the dried and chopped seaweed with sugar to make a gelatin dessert.

everything is left to chance, however. Fish farms are in operation, especially near the population centers on the north coast of Java or in western and eastern Java.
Shellfish inhabit the coral reefs, and crustaceans are caught in the Straits of Malacca as well as throughout the archipelago, south of Singapore, in the Straits of Macassar, off the south coast of Java, and south of Irian Jaya (New Guinea). Mollusks such as sea cucumbers and squid are common in the region.
With their modern fishing methods, the Japanese fishing companies which have acquired extensive fishing concessions in the eastern regions may soon come to represent a threat to Indonesian fishermen.

Beached *jukung* will float again on the incoming tide. These narrow boats come in three sizes, carrying either one, two, or three fishermen.

Pepes ikan belida
Grilled fish in banana leaf

1 mackerel, about 1¹/₄ lb (about 500 g)
2 Tsp brown sugar
salt
Juice of 2 Tbs tamarind pulp and 2 Tbs water
1 turmeric leaf, thinly sliced
2 stems knotgrass (Vietnamese coriander) *(daun kesum)* (see page 147), leaves only, chopped
1 banana leaf, blanched
3 Tbs oil

Spice paste
8 chili peppers, cleaned and sliced into rings
4 shallots, peeled and minced
2 garlic cloves, peeled and quartered
1 piece turmeric root, ¹/₂ in (1 cm) thick
2 stems lemongrass, only the lower parts, sliced into thin slices
1 piece galangal root, ¹/₂ in (1 cm) thick

First make the spice paste. Crush the chili peppers, shallots, garlic cloves, fresh turmeric, lemongrass, and galangal root to a paste using a pestle and mortar. Heat the oil in a skillet and fry the paste until the aromas start to develop. Dilute the tamarind pulp with 2 tablespoons of water, press through a sieve, and then add to the spice paste, together with sugar and salt. Simmer gently until some of the liquid has evaporated and the mixture can be spread easily. Remove from the heat and leave to cool. Cut the banana leaf into a sufficiently large rectangle, and use half of the spice

paste, half the finely chopped turmeric leaf, and half the chopped Vietnamese coriander leaves, to form a bed for the fish on the banana leaf. Place the fish on top and spread the rest of the mixture and the herbs over the fish. Fold the leaf over the fish to make a package and secure the ends with cocktail sticks. Grill or barbecue over charcoal or broil under a gas or electric broiler for 25-30 minutes.

The banana leaf may be replaced by aluminum foil, although this does mean the loss of an aromatic element. Knotgrass *(daun kesum)* has a sharp, eucalyptus-like aroma.

The fishermen return to their villages at dawn and unload the night's catch on the beach.

The fish which are to be dried are processed as soon as they are brought on land.

Using salt and sun

Preserving fish

Directly after sunrise, the beaches of the fishing villages come to life. The boats return with the night's catch, and the fishermen are met by their families who have come to join in the work to be done. The men load the fish from the boats into shallow bowls, which are obviously best carried on the head. Once on land, the fish is first weighed and then either sold directly on the beach, or taken to market. However, a large proportion of the catch is preserved before being sold at market. This involves heating seawater in wide, shallow tubs, adding the freshly caught fish, and bringing it briefly to the boil. Then it is immediately laid out to dry for about 15 hours. The drying process is crucial: if the fish are not dry enough they will rot, and every hour they dry too long means a loss of income to the fisherman, who sells his wares by weight.

Sharks and other large fish are usually bought up by the fish factories situated in the vicinity; they then undertake the salting process themselves. This means storing the fish for three days in large tubs of brine before they are cleaned and also dried in the sun.

Sambal ikan asin
Sambal with salted dried fish

5¹/₂ oz (150 g) salted dried fish (one small fish or pieces of a larger one
3 fresh red chili peppers, seeds discarded
3 fresh green chili peppers, seeds discarded
2 garlic cloves, peeled and quartered
2 shallots, peeled and chopped
3 Tbs oil
Juice from 2 Tsp tamarind pulp and 3 Tbs water
1¹/₂ Tsp sugar

Dice the pieces of a big fish, or if the fish is small, use it whole. Rinse the dried fish and pat it dry.
Heat 1 tablespoon of oil, add the fish and brown it, remove from the heat and place to one side.
Crush the chilies, garlic cloves, and shallots using a pestle and mortar. Heat the remaining oil, add the crushed ingredients, and fry them until the aromas start to develop. Add the tamarind juice, the fish, and the sugar. Stir well for 1 minute, or until the sugar has dissolved.
Because *Sambal ikan asin* is very salty and the flavor is very strong, it is only used sparingly as a condiment, especially for seasoning rice.

What the fishermen catch

Marine fish
Aya kurik: Pacific tuna *(Euthynnus affinis)*
Bawal: Pampel; various types, some very sought-after and thus very expensive, with tender flesh
Cakalong: Real tuna, striped tuna *(Katsuwonus pelamis)*; less dry flesh than most tuna
Cucut martil: Hammerhead shark *(Sphyrna blochii)*
Kakap merah: Red snapper; very sought-after fish
Kembung: Indian mackerel; used in a variety of dishes
Kerapu: perch; red types are the most popular
Madidihan: Yellow-finned tuna, albacore *(Thunnus albacares)*
Tajur, selayur: the pieces right behind the head are the best.
Tenggiri: King mackerel; firm, tasty flesh
Tongkol: False tuna, frigate mackerel *(Auxis thazard)*

Freshwater fish
Ikan lele: Catfish; good for cooking - will tolerate strong spices
Ikan mas: Carp-like fish *(Cyprinus carpio)*
Tilapia: a Nile fish, easy to farm.

Brine is heated in shallow tubs, and the fish are boiled briefly in it.

The small salted fish are spread on large trays. They take about 15 hours to dry sufficiently; if they dry for too long, they will lose too much weight.

Only small fish can be dried whole; larger ones have the head removed, are opened up along their spines down to the tail-fin, then gutted and spread out in butterfly fashion.

Shrimp

The larger varieties of shrimp are a lucrative business for fishermen; hotels and restaurants are always keen buyers, since the larger varieties of these crustaceans are the expensive ingredient of the special diet of a minority. The majority of the population can rarely afford them. Usually, all they can buy is a handful of tiny bay shrimp for a *nasi goreng*. Jumbo shrimp are sold at markets whole and raw. Many recipes require them to retain their shells for frying or broiling. They are generally only removed for boiling.

Udang bakar
Grilled shrimp

12 jumbo shrimp
3 fresh red chili peppers, cleaned and sliced into rings
2 garlic cloves, peeled and quartered
3 Tbs light Soy sauce
Juice of 1 Tsp tamarind pulp and 2 Tbs water
salt to taste
1 Tsp brown sugar
1 Tbs oil

Remove the heads from the shrimp. Slit open the tail section of the shells along the back and remove the dark "vein". Clean the shrimp tails and reserve them. Crush the chili peppers and garlic cloves using a pestle and mortar and mix with soy sauce, tamarind juice, salt, sugar and oil. Marinate the shrimp in the mixture for 30 minutes, then cook over charcoal or under an electric broiler, brushing the marinade over them while they are cooking.

Gulai udang merah
Shrimp in coconut milk

1¼ lb (500 g) jumbo shrimp
½ coconut, grated (2 cups (250 g))
2 cups (500 ml) water, combined with the grated coconut and squeezed, milk reserved
5 shallots, peeled and chopped
2 garlic cloves, peeled and quartered
1 slice ginger root, ½ in (1 cm) thick
3–4 fresh red chili peppers, cleaned and sliced into rings
1 slice galangal root (½ in (1 cm thick)), lightly crushed
1 stem lemongrass, lightly crushed
1 small turmeric leaf
1 Kaffir lime leaf
1 Tomato, sliced into rounds
salt

Shell the shrimp, clean the tails, and devein. Crush the shallots, garlic, ginger, and chili peppers using a pestle and mortar. Combine the paste and the coconut milk and bring to the boil, together with the galangal root, lemongrass, fresh turmeric, and kaffir lime leaf. Add the shrimp, tomato slices, and salt and leave to simmer until the shrimp are cooked.

Opposite: *Udang harimau*, the ship's keel shrimp, has firm flesh and tastes good.

Udang garam asam
Shrimp in tamarind sauce

17½ oz (500 g) jumbo shrimp
5 fresh red chili peppers, cleaned and sliced into rings
2 slices galangal root, about ½ in (1 cm) thick
1 slice fresh turmeric root, ½ in (1 cm) thick
1 piece shrimp paste *(trassi)*, ½ x ½ x ½ in (1 x 1 x 1 cm)
5 candlenuts
8 Tbs oil
1 stem lemongrass, lightly crushed
juice of 1 Tbs tamarind pulp and 2 cups (500 ml) water
1 ½ Tbs sugar
salt to taste

Separate the shrimp tails, peel and devein them. Crush the chili peppers, galangal root, fresh turmeric, shrimp paste and candlenuts using a pestle and mortar. Heat the oil, add the crushed ingredients and the lemon grass, and fry until the aromas begin to develop. Reduce the heat and add the shrimp with part of the tamarind juice. Stir and add the remaining tamarind juice, the sugar and the salt. Simmer for about 10 minutes.

Pais udang
Spicy shrimp in a banana leaf.

1¼ lb (500 g) small shrimp, peeled
1 slice ginger root
1 slice galangal root
2 fresh red chili peppers, cleaned and sliced into rings
2 candlenuts
3 slices fresh turmeric root
salt
1 sprig basil, leaves finely chopped
1 salam leaf
1 square-shaped piece of banana leaf, blanched

Crush the ginger and galangal root, chili peppers, candlenuts, and fresh turmeric using a pestle and mortar. Season with salt and mix with the shelled shrimp. Place the mixture on the banana leaf, scatter chopped basil over the mixture, and place the salam leaf on top. Then fold the banana leaf to make a rectangular parcel and secure the ends with toothpicks. Steam the parcel for 15 minutes (until the contents are firm) and then broil for 10 minutes under a broiler or over grill over charcoal.

Pais udang – Spicy shrimp in a banana leaf

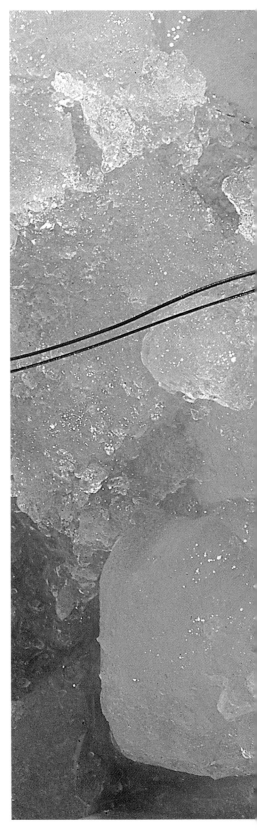

The best shrimp to be found in Indonesian and Malaysian waters

Udang harimau: Ship's keel, also known as bear shrimp *(Penaeus monodon)*, recognizable by its dark coloring with bright lateral stripes, and green tiger shrimp *(P. semisulcatus)*; the former can grow up to 13 in (33 cm), the latter around 9 in (22 cm) long (size indications relate to the whole creature; females are often larger than males). Both are especially popular in Asia because of their firm, aromatic flesh.

Udang kulit keras: Rainbow shrimp *(Para peneopsis sculptilis)*; their hard shell means that these shrimp, up to 7 in (17 cm) long, are best grilled or broiled.

Udang merah ros: Smooth-back shrimp *(Metapenaeus ensis)* prefer muddy waters. Their firm flesh has a strong flavor and is best appreciated when steamed or pan-fried. Females are up to 7 in (16 cm) long. In Malaysia, this shrimp is also farmed.

Udang putih: the Banana shrimp *(Penaeus merguiensis)* has a soft shell and is therefore good for stewing and steaming. This 9 in (24 cm), relatively plump shrimp, owes its name to its yellow coloring.

Udang susu: the Western king shrimp *(Penaeus latisulcatus,* with its hard shell, it is particularly suitable for grilling and broiling. It is caught in muddy and sandy areas. Females can be up to 8 in (19 cm) long.

Cumi-cumi isi
Stuffed squid in spicy sauce

Squid

On moonlit nights, the squid rise to the surface of the water so that the fishermen can almost scoop them up in their nets. But if the nights are dark, the fishermen trick the moon-hungry squid or calamari by illuminating their boats.

Squid have an important place on any menu, for they are so versatile. They can j be fried with spices, or marinated in spices and grilled or broiled. They are simmered in soy sauce or coconut milk, and the pouches can also be stuffed. There is also a recipe in which the squid are cooked in their own ink.

Cumi-cumi goreng – Fried squid

"Ready-to-cook squid"

In the West, squid are usually bought ready to cook. In fact, the shopper usually has no choice, all the squid that are sold in supermarkets and farmers' markets are ready for the pan. However, if you can get hold of really fresh squid, straight from the sea, you should do so, even if preparing squid initially takes some effort.

After the squid has been thoroughly washed, the speckled outer skin of the pouch is removed. This means gripping the skin firmly (but do not pull too hard, otherwise the ink sac inside, whose size depends on the type and age of the squid, could be damaged).

Then, take hold of the tentacles with one hand and the pouch with the other and slowly but firmly pull out the tentacles, plus the head and innards. Squid contain a narrow transparent cuttle bone, also known as the quill, which must also be removed. The pouch must be completely empty. Both external fins can be cut or pulled off. The head and eyes must be severed from the tentacles in such a way that they remain connected by a thin ring of muscle. The jaws situated in the middle of the tentacles should be pushed through and cut out. (Most of the recipes listed here do not use the tentacles.)

Cumi-cumi masak kecap
Squid in soy sauce

5¼ oz (500 g) ready-to-cook squid
1 slice fresh turmeric root, ½ in (1 cm) thick
¼ Tsp salt
3 Tbs lime juice
4 Tbs oil
4 slices ginger root, about ¹/₁₆ in (2 mm) thin
3 garlic cloves, sliced into thin slices
10 shallots, peeled and thinly sliced
4 Tbs dark soy sauce

Make one or two cuts in each side of the squid. Crush the fresh turmeric with salt. Add 1 tablespoon of lime juice and stir. Coat the squid with the mixture. Heat 2 tablespoons of oil in a pan and fry the squid until they are half cooked (cover the pan to prevent the fat spitting). The liquid should not completely evaporate. Then take out the squid and place to one side.

In a second pan, heat the remaining oil, add the ginger, garlic, and shallots and fry until golden-brown. Stir in the dark soy sauce and the rest of the lime juice. Add the squid, stir, and cook through. Serve immediately.

Indonesian cuisine mainly uses dark soy sauce (*kecap manis*), which is milder and slightly sweet. *Kecap asin* is also available; this is a light, saltier soy sauce of the Chinese type.

Cumi-cumi isi
Stuffed squid in spicy sauce

8 ready-to-cook squid
3 Tbs oil
½ coconut, grated (about 2 cups (250 g))
3 cups (750 ml) water, combined with the coconut, squeezed out, milk reserved
salt

Spice paste

8 fresh red chili peppers, sliced into rings, seeds
10 shallots, peeled and chopped
½ Tsp shrimp paste *(trassi)*
4 candlenuts
1 stem lemongrass, only the lower part, thinly sliced
2 slices galangal root, about ¹/₁₆ in (2 mm) thick

Filling

10 large shrimp, flesh removed
squid tentacles
1 sprig fresh coriander (cilantro), leaves minced
pepper
salt

Crush the chili peppers, shallots, shrimp paste, candlenuts, lemongrass, and galangal root to a paste using a pestle and mortar.

To prepare the squid, clean the separated tentacles carefully, and reserve. Rub the inside of the squid thoroughly with salt.

Chop the tentacles very finely. Dice the shelled shrimp likewise. Combine, stir in the coriander leaves, and season with salt and pepper.

Fill the squid pouch with the shrimp mixture and secure the pouch closed with cocktail sticks.

Fry the stuffed squid in a little oil for 2-3 minutes, then remove from the pan and place to one side. Heat the remaining oil, add the spicy paste, and fry until the aromas start to develop. Pour the coconut milk into the pan and season with salt. As soon as the mixture boils, add the stuffed squid to the pan and simmer until the liquid has almost completely evaporated. Serve immediately.

Cumi-cumi goreng
Fried squid

1 lb 5 oz (600 g) ready-to-cook squid
3 Tbs oil
1 Tsp ground turmeric
1 stem lemongrass
2 dried tamarind slices, soaked in water
salt
1 Tsp dark brown sugar

Spice paste

6 fresh red chili peppers, cleaned and sliced into rings
6 shallots, peeled and chopped
2 garlic cloves, peeled and quartered
1 slice galangal root, ½ in (1 cm) thick
5 candlenuts

Make one or two cuts in each side of the squid. Crush the chili peppers, shallots, garlic, galangal root, and candlenuts to a paste using a pestle and mortar. Heat the oil in a pan, add the spicy paste, and the turmeric, lemongrass, and tamarind slices, and fry until the aromas start to develop. Season with salt and sugar, then add the squid and stir. As soon as they are cooked, remove the pan from the heat and serve immediately.

It is easy to cook the squid for too long, which makes the flesh tough (leaving the cooked dish standing can have the same effect); so be sure not to cook the squid for a moment longer than is necessary.

Gulai cumi-cumi
Squid in coconut milk

1¼ lb (500 g) ready to cook squid
5 fresh red chili peppers, cleaned and sliced into rings
½ small turmeric leaf
2 dried tamarind slices, soaked in water
1 sprig basil
½ coconut, grated (2 cups (250 g))
1 cup (250 ml) water, combined with the grated coconut and squeezed, milk reserved
salt

Spice paste

6 shallots, peeled and chopped
2 slices turmeric root, about ½ in (1 cm) thick
2 slices ginger root, ½ in (1 cm) thick

Crush the shallots to a paste with the fresh turmeric and ginger, using a pestle and mortar.

Cut the squid into strips and cook in a pan with the chili peppers, half the turmeric leaf, the tamarind slices, and the spice paste, until all the liquid has evaporated. Now add the coconut milk, add the basil, season with salt, stir, and leave to simmer until the squid is cooked and the sauce is thick.
Serve immediately.

Battle-hardened food

Chicken

Chickens are kept in most villages; during the day they run around unfettered, but are locked in baskets at night; these are hung up inside the house or elsewhere so that they cannot be reached by rats. The usually peaceful chickens primarily satisfy the villagers' own needs, but are also bred for the market.

The fighting cocks bred especially for cockfights are less peace-loving. These too are seen in every village. Their owners spoil them with all kinds of tidbits and give them baths and massages. They carry them around under their arms and give them treats as if they were domestic pets. The fights, at which bets are also placed, are very lively.

On Bali, cockfights are only permitted for ritual purposes, so as to drive out evil spirits from the temple areas. They are therefore a fixed component of all festivities around the temple. If there appear to be a good many more places from which evil spirits need to be driven, not too many questions are asked...

Shortly before the fight begins, the men appear with the roosters under their arms or in baskets. At this stage they are still trying to calm their birds by stroking them. Usually, equally-matched opponents are chosen for the fights, since this increases the excitement. The audience forms a circle, which increases in size as more people gather. Some of the cocks behave extremely aggressively as soon as they see themselves confronted with their potential opponents, while others react calmly. When a suitable pair has been chosen, the owners fasten a sharp spur to the leg of each bird. This is when the bets are taken. Right before the start of the fight, the uproar suddenly dies down and there is silence. The cocks are placed face to face: there is loud clamoring, a wild flurry of feathers, and the fight is over in no time. The defeated bird lies wounded — often fatally — on the ground and is carried home by its owner, where it often ends up being eaten for dinner. The winnings are paid out, and after a short time the next fight takes place.

The Indonesians love fried or broiled chicken, *ayam goreng*. And as with all of the

The sharpest of spurs make the rooster's attacks even more deadly.

The spur is secured very carefully. The bird must not lose it, but should not be impeded in its movements or it is bound to lose the fight.

Many roosters are so aggressive that they volun-
tarily for both competitors.

Frenzied fluttering of wings, terrible screeches,
and flying feathers — the fight is quickly over.

most popular dishes, there is not one single recipe, but countless regional variations. What they all have in common is that the chicken is not simply cooked in oil until it is dry, but it is first boiled with herbs and spices in water and coconut milk (or tamarind juice, or soy sauce) before being fried, broiled, or grilled. This makes the chicken crisp on the outside but tender and juicy inside.

Ayam goreng bumbu
Fried chicken with spices
Serves 4-6

1 chicken, about. 2 lb 3 oz (1 kg) , cut into serving pieces
1 stem lemongrass, lightly crushed
2 salam leaves
water
oil for frying
1 Tbs ground coriander
salt
sugar

Spice paste

6 shallots, peeled and chopped
3 garlic cloves, peeled and quartered
8 candlenuts
1 piece galangal root, 1 in (2 cm) thick
1 piece fresh turmeric root, 1 in (2 cm) thick

Crush the shallots, garlic, candlenuts, galangal, and fresh turmeric to a paste using a pestle and mortar. Place the chicken parts, spice paste, lemongrass, salam leaf, salt, and sugar in a pan and just cover with water. Boil until the chicken is tender and the liquid has evaporated.
Heat oil for frying and fry the chicken until golden brown. Drain off the surplus oil and serve with the spice paste.

Ayam goreng Kalasan
Fried chicken kalasan
Serves 4-6

1 chicken, about. 2 lb 3 oz (1 kg) , halved
3 cups (750 ml) coconut water from young coconuts (or substitute canned coconut water)
5 shallots, peeled and minced
3 garlic cloves, peeled and minced
1 piece galangal root 1 in (2 cm), lightly crushed
1/4 Tsp turmeric
salt
oil for frying

Mix coconut water, shallots, garlic, galangal root, turmeric, and salt in a pan, and cook the halved chicken in the liquid. As soon as it is tender, take it out, and leave to cool. Reserve the spice mixture.
Heat oil for frying and brown the chicken halves. Remove them from the oil, spread the spices over the top, and serve.

A wild flutter of wings, a terrible screech, and flying feathers — the fight is soon over.

Ayam goreng bumbu
Fried chicken with spices

Beef, pork, and goat — all on a skewer
Meat dishes

Cattle and water-buffalo serve as draught animals in the fields and on the roads. They also provide milk and manure, and needless to say, they are also used for their meat. Water-buffalo are more or less indispensable in more than one respect in areas with short dry periods and muddy, heavy soil, such as western Java. Beef cattle, on the other hand, are seen more frequently in the dry regions with lighter soil which is easier to work, such as in most of Java, Bali, Lombok, and Madura. On some islands, there is a breed of small beef cattle similar to chamois goats; they are known as gem buffalo. The Hindu Dharma creed, to which only the Balinese belong, permits the eating of beef, deviating from pure Hindu doctrine.

Since water-buffalo meat is noticeably tougher than that of beef cattle, recipes have been devised which take account of this, allowing longer cooking times with lower to medium temperatures. One of these is rendang, in which the meat is braised gently in coconut milk and spices until only oil remains from the coconut milk, in which the meat is finally fried. By then it should be dark brown and give off a delicious aroma. Due to the long cooking time, it is more economical to cook rendang in large quantities, especially since it can be prepared in advance.

To make rendang, cook 2¼ lb 4 oz (1 kg) water-buffalo meat in 2 quarts (2 l) coconut milk with galangal root, turmeric leaves, lemongrass, and a spice paste made from 10 shallots, 10 red chili peppers, 2 garlic cloves, and a piece of root ginger.

Satay (saté) is available almost everywhere in Indonesia: at simple warung (mobile snack bars), in good restaurants and in superior hotels. Satay and sauce vary little from region to region. In general, beef is used to make it, but also chicken, mutton or offal are possible. The Indonesians are particularly fond of offal. On Bali, a special satay of minced pork with coconut milk, grated coconut and spices is prepared for festive occasions. Cooked over red-hot charcoal, satay kabobs taste best.

Saté manis
Spicy grilled beef kabobs

1¼ oz (500 g) chuck steak, diced or sliced
2 Tsp ground coriander
1 Tsp dark brown sugar
salt to taste
1 Tbs light soy sauce
Juice of 2 Tsp tamarind pulp and 2 Tbs water
2 Tbs oil

Spice paste

6 shallots, peeled and chopped
2 garlic cloves, peeled and quartered
3 fresh red chili peppers, sliced into rings
1 slice galangal root ½ in (1 cm) thick
1 slice turmeric root, ½ in (1 cm) thick
1 slice ginger root, ½ in (1 cm) thick

Crush the shallots, garlic, chili peppers, galangal, fresh turmeric, and ginger to a paste using a pestle and mortar. Mix the paste with coriander, sugar, salt, soy sauce, tamarind juice, and oil. Marinate the diced beef or beef slices in the mixture for 1–2 hours. Arrange the meat on bamboo skewers (4–5 pieces per skewer) and broil or grill over charcoal, brushing with the remaining marinade.
Serve with peanut sauce.

Sambal kacang
Peanut sauce

2 cups (250 g) shelled peanuts
4 Tbs oil
1 Tsp dark brown sugar
1 Tsp dark soy sauce
juice of 1 Tsp tamarind pulp and 1 Tbs water
salt to taste
2 cups (500 ml) water

Spice paste

4 fresh red chili peppers, seeds discarded
4 shallots, peeled and chopped
2 garlic cloves, peeled and quartered
1 piece shrimp paste (trassi), ½ x ½ x ½ in (1 x 1 x 1 cm)

Crush the chili peppers, shallots, garlic, and shrimp paste to a pulp using a pestle and mortar. Fry the peanuts in 2 tablespoons of oil, drain, and cool, then crush. Heat the remaining oil, add the spice paste, and fry it until the aromas start to develop. Add sugar, soy sauce, tamarind juice, salt, and water and bring to the boil.
Add the peanuts, reduce the heat, and simmer until the sauce is creamy. Stir occasionally.

Pigs are of course only bred and eaten in the islands which do not practice Islam — Bali, Lombok, Flores, the Batak district of Sumatra) and Toraja Land on Celebes (Sulawesi). In many village communities, the people still breed their own pigs. In the Batak district, *babi panggang* is a speciality of numerous restaurants. It consists of strips of pork belly which, seasoned only with salt, are broiled or grilled over an open flame. They are sliced and served with a sauce, made of chili peppers, lemongrass, onions, lime juice, and salt, all cooked in pig's blood.

Babi guling is a suckling pig aged three to six months which is stuffed with a mixture of chopped chili peppers, garlic, onion, fresh turmeric, ginger, and herbs. The carcass is sewn up and the pig is spit-roasted on a long wooden spike. To give the skin a golden hue, it is brushed with water in which a piece of fresh turmeric has been crushed. The pig is then roasted over charcoal or a fire made of coconut palm bark and wood. The pig is turned slowly and constantly on the spit, so that it may take two to three hours before the meal—consisting of meat, crackling, stuffing, and rice (as a side-dish)— is ready to be enjoyed. Suckling pig is only served on special occasions.

Sometimes, the contents of the cooking pot reveal religious affinities (or their absence): pork will only be found where there are no Moslems.

In this regard, the goats are an inadequate clue. At best, they identify their owners as meat-eaters and milk-drinkers.

Goats are kept primarily for their meat; their milk is of secondary importance. It is a common sight to see them wandering through a village, along a street, eating anything that takes their fancy, just like their European counterparts. Goat meat is mainly used for curry dishes (*gulai*) and *satay*, but for very special occasions, a goat may also be roasted whole. The Indonesians describe everything which is cooked on a spit and turned in the process as *"guling"*, and so *kambing guling* (spit-roast goat) is the culinary counterpart of *babi guling* (spit-roast sucking pig).

Before the goat is skewered on the spit, it is marinated in a mixture of spices, including coriander, galangal root, pepper, and fresh turmeric. During roasting, it should be brushed regularly with oil. A young goat takes about an hour and a half to cook through over hot charcoal. It is served with a peanut sauce or *kecap* (soy sauce).

Kambing guling, spit-roast goat, can feed around 30 people at a festive meal.

Rijstafel

In Indonesian households of old, it was not unusual to serve rice with a whole variety of side-dishes. However, Dutch plantation owners made such varied menus even more opulent. Their efforts were designed to impress their peers who were guests at the balls and house parties. The large number of staff employed ensued that these banquets did not pose a problem.

Rijstafel, a Dutch expression literally meaning, "rice table" and similar to the Sumatran *nasi padang* from Sumatra, is a sort of buffet. The Peranakan in Malaysia and Singapore serve large meals in a similar way and call it *tok panjang*.

In colonial villas and mansions, the dishes were served by a bevy of servants. In a modern Indonesian *rijstafel*, a procession of eleven young women, led by a matron who is familiar with the dishes and their preparation, each carries one dish. The older woman serves a portion of rice to each guest at the table. Her assistants follow her, and each of them serves up her particular dish. In the process, the older woman praises the special attributes of each individual dish. When the last woman's turn comes, each person has already been served with ten different dishes in addition to the rice.

The meal begins with a soup, followed by a plate of raw vegetables, accompanied by sauce dips and crackers. Then comes a succession of dishes, including chicken, fish, beef, vegetables, egg, and a selection of various *sambals*. The finale is the dessert, followed by coffee or tea with *manisan*, for instance in the form of sweet rice cakes or tamarind candies. Although it is by no means considered unsophisticated to take a second helping, hardly anyone is capable of doing so!

During the colonial era, *rijstafel* was served at the fashionable hotels as a Sunday brunch. Even in post-colonial days, the old Raffles Hotel in Singapore still serves *rijstafel* as the Sunday brunch.

A traditional *rijstafel* takes the diner back to times where staff were plentiful and one waitress per dish did not appear to be an excessive luxury.

Nasir putih: Steamed white rice, is parboiled then finished over steam in a double boiler.

Kimlo: Clear chicken soup. Mushrooms, carrots, and leeks are then added to the broth with shallots, garlic, cloves, nutmeg, and dark soy sauce. The garnish is onion rings and coriander.

Tahu isi: Steamed tofu with a filling made of ground chicken, shrimp, chives, and beaten egg. The sauce consists of a paste of cooked chili peppers and garlic, flavored with vinegar and sugar.

Lalapan: This dish, consisting of raw vegetables with two sauce dips, has been influenced by the West, as evidenced by the grissini and the avocado dip. Indonesian cuisine is represented by a chili dip and *krupuk udang dan ikan* (shrimp and fish crackers).

Ayam tim: Chicken pieces, cooked in broth with ginger, star anise, shallots, and garlic, are served with carrots and green vegetables, cooked separately.

Ikan belado: Fish fillets, cut into bite-size pieces and fried, are covered in a cooked sauce made of crushed chili peppers, shallots, garlic, sugar, salt, and water.

Dendeng ragi: Slices of lean beef, braised with sugar and coriander, are served with grated coconut simmered in water and tamarind juice. A spice paste is added consisting of shallots, garlic, coriander, galangal, salam leaf, and lemongrass. The mixture simmers until the water evaporates and starts to fry in the remaining coconut fat.

Lumpia: Fried spring rolls. These are usually filled with stir-fried matchstick strips of carrot and green beans, and shredded cabbage.

Sate ayam dan sapi:
Kabobs of marinated chicken and beef are served with *sambal kacang,* a cooked sauce made of roasted peanuts, shallots, garlic, shrimp paste, sugar, soy sauce, water, and tamarind juice.

Orak-arik campur: Braised carrots sliced in julienne strips with beansprouts, seasoned with shallots, garlic, salt, and pepper, and bound with beaten egg.

Aneka sambal: The choice of sauces includes *sambal tomat* (tomatoes, chili peppers, shallots, shrimp paste, and galangal), *sambal goreng* (tomatoes, chili peppers, shallots, garlic, salt, sugar), *sambal trassi* (shrimp paste, chili peppers, tomatoes, sugar, and lime juice) and *sambal bajak* (chili peppers, shrimp paste, palm sugar, tomatoes, and lemongrass).

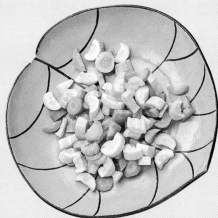

Acar campur: Blanched carrot and cucumber pieces are served in acidulated water, flavored with chili powder, sugar, and salt.

Rempeyek: Peanut crackers made from a rice flour and water batter, with garlic and candlenut.

Sambal goreng dadar telur: Omelet strips in sweet-and-sour chili sauce served with snowpeas or sugar snap peas which are cooked separately

Serundeng: Toasted coconut to which peanuts, shallots, garlic, sugar and salt are then added. The dish requires constant stirring while cooking.

Vegetables

The fertile soil, and variety of altitudes across the Indonesian archipelago, makes it possible to cultivate a huge variety of vegetables. In Berastagi, in northern Sumatra, the cool climate and the volcanic soil are ideal for growing vegetables which are native to northern latitudes, such as carrots, potatoes, beans, cucumbers, cabbage, and corn. In the lower-lying regions, sweet potatoes, yams, eddoes, cassava (yuca), potatoes, peanuts, and soybeans are grown. In some regions, a rotation between soybeans and rice is practiced successfully. In the Javan plains, spinach, water-spinach and Chinese (Napa) cabbage are grown. In village communities, every family cultivates its own chili peppers, ginger, herbs, and the other ingredients which are needed every day in the kitchen.

The vegetable varieties available in Indonesia are scarcely different from those eaten in Singapore and Malaysia, especially since Singapore, which as a city-state has scarcely any agricultural land, also imports its vegetables from Indonesia.

The best way to prepare vegetables is to boil them in rich coconut milk sauces or in light, sweet-and-sour sauces with tamarind and tomatoes, as well as in stir-fries with shallots, garlic, chili peppers, shrimp, or shrimp paste (trassi). Using raw vegetables or a mixture of cooked and raw vegetables, salads are prepared which are served with sauces, sambal for dipping, or a spicy dressing made of grated coconut.

In addition to the vegetable varieties which you could find at home in any farmer's market, there are also some unusual ones. Every type of yam, eddo, collocasia and similar tropical tubers are available, as well as the sprouts and leaves of sweet potatoes, the leaves of the melinjo tree, and daun pakis, a tender, fern-like plant which grows wild in the highlands of Java, Bali, and Sumatra. Since its consumption is limited to private households, it is however scarcely likely to be encountered on trips where one is dependent on restaurants and hot food stalls.

Acar kuning
Preserved yellow vegetables

7 oz (200 g) carrots, peeled
7 oz (200 g) cucumbers, seeds discarded
7 oz (200 g) green beans, trimmed
salt
2 Tbs oil
10 round, fairly large shallots or pearl onions
1 cup (250 ml) water
2 Tbs vinegar
1 Tsp sugar

Spice paste

1 fresh red chili pepper, trimmed and sliced into rings
2 garlic cloves, peeled and quartered
1 slice fresh turmeric root, 1/2 in (1 cm) thick
1 slice ginger root, 1/2 in (1 cm) thick
3 candlenuts

Crush the chili pepper, garlic, fresh turmeric, ginger root, and candlenuts to a paste, using a pestle and mortar. Cut the carrots and cucumber into strips 4 cm (2 in) long and 1/2 in (1 cm) thick, and the beans into 2 in (4 cm) pieces. Sprinkle the chopped vegetables with salt, stir well, and soak in water for 20 minutes. Then rinse and drain well. Heat the oil in a pan, add the spice paste, and fry until the aromas begin to develop; then add water and vinegar. Add sugar and salt and bring to the boil, then add the vegetables and stir. Reduce the heat and simmer the vegetables until they are al dente.

Acar does not have to be eaten hot. When cold, it can be stored in the fridge for several days. It serves as an appetizer, accompanied by other dishes.

Gulai daun ubi
Sweet potato leaves in coconut milk

17 1/2 oz (500 g) young sweet potato leaves (or substitute spinach)
1/2 coconut, grated (2 cups (250 g))
3 cups (750 ml) water, combined with the coconut and squeezed, milk reserved
salt to taste

Spice paste

2 fresh red chili peppers, sliced into rings seeds discarded
4 shallots, peeled and chopped
2 Tbs dried shrimp, soaked briefly

Crush the chili peppers and shallots to a paste, using a pestle and mortar, then add the dried shrimp and work them in.

Wash the sweet potato-leaves and remove the stalks. Blanch the leaves in slightly salted water, drain and leave to cool, then cut into 2 in (5 cm) strips.

In a pan, combine the prepared leaves and the spice paste with the coconut milk and salt, and bring to the boil. Reduce the heat and simmer the vegetables for 10 minutes, stirring frequently.

Acar kuning – Preserved yellow vegetables

Sayur lodeh
Mixed vegetables in coconut milk
Serves 2 or 4

5¹/₄ oz (150 g) Japanese eggplant, halved and cut into 1 ¹/₂ in (3 cm) slices
1 coconut, grated (2 cups (500 g))
3 cups (³/₄ l) water,combined with the grated coconut, squeezed, milk reserved
1 salam leaf
1 slice galangal root, ¹/₂ in (1 cm) thick, lightly crushed
3 fresh red chili peppers, sliced into rings, seeds discarded
salt
5¹/₄ oz (150 g) asparagus beans, sliced into 1 in (2.5 cm) pieces
¹/₄ cup (60 g) canned bamboo shoots, drained and cut into pieces
3¹/₂ oz (100 g) cabbage, shredded

Spice paste

2 shallots, peeled and chopped
1 garlic clove, peeled and quartered
¹/₄ Tsp shrimp paste (trassi)
2 candlenuts
1 Tsp ground coriander

Crush the shallots, garlic, shrimp paste, and candlenuts to a paste, using a pestle and mortar, and combine with the ground coriander.
Soak the eggplant pieces in salt water until they are soft. Rinse and drain. Bring the spice paste, the coconut milk, salam leaf, galangal root, chili peppers, and salt to the boil in a pan. Reduce the heat and add the beans and bamboo shoots. Only when the beans are almost cooked, add the eggplant pieces and the cabbage and stir. As soon as the eggplant pieces are cooked through, the dish is ready.

Sayur lodeh can also be served with ketupat (pressed rice) as a meal in itself, in which case the quantities will serve two.

Tumis buncis
Fried green beans

1¹/₄ lb (500 g) green beans, cleaned
2 fresh red chili peppers, cleaned
2 Tbs oil
3 shallots, peeled and sliced into rings
2 garlic cloves, peeled and thinly sliced
4 Tbs water
salt
pepper

Slice the beans and chili peppers diagonally into 1 in (2.5 cm) pieces.
Heat the oil in a wok, add the shallots, garlic, and chili peppers, and stir-fry for 1 minute. Add the beans, season with salt and pepper, and stir-fry for 2 minutes. Add the water, reduce the heat, cover the wok, and braise the vegetables for 5 minutes. Remove the lid, stir the beans, and cook uncovered, until they are tender but still al dente.

Kacang asam pedas
Asparagus beans in hot sauce

7 oz (200 g) asparagus beans, cleaned
2 cups (500 ml) water
salt
²/₃ cup (150 g) shrimp, peeled and deveined
2 tomatoes, quartered

Spice paste

4 fresh red chili peppers, seeds discarded
4 shallots, peeled and chopped
1 garlic clove , peeled and quartered
1 slice galangal root, ¼ in (5 mm) thick
1 slice fresh turmeric root, ¼ in (5 mm) thick
1 slice ginger root, ¹/₁₆ in (3 mm) thick

Using a pestle and mortar, crush the chili peppers, shallots, and garlic with the galangal, turmeric, and ginger to make a paste. Cut the beans into 2 in (5 cm) pieces. Add the spice paste and salt to a pan of water and bring to the boil. Add the shrimp and tomatoes and cook for 1 minute, then add the beans and simmer until they are cooked but still al dente.

Terung belado
Eggplant in chili sauce

1¹/₄ lb (500 g) long, thin eggplants
oil for frying
juice of 4 limes
salt
3 Tbs oil

Spice paste

4 fresh red chili peppers, cleaned and sliced into rings
4 fresh green chili peppers, cleaned and sliced into rings
1 onion, peeled and chopped

Crush the chili peppers and onion to a paste using a pestle and mortar. Remove the stalk ends from the eggplant. Then slice them almost in half lengthwise. Fry until cooked, drain, and place in a bowl. Heat the oil in a pan, add the spice paste and salt, and fry until the aromas start to develop. Pour the lime juice over them, stir, add the fried eggplant, and pour the sauce over the eggplant. Serve immediately.

Tumis buncis – Fried green beans

Cassava

While the inhabitants of the western provinces of Indonesia consider rice to be their staple food, their fellow citizens in the eastern provinces have come to view cassava *(Manihot esculenta;* Indon.: *singkong;* Mal.: *ubi kayu)* in the same way, along with taro, maize, sago and plantains. Cassava (also known as manioc or yuca) is boiled, steamed, or cooked for several hours on hot stones. As a starchy staple, it is served with salted roasted fish or meat for breakfast or lunch. In times of shortage, this South American root has helped the people of southeast Asia to survive, for apart from its high starch content, it also contains protein, trace elements, and vitamin C.

Since cassava cannot be stored raw, it has to be processed in some way. One possibility is to peel and chop it and dry it in the sun or on hot plates. It is then crushed to make cassava meal. The alternative method of wet-grinding the chopped tuber yields pure extracted starch as a dried end product.

Another possibility is to cut cassava into thin slices or strips and fry them to make chips. However, cassava is more often processed into cassava meal.

Cassava can also be fermented to make naturally sweet, slightly fermented *tapé.* For this, the peeled tubers are boiled and cooled. Yeast *(ragi)* is added and the mixture is left to stand for two days. The tapé is then ready for eating. *Es tapé* is the name of a drink made from fermented cassava.

Getuk ubi
Cassava with palm sugar

1 1/4 lb (500 g) cassava, peeled
1/2 coconut, grated (about 2 cups (200 g), brown husk removed
5 1/4 oz (150 g) palm sugar
2 Tbs water

Chop the cassava finely and cook in salted water. Drain and dry in a pan over a low heat. Steam the grated coconut with a pinch of salt. Heat the palm sugar with the water and dissolve to make syrup. Remove the fibrous parts of the cassava and crush the rest, working in the syrup. Place the mixture in a shallow bowl, smooth it flat, and press down firmly. To serve, cut out squares and coat them in grated coconut.

For processing into flour, the skin is first removed from the tuber.

In the second stage of the process, the vegetables are chopped finely so as to remove all the fibers which would make them impossible to shred or grate.

The brown tubers are turned into white granules which are ground after drying.

Kue talam ubi
Steamed cassava cake
Serves 6 - 8

Bottom layer

1 lb 5 oz (600 g) grated cassava, excess water drained away
2 Tbs tapioca
1 cup (225 g) sugar
1/2 coconut, grated (about 1 cup (220 g), brown husk first removed
1 cup (250 ml) water, combined with the grated coconut, squeezed, milk reserved
a few drops of yellow or green food coloring

Top layer

1/3 cup (80 g) tapioca
31/2 cups (50 g) rice flour
1 coconut, grated (4 cups (450 g)), brown husk previously removed
11/2 cups (375 ml) water, combined with the coconut and squeezed, milk reserved
1/4 Tsp sugar

Line a flat oven dish about 10 in x 7 1/2 in (20 x 15 cm) in size with a banana leaf, or grease it.
For the lower layer, mix the cassava with tapioca, sugar, and coconut milk. Then stir in the color evenly. Cook the mixture over a low heat, stirring constantly, until it thickens. Pour the mixture into the oven dish and steam for about 20 minutes, by which time it should be half-cooked. For the upper layer, mix all ingredients well and pour carefully over the half-cooked lower layer. Steam for 25 minutes, or until firm. When cool, cut into squares.

Above: *Tapé* is one way of preserving the easily perishable raw cassava.

Kue bingka ubi
Baked cassava cake
Serves 4 - 6

11/4 lb (500 g) cassava, grated excess moisture drained away
1 coconut, grated (4 cups (450 g), brown husk first removed
1 cup (270 ml) thick coconut milk
3/4 cup (180 g) sugar
1/4 Tsp salt
1 egg, beaten
a few drops vanilla extract

Preheat the oven to 350°F (180°C).
Squeeze the milk out of the grated coconut without adding any water. If the quantity of milk produced is insufficient, add a little water and squeeze the coconut again until the required quantity of coconut milk has been obtained.
Grease a 9 in x 9 in (18 x 18 cm) oven dish and warm it in the oven for 5 minutes.
In a bowl, combine the cassava thoroughly with the sugar, salt, egg, coconut milk, and vanilla extract.
Remove the dish from the oven and pour in the mixture. Bake for about 50 minutes until the cake is firm and a golden-brown crust has formed on the top.
Do not cut the cake into pieces until it has cooled completely.

Street sales of *tapé* are good business in some provinces of Indonesia.

Starch and hydrocyanic acid

Cassava (*manihot utilissima*) is a member of the spurge family (*Euphorbiaceae*) of which there are 150 varieties, sweet and bitter. The sap of these plants contains hydrocyanic acid and so do the tubers which are otherwise edible. When the plant is damaged, the enzyme linase, present in the cell tissue, splits the glycoside and releases the hydrocyanic acid as a gas. For this reason, cassava cannot be eaten raw, particularly the bitter cassava, and is only safe when well cooked. The cassava tuber is very rich in starch and trace elements but has a lower protein content than other staples, so it is always supplemented by a protein-rich food.

Salad

In an Indonesian menu, salads are not served separately or as an appetizer but are one of the selection of dishes accompanying the rice. They are thus eaten alternately with all the dishes on offer. However, there are some salads which are accorded a certain separate existence, such as *gado-gado*, which is even served as an entrée, or which can be eaten as a snack. The same is true of *asinan buah*, a fruit salad, or *asinan sayur*, a vegetable salad.

In Indonesian salads, vegetables are either used raw, or boiled for a few minutes. Almost all the dressings contain crushed chili peppers. Limes, tamarind, or vinegar create the acidity. Peanuts, shrimp paste, palm sugar, or special herbs add variety and subtle flavoring.

Gado-gado
Java salad
Serves 6 - 8 as a side-dish
Serves 4 as an entrée

4 1/2oz (125 g) asparagus beans, cut into 1 in (2.5 cm) pieces
4 1/2 oz (125 g) cauliflower flowerets
4 1/2 oz (125 g) coarsely shredded cabbage
1/2 cup (125 g) beansprouts, roots trimmed
1 cucumber, peeled and sliced
2 potatoes, boiled, peeled and sliced
2 hardboiled eggs, sliced

Peanut dressing
1 Tbs tamarind pulp
3/4 cup (200 ml) water, boiled and cooled
6 fresh red chili peppers, sliced into rings
1/4 Tsp shrimp paste (*trassi*) toasted in a dry skillet
1 cup (250 g) roasted peanuts, finely chopped
2 Tbs palm sugar, or substitute dark brown sugar
salt

Garnish
shrimp crackers (2 large or 4 small)
fried onion rings

Boil the asparagus beans, cauliflower, cabbage, and beansprouts until they are just cooked. Arrange the vegetables, cucumber, potatoes, and eggs on a serving platter.

Mix the tamarind pulp with 2 tablespoons of water from the total volume indicated, and strain through a sieve. Crush the chili peppers and shrimp paste using a pestle and mortar. Add the tamarind juice and the remaining water and mix with the chopped peanuts. Season to taste with palm sugar and salt.

Pour the dressing over the vegetables just before serving. Garnish with shrimp crackers and onion rings.

Asinan
Fruit and vegetable salad

2 carrots, scraped and sliced into 2 in (4 cm) long strips
2 cucumbers, peeled and sliced into 2 in (4 cm) long sticks
4 1/2 oz (125 g) cabbage, sliced into 1/2 in (1 cm) wide strips
7 oz (200 g) beansprouts, roots trimmed
2 starfruits (carambola), halved and sliced
5 1/4 oz (150 g) papaya (barely ripe), cut into rounds

Dressing
3 Tbs palm sugar, or substitute raw brown sugar
2 Tbs water
2 Tbs dried shrimp, soaked
2 fresh red chili peppers, sliced into rings
4 birdseeye chili peppers
1/2 cup (120 g) roasted peanuts, coarsely chopped
1 cup (225 ml) malt vinegar
1 Tsp salt

To make the dressing, dissolve the palm sugar in water. Crush the shrimp, red chili peppers, and birds-eye chilis using a pestle and mortar. Work in the peanuts and the salt. Combine this paste with the vinegar and palm sugar syrup in a salad bowl. Add the finely chopped vegetables and fruit and toss well. Alternatively, vegetables and fruit may first be marinated for 1 hour in vinegar and then drained. Then continue as described above. This method may require additional sugar.

Other varieties of fruit and vegetables may be combined to make this salad. However, the fruit must be firm and should not be mushy or overripe.

Gado-gado – Java salad

Asinan – Fruit and vegetable salad

Urap

Vegetable salad with coconut dressing
Serves 4 - 6

1/2 cup (125 g) beansprouts, roots trimmed
1/2 cup (125 g) green beans, cleaned and cut into 1/2 in (1 cm) slices
1/2 cup (125 g) carrots, peeled and sliced
1/2 cup (125 g) coarsely shredded cabbage

Dressing

1/2 coconut, grated 15 Tbs (225 g), brown husk previously removed
salt
juice of 2 limes

Spice paste

2 Tbs dried shrimp, soaked
5 fresh red chili peppers, sliced into rings
1 garlic clove , peeled and quartered

Boil the vegetables for 3-5 minutes and drain well. They should all still be slightly crunchy. Crush the shrimp, chili peppers, and garlic to a paste, using a pestle and mortar.
Cook the grated coconut, spice paste, and salt in a skillet or wok and stir-fry over a low heat until the aromas begin to develop. Combine the fried grated coconut mixture with the lime juice in a bowl. Add the cooked vegetables, and toss well.

Urap can also be prepared with raw vegetables. This means grating them finely or slicing them thinly. For the dressing, all the ingredients are mixed raw.

Anyang pakis

Fiddlehead salad

1 1/4 lb (500 g) *daun pakis* (fiddlehead ferns)
1/2 coconut, grated (about 1 1/2 cups (200 g), brown husk previously removed
2/3 cup (150 g) beansprouts, roots trimmed
5 shallots, peeled and sliced into thin rings

Spice paste

5 fresh red chili peppers, sliced into rings, seeds discarded
1 slice ginger root, 1/8 in (5 mm) thick
1 stem lemongrass, lower part only, thinly sliced
Fruit pulp of 1 lime
sugar
salt

Grind the chili peppers ginger, lemongrass, and lime pulp in a mortar, with sugar and salt to taste.
Toast the grated coconut in a dry skillet, stirring frequently, until it is a uniform light brown all over; then crush it in a pestle with a mortar. Reserve it.
Blanch the beansprouts and drain them well.
Combine the crushed toasted coconut with the spice paste in a bowl, add the beansprouts and fiddlehead ferns and toss thoroughly.

Note: many types of fern that grow wild in Europe and the U.S. are poisonous. Make sure you only use the young fiddleheads and that they are from an edible variety of fern.

Markets are not just a place to shop, they also make a very artistic display.

Desserts

A dessert does not always have to be something sweet, and it certainly does not have to be eaten at the end of a meal. The strict sequence of dishes to which royal banquets and other formal occasions were once subjected has long since become more relaxed. Steamed rice cakes, fried banana, fruit salad—these delicacies have all passed into the popular culture, and are now sold from pushcarts or by peddlars in the street. Anyone who suddenly fancies a snack need only listen out for the familiar cries which announce the arrival of the food-seller. The Indonesians have an interesting name for these sweet snacks — *cuci mulut*, which means roughly "something with which to cleanse the palate."

Pisang goreng
Fried bananas

4 eating bananas *(pisang raja)*
2 cups (250 g) rice flour
1/4 Tsp salt
2/3 cup (150 ml) water
oil for frying

Combine the rice flour with the salt and water to make a smooth batter. Heat enough oil for frying shallot (about 4 Tbs). Coat the bananas in the batter and fry until they are golden-brown. Drain and serve.
A stronger flavor can be obtained by mixing the rice flour with coconut milk instead of water. Alternatively, the batter may also be made from all-purpose flour, beaten egg, and water. Rice flour makes for a particularly crispy batter. If you want this consistency with all-purpose flour, use equal quantities of rice flour and all-purpose flour.

Onde-onde
Sticky rice flour dumplings filled with beans

Filling
2/3 cup (150 g) dried lima beans, soaked overnight
2/3 cup (150 g) sugar
salt
1 pandanus leaf

Dough
7 oz (200 g) sticky rice flour *(mochi)*
3 1/2 Tbs (50 g) cornstarch
1 pinch salt
1/4 coconut, grated (about 2/3 cup ((100 g), brown husk previously removed
3/4 cup (200 ml) water, mixed with grated coconut, squeezed, milk reserved
6 1/2 Tbs (100 g) sesame seeds
oil for frying

For the filling, drain the soaked beans, rinse, and drain again. Place in a pan, cover with water, and cook until half-cooked, or until the bean skins burst. Remove from the heat and stir with a wooden spoon to release the skins. Remove the skins by rinsing the beans in water.

Pisang goreng – Fried bananas

Steam the skinned beans until they are soft. Then crush them and mix with sugar, salt, and the pandanus leaf. Stirring constantly, allow the remaining moisture to evaporate in the pan. Remove the pandanus leaf. Divide the mixture into 12 portions. The filling may be prepared a day in advance.

To make the dough, combine the sticky rice flour with the cornstarch and salt. Gradually add enough coconut milk to make a firm dough. Knead the dough until it is no longer sticky. Divide into 12 equal portions. In the palm of the hand, press each portion flat to make a 1/4 in (5 mm) thick disk. Place a portion of filling on the disk, fold the dough over it, and roll into a ball. Toss the dumplings in the sesame seeds until the surface is completely covered, then fry until golden brown in oil which should not be too hot. The sesame seeds may need to be cleaned before use. They may contain small stones or other pieces of debris.

Urap pisang
Bananas with grated coconut

6 ripe plantains (pisang kepok)
1/3 coconut, grated (1 1/3 cups (150 g)), brown husk previously removed
1/4 Tsp salt
1 1/4 Tbs sugar

Wash the bananas in their skins and steam for 15 minutes. Then peel the bananas and cut into pieces. Mix the grated coconut with salt and sugar and toss the banana pieces in the mixture.

Rujak
Fruit salad with spicy dressing
Serves 4 - 6

1 pineapple
1 mango (not quite ripe)
1/2 pomelo
1/2 cucumber
1/2 yam bean

Dressing
2 red chili peppers, cleaned and finely chopped
1/2 Tsp shrimp paste (trassi), toasted in a dry skillet and grated
4 Tbs palm sugar, or use dark brown sugar
2 Tbs malt vinegar or lemon juice

Chop the pineapple, mango, and yam bean into bite-sized pieces. Peel the pomelo and discard all the white parts. Cut the cucumber in half lengthwise, then cut the halves crosswise into strips.
Combine all the ingredients for the dressing and pour it over the fruit and vegetables. Toss well.

Although this is called a fruit salad, it also includes vegetables such as cucumber and yam bean. Any fruit may be used provided it is firm and not overripe or mushy. Crispy tropical fruits and vegetables, such as sapote, mamey apple, and bitter gourd are ideal for this salad.

Urap pisang
Bananas with grated coconut

Onde-onde
Sticky rice flour dumplings with bean filling

293

Coconut water you can cut with a knife

Nata de Coco

A combination of coconut water, the liquid inside a young coconut — not to be confused with the "milk" pressed from grated coconut — plus sugar, acidophilus bacteria, and a little ordinary physics, chemistry, and mechanics, result in a unique and delicious food.

As with yeast dough starter and sourdough, the bacteria has to have something to feed upon, so first of all, the "starter" or "leaven" must be made from coconut water and sugar.

What has actually been started will be seen by boiling up sugar with a large quantity of coconut water, cooling it, then adding acetic acid bacteria (*Acetobacter xylinum*) before covering with a lid and leaving to stand for five days in shallow rectangular tubs. After four days, the coconut water slowly begins to solidify, and on the fifth day it can be removed as a solid from the container. The coconut is then trimmed neatly at the edges and surface so that no unsightly fermentation residue impair the milky-white purity of the jelly. The individual slabs are now cut mechanically into 1 in (2 cm) cubes, boiled in water for ten minutes, and then sealed in perforated bags. These bags are then placed in a press and subjected to gentle pressure so that the liquid they have absorbed during boiling will flush out some of the acid, which is now no longer needed. This procedure is repeated until the gelatin is a translucent shimmering white, slightly springy to touch, and pleasant to taste.

Finally, the gelatin cubes are pasteurized in a syrup flavored with pandanus leaves or vanilla. Pasteurization increases the shelf life to two years.

Nata de coco, originates from the Philippines, hence the Spanish name meaning "cream of coconut.".Today, it is exported to Europe, Asia, and the United States.

Opposite: Layers of milky-white coconut gelatin are mechanically diced.

To solidify the coconut water, a little is combined with sugar to make a starter for the fermentation process.

The processed coconut water is left in shallow dishes for five days before being diced.

The cubes are boiled for 10 minutes in water before being sealed into bags and placed in a press.

Before the gelatin is finished, it must be boiled and pressed several times.

Packaged, filled with syrup, and pasteurized; two forms of the finished product for sale in a store.

Soft drinks

Air durian balanda: A refreshing juice made from the acidic soursop *(sirsak).*

Air jeruk nipis: Lime juice is diluted with water and sweetened with syrup as a soft drink.

Bandung: A pink syrup topped up with condensed milk.

Es apocat: Sweetened puréed avocado, diluted with water.

Es buah, es campur: A varied mixture of fruits, syrup, condensed milk, and crushed ice.

Es cendol: Jackfruit and other fruits in a mixture with palm sugar, coconut milk and green gelatin-like particles made from mung bean flour, topped up with crushed ice. There are numerous variations on this drink, one of which contains boiled kidney beans. It is also sold in cans.

Es juice: A glass of juice of one or several tropical fruits is topped up with ice.

Es tapé uli: A drink made of fermented rice and fermented cassava.

Markisah: Bottled syrup or freshly squeezed passion fruit juice is diluted with water. There are also *markisah* drinks which contain mango or tree tomatoes (tamarillo).

Salak juice: This is prepared from the flower essence of the *salak*, the snakeskin fruit.

Foreground: A large glass of *es cendol* has to be spooned rather than drunk from the glass.

Tuak (palm wine), the fermented sap of the sugar palm buds, has a low alcohol content.

But if it is distilled, in homemade stills like this, to make *arrak*, it should be drunk with care!

Drinks

Cold refreshments

The heat undoubtedly provides many street-sellers with a profitable business in sweet, ice-cold drinks. Hardly anyone can resist the fascination of the pitchers lined up in a row and filled with colorful syrups, coconut milk, coconut water, fruits, and gelatin, from which drinks are mixed that sometimes look like desserts.

Tuak

Palm wine is obtained from the sap of the sugar palm bud (the sugar palm also produces palm sugar and *gula jawa*). The time at which the sap was collected makes all the difference; sap gathered in the morning is different from sap gathered in the afternoon or at night, when it has already begun to ferment. The early juice is sweeter and has a lower alcohol content; sap gathered later in the day is drier. Because *tuak* turns to vinegar after just two to three days, it must be drunk fresh and is only suitable for local consumption. In Malaysia and Singapore it is known as *toddy*.

Arrak

This is distilled from *tuak* or rice wine, and since the Balinese are not prohibited from drinking alcohol by their religion, the majority of the production takes place on Bali. Home-made *arrak* can be so rough that even many Balinese prefer *tuak* and would rather sell bottled *arrak* to hotels, unless, as usual in traditional medicine, it is used externally. It is also deployed in religious ceremonies, although only the lowest quality is used, either because it is assumed that the gods or demons do not have human tastes, or for more practical reasons.

Tuak intended for distillation is mixed with coconut fiber to speed up fermentation, and is left to stand for two to three days. When sufficient liquid has been collected, it is poured into a pan in which it is boiled and distilled and then sealed. The product of the first distillation process has the best quality. Tourists to Bali will encounter the clear, colorless, high-proof beverage in cocktails such as Arrak Attack, Arrak Coke, Arrak Orange or Arrak Madu (a mead-like drink made of *arrak* and honey).

Brem Bali

Brem, rice wine, is a product made of 75 percent white and 25 percent black sticky rice (which is also distilled to make *arrak*.) Production begins by soaking the cleaned rice for 24 hours before steaming it for two and a half hours in large aluminum cookers. During this time, it may be necessary to add more hot water, since during this phase, the rice must not be allowed to become too dry. It is also stirred at regular intervals so that it cooks evenly. After steaming, the rice is poured into baskets and left to stand for one hour so as to cool down to room temperature. Only then can yeast cultures be added, for these react sensitively to excessive heat, rendering them ineffectual. The damp, prepared rice is poured back into the sieve inserts in the aluminum containers, and left to ferment. After just five days, the liquid produced can be drawn off, the rice pressed, and the liquids combined to make the rice wine. The rice residue is fed to the pigs, so nothing is wasted.

The liquid obtained in this way must ferment for a further 15 days before it is put in plastic tanks for fining. It remains in the

Brem Bali (rice wine) ready for shipping, bottled, sealed, and labeled, as seen in Indonesia. Alcoholic drinks are made and drunk by the non-Moslems.

tanks for six months. The wine is then bottled. Like the sealing and labeling, this is still often performed by hand, since home production of *brem* is still widespread.

The finished product is a very sweet wine which is served chilled. It can be served plain and undiluted with desserts, or mixed with *arrak*. It is also used for temple offerings. Sensibly, at religious ceremonies, the Balinese use a low-quality wine and for ritual offerings.

Sanur Sunrise

½ jigger Brem Bali
1 jigger Vodka
½ jigger fresh lime juice

Shake vigorously with ice cubes in a cocktail shaker and serve in cocktail glasses with a slice of orange.

Brem Sour

2 jiggers Brem Bali
½ jigger lime juice

Shake vigorously with ice cubes in a shaker and serve in cocktail glasses with a slice of orange.

White and black sticky rice is first soaked for 24 hours before being steamed.

After two and a half hours of steaming, the rice is as it should be: the stage of cooking and the color are

Before yeast cultures can be added, the rice must cool down to room temperature.

The rice is fermented in containers like these for a further five days before the liquid is drawn of.

Once mature, it is bottled as dark golden, 5% volume, light rice wine.

The bottles are sealed, labeled by hand - and dedicated to Dewi Sri, the rice goddess.

Wine? Wine!

The production of palm and rice wine on Bali is traditional and therefore not surprising. However, who would expect to see a vineyard here? And yet, in Sanur, grapes grown in Singaraja in the north are used to produce wine. It has not been easy, and Mother Nature has not been particularly helpful either, for precisely the one element which is beneficial in so many respects, namely the climate, is only suitable for wine-growing to a limited extent. First, attempts with European varieties of *Vitis vinifera* failed when it emerged that the grapes cannot come into bud unless there is a period of sufficiently cold weather. A long cold snap simply cannot be relied upon in such tropical latitudes. The American Red Isabella vine, a *Vitis labrusca*, however, is also capable of flowering in a constantly warm climate, indeed it flowers five times in two years. Although it can only

be used to make a light rosé, nonetheless it is a wine.

The sorted grapes are trampled by foot and left to stand until contact with the colorant contained in the skin turns the liquid to the required red. Only then will the grapes be pressed. The must is then stored in tanks equipped with cooling pipes so that, in this hot climate, the correct temperature can be obtained to enable settling of the sediment. The clear must is then pumped into another tank and left there to ferment for a further week. The tanks are not insulated, and the wine has to spend two weeks being stabilized at a cool temperature. During this time, it is filtered three times. After the second filtering process, sugar is added, following which it is sterile-filtered and then bottled.

The wine is ready to drink after just five to six weeks. Champagne is also produced from the same grape, and both products find willing purchasers in the local hotels and restaurants.

The light rosé produced on Bali is beautifully clear.

ROSÉ

An aromatic medium dry tropical wine for all occasions. Serve chilled.

Produced by Fa. "UDIYANA" SANUR BALI

±11% Alc/Vol

750mL

PRODUCE OF INDONESIA

DEP. KES. RI. MD 10012002018

WINES

At major temple festivals, such as the annual festival (*odalan*), Balinese women carry artistically arranged towers of produce on their heads as temple offerings.

In order to model such cakes free-hand, you need the right dough and a lot of practice.

A special flour mixture is combined with water and a generous portion of bright food coloring.

The dough must be kneaded energetically so that it acquires an even color and the right consistency.

The brightly-colored rice cakes not only serve as sacrificial offerings but are also eaten with freshly grated coconut.

To make a tray, pliable coconut leaves are cut lengthwise.

The strips which are to be folded are then separated.

For the base of the tray, the strips are laid side by side so that they overlap.

To secure them, the middle rib of several other leaves is removed.

Using quick "stabs" with the middle rib, the strips can be "stapled."

The base of the tray is strengthened by the addition of a rim.

The decorative rim is made of one strip, turned, folded, and pinned.

The finished tray can then be lined with a piece of banana leaf.

Sacrificial offerings

In Bali, small, brightly colored sacrificial offerings can be discovered in the most unusual places, for the Balinese must at all times be mindful of their duty to pay their gods and spirits due attention. When a housewife has finished cooking in the morning, she will place small coconut-leaf bowls containing cooked dishes at the house shrines and other strategically important points in the house and yard. Offerings can be found outside the gate or perhaps on a step. The women spend a lot of time producing and preparing these offerings, many of which are beautifully crafted, for the numerous religious ceremonies which take place on the occasion of births and deaths, or for the consecration or cleansing of temples, which takes several days.

The time-consuming festival preparations are community tasks, and so the women have combined to form clubs, the *anyaman (alad)*, just as the men meet together in *subak*. They meet to prepare rice cakes, to make offerings for the temple, as well as to play music or discuss family matters. These clubs therefore play a social role.

The women are very skilled at making containers and decorations out of young coconut leaves. The leaves are cut to the right shape, bent, folded, and made into the right form and the right size. The results of their work are cake boxes, flower vases, and containers for sacrificial offerings, as well as decorations for bamboo poles (*penjor*) used to offer thanks for the harvest, and from which fruits, cakes, and rice are hung as fertility symbols.

Bali has an astounding number of temples, for besides the village temples there are shrines for rice farmers, fishermen, and other occupational groups (with around 20,000 registered temples, this means six temples per square mile, not including family altars). As for the extravagance of the respective sacrificial offerings, this depends on the occasion. Particularly grand offerings are carried to the temple to express gratitude for a favor granted. At *odalan*, the anniversary of the village temple consecration, the towers of rice cakes, fruits, and flowers, interspersed with the odd roast chicken, may be yards high and weigh up to 50 pounds!. These precarious structures only stay in one piece thanks to a central wooden support. Balancing the towers on their heads, the women carry them to the temple, accompanied by musicians beating drums, gongs, and cymbals. In view of all the food involved, it is a good thing that the gods to whom these offerings are made content themselves with the ideal essence, which is passed to them by the priests with the aid of incense; this leaves the worldly components for consumption by their bearers once the festival is over.

Jajanan (Jaja)

The dough for these cakes consists of a mixture of sticky rice and tapioca flour, which is kneaded with water and brightly colored food colorant. The women need no aids such as pastry cutters or patterns; the frilly shapes are simply created by their own hands, and at most they will use a leafstalk. They many shapes of cake are steamed and served with grated coconut and palm sugar, for what the gods leave behind is just the thing for the believers.

A whole range of colorful hand-shaped rice cakes are produced without the help of a mold or cookie-cutter.

Glossary

Abalone (*Haliotidae*) Also known as ormers or sea-ears; they belong to *Haliotis* family, are very sought-after as a delicacy, and are thus already almost extinct. Around 100 types are known; they live in the surf areas of all warm seas. The sucking power of their feet, with which they cling to stones and rocks, is exceptionally strong for this reason, meaning that collectors have great difficulty releasing them. Their flesh is similar to that of the scallop, but is somewhat firmer. If not handled correctly, and particularly if cooked for too long, the flesh quickly becomes tough. It is difficult to find them fresh, they are usually sold frozen or canned. If canned, they are ready for use, while dried abalone takes a lot of preparation before it can be incorporated into a recipe.

adas (Indon.) Fennel leaves, blossom and seeds used as a spice; the white bulbs are not usually eaten as a vegetable in Indonesia.

asam (*Mal., Indon.*) sour

asam Tamarind (*Tamarindus indicus*); this tropical tree produces a pod, the dried fruit pulp of which has a distinctive sweet-and-sour flavor which adds acidity to a dish. The pulp is always diluted with water.

asam keping (Mal.; Indon.: *asam gelugur;* Chin.: *a shen pian*) Dried tamarind slices

bawang putih (Indon.) garlic

Boxthorn fruit (*Lycium barbarum*) These are known in Chinese medicine and Chinese cuisine for their ability to lower blood pressure and cholesterol levels; they strengthen the liver and kidneys and improve eyesight. But they have even more uses than this; their healing powers are relied on for lumbago, impotence, and menopausal complaints. This hardy ornamental plant needs to be planted in the sun in an alkaline, sandy, well-drained soil. The red berries are gathered in the fall.

buah keluak (Mal.) Seeds of the pangi tree (*Pangium edule*), which is indigenous to Java and Bali. The seeds are only edible once the toxic substances they contain have been flushed out by repeatedly rinsing in water.

buah keras (Mal.; Indon.: *kemiri;* Chin.: *ma jia la*) candlenut. Found in Southeast Asia and very fatty. It is always eaten cooked.

bunga cengkih (Mal.; Indon.: *bunga cengkeh;* Chin.: *ding xiang*) Cloves (*Syzygium aromaticum*), The fully developed buds of an evergreen tree native to the Moluccas.

bunga kantan (mal.; indon.: *honje, palang;* chin.: *xiang hua*) the bud of the red ginger plant (*Phaemeria speciosa*) serves as an ingredient for salads and curries.

cabe hijau, cabe merah (Mal.) green and red chili peppers

Candlenut (*Aleurites moluccana*); a type of nut similar to the macadamia nut in appearance. However, the candlenut cannot be used raw like the macadamia, since it contains toxins which evaporate upon heating. Candlenut kernels are hard, very oily, and are crushed in small quantities to bind sauces in curries and braised dishes. The aroma which they give to dishes is unmistakeable, and they can only be replaced to a limited degree by almonds, macadamias, or Brazil nuts. Shelled, packaged *kemiri* can be purchased in oriental stores.

Cardamom (*Elatteria cardamomum*) The dried seed pods of a tall 6–10 ft (2–3 m) reed-like plant which is native to the warm and humid regions of India, Sri Lanka, and the Malabar coast. It is also cultivated in suitable locations. The aroma is hot and spicy. The pods may be green or bleached white. Ground cardamom is an ingredient in curry powders.

cecur (Mal.; Indon.: *kencur;* Chin.: *sha jiang*) This aromatic waterlily root (*Kaempferia galanga*) has a similar aroma to ginger and is used in the same way.

Chili peppers: In Southeast Asian cooking, mainly small, thin chili peppers are used. These are generally very hot, regardless of whether they are red or green. Their intensity can be somewhat reduced by removing the seeds. When doing so, and when cleaning any chili pepper, it is essential to make sure not to touch the eyes or any other mucus membranes (including those of small children) after handling them.

Coconut milk This is the liquid pressed out of grated coconut. A first pressing without added water or with only a little water added produces a thick milk, while the same grated coconut, combined with more water and pressed out, produces the thin milk. If both

types are required in a recipe, the thin milk is added first, and the thick milk is only added at the end of the cooking time. A coconut with its brown skin, grated, produces about 2 cups (500 g) grated coconut (without the skin, it weighs about 1 3/4 oz (50 g) less). In oriental grocery stores, various brands of concentrated or pulverized coconut milk are also available; these must be diluted with water.

Coconut water The watery liquid inside a young coconut, which the nut uses up as it ages. Coconut water is sold as a refreshing beverage and forms the basis of *nata de coco*.

cumi-cumi (Indon.) Squid (*Teuthoidea*); These belong to the ten-armed octopus family (eight relatively short feeding-arms with suckers, and two long fishing-arms). These mollusks are a delicacy in Asian and Mediterranean cuisine, so that in some areas overfishing is already occurring. The flesh is firm, but only becomes tough when handled incorrectly, particularly if cooked for too long at too high a temperature. Squid is very suitable for stuffing with other ingredients.

Cumin (*Cuminum cyminum*) Cumin, a one-year-old herb growing up to 20 in(50 cm) high, in the umbelliferous blooms of which the narrow, slightly bent yellow-grey [Spaltfruechte] ripen. These are dried and ground to make a vital ingredient in curry powder.

Curry leaf The 1½-2 in (4-5 cm) long, lance-shaped, dark-green leaf of the orange rue (*Murraya koenigii*; Chin.: *gah li ye*), whose essential oils give a hot and spicy aroma; the spiciness develops most when the leaves are boiled for five minutes in a dish, or fried in oil. In Indonesian cuisine, they are often replaced by salam leaves (*daun salam*).

daun bawang Mal., Indon.) Green onions (scallions) (*Allium fistulosum*) are comparable with European types (Chin.: *cong*).

daun jeruk purut (Indon.) Kaffir lime leaves.

daun kari (Mal.) curry leaf

daun kemangi (Indon.) Basil

daun kesum (Mal.; Chin.: *ku wo ye*) Knotgrass, also known as knotweed or Vietnamese coriander.

daun ketumbar (Mal.) coriander (cilantro) (Coriandrum sativum; Chin.: yan sui ye)

daun kunyit (Mal.; Chin.: *huang jiang ye*) turmeric leaf *(Curcuma domestica)* used in curries or for wrapping fish before grilling.

daun limau purut (Mal.; Indon.: *daun jeruk purut;* Chin.: *suan gan ye)* Kaffir lime leaves, the leaves of *Citrus histrix.*

daun pandan (Mal.; Indon.) pandanus (screwpine) leaves.

daun salam (Indon.) salam leaves.

daun seladeri (Mal.) celery *(Apium graveolens;* Indon.: *daun seledri;* Chin.: *qin cai>*

daun selaseh (Mal.) Basil *(Ocimum basilicum)* an oriental variety of the herb, used in curries (Indon.: *daun kemangi*).

Egg Jam. A custard made of eggs, sugar, and coconut milk, stirred over a water-bath. It is served on toast as a breakfast dish in Chinese-run coffee shops. It may also be used as a filling for little cakes and cookies.

Fermentation 1. The chemical breakdown of organic substances through the action of enzymes already present or added. Fermentation changes the appearance, taste, constituents, and nutritional value of the food. Depending on the fermentation agent and the end-product, a distinction is made, for instance, between alcohol fermentation, lactic acid fermentation, and acetic acid fermentation. 2. The biochemical process for releasing an aroma, for instance with tea or tobacco.

Five-spice powder Chinese spice mixture consisting of equal parts of Szechuan pepper, star anise, cinnamon stick, cloves, and fennel seeds. It is usually used to flavor meat dishes.

Galangal root *(Alpinia galanga,* syn. *Galanga major;* Chin.: *lan jiang*); galangal root is hot and slightly bitter. It is used like ginger root, but more sparingly.

Ginger root *(Zingiber officinale)* The smooth, light gray-brown roots sold in the stores have already had their outer layer of cork removed. The interior of the rootstock is light yellow and can be very fibrous. The taste is pleasantly hot and fresh, while the strength increases as the product ages. Top-quality ginger root should not be older than one year.

H.P. Sauce Abbreviation for "Houses of Parliament Sauce," a proprietary brandname for a spicy bottled sauce whose ingredients include tamarinds, figs, raisins, dates, oriental spices, pepper and malt vinegar. It is imade only in the United Kingdom, but the inspiration, as for most of these types of sauce, is Malay.

halia muda (Mal.; Indon.: *jahe muda;* Chin.: *nen jiang)* Young ginger, also known as stem ginger.

halia tua (Mal.; Indon.: *jahe tua;* Chin.: *jiang)* The mature ginger root, which has a more distinctive taste.

Jackfruit or **Jakfruit** *(Artocarpus heterophyllus)* A warty green fruit of an evergreen tree, native to the East Indies and India, which can weigh up to 110 pounds (50 kg).The pulp is much appreciated raw, but the fleshy yellow seed pods are used in cooking. Unripe jackfruit is used for the Indonesian speciality *gudeg.*

jahe (Indon.) ginger root

jinten (Indon.) cumin

Kaffir lime leaves *(Citrus hystrix)* This knobbly citrus fruit which is yellow but has the scent of lime is used as an ornamental in the United States. The aromatic leaves are used in cookery in Southeast Asia. Dried leaves can be bought at oriental stores.

kayu manis (Indon.) cinnamon.

kemiri (Indon.) candlenut.

kencur (Indon.) This aromatic waterlily root*(Kaempferia galanga)* has a similar aroma to ginger and is used accordingly.

Knotgrass *(Polygonum odoratum)* Also known as knotweed Vietnamese coriander; sharp and peppery citrus-like herb for rich coconut sauces.

kucai (Mal.) Garlic chives *(Allium tuberosum),* the smell of this member of the allium family is an interesting combination of the aromas of chives and garlic (Chin.: *jiu cai*).

kunyit fresh and dried turmeric

kunyit basah (Mal.) turmeric root

lada kering (Mal.) Dried chili peppers; they should first be softened in warm water; they are milder without the seeds (Indon.: *cabai/cabe kering;* Chin.: *la jiao gan)*

lada merah/lada hijau (Mal.) Fresh red and green chili peppers; the long ones are usually hotter than round ones (Indon.: *cabai/cabe* merah/hijau; Chin.: *hong/qing la jiao)*

laos (Indon.) galangal root. Sometimes sold in powdered form and called laos powder.

Lemongrass *(Cymbopogon citratus);* A shrub with onion-like thick roots and a lemony fragrance; usually, only the lower 2-4 in (5-10 cm) are used. These are cut into thin slices and mostly crushed with other spices using a pestle and mortar or the flat side of a large Chinese heavy-bladed knife. Recipes sometimes also require that the whole stems be cooked in the dish; these are, however, generally removed before serving.

lengkuas (mal.) galangal root

limau kesturi (Mal.) Limes *(Citrus aurantiifolia)* Green-skinned citrus fruits, with yellow or green aromatic flesh; the juice is used in cooking (Indon.: *jeruk nipis;* Chin.: *suan gan).*

manis (Mal., Indon.) sweet

Oyster sauce Seasoning agent based on oyster extract, boiled with sugar, salt, wheat flour, cornstarch, caramel, and water. It is used in vegetable, meat and fish dishes.

Paddi-straw mushroom *(Volvariella volvacea),* also known as rice-straw or paddy straw mushroom. These dark-brown mushrooms, about the size of a pigeon's egg when mature, are grown on a mixture of rice-straw and soil and need 30-40 days to mature for harvest. Their flavor is strongest when they are used fresh, but they are easy to find canned and are also sold dried.

pala (Indon.) nutmeg

Palm sugar (mal.: *gula melaka;* indon.: *gula jawa)* The boiled and crystallized sweet sap obtained from the unopened bud of the sugar palm *(Arenga pinnata)* and the Atta palm.

Pandanus leaves *(Pandanus odorus, P. tectorius;* Chin.: *xiang lan ye)* The narrow, lanceolate leaves of the screwpine are used mainly to give desserts an aroma reminiscent of roses or vanilla. They are used at least as frequently as vanilla is used in northern Europe; the green juice is used as a colorant.

Sago This starchy substance is extracted from the pulp of the sago palm *(Metroxylon sagu)* and ground to make flour. To make the sago pearls usually found in the stores, the dampened flour is pressed through special sieves so that tiny droplets fall onto hot, vibrating metal trays. These cause the drying starch to clump together into round grains."Sago" is produced in a similar manner,

alam leaf *(Eugenia polyantha)* These aromatic, slightly acidic leaves are used only in Indonesian cookery in the same way as bay leaves, which they are said to resemble. However, the flavor is quite different so rather than use bay as a substitute, they should be replaced by curry leaves if unavailable.

serai (Mal.; Indon.: *sereh*; Chin.: *xiang mao*) lemongrass, lemon grass.

Shiitake mushrooms *(Lentinellus edodes;* Japan. Shiitake) or winter mushrooms. The caps are 2-4 in (5-10 cm) in diameter and of various shapes. They are colored brownish-gray to red-brown, often with whitish scales. The gills are close-set and the stem has a distinctive ring. The fungi are first whitish in color, later slightly yellow, and finally reddish-brown, with a short, fairly thin stem. The flesh is firm and the flavor strong. Those who do not like it claim it tastes of burned rubber. Shiitake are available both fresh and dried.

Shrimp The name is used for a large family of crustaceans related to the lobster which vary in size from very tiny (bay shrimp) to 5-6 in (15-17.5 cm) long (jumbo shrimp). Shrimp live in cold and warm waters, but of course the varieties used in Southeast Asian cooking live in the tropics. Although there are recipes in this book which call for live shrimp, for reasons of public health, shrimp are never sold live, except perhaps where they are caught. The best you can hope for are uncooked or "green" shrimp. If you need live shrimp you may have to catch them yourself. They live in the tidal waters off the coast, particularly among rocks.

Shrimp paste (Mal. *blacan;* Indon. *trassi*) This is creamy, dark paste, similar to yeast extract. The odor is strong and pungent but only small quantities are ever used. The paste is added as a flavoring to savory foods, in conjunction with other spices. For western palates, the prescribed quantities may be too salty, especially as the Malay or Indonesian version may be hard to find abroad. It can be replaced by a comparable Sri Lankan or Thai product but this may have slightly different ingredients. Care should be taken not to use too much shrimp paste and to gradually get a feel for the right quantity for a particular dish.

Soy sauce Probably the best-known Asian seasoning agent, based on fermented soya beans. Apart from numerous special flavours, it is sold in a dark, milder version and a light, more salty version.

Spice paste There is no standard mixture for spice paste, but a paste of varying ingredients consisting of dried and fresh spices which

acquire their characteristic consistency by being crushed together using a pestle and mortar. Ideally, all ingredients should combine to form an homogenous mass (which, admittedly, can be achieved with far less effort using a kitchen appliance). The paste is fried in hot oil until the aromas have developed.

Sticky rice Also known as glutinous rice. A medium-grain rice which has a particularly high starch content, but whose stickiness also depends on how it is prepared. When steamed, the grains remain separated, but if cooked until very soft, using twice as much water as is normally required, it turns into a sticky mass which can almost be shaped like dough. Much used for sweet dishes as well as with fish and to make dumplings.

Stir-frying Finely chopped ingredients are fried in a wok in a little extremely hot oil, stirring constantly; because of the great heat, they cook rapidly and the taste and nutritional value of the food is preserved.

Straw mushrooms *(Volvaria bombycina,* Rice straw mushrooms) *See* Padi-straw mushrooms.

Szechuan pepper The red and yellow capsules of *Zanthoxylum piperitum,* with the seeds removed. The tree is not related to the pepper tree but the seeds are used in the same way. The aroma, besides being hot, also has lemony undertones..

tahu (Indon.) Fermented soybean tofu.

Tamarind: The tamarind fruit *(Tamarindus indicus)* bears a pod whose tough, dark brown or blackish pulp is available dried and pressed into blocks in oriental grocery stores. The quantity indicated in the recipe is dissolved in hot water, the pulp is strained thoroughly, and the acidic liquid is used for flavoring (it is also a good binding agent). The acidity is due to a mixture of tartaric acid, citric acid, lactic, and malic acid, as well as several other elements, and makes up about 20 percent of the fruit. In Europe, tamarind is used to flavor Worcestershire Sauce, HP Sauce (*q.v.*) and other sauces based on Southeast Asia dipping sauces. Tamarind has a slightly laxative effect.

Tempeh A type of soybean cheese made of fermented soybeans, the shape of which can be seen in the finished product, but which have lost their structure. In Indonesia, *tempeh* is used more often than tofu.

Thousand-year eggs (Chin.: *Pi Dan*) Duck eggs stored in a mixture of chalk, ash, salt, and rice husks for 2-4 months, until the egg

white is translucent black and the yolk is grayish green. Quarters or eighths of an egg are used, for instance, as a garnish for cold hors d'oeuvres or rice gruel. These preserved eggs are used exclusively in Chinese cooking.

Tofu Beancurd made from soya milk, obtained from soaked, ground and boiled soybeans. Hard, soft and smoked tofu are available in oriental and health food stores.

Turmeric, fresh *(Curcuma domestica;* Chin.: *huang jiang*) the root is used fresh like ginger, but is also sold dried, cut in pieces, or as a powder. Turmeric, a vital constituent of curry powder, gives dishes a bright yellow coloring, a quality which the spice retains for much longer than its aroma. Yellow is considered a sacred color throughout southeast Asia, which is why fresh turmeric is used particularly generously at festive meals. For the sake of clarity, in the recipes in this book "fresh turmeric" refers to the fresh product, while "turmeric" used alone refers to the powder.

Tumeric root In order to make a clear distinction, in these recipes, "turmeric" is always used to refer to the ground powder, whereas fresh turmeric refers to the root.

Wok The bowl-like shape of this pan means that the heat is evenly distributed; the high-sloping edges and the oil gathering only in a small area in the center is perfect for stir-frying. This is a way of cooking finely-chopped ingredients which preserves their taste and nutritional value and takes the shortest amount of time.

Introduction to Chinese nutritional theory

By Andrea Fülling

What is healthy nutrition? This question is answered differently in China from the way in which it is answered in the West, where food is classified by nutrients and calories. To be able to do justice to the question from a Chinese perspective, we must look in more detail at some concepts which run through the whole of Chinese thinking and which arose from several thousand years' experience of life and everyday routine.

Yin and yang

The dual concept of yin and yang relates to the bipolar forces which are present everywhere in the microcosm and macrocosm. The contrast between them is not absolute, in the sense of "being and not being," or "good and evil," but they determine and complement one another, and can only be effective together. The one is inconceivable without the other. Yin and yang are not constant dimensions, but are caught up in a constant rhythmical exchange. What dominates is the principle of alternation, meaning that the active forces of yin and yang take turns at assuming predominance.

Yin stands for the feminine, dark principle, and describes characteristics such as quiet, cold, or passivity. It is associated with the night. Yang describes the masculine, light principle and stands, amongst other things, for warmth, activity, and the day.

Since yin and yang have their effects both in the microcosm and the macrocosm, they of course also regulate the human body. Yin makes up the substances of the body such as blood, bodily fluids, tissue, muscle and bones, while yang provides the energy which the body needs to keep warm and for all its functions. Via fine pathways, also known as meridians, the organs are supplied with substance (yin: bodily fluids, blood) and energy (yang). If yin and yang are no longer balanced, then a person will become sick. Traditional Chinese medicine distinguishes between yin root and yang root disturbances in a person. If the yang root is damaged, then in the early stages of illness there may be a lack of chi, i.e. a reduction in energy, or in the advanced stages, a lack of yang, i.e. a lack of energy. If there is too much energy or heat in a body, this is referred to as an excess of yang. If the yin root is impaired, this creates a lack of blood or a lack of yin or an excess of yin. Lack of blood covers any illness which has a negative influence on the quality, quantity, or function of the blood. Where there is a lack of yin, the bodily fluids are severely reduced to a varying extent, while on the other hand, where there is an abundance of yin, too much mucus, water, or fat has accumulated in the body.

The three warmers

The three warmers form the system of organs, consist of three levels on which energy and warmth are passed from organ to organ. One of the roles of this system is to extract energy from the air and from foods.

The kidney is the lower warmer. One of its most important functions is to store the prenatal chi, the yuan-chi. It is not formed by the organs, but comes into being with the birth of each individual. Each day, the body emits a little of its yuan-chi, a mechanism by which the Chinese explain the ageing process. Once it is used up, we die. Its quality and quantity are determined individually and are thus not renewable. The quantity of yuan-chi excreted by the kidneys can, however, be influenced by a healthy lifestyle and good nutrition.

A further task of the kidneys is to pass on energy and warmth to the middle warmers — the spleen and the stomach. By means of this energy, they can extract the chi and essence from foods. In this way they produce the first portion of postnatal energy.

From the middle warmer, energy is in turn passed on to the upper warmer to supply the lungs and heart. Its task consists of obtaining the second portion of postnatal energy by making energy from the breath available to the body. The two components of postnatal chi consist of the chi of food and breath. The more postnatal chi available to the body from the organism, the less of its prenatal energy source it needs to use up. The kidneys also store excess chi from the postnatal energy obtained and they can transmit it to the organism when required.

The warming effect of foods

If the effects of the cosmic forces are universal, then foods are very much part of this system. Moreover, each food is characterized by a particular energy effect, through which it is possible to harmonize, strengthen, and restore the organs, their functions and the chi which flows through them from a state of imbalance.

The Chinese classify all foods in accordance with five energy states: hot, warm, neutral, refreshing, and cold.

Hot and warm foods are eaten to prevent a lack of yang or to balance yang, for they can protect the body against cold and are therefore also preferred in winter. Anyone who feels the cold particularly acutely, should eat more of these foods. Vegetable and meat broths have an especially good record in this regard. But an excess of these hot and warm dishes is not healthy either and may lead to a yin deficiency.

Hot foods include fennel, lamb, hard liquor, hot water, hot spices, such as chili peppers and pepper, but also milder ones such as cloves, cinnamon, and nutmeg. Warm foods also include fish such as perch, salmon, and trout, as well as poultry and game; vegetables include carrots, pumpkin, leek, onions, garlic, and the winter vegetables; spices are coriander, caraway, paprika, ginger, marjoram, and all dried spices. Red wine and coffee are also among the warm foods.

The easiest foods for the body to digest are all neutral. These include cereals, potatoes, beef, and pork, since they have both a harmonizing and stabilizing effect on the chi. Cooked cereal, especially maize and millet, are supposed to contain a particularly harmonious form of chi and should therefore be included as often as possible in the daily diet. Potatoes, on the other hand, do not have this particular effect. Beef tones the blood and chi equally, while pork is not so valuable in this regard.

The refreshing foods include most vegetables, for instance beans, mushrooms, courgettes, tomatoes, Chinese (Napa) cabbage, mangold, turnip, fruits, and also dairy products such as yoghurt, cheese, and butter. They play a vital role in strengthening the blood and substances of the body. In order for this to happen, the kidneys, spleen and pancreas must be supplied with sufficient energy. If the requisite energy supply is not assured, the result will inevitably be a yang deficiency (from which women suffer in particular). Foods in this category should therefore be eaten less often in autumn and winter.

Foods in this category should therefore be eaten less often in autumn and winter.

he same, but to a greater extent, of course also applies to the cold foods. They are intended to protect the body in summer against too much heat, and thus prevent an abundance of yang.

Tropical fruits, which ripen in the summer in their native countries, should also be eaten in summer in the West. Other cold foods are, for instance, salads, herb teas such as peppermint or camomile, black tea, mineral water and all cold drinks, ice cream, and salt. Since, when it is very hot, people tend to eat a large amount of cold food, it is important particularly in summer to guard against an energy loss in the middle warmer (spleen and stomach).

As a rule of thumb, one can remember that the aim should be to cover one's daily nutritional needs mainly from neutral, warm, and refreshing foods. Hot and cold foods only serve as a supplement.

Moreover, if you prepare your food from seasonal fruit and vegetables, this is a very healthy way to eat, not only from a Chinese point of view. The indications as to the thermal effect of foods always relate to the food as prepared for inclusion in a meal.

The five elements

The five phases of change are subject to the control of yin and yang and thus to the doctrine of the Five Elements. This is based on the theory that natural sequences are subject to a subtle system of balance between various processes which, depending on the situation, support, inhibit, or block.

These five elements — wood, fire, earth, metal, and water, form a further universally active system in the holistic Chinese way of thinking, whereby natural processes are explained and which accordingly play a major role in the choice and composition of foods. They may support, inhibit, or block one another, depending on the situation. Each element is, amongst other things, allocated to a particular type of flavor, a specific form of energy, a specific color, and one or more of the organs of the body.

Thus, wood has a sour flavor attributed to it, as have the liver and gall bladder, and the color green. All sour and/or green foods thus have a beneficial effect on those organs associated with wood, even if in terms of flavor they might be allied to other elements. Duck, chicken, turkey, wheat, spelt, and unripe grain also have a positive effect on the liver and gall bladder. Sour-tasting foods almost always additionally contain a refreshing thermal energy, which has a balancing effect on the liver in the

case of a deficiency of fluids and excess heat. A person who sweats heavily should drink rosehip, malva, and hibiscus tea which will provide refreshment and help balance the bodily fluids.

The heart and small intestine and the colour red belong to the element of fire, which is said to have a bitter flavor. This bitterness has a direct influence on the digestive tract. That is why bitter aperitifs stimulate the appetite, and bitter liqueurs aid the digestion after a heavy, rich meal. Cold fire foods, which moreover have a refreshing energy, protect against excess heat in the heart and help to build up bodily fluids, while the bitter-warm flavor of cocoa, coffee, and red wine is drying and protects the body in damp and cold weather. Lamb and goat meat, as well as rye, buckwheat, sweet cherries, red grapes, and peppers (capsicums), to name but a few, belong to the fire element.

The spleen and stomach and the color yellow are said to have a sweet flavor and belong to the earth element.

Sweet foods strengthen *chi*, moisten and harmonize the body and give it energy. To avoid any misunderstandings right away: this does not apply to mass-produced candies and desserts which are store-bought but only to untreated, prepared foods such as grains and sweet-tasting vegetables like pumpkin, carrots, or sweet potatoes. Millet and maize are best for strengthening the spleen and stomach. Oats are able to balance the *chi* in the earth organs. Sweet, cold, or refreshing fruits and vegetables moisten and have a cooling effect. Too much sweet and cold food, however, weakens the spleen and stomach *chi*.

Meat, carrots, fennel, and pumpkin are sweet and warm foods and thus have a warming and toning effect on the earth organs.

A sharp taste, the organs lung and large intestine, and the color white belong to the element of metal. Sharp, warm foods help to open the pores and protect against cold. For colds, mulled wine, and ginger tea are thus a tried and tested household remedy, for only if the pores are opened can the cold which has penetrated escape. Too many metallic foods, however, can lead to overheating of the body, which may have a particularly damaging effect on the liver. The lungs react to this by coughing. Foods considered sharp and refreshing, such as kohlrabi, cress, radish, or whole-grain rice, moisten the lungs and put color in the cheeks.

Water forms the last element in this cycle. The kidneys and bladder are dependent on it, as is a salty flavor and the color black. Salt has an expectorant, softening, and laxative effect, so that, taken in the right doses, it binds and enhances bodily fluids, but when taken to excess, it dries the organs out, an unbalanced

state which can be corrected with sweet foods. The kidney yang is strengthened through warm, salty foods. Many types of fish and seafood have this warming effect.

Some pulses are neutral in terms of salt and strengthen *chi*. A combination of salty and refreshing elements has a balancing effect on the kidney fluids, while salty and cold protects against the fire element being too strong in the kidneys. Shrimp, fish roe, and mineral water are among the salty and cold foods.

In this way, all foods impact upon one another through a complex system, and anyone wishing to prepare a balanced or balancing meal at a particular time of year on the basis of these criteria, can combine various flavors which may be surprising to someone with a western understanding of the harmonious sequence of dishes. From the Chinese point of view, the effects of a meal are at least as important as its flavor — an attitude from which undoubtedly we in the West could benefit in our approach to food.

Acknowledgements

The publishers would like to express their thanks for the support and assistance received. These thanks are also extended to those individuals and institutions which have helped in realizing the project without being known by name to the publishers.

Singapore

Aziza's Restaurant
Charming Garden Restaurant Pte Ltd
Chin Nee Chin Confectionery
Chin Guan Hong (Sharksfin) Pte Ltd
Eng Soon Dry Bean Curd Mfg. Pte. Ltd
Eu Yan Sang (Singapore) Pte Ltd
Everbloom Mushroom Pte Ltd
Gourmet Popiah, Coronation Shopping Plaza
Heng Lung Duck Farm
Hiap Giap Noodle Manufacturers
Hong Reng Tang Imperial Kitchen (S) Pte Ltd
(Imperial Herbal Restaurant) Metropol Hotel
Horng Dar Marine Enterprise (Pte) Ltd
Zarina Ibrahim
Joo Chiat Bak Chang
Kaiyen Co. Pte. Ltd
Kelong Thomson Restaurant
Khye Soon (Pte) Ltd
Kia Hiang Restaurant
King's Hotel
Lim Luan Seng Foods Industries Pte Ltd
Lim Seng Lee Duck Rice Restaurant
Raffles Hotel
See Lian Confectionery
Seng Choon Farm Pte Ltd
Agro Technology Park
Sinchong Meheco Ltd, Pearls Centre
Singa Inn Seafood Restaurant
Sinsin Food Industries Pte Ltd
Siti Hawa Janamin
Soubrite Pte Ltd
Unicurd Food Company (Pte) Ltd
Mr C O Wong, Onn Fat Hong

Malaysia

Hong Kat Yean, Bidor, Perak
Hup Soon Sing Co., Pangkor
Jabatan Perikanan Negeri Perak (State Fisheries Department)
Jabatan Pertanian Negeri Perak (State Agricultural Department)
Khasiba Enterprise, Perak Darul Ridzuan
Khim Tat Marine Products, Kuala Sepetang
Kulai Palm Oil Factory, Kulai, Johore
Lee Pineapple Co. Pte. Ltd., Johore
Maju Goat Farming & Trading Sdn. Bhd., Selangor Darul Ehsan
Riviera Bay Resort, Malacca
Sarawak Cultural Village, Kuching, Sarawak, East Malaysia
Sin Tai Hing Oyster & Shrimp Sauce Factory Sdn. Bhd., Selangor Darul Efsan, West Malaysia
Sungai Palas Tea Estate, Cameron Highlands
Mr. Tan Ah Too; Pangkor
Toon Yew Fee & Sons Co., Ipoh

Indonesia

ATI, Medan, Sumatra Utara
Campur Sari, Yogyakarta
Mr. Hidayat, Jakarta
Huler Gabah ›DR‹, Tasikmalaya
Ibu Nihaya, Jakarta Timur
Kripik Balado, Padang
Margo Utomo (Homestay), Kalibaru
Oasis Restarant, Jakarta
Pengolahan Coklat, Medan, Sumatra Utara, & Pematang Siantar, Sumatra Utara
Perkebunan Helvetia, Medan, Sumatra Utara
Perusahaan Daerah Taru Martani, Yogyakarta
Pyramid Unta, Peceren Brastagi, Sumatra Utara
P.T. Sari Segar Husada, Pasir Putih, Tarahan, Lampung Selatan
Restaurant Garuda, Bandar Lampung
Taman Buah Mekarsari, Bogor
Toko Manisan Situ Indah, Cianjur Jabar
Fa. Udiyana, Sanur
Restaurant Garuda, Bandar Lampung
Taman Buah Mekarsari, Bogor
Toko Manisan Situ Indah, Cianjur Jabar
Fa. Udiyana, Sanur

Photo Credits

All photos, including back cover:

© Könemann Verlagsgesellschaft / Günter Beer, apart from:

© Könemann Verlagsgesellschaft / Ruprecht Stempell, front cover

© Uli Franz, Cologne: 68/69 (large illus..), 102 (below)

© Michael Freeman, London: 100

© Könemann Verlagsgesellschaft / Arena Studios Pte Ltd., Hartmut Gottschalk, Singapore: 34/35, 36, 44/45, 60/61, 70/71 (larger illustration), 72 bottom, 73, 102 (top), 148/149, 151 (bottom, 156/157, 159 (smaller illustration), 164/165, 175 (right), 187, 188/189, 193 (right, from top to bottom), 198/199, 204/205, 223 (bottom), 226/227, 268/269, 274 (bottom), 276/277, 286/287, 292/293

© Könemann Verlagsgesellschaft / Klaus Arras Fotodesign, Cologne: 32/33, 142/143

Straits Times Library Pictures / Singapore Press Holding, Berita Harian, Singapore: 200, 201

© Hu Yong – Sigma, Paris: 82 (large ill.) 83

Index

Figures in bold refer to pages on which there is an extensive entry in the text. Recipes are indexed separately.

Recipe Index